THE COMPLETE PRACTICAL GUIDE TO SUCCESSFUL

HOUSEPLANTS, WINDOW BOXES
HANGING BASKETS, POTS & CONTAINERS

THE COMPLETE PRACTICAL GUIDE TO SUCCESSFUL

HOUSEPLANTS, WINDOW BOXES
HANGING BASKETS, POTS & CONTAINERS

A PRACTICAL GUIDE TO SELECTING, LOCATING, PLANTING AND CARING FOR YOUR POTTED
PLANTS BOTH INDOORS AND OUTDOORS, WITH DETAILED DIRECTORIES, TECHNIQUES
AND TIPS, RICHLY ILLUSTRATED WITH MORE THAN 2200 STUNNING PHOTOGRAPHS

STEPHANIE DONALDSON & PETER MCHOY

southwater

This edition is published by Southwater, an imprint of Anness Publishing Ltd,
Blaby Road, Wigston, Leicestershire LE18 4SE; info@anness.com

www.southwaterbooks.com; www.annesspublishing.com

If you like the images in this book and would like to investigate using them for publishing, promotions
or advertising, please visit our website www.practicalpictures.com for more information.

Publisher: Joanna Lorenz
Project Editor: Felicity Forster
Designers: Janet James and Peter Butler
Photographers: Marie O'Hara, Janine Hosegood and John Freeman
Illustrator: King & King Associates
Stylist: Stephanie Donaldson
Indexer: Dawn Butcher
Editorial Reader: Hayley Kerr
Production Controller: Ben Worley

ETHICAL TRADING POLICY

At Anness Publishing we believe that business should be conducted in an ethical and ecologically
sustainable way, with respect for the environment and a proper regard to the replacement of
the natural resources we employ.

As a publisher, we use a lot of wood pulp to make high-quality paper for printing, and that wood
commonly comes from spruce trees. We are therefore currently growing more than 500,000 trees in
two Scottish forest plantations near Aberdeen – Berrymoss (130 hectares/320 acres) and West Touxhill
(125 hectares/305 acres). The forests we manage contain twice the number of trees employed each
year in paper-making for our books.

Because of this ongoing ecological investment programme, you, as our customer, can have the
pleasure and reassurance of knowing that a tree is being cultivated on your behalf to naturally
replace the materials used to make the book you are holding.

Our forestry programme is run in accordance with the UK Woodland Assurance Scheme (UKWAS) and
will be certified by the internationally recognized Forest Stewardship Council (FSC). The FSC is a non-
government organization dedicated to promoting responsible management of the world's forests.
Certification ensures forests are managed in an environmentally sustainable and socially responsible
basis. For further information about this scheme, go to www.annesspublishing.com/trees

A CIP catalogue record for this book is available from the British Library.

Previously published as Container Gardens

PUBLISHER'S NOTE

Although the advice and information in this book are believed to be accurate and true at the time of going to
press, neither the authors nor the publisher can accept any legal responsibility or liability for any errors or
omissions that may have been made nor for any inaccuracies nor for any loss, harm or injury that comes
about from following instructions or advice in this book.

Contents

INTRODUCTION

Planting in containers is an easy and extremely versatile way to bring the garden inside, as well as creating beautiful displays outside, where you may not have much space. The rewards to be gained from growing your own plants are infinite, and with a little imagination you can transform any room of your home, your windows or your backyard.

This book covers all the essential techniques involved in becoming a successful container gardener. There are ideas for every kind of container you could imagine, from traditional wire hanging baskets to terracotta pots, and from stone troughs to a pair of old boots. Once you have decided on your container, the book continues to provide detailed information to ensure that your plants will always remain healthy and thriving: propagation techniques, composts (potting mixes), feeding and watering, pest and disease control, and general maintenance throughout the year.

The opening section on the container garden consists of inspiring projects for gardeners of all levels of experience. There are ideas on how to decorate

your containers, and suggestions for which plants to use for any situation – colour-themed plantings, plants suited to particular seasons, edible plants, scented plants, plants for difficult situations and dramatic, inspirational containers. There are also fun projects especially designed for children, all with step-by-step colour photographs to illustrate the stages in reaching your goal.

The next section then focuses on houseplants, with detailed guidance on how to choose and care for your indoor plants. Here you'll find flowering plants and leafy plants, both common and exotic, with information on how to care for each plant, how to create the correct environment, and how to avoid common pests and diseases.

The book also includes an illustrated A–Z directory of houseplants, providing a catalogue of all the indoor plants you are likely to find in garden centres and nurseries. Close-up photographs are there to help you identify your plants, and you will find useful information about each variety so that you'll be able to provide the right conditions for your displays.

An A–Z of common plant names and a plant guide conclude the volume, providing a quick reference section for when you want to know the name of a plant, or whether a particular plant is suited to sun or shade.

Aimed at gardeners of all levels of experience, this book has been designed to give practical help, as well as inspirational ideas, on all aspects of growing plants in containers, and is an informative source of information that you can refer to again and again.

The
Container
Garden

Techniques • Decorating containers
• Colour schemes for containers
• Seasonal planters • Edible collections
• Scented collections • Difficult situations
• Inspirational containers • The young
container gardener • Indoor containers

Introduction

Container gardening expands your horticultural horizons because it defies space and time. You do not need to be a full-time gardener with a large country garden to grow the tastiest herbs, lushest wild strawberries, or beautiful flowers for a summer evening. You don't even need any expert knowledge to be a successful container gardener – indeed, if you own a house-plant or a pot of parsley, you are already a container gardener.

The beauty of containers is that with the minimum amount of time and effort they will instantly jazz up a balcony or roof garden, extend the garden up to the back door, and liven up window-sills with colour, scent and form. They can also, of course, be used indoors, as spectacular table centrepieces, or to brighten a corner of the room.

The great advantage of gardening in containers is that, like furniture, containers can be moved around to create a new look, with pride of place given to those plants that are performing best. Unlike plants in your garden, containers can simply be moved to wherever you want them: in the foreground when flowering, and then into the background once flowering is over. If you are unhappy with a particular arrangement or combination, you only have to move the pots to try something else.

Today, good quality container-grown plants are available all through the year, and skills such as seed sowing, potting-on and taking cuttings are not always essential. There is nothing wrong with this form of "instant" gardening. By buying plants that are nearing maturity, you can save the

time-consuming and uncertain business of rearing the plants, and you can try out different shape and colour combinations before you buy the plants by simply grouping them together.

Of course, the plants are only a part of the equation, and you can be as creative as you like with your choice of containers. Shops and garden centres stock an ever-increasing range of containers to suit every budget, from magnificent Italian olive jars to humble plastic pots. Junk shops and flea markets are also a rich source of objects that can take on a new use as a planter – a blackened cooking pot with a hole in its base is useless for its original purpose, but is ideal as a container of character, and can be bought extremely cheaply. Similarly, an old basket can be completely transformed when filled with a fresh floral display. The range of possibilities is nothing short of amazing,

both for the small-scale gardener and for gardeners who work with very large areas. Containers will add to the grace and majesty of even the grandest garden designs.

In the following pages you will find scores of imaginative and innovative themed ideas for beautiful containers, with recommendations of some of the best plants around for achieving them. Don't be dismayed if you can't find exactly the plants suggested. There is nearly always an excellent alternative, and new varieties with brighter colours and bigger, longer-lasting blooms keep appearing in the nurseries. With a bit of experience, you'll soon be able to create your own eye-catching arrangements. Whether you are a novice or an experienced gardener, container gardening is a highly accessible, enjoyable and colourful way to brighten up your surroundings.

OPPOSITE: *Plants are only a part of the equation, and decorative containers are readily available.*

RIGHT: *A copper tub is a simple and yet very beautiful way to display spring bulbs such as white tulips.*

Techniques

Much of the enjoyment of container gardening comes from experimenting with different types of container and different kinds of plants. Garden centres stock a huge variety of containers, ranging from traditional terracotta pots to antique wire hanging baskets, and the range of plants available is almost limitless. Learning about propagation, composts (potting mixes), feeding, watering, and pests and diseases will ensure that your container plants stay healthy, and that you are able to spot any signs of trouble immediately. Having mastered the techniques, you'll be able to create beautiful container displays all year round.

ABOVE: *The variety of shapes and sizes of containers is as wide as your imagination – from pots and troughs to baskets and watering cans.*

Types of container

One of the challenges of container gardening is finding the right container for the right setting. You can now quite readily buy a whole range of lovely containers; for example, waist-high, Italian olive oil jars make a terrific focal point – big, bold and stylish. At the other end of the scale, you can be as imaginative as you like. You could use a Wellington boot or an old shoe for an engaging, quirky touch. In between, of course, the choice is huge: rustic terracotta, voguish metal, lightweight fibre, handmade wicker, or brightly painted tins, Mediterranean-style.

It is important to consider the final setting when you are buying a container. A rustic tub may look charming under the window of a thatched cottage, but inappropriate outside a formal town house. Bear proportions in mind; for example, choose a window box that exactly fits the sill or a hanging basket that fits high above a doorway. It is also worth noting that the weight of a container, when filled with compost (potting mix) and freshly watered, will be considerably greater than when empty. Think twice before packing your roof terrace or balcony with heavy pots: the structure may not be able to cope. Remember never to leave a container on a window-sill where it could fall down into the street.

Stone troughs

NOT SO READILY AVAILABLE, BUT DEFINITELY WORTH LOOKING AT.

Advantages – durable and attractive.

Disadvantages – very heavy and expensive.

Painted clay pots

ADD AN ADDITIONAL SPOT OF COLOUR IN THE HOUSE OR GARDEN.

Advantages – can be bought ready-painted or are fun to paint yourself.

Disadvantages – may require repainting to look their best.

Terracotta pots

AVAILABLE IN A WIDE RANGE OF SIZES AND STYLES.

Advantages – attractive and appear even better with age.

Disadvantages – heavy, and may be damaged by frost.

Wooden boxes

GIVE A WOODEN CONTAINER AN ORIGINAL LOOK WITH YOUR OWN COLOUR SCHEME.

Advantages – you can change the look to suit any new planting scheme.

Disadvantages – the boxes require occasional maintenance.

Galvanized tin

TIN HAS MOVED FROM THE UTILITARIAN TO THE FASHIONABLE.

Advantages – an interesting variation from the usual materials.

Disadvantages – drainage holes are required.

Wire baskets

MOSS LOOKS ESPECIALLY BEAUTIFUL WHEN SEEN THROUGH DELICATE WIRE.

Advantages – available in a huge variety of sizes, easy to work with, and can be moved around easily.

Disadvantages – involve careful preparation and maintenance.

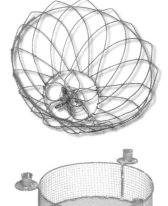

Lightweight fibre window boxes

PLAIN AND PRACTICAL.

Advantages – look rustic, and have a rich brown colour.

Disadvantages – short life-span.

Baskets

ADD A WONDERFUL COUNTRY FEEL TO ANY DISPLAY AND LOOK DELIGHTFUL PLANTED WITH SPRING BULBS.

Advantages – an unconventional and durable way to display plants.

Disadvantages – need lining before planting to prevent leakage.

Novelty containers

HUGELY UNDERRATED. USE ANYTHING FROM WATERING CANS OR TYRES TO SHOES.

Advantages – witty and fun.

Disadvantages – possible short life-span.

Propagation techniques

Most containers and plants are available from garden centres but raising your own plants from seed or cuttings is far easier than you may think and can be very rewarding. Buying young plants from mail order catalogues is an increasingly popular way of starting a collection.

Seed Sowing

One of the cheapest ways of getting a mass planting is by growing plants from seed. It is fun, can be easy (when growing marigolds, for instance), and you don't need a high-tech greenhouse. Furthermore, if you get hooked on the plants, you can collect your own ripe seed in the autumn for a spring sowing the following year.

Cuttings

If you want to increase your stock of the plants you are already growing in the garden, you can get quick results by taking spring cuttings.

When the cuttings have rooted – this will be immediately obvious because they suddenly perk up – wait for the roots to fill the pot, and then transfer to individual pots.

1 Fill the seed tray with seed compost. Gently firm and level the surface by pressing down on the compost using a tray of the same size. When sowing large seeds, such as sunflowers or marigolds, use a dibber, cane or pencil to make holes for each seed. Plant the seeds and cover with compost.

2 When sowing small seeds they should be thinly scattered on the surface of the compost and then covered with just enough sieved sand and compost to conceal them. Firm the surface, using another tray. Water from above, using a fine rose on a watering can, or by standing the tray in water until the surface of the compost is moist.

1 Remove the new soft-wood growth when it is about 10 cm (4 in) long, just above a leaf node.

2 Using a sharp knife, trim the cutting just below a node and trim away the lower leaves.

3 Dip the end of the stem in hormone rooting powder, and plant up in a small container, using cuttings compost.

4 Fill the pot with cuttings, water, and place in a warm, bright place, out of scorching sunlight.

3 Enclose the seed tray in a plastic jar or bag to conserve moisture and cover with a black plastic bag, as most seeds germinate best in a warm dark place.

4 Check daily and bring into the light when the seedlings are showing.

5 To create a moist microclimate for the cuttings, it's a good idea to enclose the pot completely in a plastic bag. Secure it with an elastic band around the pot.

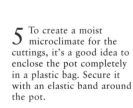

Mail Order

Send off each year for the latest seed and plant catalogues. You will invariably find a wider range than you can buy in a garden centre. Young plants are packed into special packages, which minimize damage during transit, but as they are restricted and in the dark they are initially weakened and some care is necessary to encourage vigorous growth.

Potting On

After several weeks your young plants, whether grown from seed, mail order stock or cuttings, will need potting on. This simply means giving the young plant its own larger, individual container.

1 Young plants are ready to move into larger pots when the roots start to emerge through the holes in the base of the pot. Gently remove the rootball from the pot to check. If there is more than one seedling in the pot, carefully tease away each individual rootball. (Some plants hate to have their roots disturbed. The information on the seed packet will tell you this. These seeds are best sown individually in peat pots or modular trays.) Lower the rootball of the plant into a pot marginally bigger than the existing one.

1 Open the package with care. Leaves will probably unfold from the confined space. Each plant should be intact and clearly labelled.

2 Lift the plants out of their travelling box. Labels tucked underneath the root ball reduce the necessity for handling it directly and helps to keep the compost intact.

3 Plant in a small pot. If the plants seem very wilted, remove some of the larger leaves.

2 Holding the plant carefully so as not to damage the stem, gently pour potting compost around the rootball, firming lightly.

3 Dibble the compost down the side of the pot to eliminate air spaces. It does not matter if the stem of the seedling is buried deeper than it was previously, as long as the leaves are well clear of the soil. Water, using a can with a fine rose.

Composts

Composts come in various formulations suitable for different plant requirements. A standard potting compost is usually peat-based and is suitable for all purposes. Peat and peat substitutes are relatively light in weight, and are therefore the obvious choice for hanging baskets. Regular watering is vital when using peat-based composts, as it is very difficult to moisten them again if they have been allowed to dry out completely. Different composts can be mixed together for specific plant needs.

Standard compost

The majority of composts available at garden centres are peat-based with added fertilizers.

Container compost

A peat-based compost with moisture-retaining granules and added fertilizer, specially formulated for window boxes and containers.

Ericaceous compost

A peat-based compost with no added lime, essential for rhododendrons, camellias and heathers in containers.

Peat-free compost

Manufacturers now offer a range of composts using materials from renewable resources such as coir fibre. They are used in the same way as peat-based composts.

Loam-based compost

Uses sterilized loam as the main ingredient, with fertilizers to supplement the nutrients in the loam. Although much heavier than peat-based compost, it can be lightened by mixing with peat-free compost. Ideal for long-term planting as it retains nutrients well.

THE ESSENTIAL FERTILIZER ELEMENTS

All plant fertilizers contain three key elements, nitrogen (N), phosphorous (P), and potassium/potash (K), with extra trace elements. These three promote, respectively, foliage growth, flower development, and fruit ripening and root development.

When buying a packet of fertilizer you can easily check the balance of the ingredients. It is printed as an "NPK" ratio, for instance 12:5:12. But don't be fooled into thinking that a reading of 24:10:24 is stronger, giving twice the value. It won't, of course, as the ratio is the same. A fertilizer with a ratio of 10:5:10 provides a sound, balanced diet. (You can purchase meters from garden centres that give a guide to the nutrient levels in the soil but they are not, to date, particularly accurate.)

Besides feeding, you can also trick some plants into a prolific display of flowering. Plants packed into small containers, with restricted (but not crippling) root space, feel that they are in danger of dying. Their immediate response is to do what all flowering plants are programmed to do – flower and set seed to continue the species.

Feeding container plants

It is not generally understood that most potting composts contain sufficient food for only six weeks of plant growth. After that, the plants will slowly starve unless more food is introduced. There are several products available, all of which are easy to use. Many of the projects in this book use slow-release plant food granules because they are the easiest and most reliable way of ensuring your plants receive sufficient food during the growing season. For these granules to be effective the compost needs to remain damp or the nutrients cannot be released.

Slow-release Plant Food Granules

These will keep your container plants in prime condition and are very easy to use. One application lasts six months, whereas most other plant foods need to be applied fortnightly. Follow the manufacturer's recommended dose carefully; additional fertilizer will simply leach away.

BELOW: *A variety of plant foods (clockwise from top left): liquid foliar feed, two types of pelleted slow-release plant food granules, a general fertilizer and loose slow-release plant food granules.*

TOP: *Slow-release plant food granules can be added to the compost or potting mix in the recommended quantity before filling the container and planting it.*

ABOVE: *When adding fertilizer granules to the soil, sprinkle them on to the surface of the compost and rake into the top layer. Pelleted granules should be pushed approximately 2 cm (3/4 in) below the surface.*

Watering container plants

Watering plants in containers is an acquired art, and an incredibly important one. You cannot leave it entirely to nature because rain tends to bounce off the leaves of the bushiest plants, soaking not into the pot but into the adjoining ground.

Outside, pot plants dry out very quickly on roasting hot days. Unlike plants in the ground, their roots are encircled by heat; some thirsty plants might even need two waterings a day, so keep checking. You have to get the balance right between over- and under-watering.

Trial and error is one way, but there are a few key tips, one of the best and simplest being to stick your finger deep into the soil to test for dryness. If you are unsure, wait until you see the first signs of wilting, then give the plant a thorough drink, letting the water drain out of the bottom of the pot. And always water plants either first thing in the morning or, better still, late at night, so that the moisture does not quickly evaporate. At all costs, try to avoid over-watering, which is a bigger killer than pests and diseases combined.

The best water is either rainwater or cold, boiled water, but it is not essential to use these unless your tap water is very hard, or you are growing lime-hating plants such as camellias. Don't allow your

potted plants to become waterlogged. If there is any water remaining in the saucer half an hour after watering, tip it away.

Window Boxes and Pots

Don't rush the watering. Though you might think one soaking is enough for a big window box, it might only wet the top few inches of compost. Wait until the water sluices out of the bottom. Container composts include a water-retaining gel and if the compost remains wet in cold weather it can cause the roots to rot.

Hanging Baskets

Summer hanging baskets need daily watering even in overcast weather and on a hot day should be watered morning and evening. Once they have been allowed to dry out it can be difficult for the compost to re-absorb water. In these circumstances it is a good idea to immerse hanging baskets in a large bucket or bowl of water. Winter and spring hanging baskets should be watered only when the soil is dry.

LEFT: *Houseplants enjoy being sprayed with water, but in hard water areas you should use rainwater or bottled water.*

Water-retaining Gel

One of the main problems for most container gardeners is the amount of watering required to keep the plants thriving in the growing season. Adding water-retaining gels to compost will certainly help reduce this task. Sachets of gel are available from garden centres.

1 Pour the recommended amount of water into a bowl.

2 Scatter the gel over the surface, stirring occasionally until it has absorbed the water.

3 Add to your compost at the recommended rate, and mix the gel in thoroughly before using it for planting.

MULCHES

A mulch is a layer of protective material placed over the soil. It helps to retain moisture, conserve warmth, suppress weeds and prevent soil splash on foliage and flowers.

Bark chippings

Bark is an extremely effective mulch and as it rots down it conditions the soil. It works best when spread at least 7.5 cm (3 in) thick and is therefore not ideal for small containers. It is derived from renewable resources.

Clay granules

Clay granules are widely used for hydroculture, but can also be used to mulch houseplants. When placing a plant in a *cachepot*, fill all around the pot with granules. When watered, the granules absorb moisture, which is then released slowly to create a moist microclimate for the plant.

Gravel

Gravel makes a decorative mulch for container plants, and also provides the correct environment for plants such as alpines. It is available in a variety of sizes and colours which can be matched to the scale and colours of the plants used.

Stones

Smooth stones can be used as decorative mulch for large container-grown plants. You can save stones dug out of the garden, collect your own from beaches and riverbeds or buy stones from garden centres. They also deter cats from using the soil as a litter tray.

Pests and diseases

Container plants are every bit as susceptible to aphid and slug attacks as those grown in the garden. But they are generally easier to keep an eye on, so the moment you see a pest attack, take action. Most pests multiply at a staggering rate, and once a plant has been vigorously assaulted, it takes a long time to recover.

Common Pests

Aphids

These sap-sucking insects feed on the tender growing tips. Most insecticides are effective against aphids such as greenfly or blackfly (shown above). Choose one that will not harm ladybirds.

Mealy bugs

These look like spots of white mould. They are hard to shift and regular treatment with a systemic insecticide is the best solution.

Caterpillars

The occasional caterpillar can be picked off the plant and disposed of as you see fit, but a major infestation can strip a plant before your eyes. Contact insecticides are usually very effective.

Red spider mite

An insect that thrives indoors in dry conditions. Constant humidity will reduce the chance of an infestation, which is indicated by the presence of fine webs and mottling of the plant's leaves. To treat an infestation, pick off the worst affected leaves and spray the plants with an insecticide.

Vine weevils

These white grubs are a menace. The first sign of an infestation is the sudden collapse of the plant because the weevil has eaten its roots. Systemic insecticides or natural predators can be used as a preventative, but once a plant has been attacked it is usually too late to save it. Never re-use the soil from an affected plant. The picture above shows an adult weevil.

Snails

Snails cannot generally reach hanging baskets, but are more of a problem in wall baskets and window boxes: they tuck themselves behind the container during daylight and venture out to feast at night. Use slug pellets or venture out yourself with a torch and catch them.

Whitefly

These tiny white flies flutter up in clouds when disturbed from their feeding places on the undersides of leaves. Whitefly are particularly troublesome in conservatories, where a dry atmosphere will encourage them to breed. Keep the air as moist as possible. Contact insecticides will need more than one application to deal with an infestation, but a systemic insecticide will protect the plant for weeks.

Common Diseases

Black spot – most commonly seen on roses; dark spots on leaves occur before they fall. Burn all affected foliage, and treat with a fungicide.
Botrytis – immediately evident as a pernicious, furry grey mould. Remove and burn all affected parts, and treat with a fungicide.
Powdery mildew – most likely to affect potted fruit trees. Remove and burn affected parts. Treat with a fungicide.
Rust – high humidity causes orange/dark brown pustules on the stem. Remove and burn affected parts. Treat with a fungicide.
Viruses (various) – the varied symptoms include distorted, mis-shapen leaves, and discoloration. Vigorous anti-aphid controls are essential. Destroy affected foliage.

Pest Control

There are three main types of pest control available to combat common pests.

Systemic insecticides

These work by being absorbed by the plant's root or leaf system, and killing insects that come into contact with the plant. This will work for difficult pests, such as the grubs of vine weevils which are hidden in the soil, and scale insects which protect themselves from above with a scaly cover.

Contact insecticides

These must be sprayed directly on to the insects to be effective. Most organic insecticides work this way, but they generally kill all insects, even beneficial ones, such as hoverflies and ladybirds. Try to remove these before spraying the infected plant.

Biological control

Commercial growers now use biological control in their glasshouses; this means natural predators are introduced to eat the pest population. Although not all are suitable for the amateur gardener, they can be used in conservatories for dealing with pests such as whitefly.

NATURAL PREDATORS

Aphidius – a wasp that lays eggs in young aphids; on hatching they devour the host.
Aphidoletes – a gall midge that devours aphids.
Bacillus thuringinesis – a bacterium that kills caterpillars.
Cryptolaemus montrouzieri – an Australian ladybird that eats mealy bug. It is activated by a temperature of 20°C (68°F).
Encarsia formosa – a parasitic wasp that lays eggs in the larvae of whitefly. The young wasps eat their hosts.

Metaphycus – a parasitic wasp, activated by a temperature of 20°C (68°F), that kills off soft scales.
Phasmarhabditis – a nematode that kills slugs provided the temperature of the soil is above 5°C (41°F).
Phytoseiulus persimilis – attacks red spider mite provided the temperature is 20°C (68°F).
Steinernema – kills vine weevils by releasing a bacterium into them. Needs a temperature of 12°C (53°F).

Suitable container plants

Annuals and Biennials

Whether you raise them yourself from seed in the greenhouse or on the kitchen window-sill, or buy them in strips from the garden centre for an instant effect, fast-growing annuals and biennials will quickly and cheaply fill baskets and boxes and flower prolifically all summer to produce eye-catching effects. Choose compact varieties that will not need support. Trailing annuals such as lobelia, nasturtiums and dwarf sweet peas are all invaluable for hanging baskets. Some perennial species, including petunias, pelargoniums and busy Lizzies (impatiens), are normally grown as annuals.

Tender Perennials

Beautiful tender and half-hardy plants such as osteospermums, verbenas, pelargoniums, petunias and fuchsias are ideal for containers, where their showy flowers can be fully appreciated. Raise new plants from cuttings for next season. If you buy young, tender plants from the garden centre in the spring, don't be tempted to put newly planted boxes or baskets outside until all danger of frost is past.

ABOVE: *Trailing nasturtiums make a glorious display, providing colour from early summer.*

LEFT: *Petunias and pelargoniums are tender perennials, which are often grown as annuals.*

BELOW: *Containers of spring bulbs such as these yellow tulips cannot fail to delight.*

Evergreen Perennials

Evergreen non-woody perennials such as ajugas, bergenias and *Carex oshimensis* 'Evergold' are always useful for providing colour and foliage in the winter, but look best as part of a mixed planting.

For single plantings, try *Agapanthus africanus* or *A. orientalis* with their blue flowers on tall stems. For a more architectural shape, consider one of the many different eryngiums (sea holly). *E. agavifolium* is particularly attractive, and has greenish-white flowers in late summer.

Border Perennials

Few people bother to grow perennials in containers, but if you have a paved garden, or would like to introduce them to the patio, don't be afraid to experiment. Dicentras, agapanthus, and many ornamental grasses are among the plants that you might want to try, but there are very many more that you should be able to succeed with – and they will cost you nothing if you divide a plant already in the border.

Bulbs

Bulbs, particularly the spring varieties make ideal container plants. Bulbs should be planted at twice the depth of their own length. They can be packed in as tight as you like, and even in layers, so that you get a repeat-showing after the first display. Note that when planting lilies (the white, scented, fail-safe *Lilium regale* is a fine choice if you have never tried them before), they need excellent drainage, so put in an extra layer of grit at the bottom. And to prevent spearing the bulb later on with a plant support, insert this in the compost at the same time.

Shrubs for Tubs

Camellias are perfect shrubs for tubs, combining attractive, glossy evergreen foliage with beautiful spring flowers. *Camellia* x *williamsii* and *C. japonica* hybrids are a good choice. Many rhododendrons and azaleas are also a practical proposition, and if you have a chalky soil this is the best way to grow these plants – provided you fill the container with an ericaceous compost.

Many hebes make good container plants (but not for very cold or exposed areas), and there are many attractively variegated varieties. The yellow-leaved *Choisya ternata* 'Sundance' and variegated yuccas such as *Yucca filamentosa* 'Variegata' and *Y. gloriosa* 'Variegata' are also striking shrubs for containers.

For some winter interest, try *Viburnum tinus*.

Topiary for Pots

Topiarized box is ideal for a pot. However, it is relatively slow growing at about 30 cm (12 in) a year. It may be best to buy a mature, ready-shaped plant, although you miss the fun of doing the pruning.

ABOVE: *If your garden cannot support lime-hating rhododendrons, do not despair. They can easily be grown in pots, in ericaceous compost, giving colour from autumn, through winter, to summer.*

LEFT: *Pots on plinths and fruit trees in tubs create a marvellous architectural effect, with plenty of striking verticals.*

Trees for Tubs

Trees are unlikely candidates for containers, particularly for small gardens. Fortunately, the restricted root-run usually keeps them compact and they never reach the proportions of trees planted in the ground. Even in a small garden, some height is useful.

Choose trees that are naturally small if possible. Laburnums, crab apples (and some of the upright-growing and compact eating apples on dwarfing rootstocks), *Prunus* 'Amanogawa' (a flowering cherry with narrow, upright growth), and even trees as potentially large as *Acer platanoides* 'Drummondii' (a variegated maple) will be happy in a large pot or tub for a number of years. Small weeping trees also look good. Try *Salix caprea pendula* or *Cotoneaster* 'Hybridus Pendulus' (which has cascades of red berries in autumn). Even the pretty dome-shaped, grey-leaved *Pyrus salicifolia* 'Pendula' is a possibility.

These must have a heavy pot with a minimum inside diameter of 38 cm (15 in), and a loam-based compost. Even then they are liable to blow over in very strong winds unless you pack some other hefty pots around them during stormy weather.

Planting pots

Planting up a container of any size could not be easier, as long as you follow a few basic rules. First, terracotta pots need a layer of material at the bottom to help the water drain away quickly. Plastic pots usually have sufficient drainage holes. Second, always plant into the appropriate size pot; that is, slightly larger than the rootball. Putting a small plant into a large pot is counter productive. The plant will put on good root growth at the expense of flowers and foliage. Since the hungry root system will drink up water rapidly in summer, check regularly that the soil is not too dry.

ABOVE: *Beautiful, elegant urns do not always need the finest flowering plants. As these twin pots show, even a modest planting works well. Indeed, it is often preferable because it does not detract from the gorgeous containers.*

Maintaining Plants

Large plants can grow in surprisingly small containers. They will not grow to the same height as if they were given a free root run, but should be impressive nonetheless. If possible, remove the top layer of soil every year, and replace it with fresh compost. There comes a time, however, when most plants finally outgrow their containers. What then? You can replace the mature plant with a cutting and start again. Alternatively, stick instead to plants that are slow-growing, or which will not rapidly fill their pots with roots. Or root prune.

Root pruning is a remarkably easy technique, which involves removing the plant from the pot in spring, when it is beginning to put on good growth. Either slice away the exterior of the rootball quite boldly, or snip at it with secateurs. Then replace in the existing pot, filling the gap with fresh compost.

Overwintering

Remember that while tender plants may just survive winter outside in your area, with their roots protected deep below ground, those in pots are much less likely to survive. The roots will be just the width of the pot (a few centimetres) away from encircling snow or icy winds. Bring these plants indoors or, if you do not have room, take cuttings before the end of the season.

Planting in Terracotta

Terracotta containers are always popular, but need some preparation before planting.

1 With terracotta it is essential to provide some form of drainage material in the base of the container. When planting in large pots or boxes, recycle broken-up polystyrene plant trays as drainage material. Lumps of polystyrene are excellent for this purpose and as they retain warmth they are of additional benefit to the plant.

2 In smaller pots the drainage material can be broken pieces of pot, known as crocks, or gravel.

Planting in Plastic

When buying plastic pots or boxes, check that the drainage holes are open. Some manufacturers mark the holes but leave it to the purchaser to punch or drill them out as required.

Plant Supports

Climbing plants in containers will need support. This can be provided by one or more canes which are pushed into the pot, a free-standing plant frame or a trellis fastened to a wall behind the container.

Planting in Wicker Baskets

If you wish to use a more unconventional container as a window box you may need to seal it with a sheet of plastic to prevent leakage.

1 Line the basket with a generous layer of moss which will prevent the compost leaking away.

2 Fill the basket with compost, and mix in plant food granules or any organic alternative you wish to use.

Saucers and Feet

Saucers are available for plastic and clay pots. They act as water reservoirs for the plants, and are used under houseplants to protect the surface they are standing on. Clay saucers must be fully glazed if they are used indoors or they will leave marks. Clay feet are available for terracotta pots. They will prevent the pot becoming waterlogged, but this also means that in a sunny position the pot will dry out very quickly and may need extra watering.

Plastic plant saucers can be used to line and protect containers which are not waterproof, such as this wooden apple-basket.

Hanging gardens

When you want colour high up or relating closely to the building, the easiest way is to create a hanging garden, either in baskets or in wall-mounted containers. A purpose-made hanging basket is designed so that as the flowers grow, they cascade through the side and spill over the edge in a joyous show of colour, covering the whole basket. An alternative is to make the basket or container part of the display. Ordinary shopping baskets, buckets, agricultural containers, even kitchen equipment such as colanders, pots and pans, can be used.

Planting and Positioning Hanging Baskets

One hanging basket, alone on a wall, can look rather insignificant. Far better to plant up baskets in pairs, either with similar plants to create an echoing effect, or with clashing, contrasting colours. For a really stunning effect, entirely cover a wall with baskets, but remember that they are very demanding, and will need prolific watering in a dry mid-summer.

If the container is large and in danger of getting too heavy for its support, one trick is to put a layer of broken-up expanded polystyrene (from plant trays or electrical goods packaging) in the bottom of the container. This is lighter than the equivalent amount of compost and provides good drainage. Containers should have drainage holes, and baskets will need lining to stop the soil from being washed out while you are watering. Liners can

be home-made from pieces of plastic sheet cut to size, with a layer of moss tucked between the basket and plastic for a more decorative look. Alternatively, you can use a proprietary liner, made from paper pulp, to fit purpose-made hanging baskets, or coconut matting – which comes in a variety of shapes and sizes to adapt to all kinds of baskets.

Whichever type of container you choose, it needs to be filled with a good compost, and adding fertilizer granules and water-retaining gel can also help promote lush results and make care and maintenance a little easier.

RIGHT: *Hanging baskets filled with pansies create a lovely focal point of gentle colour.*

Preparing Hanging Baskets

The key to successful hanging baskets is in the preparation. Time taken in preparing the basket for planting will be rewarded with a long-lasting colourful display. Slow-release plant food granules incorporated into the compost when planting ensure that the plants receive adequate nutrients throughout the growing season. It is essential to water hanging baskets every day, even in overcast weather, as they dry out very quickly. There are various ways to line a hanging basket.

Choosing a Lining

1 When buying a hanging basket, make sure that the chains are detachable. By unhooking one of the chains, they can be placed to one side of the basket, allowing you to work freely. Either rest the basket on a flat surface, or sit it on a flowerpot.

2 Traditionally, hanging baskets are lined with sphagnum moss. This looks very attractive and plants can be introduced at any point in the side of the basket. As sphagnum moss tends to dry out rather faster than other liners, it is advisable to use a compost containing water-retaining gel with this lining.

3 Coir fibre liners are a practical substitute for moss. Although not as good to look at, the coir will soon be hidden as the plants grow. The slits in the liner allow for planting in the side of the basket.

4 Cardboard liners are clean and easy to use. They are made in various sizes to fit most hanging baskets.

5 Press out the marked circles on the cardboard liner if you wish to plant into the side of the basket.

Underplanting a Hanging Basket

Underplanting helps to achieve a really lush-looking basket and soon conceals the shape of the container under flowers and foliage.

1 Line the lower half of the basket with a generous layer of moss.

2 Rest the rootball on the moss and gently guide the foliage through the side of the basket.

3 Add more moss to the basket, tucking it carefully around the plants to ensure that they are firmly in place. Add a further row of plants near the top edge of the basket, if required, and continue to line the basket with moss, finishing off with a collar of moss overlapping the rim of the basket. Fill with compost.

Year-round containers

Containers are traditionally used for creating extra, lavish colourful effects in summer. With a little thought and careful planning you can enjoy delightful containers all year round.

First Signs of Spring

Early spring bulbs burst into life as soon as winter loosens its grip. Even on chilly, rainy days, pots planted with small bulbs – snowdrops, crocuses, scillas and *Iris reticulata* – will provide splashes of clear colour on the patio or window-sills, and can be briefly brought indoors, if you like, for an early taste of spring. Primulas and polyanthus look great in containers, too. If you grow lily-of-the-valley in the garden, pot up a few roots and bring them inside: they'll come into bloom weeks early.

ABOVE AND LEFT: *Plants might not flourish in the garden border all year round, but you can still have some delightful plants every day of the year. Here, small pots of lily-of-the-valley, dwarf irises, crocuses and primroses brighten up a warm day in early spring.*

Summer Blooms

Summer is, of course, the highlight of the container gardener's year, giving the opportunity for lovely creative plantings. Deciding which plants to use is an enjoyable task.

RIGHT: *For a really eye-catching container, be different. A large potted mix, featuring summer bedding plants topped by a lanky white fuchsia, is encircled by a rustic woven sheep feeder. The effect is heightened by tufts of grass packed into the gaps.*

FAR RIGHT: *A flamboyant show of billowing annuals.*

Autumn Highlights

Grow one or two autumn-glory shrubs in tubs that you can bring out when you need a final burst of colour on the patio.

Ceratostigma willmottiamum has compact growth and lovely autumn foliage tints while still producing blue flowers. Berries can also be used as a feature, and you can usually buy compact gaultherias already bearing berries in your garden centre.

ABOVE: *Potted chrysanthemums (here flanked by ericas) are an easy and excellent way of prolonging bright summer colours into autumn.*

Winter Colour

Some winter-flowering shrubs can be used in tubs, such as *Viburnum tinus* and *Mahonia* x *media* 'Charity'. Try being bold with short-term pot plants such as Cape heathers (*Erica hyemalis* and *E. gracilis*) and winter cherries (*Solanum capsicastrum* and similar species and hybrids). You will have to throw them away afterwards, but they will look respectable for a few weeks even in cold and frosty winter weather.

HOW TO PROTECT PLANTS FROM FROST

Many of the most dramatic summer patio shrubs – like daturas and oleanders – must be taken into a frost-free place for the winter. Others that are frost-tolerant but of borderline hardiness in cold areas, like the bay (*Laurus nobilis*), or that are vulnerable to frost and wind damage to the leaves (such as *Choisya ternata* 'Sundance') need a degree of winter protection. It is a pity to lose these magnificent patio plants for the sake of a little forethought as autumn draws to a close. Shrubs that are fairly tough and need a little protection from the worst weather can be covered with horticultural fleece, or bubbly polythene. If you use fleece, you may be able to buy it as a sleeve (ideal for winter protection for shrubs in tubs).

1 Insert four or five canes around the edge of the pot. Cut the polythene to size. Allow for an overlap over the pot.

2 Wrap it around the plant, allowing a generous overlap. For particularly vulnerable plants, use more than one layer. Securely tie the protection around the pot. For very delicate plants, bring the material well down over the pot, to keep the rootball warm. Leave the top open for ventilation and to permit watering if necessary.

GARDENER'S TIP

If covering with fleece, tie the top together (moisture will be able to penetrate, and tying the top will help to conserve warmth).

OPPOSITE: *Smooth, topiarized box balls and pyramids catch the eye at any time of year. You can buy them ready styled or, better still, raise your own cuttings and shape them as you wish.*

Colour-theme plantings

Create impact in the garden by colour-theming seasonal planting to tune in with their surroundings. This works best with plants in containers as the containers can be chosen to tone and blend with the walls, then planted with flowers in complementary colours. Once the blooms are over, they can be replaced by new plantings for the next season. You do not always have to match the colours; you may decide to use contrasting colours instead. In this way, the garden looks fresh and bright all year round and you have several scene changes to enjoy as the seasons pass.

ABOVE: *The blue-green and purple tones of ornamental cabbage look fabulous in a galvanized grey bucket, set against the blue-green of a painted fence.*

OPPOSITE: *An orange-yellow poppy and cream-coloured violas look stunning planted in beige pots, set against the warm ochre shades of a brick wall.*

ABOVE: *This pot has been painted in stripes to link the green background and pink blooms of a wonderful hebe.*

Colour-splash plantings

Just as you can decorate the inside of your home with colourful flower arrangements, so you can do the same outside. Use pots of flowering plants to provide a colourful splash in a prominent part of the garden or to decorate the outdoor living area when entertaining. Create an immediate colour impact by choosing a colour theme and teaming containers and plants in toning shades. Try painting some terracotta pots specially to match your favourite flowers. You could also make a tablescape for a special occasion, using a variety of containers and seasonal flowering plants in hot clashing colours or in cool shades of blue, purple and white.

ABOVE: *Simple and magical, it is as though the rich colouring of the tulips has leaked out of the petals and dripped down the side of the pots.*

ABOVE: *Even a couple of ordinary terracotta garden pots hanging on the wall make interesting decorative detail, especially when they are both planted with a froth of white blooms.*

LEFT: *The papery white flowers of the petunias are underplanted with white lobelia and surrounded by silver Helichrysum. The basket looks wonderful in the pale light of a summer's evening.*

ABOVE: *Bright, bold, hothouse colours are very effective in groups.*
Try to find equally brightly coloured planters and containers.

Creating cameo gardens

If you are lucky enough to have a spare part of the garden where nothing is going on, liven it up by introducing a set theme. It can be witty and original, or have a theme to merge with the rest of the garden. Or it could even be a special private area packed with all your favourite pots.

Cameo gardens can provide a surprise in a small corner, embellish an under-used area or even provide a miniature project for children, who love to have a space of their own. The idea is to find a theme – herbs, perhaps, or pansies, miniature vegetables or lavender – then make up a "sampler", providing a different container for each variety. Alternatively, you can make the containers the

theme, choosing watering cans, culinary pots, pans and colanders, enamelware or terracotta in different shapes and sizes. Another idea is to design a miniature formal garden, perhaps taking inspiration from the classic Italian style. Choose a piece of small statuary as a focal point, then clip some young box plants into a miniature hedge surround and fill in with dwarf lavender.

LEFT: *For a seaside-type garden, use a stone-coloured pot and grey-leaved plants to blend in with the sandy background.*

Pots for Privacy

To be able to relax totally in the garden, you need to satisfy two basic requirements: privacy and shelter. Without the benefit of enclosed spaces, especially in built-up areas, these considerations can be problematic. However, there are ways of achieving them. Trellis can be fixed on top of walls and fences to create extra height. You can then grow decorative climbers to provide a wonderful natural wallpaper. And within this enclosure you can create a special atmosphere with the use of gorgeous pots. In fact, pots score over plants in beds because they can be swapped round with other containers in the rest of the garden, giving a constant change of scenery.

One way of conveying privacy is by furnishing this area like a real room. A row of shelves for a collection of, say, pelargoniums, pouring out rich red and magenta flowers and subtler hues. Verbenas make an

excellent alternative, and can either be left to tumble, or trained up miniature wigwams of green sticks to provide a side-show in blues, mauves and purples, interspersed with white. Violas are equally small-scale and domestic, with the added advantage that, being placed at eye level, their amazingly exquisite, detailed patterning can be fully appreciated. But perhaps the best container plants for outdoor shelving, or even an old, brightly painted open kitchen display unit, are auricula primulas.

Auriculas impart a strong Victorian feel (although they were actually introduced in the late 16th century) with their ornate faces, which are so exquisite that they used to be displayed inside an empty picture frame. One by itself is always an eye-catcher, leaving the viewer demanding more. Visit a specialist nursery to see a wide range.

Scented Pots

An enclosed area with no wind is the perfect place to grow scented pot plants where the perfume can hang in the air. You can have anything from marzipan to the smell of melting, rich brown chocolate. Just place the pots around a chair, sit back and relax.

Daphne odora 'Aureomarginata' makes a perfect shrub for a tub. It grows quite slowly to about 1.5m (5ft), and has purplish flowers, and the most ravishing scent imaginable. Feed well, place in the sun, and add plenty of grit to the soil for quick drainage.

Jasminum officinale is a fast, vigorous climber; it will quickly race up the side of a house or, with a restricted root run, can be trained round a large frame. Give it a hot sunny spot, water well, and inhale. Lilies have equally strong scents. The range is huge, running from the highly popular and reliable *Lilium regale* to the various, multi-coloured hybrids like 'Black Dragon' and 'Green Dragon', to the stunning strain called Imperial Crimson, with white flowers speckled red. Good drainage is the secret of success.

For a talking point, choose the unusual but wonderful *Cosmos atrosanguineus* which has dark maroon flowers and a whiff of chocolate on hot, sunny days. For marzipan, try an old-fashioned heliotrope like 'Princess Marina'. And for an unusual small black flower and the scent of summer fruits, plant up *Salvia discolor*.

RIGHT: *Thyme-filled gardens have a distinguished history, and have been popular since the medieval period. The trick is to choose a selection, with round and needle-like leaves, to create a rich tapestry in shades of green, gold and silver.*

Novel Themes

Edible gardens are always popular, and besides growing potted fruit trees and strawberries, it is worth experimenting with different kinds of salad. Lettuces now come in a wide range of shapes and colours and the more ornamental forms of herbs like basil and sage are just as delicious as the green varieties.

You can also grow a range of potted plants with different textured foliage. Smooth and svelte, sharp and pointed, rubbery and mounded, are all available. When next visiting a garden centre, do not just go in with your eyes open but with a stroking, extended hand. Plants appeal to more senses than one.

ABOVE: *A marvellous concoction made from the simplest of easily gathered materials. A scattering of wet beach pebbles frames a circular pattern, backed up by a group of small pots and chimney pots, planted with a wide selection of succulents.*

TOP: *Serried ranks of watering cans in the soft greys of weathered, galvanized metal make a beautiful feature in themselves. Planted up with hostas and violas, they become a highly original cameo garden.*

ABOVE: *This terracotta garden is focused around tall, long-tom pots planted with hostas, ivies and clematis let loose so that it behaves like a trailer, rather than a climber. Old drain covers and edging tiles add character.*

LEFT: *Potted plants always give plenty of impact when arranged in groups and one way to display them is on old baker's shelves in rows and rows of pots.*

RIGHT: *Themed gardens do not come much better than this. A sensational group of battered, wizened old boots double up as containers. The sumptuous profusion of pelargoniums in full blast obviously couldn't be happier.*

Potted table decorations

Outdoor table decorations are easy to put together and are at their most successful when they complement their surroundings. Simply gather together some of the smaller pots from around the garden, you may plunder the garden for a few cut flowers or foliage to add, or even add fruit and vegetables to complete the effect. The concentration in one place of what grows in naturally looser arrangements throughout the garden focuses the overall look.

BELOW: *Spring narcissi are perfectly in scale for a table setting. And with so many varieties having strong scents, there's nowhere better to appreciate them while relaxing over a long cold drink?*

RIGHT: *Ornamental cabbages, complemented by individual cabbage leaves used decoratively on the napkins and a miniature arrangement in a small jar, make an unusual centrepiece.*

BELOW: *A wire basket with raffia interwoven round its base gathers together pots of verbena surrounded by tiny pots of variegated ivy. The end result is an outdoor casualness perfectly in accord with its surroundings.*

LEFT: *In summer, a couple of potted strawberry plants are transformed into an original decoration when arranged in a wire jug with some extra ripe fruits.*

Location plantings

Finding the right place for the right plant is the key to successful container gardening. One way of tackling the problem is to see container plants as a way of extending the garden into areas where plants do not normally grow. Once you have made a list of such areas, and it is always far longer than you would initially imagine, decide which kind of plants you would like growing there – climbers, scented plants, or plants to screen unsightly areas.

BELOW: *A classical, clipped, mop-head bay tree* (Laurus nobilis) *makes a smart entrance, and adds to the sense of formality. Its geometric shape is cleverly offset by a massed underplanting of lovely pink-flowering fuchsias.*

Entrance Containers

A bare porch can be made to look far more welcoming and attractive by the addition of one large plant in a pot or urn. In warm, sheltered parts of the country you could try growing an exotic scented plant like one of the more tender daphnes (eg the evergreen *D. bholua* 'Jacqueline Postill') in a bright, south-facing spot.

If space is limited, you could hang smaller, ornate terracotta pots on the wall, one above the other, each with attractive, trailing growth. Or fix one or two hanging baskets just outside the porch, to provide aerial colour. But if you live in a particularly cold area, stick to summer bedding plants in the growing season, and for the rest of the year be content with one large, attractive urn. Even when unfilled, it can still be quite a feature.

RIGHT: *An excellent way of livening up a typical suburban porch. Tropical, strap-shaped leaves add height and structure to a mass of smaller evergreens.*

Containers for Corners

Bare corners are all too often taken for granted, a kind of necessary evil. But there is no reason why they cannot add to the garden's glamour. Corners that are paved or covered with stony shingle make the perfect stage for a group of pots whose foliage and flowers mix and mingle, creating striking effects.

The key principle is to place the smaller plants at the front where they can be seen, with the medium-high plants behind, and the tallest at the back. Alternatively, choose a small group of elegant containers, using the plants in a more restrained way. A trailer growing from a pedestal container with a cluster of distinctive smaller plants round the base can be as stunning as a large group.

BELOW: *Antique stone urns like this are ideal for sharp corners where they both create a special feature and help soften a stark 90° angle with curves, colour and interest.*

1 This shady area next to a driveway has been gravelled to break up the effect of a large area of paving but still looks bleak and uninteresting.

2 Plants in containers have transformed this corner. Even though the plants may not completely conceal the wires and downpipe, there is now so much else to interest the eye that they are easily overlooked.

Pots for Steps and Walls

Steps and wall tops are too often left bare when they actually make a perfect platform for a row of colourful pot plants. The outside steps rising up to the top floor of a barn, for example, like a series of rising plinths, make a perfect stage for a series of pot plants, each tumbling colour on to the step below.

ABOVE LEFT: *The severe, formal Georgian entrance to this town house is wonderfully softened by the use of a row of containers on a ledge, packed with white-flowering fuchsias. Note how they complement the colour scheme.*

ABOVE: *Miniature violas, one plant to a pot, make an enchanting decoration for old stone steps.*

1 This terrace of old brick and stone is attractive in its own right, but is not as colourful as it might be.

2 The addition of a variety of containers with flowering plants completes the picture and adds colour and depth to the scene.

Containers as Screens, and with Arbours and Arches

Where you have a garden eyesore, such as a crumbling outhouse or drainage pipe, use ingenuity and imagination to hide it. You do not need to go overboard. A large pot containing a prolific marguerite (argyranthemum) will produce hundreds of daisy-like blooms all summer. You could even grow this plant as a standard, with a mop-head of growth on a 90cm (3ft) high single stem. A planted container, whether hanging or on the ground, is a lovely finishing touch to a garden arch or arbour.

TOP: *This arbour would look very bare without its glorious hanging basket of petunias.*

ABOVE: *A pair of formal containers planted with fuchsia standards, complement this garden archway perfectly.*

LEFT: *A colourful window box is used here to mark the edge of a border.*

Decorating containers

One of the joys of container gardening is decorating your own pots, giving them exactly the right colour scheme to suit the plants and their surroundings. Decorating pots is an undervalued and under-explored art. The majority of plant pots sold in garden centres are plain brown, which people assume is the colour they have to be. As the following projects show, plant pots are like empty canvases. You can turn them into bright, colourful containers with a Mediterranean feel, or much subtler pots in the softest of tones. It is also worth experimenting with more unusual containers such as tin cans and buckets.

ABOVE: *Terracotta pots decorated with simple geometric shapes in yellow and green make perfect containers for spring bulbs.*

Tin can plant nursery

Seedlings can be decorative in themselves, so prick them out from their seed trays into a collection of shiny aluminium cans mounted on to a plaque. They can grow there until they are ready to be planted out. The plaque itself looks wonderful made from ordinary aluminium cans, but if you want to add a bit more colour, scour the shelves of delicatessens for some unusual printed cans and enjoy some culinary treats at the same time.

MATERIALS

Piece of board, about
  60 x 30 cm (24 x 12 in)
Undercoat
Coloured gloss paint
Decorating brush
Can opener
Variety of empty
  aluminium cans with
  the labels removed

Metal snippers
Pliers
Nail
Hammer
Tin tacks

1 Apply an undercoat followed by a coat of gloss paint to the board, allowing each coat to dry completely.

2 Use the can opener to remove the top of each can if this has not already been done. Wash out the cans thoroughly.

3 Using metal snippers, cut down the side of each can and cut off half of the bottom.

4 Open out the sides with pliers and snip a V-shape into each one. Pierce the bottom of each can, using a nail and hammer.

5 Try out the arrangement of the cans on the board. Then, using one tin tack at each side point of the cans, nail into position.

Mexican painted pots

A series of traditional folk-art motifs painted over stripes of vibrant colours gives simple pots a rich Mexican look. Enhance the effect by allowing some of the untreated terracotta colour show through, especially if you use pots with a fluted top like this one. Planted up with pelargoniums in hot summer colours, and stacked together, they make a lively garden feature.

MATERIALS

Terracotta pot with fluted-top
Masking tape
White undercoat
Small decorating brush
Artist's gouache paints
Fine and medium artist's brushes
Polyurethane matt varnish

1 Mark the stripes on the pot using masking tape. Cut some lengths into narrower widths to get variation in the finished design. Bear in mind that the areas covered by masking tape will remain natural terracotta.

2 Paint the body of the pot with undercoat, avoiding the fluted rim. Allow to dry completely.

3 Paint the coloured stripes with gouache paints, changing colour after each band of masking tape. Allow to dry completely.

4 Peel off the masking tape to reveal coloured stripes alternating with terracotta stripes.

5 Using the fine artist's brush and white undercoat, paint simple motifs over the stripes. When completely dry, coat with matt varnish.

Verdigris bucket

There is something irresistible about the luminous, blue-green tones of verdigris. It is a colour that always complements plants and is not difficult to reproduce on a cheap galvanized bucket. To make the rust bucket shown behind the verdigris one, follow the steps below, but substitute rust-coloured acrylic paint for the aqua paint.

MATERIALS

Galvanized bucket
Medium-grade sandpaper
Metal primer
Small decorating brush
Gold paint
Amber shellac
Artist's acrylic paint in white and aqua-green
Water for mixing
Natural sponge
Polyurethane matt varnish

1 Sand the bucket, then prime with metal primer. Allow to dry for 2–3 hours. Paint with gold paint and allow to dry for 2–3 hours.

2 Paint with amber shellac and allow to dry for 30 minutes. Mix white acrylic paint with aqua-green and enough water to make a liquid consistency.

3 Sponge on the verdigris paint and allow to dry for 1–2 hours. Apply a coat of varnish.

Lead chimney

The wonderful chalky tones of lead have made it a popular material for garden containers down the centuries. However, lead is incredibly heavy and very expensive, so here is a way of faking it, using a plastic, terracotta-coloured chimney and some simple paint effects.

MATERIALS

Plastic, terracotta-
  coloured chimney
Sandpaper
Acrylic primer
Large artist's brush

Emulsion (latex) paint in
  charcoal grey and white
Acrylic scumble glaze
Water
Decorating brush
Polyurethane matt varnish

1 Sand the chimney to give it a key. Paint with one coat of acrylic primer and allow to dry for 1–2 hours.

2 Apply one coat of charcoal-grey emulsion and allow to dry for 2–3 hours.

3 Tint the scumble glaze with white emulsion and thin with water. Paint over the chimney randomly. Wash over with water and allow to dry.

4 Add more of the white scumble mixture to parts of the chimney for extra colour and "age". Varnish with polyurethane matt varnish when dry.

A shell window box

Decorated window boxes provide a delightful finish to windows, almost bringing the garden into the house. Being flat-fronted, they are also easier to decorate than round pots. Here, mussel shells lend impact to a co-ordinated planting of lavender and violas. Experiment with different shapes, using some mussel shells face-up and others face-down.

MATERIALS

Small terracotta window box
Mussel shells
Glue gun and all-purpose glue
 sticks
Crocks or pebbles
Compost
Water-retaining gel
Slow-release plant food granules
2 lavender plants
Tray of young viola plants

1 When you are satisfied with your design, fix the shells in position on the window box, using a glue gun.

2 Place crocks or pebbles over the drainage holes inside the window box.

3 Partly fill the box with compost, adding water-retaining gel and plant food granules as you go.

4 Place the lavenders at the back of the box. Press extra compost in front of them until it is the right height for the violas. Plant the violas on this "raised bed".

5 Press more compost firmly around all the plants and water generously.

Colour schemes for containers

*The artistry of container gardening lies in the way in which you arrange and combine
all your raw materials: not just the plants themselves, but the container and the
site you choose for it. Above all, sensitive colour co-ordination can make the difference
between a planting scheme that is just pretty and one that draws gasps of admiration.
The plants and the container need to enhance each other: lavender with blue violas in a
stone urn, for instance, or fiery nasturtiums in terracotta pots. Think about
the background, too – the colour of the surrounding walls, the paint on the window
frame – and make the picture work as a whole.*

*Single-colour schemes can be striking, emphasizing the contrasting forms of
the flowers and foliage, but so can strong contrasts of colour or tone. Let the glowing
palette presented on the following pages inspire you to new heights of creativity.*

ABOVE: *Pure white petunias and lobelia planted with a touch of grey
foliage make a sophisticated display.*

A delicate antique basket

An antique basket is not essential for this scheme, but the bowl shape makes an interesting variation. A small variety of dahlia, known as a dahlietta, has large white flowers that blend with trailing verbenas and a begonia. Silver-leaved marguerites, with soft pink flowers, add a subtle touch of colour.

VERBENA

DAHLIETTA

ARGYRANTHEMUM

MATERIALS

36 cm (14 in) hanging basket
Sphagnum moss
Compost
Slow-release plant food granules

PLANTS

White Begonia semperflorens
3 white dahliettas
3 white trailing verbenas
3 marguerites (Argyranthemum
'Flamingo')

BEGONIA

1 Line the basket with moss and fill with compost. Mix a teaspoon of slow-release plant food granules into the top of the compost.

2 Plant the begonia in the centre and position and plant the dahliettas around the begonia.

3 Plant a verbena to one side of each of the dahliettas. Plant the marguerites, angling them so they will trail over the edge of the basket. Water well and hang in a sunny position.

GARDENER'S TIP

Regular dead-heading of the flowers will keep the basket in tip-top condition. The slow-release plant food granules will give the flowers a regular supply of nutrients provided the basket is not allowed to dry out.

PLANT IN LATE SPRING OR EARLY SUMMER

An all-white window box

A painted wooden window box filled with a white pelargonium, verbenas, marguerites, bacopa, and silver senecio is an ideal combination for a summer wedding celebration in the garden.

MATERIALS

45 cm (18 in) slatted wooden window box
Sphagnum moss
Compost
Slow-release plant food granules

PLANTS

White pelargonium
2 white marguerites (argyranthemums)
2 white trailing verbenas
2 Senecio cineraria 'Silver Dust'
White bacopa

SENECIO

BACOPA

PELARGONIUM

MARGUERITE

VERBENA

1 It is a good idea to line slatted wooden containers with moss before planting to prevent the compost from leaking out when the box is watered.

2 Fill the moss-lined window box with compost, mixing in 2 teaspoons of slow-release plant food granules. Plant the pelargonium in the centre of the window box towards the back.

3 Plant the marguerites on either side of the pelargonium.

4 Plant the trailing verbenas in the two back corners of the window box.

5 Plant the senecios in the front two corners of the window box to frame the bacopa.

6 Plant the bacopa centrally in the front of the box. Water the arrangement thoroughly and stand in a sunny position.

GARDENER'S TIP

To prolong the life of wooden containers it is advisable to empty them of compost before winter and store them under cover until spring.

PLANT IN LATE SPRING OR EARLY SUMMER

White flowers and painted terracotta

There are plenty of inexpensive window boxes available, but they do tend to look rather similar. Why not customize a bought window box to give it a touch of individuality? This deep blue painted window box creates an interesting setting for the cool white pelargonium and verbenas.

MATERIALS

45 cm (18 in) terracotta window box painted blue
Crocks or other suitable drainage material
Compost
Slow-release plant food granules

PLANTS

White pelargonium
2 variegated felicias
2 white trailing verbenas

FELICIA

1 Cover the base of the window box with a layer of crocks or similar drainage material.

VERBENA

2 Fill the window box with compost, mixing in 2 teaspoons of slow-release plant food granules. Plant the pelargonium in the centre of the window box.

PELARGONIUM

3 Plant a felicia on either side of the pelargonium at the back of the container. Plant a verbena on either side of the pelargonium at the front of the window box. Water well and stand in a sunny position.

GARDENER'S TIP

White pelargoniums need regular dead-heading to look their best.
Old flowerheads discolour and quickly spoil the appearance of the plant.

PLANT IN LATE SPRING OR EARLY SUMMER

Wedding fuchsias

MATERIALS

Wire basket
Sphagnum moss
Garden twine

PLANTS

3 Fuchsia *'Happy Wedding Day'*
3 *busy Lizzies (impatiens)*
  (optional)
3 *white lace-cap hydrangeas*
  (optional)

'Happy Wedding Day' is a modern fuchsia which produces very large, round flowers. The lax growth makes it highly suitable for use in a decorative wire basket. As its name suggests, this fuchsia is ideal for a wedding display. Other white-flowered plants can be used to make a really imposing display, and to reinforce the lively impact of the fuchsia's fresh white bells.

FUCHSIA

1 Make a hand-sized pad of sphagnum moss and start to cover the outside of the plastic pot containing the fuchsia.

2 Use a long piece of twine to start tying the moss in place. Leave the ends loose.

3 Continue working around the pot, using small pads of moss.

4 Use the long ends of the piece of twine to secure the moss as you work round the pot.

5 Completely cover the pot with moss. Repeat for the other plants. Group the pots together for a finished display.

GARDENER'S TIP

To ensure that you have a vigorous display with lots of flowers on the wedding day, you will need to stop the plants at least eight weeks before. This involves pinching out the sideshoots and growing tips with your fingers. It will encourage extra bushy growth, and the development of even more flower buds.

PLANT IN SPRING OR SUMMER

A silver and white wall basket

The helichrysum's silvery foliage and cool blue lavender flowers give a delicate colour scheme which would look good against a weathered background.

MATERIALS

30 cm (12 in) wall basket
Sphagnum moss
Compost
Slow-release plant food granules

PLANTS

2 lavenders (Lavandula dentata var. candicans)
Osteospermum *'Whirligig'*
2 Helichrysum petiolare

OSTEOSPERMUM

LAVENDER

HELICHRYSUM

GARDENER'S TIP

The lavender used in this project is fairly unusual – if you wish, you can substitute a low-growing variety such as 'Hidcote'.
Keep the helichrysum in check by pinching out its growing tips fairly regularly or it may take over the basket.

PLANT IN SPRING

1 Line the basket with moss and half-fill it with compost.

2 Mix in a half-teaspoon of plant food granules. Plant the lavenders in each corner.

3 Plant the osteospermum in the centre of the basket then add the helichrysums on either side.

4 Angle the plants to encourage them to trail over the side of the basket. Fill with compost. Water the basket and hang.

An informal wall basket

The strong pink of the dahlietta flower is echoed in the leaf colouring of the pink-flowered polygonums in this country-style basket. Silver thymes and white lobelias provide a gentle contrast.

MATERIALS

36 cm (14 in) wall basket
Sphagnum moss
Compost
Slow-release plant food granules

PLANTS

5 white lobelias
3 Polygonum 'Pink Bubbles'
2 thymes (Thymus 'Silver Queen')
1 pink dahlietta (miniature dahlia)

LOBELIA

THYME

POLYGONUM

DAHLIETTA

GARDENER'S TIP

To prevent the thyme getting leggy, trim off all the flowerheads after flowering – this will help to maintain a dense, well-shaped plant.

PLANT IN SPRING

1 Line the back and the base of the basket with moss, and position three lobelias around the side of the basket near the base.

2 Plant two of the polygonums into the side of the basket above the lobelia. Rest the root-balls on the moss, and gently feed the foliage through the basket.

3 Fill the basket with compost. Mix a half-teaspoon of slow-release plant food granules into the top of the compost. Plant the thymes into the corners of the basket, angling them so that they tumble over the sides.

4 Plant the dahlietta in the middle of the basket and the remaining polygonum in front of the dahlietta. Plant the remaining lobelias. Water well and hang in a sunny position.

A medley of pinks

In this basket-weave stone planter sugar-pink petunias are planted with ivy-leaved pelargoniums and shaggy-flowered pink dianthus with a deep-red eye. None of these plants requires much depth for its roots and, provided the plants are fed and watered regularly, they will be happy.

MATERIALS

60 cm (24 in) window box
Gravel
Compost
Slow-release plant food granules

PLANTS

2 pink-flowered ivy-leaved
  pelargoniums
3 sugar-pink petunias
6 pink dianthus

DIANTHUS

PETUNIA

PELARGONIUM

1 Fill the base of the window box with a layer of washed gravel or similar drainage material.

2 Fill the window box with compost, mixing in 2 teaspoons of plant food granules.

3 Plant the two pelargoniums 10 cm (4 in) from either end of the window box.

4 Plant the petunias, evenly spaced, along the back edge of the window box.

5 Plant four dianthus along the front edge, and the other two on either side of the central petunia.

6 Spread a layer of gravel around the plants; this is decorative and also helps to retain moisture. Water well and stand in a sunny position.

GARDENER'S TIP

Once the summer is over, the petunias and pelargoniums will need to be removed, but the dianthus will overwinter quite happily. Cut off any flower stems and add a fresh layer of gravel.

PLANT IN LATE SPRING OR EARLY SUMMER

A wall basket in shades of pink

Trailing rose-pink petunias provide the main structure of this wall basket and are combined with two colourful verbenas and white alyssum. On their own, the pale petunia flowers could look somewhat insipid but they are enhanced by the deeper tones of the verbenas.

MATERIALS

36 cm (14 in) wall basket
Sphagnum moss
Compost
Slow-release plant food granules

PLANTS

4 white alyssum
2 cascading rose-pink petunias
2 Verbena 'Pink Parfait' and 'Carousel', or similar

ALYSSUM

VERBENA

PETUNIA

1 Line the back of the basket and half-way up the front with moss. Plant the alyssum into the side of the basket, resting the rootballs on the moss and feeding the foliage through the sides.

2 Fill the basket with compost and mix a half-teaspoon of slow-release plant food granules into the top of the compost. Plant the petunias in each corner.

3 Plant the verbenas one in front of the other, in the middle of the basket. Water thoroughly and hang in a sunny position.

GARDENER'S TIP

If, like these petunias, some of the plants are more developed than others, pinch out the growing tips so that all the plants grow together and one variety will not smother the others.

PLANT IN LATE SPRING OR EARLY SUMMER

'Balcon' pelargoniums

Traditionally planted to cascade from balconies in many European countries, these lovely pelargoniums are now increasingly and deservedly popular. They are seen at their best when planted alone, as in this basket, where the only variation is of colour.

MATERIALS

40 cm (16 in) hanging basket
Sphagnum moss
Compost
Slow-release plant food granules

PLANTS

5 'Balcon' pelargoniums
('Princess of Balcon' and 'King of Balcon' were used here:
the former is now often known as 'Roi des Balcons Lilas', and the latter as 'Hederinum')

'BALCON'
PELARGONIUMS

GARDENER'S TIP

Take cuttings from non-flowering stems in the autumn to use in next year's basket. Pelargonium cuttings root easily and the young plants can be kept on a window-sill until spring.

PLANT IN LATE SPRING OR EARLY SUMMER

1 Fully line the basket with moss. Fill with compost. Mix a teaspoon of slow-release plant food granules into the top layer of the compost.

3 Plant the other four pelargoniums round the edge of the basket, and remove any supporting canes to encourage the plants to tumble over the side. Water well and hang the basket up in a sunny spot.

2 Plant one of the pelargoniums in the centre of the basket.

Sugar and spice

The candy-floss colour of the petunias is enriched by combining them with deep crimson ivy-leaved pelargoniums. Slower-growing silver-leaved snapdragons and a variegated pelargonium will add further colour later in the summer.

MATERIALS

36 cm (14 in) hanging basket
Sphagnum moss
Compost
Slow-release plant food granules

PLANTS

3 snapdragons (Antirrhinum
  'Avalanche') (optional)
Ivy-leaved Pelargonium 'Blue
  Beard'
Ivy-leaved Pelargonium
  'L'Elégante'
  (optional)
3 pink petunias

SNAPDRAGON

PELARGONIUMS

PETUNIA

GARDENER'S TIP

It is a good idea to include a number of different plants. This creates a more interesting picture and ensures that if one plant does not thrive, as happened to the snapdragons in this basket, the other plants will still make a good display.

PLANT IN LATE SPRING OR EARLY SUMMER

1 Line the lower half of the basket with moss. Plant the snapdragons in the side of the basket, resting the rootballs on the moss and guiding the foliage through the side of the basket.

2 Line the remainder of the basket with moss, tucking it carefully around the underplanted snapdragons.

3 Fill the basket with compost, mixing a teaspoon of slow-release plant food granules into the top layer of compost. Plant the *Pelargonium* 'Blue Beard' at the back of the basket.

4 Plant the *Pelargonium* 'L'Elégante' at the front of the basket. Plant the petunias around the pelargoniums. Water thoroughly and hang in a sunny position.

Three tiers of colour

Scented petunias, delicate white marguerites and starry isotoma make a stunning layered arrangement. Use veined petunias, as they have the strongest scent.

MATERIALS

36 cm (14 in) terracotta window box
Crocks or other suitable drainage material
Compost
Slow-release plant food granules

PLANTS

2 white marguerites (argyranthemums)
3 petunias
3 isotoma

ISOTOMA

MARGUERITE

PETUNIA

GARDENER'S TIP

Try to position flowers where they can be seen at dusk, when their colours become far more intense and are a treat not to be missed.

PLANT IN LATE SPRING OR EARLY SUMMER

1 Cover the base of the window box with crocks. Fill with compost, mixing in 2 teaspoons of slow-release plant food granules.

2 Plant the marguerites on either side of the centre towards the back of the window box.

3 Plant one petunia in the centre and the other two at each end of the window box.

4 Plant the isotoma along the front edge of the window box. Water the arrangement well and stand in a sunny position.

Divine magenta

The gloriously strong colour of magenta petunias is combined with blue *Convolvulus sabatius*, heliotropes, which will bear scented deep purple flowers, and a variegated scented-leaf pelargonium, which will add colour and fragrance later in the summer.

MATERIALS

45 cm (18in) basket
Sphagnum moss
Compost
Slow-release plant food granules

PLANTS

Scented-leaf Pelargonium
'Fragrans Variegatum'
3 purple heliotropes
3 Convolvulus sabatius
5 trailing magenta-flowered
petunias

HELIOTROPES

PELARGONIUM

CONVOLVULUS

PETUNIA

1 Carefully line the hanging basket with a thick layer of moss.

2 Fill the basket with compost, mixing a teaspoon of slow-release plant food granules into the top layer.

3 Plant the scented-leaf pelargonium in the middle of the hanging basket.

4 Plant the heliotropes, evenly spaced, around the central pelargonium.

5 Plant the blue convolvulus, evenly spaced, around the edge of the basket.

6 Plant the petunias in the spaces between the convolvulus and the heliotropes.

GARDENER'S TIP

Baskets with flat bases like this one can be stood on columns rather than hung from brackets. This is a useful solution if fixing a bracket is difficult.

PLANT IN LATE SPRING OR EARLY SUMMER

A peachy pink wall basket

The vivid flowers of the petunias and pelargonium contrast dramatically with the greeny-yellow lamiums. This basket is seen to best effect against a dark background.

LAMIUM

PETUNIA

PELARGONIUM

MATERIALS

30 cm (12 in) wide wall basket
Sphagnum moss
Compost
Slow-release plant food granules

PLANTS

3 Lamium 'Golden Nuggets'
Peach/pink zonal Pelargonium
  'Palais', or similar
3 petunias

1 Line the back and lower half of the front of the basket with moss. Plant the lamiums by resting the rootballs on the moss, and feeding the foliage through the side of the basket. Line the rest of the basket with moss.

2 Fill the basket with compost, mixing a half-teaspoon of slow-release plant food granules into the top layer. Plant the pelargonium in the centre of the basket against the back edge.

3 Plant one petunia in each corner and the third in front of the pelargonium. Water well and hang on a sunny wall.

GARDENER'S TIP

For a gentler colour scheme, the lamium can be replaced with the silver-grey foliage of *Helichrysum microphyllum*.

PLANT IN LATE SPRING OR EARLY SUMMER

A small pelargonium basket

Ivy-leaved pelargoniums are lovely plants for hanging baskets, and one plant will fill a small basket like this by the middle of summer. The silver-leaved helichrysum and lilac diascias add the finishing touches to this pretty pink-and-silver theme.

MATERIALS

25 cm (10 in) hanging basket
Sphagnum moss
Compost
Slow-release plant food granules

PLANTS

2 Diascia *'Lilac Belle'*
Ivy-leaved Pelargonium *'Super Rose'*
2 Helichrysum microphyllum

DIASCIA   HELICHRYSUM

PELARGONIUM

GARDENER'S TIP

If you like some height in your hanging basket, use small canes to support some of the pelargonium's stems; if you prefer a cascading effect, leave the pelargonium unsupported.

PLANT IN LATE SPRING OR EARLY SUMMER

1 Line the bottom half of the hanging basket with moss.

2 Plant the diascias into the side of the basket by resting the rootballs on the moss, and gently feeding the foliage between the wires. Add some compost.

3 Line the rest of the basket with moss, top up with compost and mix a teaspoon of slow-release plant food granules into the top layer. Plant the pelargonium in the centre of the basket.

4 Plant the helichrysums on either side of the pelargonium. Water the basket well and hang in a sunny position.

Luxury basket

Fuchsia 'Pink Galore' is a beautiful cultivar for a luxury hanging basket. The dark glossy green foliage is a perfect foil for the very full, soft rose-pink flowers. A plastic basket with a fixed reservoir has been used to facilitate growth and watering, and the curtain of stems will soon hide the basket from view.

FUCHSIA

MATERIALS

36 cm (14 in) plastic hanging basket with fixed reservoir
Compost
Slow-release plant food granules

PLANTS

5 Fuchsia *'Pink Galore'*

1 To avoid the plants becoming tangled in the chain, pull it to one side while planting up the basket.

2 Put a layer of compost with a half-teaspoon of slow-release plant food granules into the bottom of the hanging basket.

3 Arrange four of the plants around the edge of the basket in a symmetrical pattern. Place the last plant centrally.

4 Remove each fuchsia plant from its pot, and gently ease the rootball into the compost.

5 Carefully fill the spaces between the plants with more compost mixed with plant food granules. Firm the compost with your hands.

6 Tease the stems and the foliage around the chains as they are lifted into position.

GARDENER'S TIP

Always use an odd number of plants to achieve the best effect.
A plant placed centrally will prevent a gap appearing as the plants begin to cascade downwards.

PLANT IN EARLY SUMMER

In the pink

The common name for *Dianthus deltoides* is the pink. Its delightful deeply coloured flowers and silvery grey foliage work very well in a hanging basket combined with prostrate thymes, pink-flowered verbena and an osteospermum.

MATERIALS

36 cm (14 in) hanging basket
Sphagnum moss
Compost
Slow-release plant food granules

PLANTS

6 Dianthus deltoides
Osteospermum *'Pink Whirls'*
Verbena *'Silver Anne'*
3 thymes (Thymus *'Pink Chintz'*
or similar prostrate variety)

PINKS

THYME

VERBENA

OSTEOSPERMUM

1 Line the bottom half of the basket with moss and fill with compost. Plant three of the pinks into the side of the basket, resting the rootballs on the compost and feeding the leaves carefully through the wire.

2 Line the rest of the basket with moss and fill with compost. Mix a teaspoon of slow-release plant food granules into the top of the compost. Plant the osteospermum in the centre of the hanging basket.

3 Plant the verbena to one side of the osteospermum on the edge of the basket and the thymes, evenly spaced, around the unplanted edge.

4 Plant the remaining three pinks between the thymes and the verbena. Water well and hang in a sunny position.

GARDENER'S TIP

Pinch out the growing tips regularly to prevent plants such as the osteospermum growing too vigorously upwards and unbalancing the look of the basket. It will be bushier and more in scale with the other plants as a result.

PLANT IN SPRING

Bright splashes of colour

MATERIALS

76 cm (30 in) plastic window box with drainage holes
Compost
Slow-release plant food granules

PLANTS

2 yellow gazanias
3 Alaska nasturtiums
3 Brachycome 'Lemon Mist'
2 yellow snapdragons (antirrhinums)

The leaves of the Alaska nasturtium look as if they have been splattered with cream paint. In this box they are planted with yellow-flowered snapdragons, gazanias and brachycome daisies.

BRACHYCOME

NASTURTIUM

SNAPDRAGONS

GAZANIA

GARDENER'S TIP

Nasturtiums are among the easiest plants to grow from seed. Start them off about 4–6 weeks before you plant your window box, potting them on to keep them growing vigorously.

PLANT IN THE SPRING

1 Fill the window box with compost, mixing in 2 teaspoons of plant food. Plant the gazanias either side of the centre.

2 Plant the nasturtiums at either end and in the centre of the window box.

3 Plant the three brachycome plants, evenly spaced, along the front of the window box.

4 Plant the two snapdragons on either side of the central nasturtium. Water thoroughly and stand in a sunny position.

Fire and earth

The earth tones of this small decorative terracotta window box are topped with the fiery reds and oranges of the plants – the fuchsia with its orange foliage and tubular scarlet flowers, the orange nasturtiums and the red claw-like flowers of the feathery-leaved lotus.

MATERIALS

36 cm (14 in) terracotta window box
Clay granules or other suitable drainage
 material
Compost
Slow-release plant food granules

PLANTS

Fuchsia *'Thalia'*
3 orange nasturtiums
2 Lotus berthelotii

NASTURTIUM

FUCHSIA

LOTUS

1 Cover the base of the window box with drainage material. Fill with compost, mixing in a teaspoon of plant food granules.

2 Plant the fuchsia in the centre of the window box.

3 Plant the nasturtiums along the back of the window box.

4 Plant the two lotuses in the front of the window box on either side of the fuchsia. Water thoroughly, leave to drain, and stand in a sunny position.

GARDENER'S TIP

This stunning fuchsia is worth keeping for next year.
Pot it up in the autumn, cut back by half and overwinter on a window-sill or in a heated greenhouse.

PLANT IN LATE SPRING OR EARLY SUMMER

Fruit and flowers

Bright red petunias become even more vibrant when interplanted with variegated helichrysums and underplanted with alpine strawberries. With their delicate trailing tendrils, the strawberry plants soften the lower edge of the basket.

MATERIALS

30 cm (12 in) hanging basket
Sphagnum moss
Compost
Slow-release plant food granules

PLANTS

3 alpine strawberry plants
3 bright red petunias
3 Helichrysum petiolare
'Variegatum'

HELICHRYSUM

ALPINE STRAWBERRY

PETUNIA

1 Line the lower half of the basket with moss.

2 Plant the alpine strawberries by resting the rootballs on the moss, and guiding the leaves through the side of the basket.

GARDENER'S TIP

The tendrils, or runners, sent out by the strawberries are searching for somewhere to root. If you can fix a pot in a suitable spot, pin the plantlet into the compost while it is still attached to the parent plant. As soon as it has rooted it can be cut free.

PLANT IN LATE SPRING OR EARLY SUMMER

3 Line the rest of the basket with moss and fill with compost. Mix in a teaspoon of slow-release plant food granules. Plant the petunias, evenly spaced, in the top of the basket.

4 Interplant the petunias with the helichrysums. Water thoroughly and hang in full or partial shade.

Flame-red flowers in terracotta

The intense red flowers of the pelargoniums, verbena and nasturtiums are emphasized by a few yellow nasturtiums and the variegated ivy, but cooled slightly by the soothing blue-green of the nasturtium's umbrella-shaped leaves.

NASTURTIUM

VERBENA

IVY

PELARGONIUM

MATERIALS

50 cm (20 in) terracotta window
    box
Crocks or other suitable drainage
    material
Compost
Slow-release plant food granules

PLANTS

2 red zonal pelargoniums
2 nasturtiums – 1 red, 1 yellow
Red verbena
2 variegated ivies

1 Place a layer of crocks or other suitable drainage material in the base of the window box.

2 Fill the container with compost, mixing in 3 teaspoons of slow-release plant food granules.

3 Plant the pelargoniums either side of the centre of the window box.

4 Plant a nasturtium at each end of the window box, in the back corners.

5 Plant the verbena in the centre of the window box.

6 Plant the ivies in front of the nasturtiums in the corners. Water well, leave to drain, and place in a sunny position.

GARDENER'S TIP

Nasturtiums are prone to attack by blackfly. Treat at the first sign of infestation with a suitable insecticide and the plants will remain healthy.

PLANT IN LATE SPRING OR EARLY SUMMER

Sunny daisies and violas

Osteospermum daisies are sun-worshippers, keeping their petals furled in cloudy weather. In this window box they are combined with yellow violas and tumbling white bacopas.

VIOLA

BACOPA

OSTEOSPERMUM

MATERIALS

45 cm (18in) fibre window box
Polystyrene or other suitable drainage material
Compost
Slow-release plant food granules

PLANTS

Osteospermum 'Buttermilk'
3 yellow violas
2 white bacopas

1 Line the base of the box with polystyrene or other suitable drainage material and fill with compost.

2 Mix in 3 teaspoons of plant food granules. Plant the osteospermum in the centre.

3 Plant two of the violas at each end of the window box and the third in front of the osteospermum.

4 Plant the two bacopas on either side of the osteospermum. Stand in a sunny spot and water thoroughly.

GARDENER'S TIP

Pinch out the growing tips of the osteospermum regularly to encourage a bushy rather than a leggy plant.

PLANT IN SPRING

A floral chandelier

MATERIALS

36 cm (14 in) hanging basket
Sphagnum moss
Compost
Slow-release plant food granules

PLANTS

3 yellow lantanas, 2 variegated,
* 1 green-leaved*
2 Bidens ferulifolia
5 African marigolds (tagetes)

The chandelier shape is a result of combining the spreading bidens with upright lantanas and marigolds. Since the variegated-leaf lantanas proved very slow to establish, a more vigorous green-leaved form was added later. As the season progresses, the strongly marked leaves of the variegated plants will become more dominant.

AFRICAN MARIGOLDS

LANTANA

BIDENS

1 Line the basket with moss. Fill it with compost, mixing a teaspoon of slow-release plant food granules into the top layer. Plant the lantana in the centre.

2 Plant the two bidens opposite one another at the edge of the basket.

3 Plant the African marigolds around the lantana plants. Water thoroughly and hang in a sunny position.

GARDENER'S TIP

To complete the chandelier, make candle holders by twisting thick garden wire around the base of yellow candles and add them to the hanging basket.

PLANT IN LATE SPRING OR EARLY SUMMER

Vibrant reds and sunny yellows

This basket is an exciting mix of glowing colours and contrasting leaf shapes. A bright red verbena and the pineapple-scented salvia tumble from the basket, intertwined with red and yellow nasturtiums and a striking golden grass.

MATERIALS

36 cm (14 in) hanging basket
Sphagnum moss
Compost
Slow-release plant food granules

PLANTS

4 trailing nasturtiums
Golden grass Hakonechloa 'Alboaurea', or similar
Salvia elegans
Verbena 'Lawrence Johnston'

1 Line the bottom half of the basket with moss.

NASTURTIUM

VERBENA

SALVIA

GOLDEN GRASS

2 Plant three of the nasturtiums into the side of the basket by resting the rootballs on the moss, and carefully feeding the leaves through the basket.

3 Line the rest of the basket with moss and fill with compost. Mix a teaspoon of slow-release plant food granules into the compost. Plant the golden grass to one side of the basket.

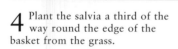

4 Plant the salvia a third of the way round the edge of the basket from the grass.

5 Plant the verbena at an equal distance from the salvia and the golden grass.

6 Plant the remaining nasturtium in the centre. Water well and hang in a sunny position.

GARDENER'S TIP

Nasturtiums are wonderful plants for hanging baskets – vigorous, colourful and undemanding – but they can be disfigured by blackfly. Spray at the first sign of an infestation with an insecticide which will not harm beneficial insects.

PLANT IN LATE SPRING OR EARLY SUMMER

Summer carnival

The orange markings on the throats of some of the mimulus flowers look wonderful with the orange-flowered pelargonium in this colourful basket. By the end of the season, trails of lysimachia leaves will form a waterfall of foliage around the base.

MATERIALS

36 cm (14 in) basket
Sphagnum moss
Compost
Slow-release plant food granules

PLANTS

Orange-flowered zonal
* pelargonium*
3 Lysimachia nummularia 'Aurea'
3 mimulus

LYSIMACHIA

MIMULUS

1 Line the basket with moss and fill it with compost, mixing a teaspoon of slow-release plant food granules into the top layer. Plant the pelargonium in the centre of the basket.

PELARGONIUM

GARDENER'S TIP

Dead-head the flowers regularly to encourage repeat flowering, and if the mimulus start to get leggy, cut back the offending stems to a leaf joint. New shoots will soon appear.

PLANT IN LATE SPRING OR EARLY SUMMER

2 Plant the lysimachia, evenly spaced, around the edge of the basket, angling the plants so they will trail over the sides.

3 Plant the mimulus between the lysimachia. Water the hanging basket thoroughly and hang in a sunny spot.

Tumbling violas

Violas can be surprisingly vigorous plants and, given the space, will happily tumble over the edge of a wall basket. Combined with curly-leaved parsley and the daisy-like flowers of asteriscus the effect is delicate but luxuriant.

MATERIALS

30 cm (12 in) wall basket
Compost
Sphagnum moss
Slow-release plant food granules

PLANTS

5 parsley plants
5 yellow violas
Asteriscus 'Gold Coin'

PARSLEY

ASTERISCUS

VIOLA

1 Line the back and lower half of the front of the basket with sphagnum moss.

2 Plant three of the parsley plants into the sides of the basket by resting the rootballs on the moss, and feeding the foliage through the wires.

4 Finish lining the basket with moss and fill with compost, mixing a half-teaspoon of slow-release plant food granules into the top layer. Plant the asteriscus in the centre of the basket, and surround with the remaining parsley and viola plants.

GARDENER'S TIP

To keep the violas flowering all summer they need regular dead-heading – the easiest way to do this is to give the plants a trim with a pair of scissors rather than trying to remove heads individually.

PLANT IN SPRING

3 Add another layer of moss and plant two of the viola plants in the side of the basket using the same method.

Mediterranean mood

The lantana is a large shrub which thrives in a Mediterranean or sub-tropical climate, but it is increasingly popular in cooler climates as a half-hardy perennial in borders and containers. This multi-coloured variety has been planted with yellow bidens and orange dahliettas.

DAHLIETTA

BIDENS

LANTANA

MATERIALS

36 cm (14 in) hanging basket
Sphagnum moss
Compost
Slow-release plant food granules

PLANTS

Orange/pink lantana
3 orange dahliettas (miniature dahlias)
3 Bidens aurea

1 Line the basket with moss. Fill the basket with compost, mixing a teaspoon of slow-release plant food granules into the top layer. Plant the lantana in the centre of the basket.

2 Plant the dahliettas, evenly spaced, around the lantana.

3 Plant the bidens between the dahliettas. Water thoroughly and hang in a sunny position.

GARDENER'S TIP

To encourage a bushy plant, pinch out the growing tips of the lantana regularly. Like many popular plants, the lantana is poisonous, so treat it with respect and do not try eating it.

PLANT IN LATE SPRING OR EARLY SUMMER

A sunny wall basket

30 cm (12 in) wall basket
Sphagnum moss
Compost
Slow-release plant food granules

PLANTS

2 Lysimachia congestiflora
3 Alaska nasturtiums
3 mixed colour African marigolds
(tagetes)

The vibrant yellows, oranges and reds of the flowers in this basket glow richly amongst the variegated leaves of the nasturtiums. As the season progresses the underplanted lysimachia will bear deep yellow flowers and add another layer of colour.

LYSIMACHIA

NASTURTIUM

AFRICAN
MARIGOLDS

1 Line the back of the basket and half-way up the front with moss. Plant the lysimachia by resting the rootballs on the moss and feeding the foliage between the wires.

2 Line the rest of the basket and fill with compost, mixing in a half-teaspoon of plant food granules. Plant the nasturtiums along the back.

3 Plant the African marigolds in front of the nasturtiums. Water the basket well and hang it up in a sunny spot.

GARDENER'S TIP

If you have a large area of wall to cover, group two or three wall baskets together. This looks very effective, especially when they are planted with the same plants.

PLANT IN SPRING

Dark drama

The intense purple of the heliotrope usually dominates other plants, but here it is teamed with a selection of equally dramatic colours – *Dahlia* 'Bednall Beauty', with its purple foliage and dark red flowers, black grass and red and purple verbenas – to make a stunning display.

MATERIALS

60 cm (24 in) terracotta window box
Broken polystyrene or other suitable drainage material
Compost
Slow-release plant food granules

PLANTS

Heliotrope
2 Dahlia 'Bednall Beauty'
Black grass (Ophiopogon planiscapus 'Nigrescens')
2 purple trailing verbenas
2 red trailing verbenas

BLACK GRASS

VERBENAS

DAHLIA

HELIOTROPE

1 Fill the bottom of the window box with broken polystyrene or other suitable drainage material.

2 Fill the window box with compost, mixing in 3 teaspoons of slow-release plant food granules. Plant the heliotrope centrally at the back of the window box, gently teasing apart the roots, if necessary.

3 Plant the dahlias in the back corners of the window box.

4 Plant the black grass in front of the heliotrope.

5 Plant the purple verbenas at the back between the heliotrope and the dahlias.

6 Plant the red verbenas at the front in either corner. This is a large container so it is best to position it before watering. Put it where it will benefit from full sun, then water thoroughly.

GARDENER'S TIP

Dahlias can be overwintered by digging up the tubers after the first frosts, cutting the stems back to 15 cm (6 in) and drying them off before storing in slightly damp peat in a frost-free shed. Start into growth again in spring and plant out after all danger of frost is past.

PLANT IN LATE SPRING OR EARLY SUMMER

A cascade of lilac and silver

Petunias and violas are surrounded by a cascading curtain of variegated ground ivy and silver-leaved senecio in this softly coloured hanging basket.

MATERIALS

30 cm (12 in) hanging basket
Sphagnum moss
Compost
Slow-release plant food granules

PLANTS

3 deep blue violas
3 soft blue petunias
Variegated ground ivy (Glechoma hederacea *'Variegata'*)
3 Senecio cineraria 'Silver Dust'

SENECIO

IVY

PETUNIA

VIOLAS

GARDENER'S TIP

If the ground ivy becomes too rampant and threatens to throttle the other plants, prune it by removing some of the stems completely and reducing the length of the others.

PLANT IN LATE SPRING OR EARLY SUMMER

1 Line the lower half of the basket with moss. Plant the violas in the side by resting the rootballs on the moss, and carefully guiding the foliage between the wires. Line the rest of the basket with moss and fill with compost, mixing a teaspoon of slow-release plant food granules into the top layer.

2 Plant the three petunias, evenly spaced, in the top of the basket. Plant the ground ivy on one side to trail over the edge of the basket.

3 Plant the three senecios between the petunias. Water well and hang in a sunny position.

Violas and verbenas

Deep blue violas are surrounded by trailing
purple verbenas to make a simple but attractive
basket. Trailing verbena is a particularly good
hanging-basket plant with its feathery foliage
and pretty flowers.

VERBENA

MATERIALS

30 cm (12 in) hanging basket
Sphagnum moss
Compost
Slow-release plant food granules

VIOLAS

PLANTS

9 blue violas
3 purple trailing verbenas

1 Line the lower half of the
basket with moss. Plant five of
the violas into the side of the
basket by resting the rootballs on
the moss and guiding the foliage
through the side of the basket.

2 Line the rest of the basket with
moss and fill with compost,
mixing a teaspoon of slow-release
plant food granules into the top
layer. Plant the verbenas around
the edge of the basket.

3 Plant the remaining violas in
the centre of the basket. Water
well and hang in partial sun.

GARDENER'S TIP

If the violas grow too tall, pinch out
the main stems of the plants to
encourage the spreading side shoots.

PLANT IN SPRING

An instant garden

There is not always time to wait for a window box to grow and this is one solution. Fill a container with potted plants and, as the season progresses, you can ring the changes by removing those that are past their best and introducing new plants.

MATERIALS

64 cm (25 in) galvanized tin
window box
Clay granules
5 1-litre (5 in) plastic pots
Compost

PLANTS

Lavender (Lavandula pinnata)
2 blue petunias
Convolvulus sabatius
Blue bacopa
Helichrysum petiolare
Viola *'Jupiter'*

HELICHRYSUM

PETUNIA

CONVOLVULUS

LAVENDER

VIOLA

BACOPA

GARDENER'S TIP

When using a container without drainage holes, take care not to overwater or the roots will become waterlogged.
Check after heavy rain, too, and empty away any excess water.

PLANT IN LATE SPRING OR EARLY SUMMER

1 Fill the base of the container with clay granules or similar drainage material.

2 Pot up the lavender into one of the pots.

3 Pot up one of the petunias with the convolvulus.

4 Pot up the other petunia with the bacopa.

5 Pot up the helichrysum.

6 Pot up the viola and arrange the pots in the window box.

Showers of flowers

Deep, velvety purple pansies and purple sage are surrounded by pink nemesias and tumbling purple verbenas in a pretty basket hung, here, in the corner of a thatched summerhouse.

MATERIALS

40 cm (16 in) hanging basket
Sphagnum moss
Compost
Slow-release plant food granules

PLANTS

3 purple verbenas
Purple sage
3 deep purple pansies
6 Nemesia 'Confetti'

VERBENA

SAGE

PANSY

NEMESIA

GARDENER'S TIP

In summer, pansies tend to flag in hot sun, especially in hanging baskets. They will do best where they are in the shade during the hottest part of the day.

PLANT IN SPRING

1 Line the lower half of the basket with moss. Plant the verbenas in the side of the basket. Line the rest of the basket and fill with compost, mixing in a teaspoon of plant food granules.

2 Plant the sage in the middle of the basket.

3 Plant the three purple pansies around the sage, spacing them evenly. Add more compost around the pansies and press in firmly.

4 Plant three nemesias at the back of the pansies, and three nemesias between the pansies. Water and hang in light shade.

A pretty stencilled planter

This small stencilled wooden window box is full of blue flowers. In a particularly pretty mix, petunias are intertwined with brachycome daisies and trailing convolvulus. A pair of brackets hold it in place under the window.

MATERIALS

40 cm (16 in) wooden window box
Clay granules or other suitable drainage material
Compost
Slow-release plant food granules

PLANTS

3 blue petunias
2 blue brachycome daisies
Convolvulus sabatius

BRACHYCOME

PETUNIA

CONVOLVULUS

1 Line the base of the window box with clay granules or other suitable drainage material. Fill the window box with compost, mixing in a teaspoon of slow-release plant food granules.

2 Plant the three petunias, evenly spaced, towards the back of the box. Plant the brachycome daisies between the petunias.

3 Plant the convolvulus centrally at the front of the box. Water thoroughly and position in full or partial sun.

GARDENER'S TIP

If you are stencilling a wooden container for outside use, do not forget to seal the wood after decorating it. In this instance, a matt wood varnish in a light oak tint has been used.

PLANT IN LATE SPRING OR EARLY SUMMER

Marguerites and pimpernels

We are more familiar with the wild scarlet pimpernel, but in this window box its blue relative, anagallis, has been planted to climb among the stems of the yellow marguerites and snapdragons. Blue-flowered variegated felicia and golden helichrysum complete the picture.

MATERIALS

76 cm (30 in) plastic window box
Compost
Slow-release plant food granules

PLANTS

2 yellow marguerites
4 blue anagallis
3 variegated felicias
2 Helichrysum petiolare 'Aureum'
4 yellow snapdragons (Antirrhinum)

MARGUERITE

ANAGALLIS

HELICHRYSUM

SNAPDRAGONS

FELICIA

1 Check the drainage holes are open in the base and, if not, drill or punch them open. Fill the window box with compost, mixing in 3 teaspoons of slow-release plant food granules.

2 Plant the marguerites on either side of the centre, towards the middle of the window box.

3 Plant two of the anagallis in the back corners of the window box and two at the front, on either side of the marguerites.

4 Plant one felicia in the centre of the box and the other two on either side of the anagallis.

5 Plant the helichrysum in the front corners of the window box to trail over the edges.

6 Plant two of the snapdragons on either side of the central felicia and two on either side of the marguerites. Water thoroughly, drain, and stand in a sunny or partially sunny position.

GARDENER'S TIP

Dead-head the marguerites, snapdragons and felicias to keep them flowering all summer. When planting the marguerites, pinch out the growing tips to encourage bushy plants.

PLANT IN SPRING

Shades of mauve

AGERATUM

ISOTOMA

HELICHRYSUM

SCABIOUS

MATERIALS

40 cm (16 in) hanging basket
Sphagnum moss
Compost
Slow-release plant food granules

PLANTS

6 blue ageratum
Blue scabious
3 Helichrysum petiolare
3 blue Isotoma axillaris

Some unlikely plants, such as this powder-blue scabious, can do very well in a hanging basket, especially when combined, as it is here, with isotoma and ageratum in the same colour, and the trailing silver foliage of helichrysum.

1 Line the lower half of the basket with moss. Plant three ageratum by resting the rootballs on the moss, and carefully guiding the foliage through the wires.

2 Add a further layer of moss and plant the other three ageratum into the side of the basket at a higher level.

3 Fill the basket with compost, mixing a teaspoon of slow-release plant food granules into the top layer. Plant the scabious in the centre of the basket.

4 Plant the helichrysums, evenly spaced, around the edge of the basket. Plant the isotoma between the helichrysums. Water well and hang in a sunny position.

GARDENER'S TIP

At the end of the season the scabious can be removed from the basket and planted in the border to flower for many years to come.

PLANT IN LATE SPRING

Sapphires for spring

Deep blue pansies are surrounded by gentian-blue anagallis and underplanted with golden helichrysums in this richly coloured basket.

MATERIALS

30 cm (12 in) hanging basket
Sphagnum moss
Compost
Slow-release plant food granules

PLANTS

3 Helichrysum petiolare *'Aureum'*
3 *deep blue pansies*
3 *blue anagallis*

ANAGALLIS

HELICHRYSUM

PANSY

1 Line the lower half of the basket with moss before planting the helichrysums in the sides of the basket.

2 Rest the rootballs on the moss, and carefully guide the foliage through the wires.

GARDENER'S TIP

The golden-green colour of *Helichrysum petiolare* 'Aureum' is far stronger if the plants are not in full sun. Too much sun tends to fade the colouring.

PLANT IN SPRING

3 Line the rest of the basket with moss and fill with compost, mixing a teaspoon of plant food into the top layer. Plant the pansies, evenly spaced, in the top of the basket.

4 Plant the anagallis between the pansies. Water the basket thoroughly and hang in partial sun.

Seasonal planters

There's no need to confine your ideas to summer planting schemes, however exuberant. You can keep boxes and hanging baskets looking vibrant and beautiful all year round. It's a lovely reassurance that spring is on its way to see the earliest spring bulbs bursting into flower right outside your window, and judiciously planted pots can often be slipped into temporary gaps in the borders to bridge the seasons. One of the joys of container gardening is that you can put together combinations that will look their best in spring, summer or autumn, then swap them around to take centre stage at the appropriate time.

You may also have containers you don't want to move: if a stately classical urn is a focal point in your garden, give it all-year-round interest with an evergreen shrub or a beautifully clipped piece of topiary; you can ring seasonal changes by underplanting with spring and summer bedding plants.

ABOVE: *A colourful spring display underplanted with moss.*

Daffodils and wallflowers

A weathered wooden tub planted in the autumn with daffodil bulbs and wallflower plants will provide a colourful spring display. Alternatively, you can buy pots of daffodils and wallflowers in bud in the early spring and plant them for an instant show.

MATERIALS

36 cm (14 in) wooden tub
Polystyrene or other drainage
  material
Compost
Slow-release plant food granules

PLANTS

24 daffodil bulbs or 4 1-litre
  (5 in) pots of daffodils
3 bushy wallflower (cheiranthus)
  plants

1 Break the polystyrene into large pieces and fill the bottom third of the tub to provide drainage and to save on the quantity of compost used.

2 Add compost until the tub is half-full and arrange 12 of the daffodil bulbs evenly over the surface. Cover the bulbs with compost.

3 Arrange the remaining 12 bulbs on the surface of the compost. Remove the wallflower plants from their pots and place them on the compost. Don't worry if the plants cover some of the bulbs, they will grow round the wallflowers. Fill the tub with compost, pressing down firmly around the wallflowers to ensure that they do not work loose in windy weather. Sprinkle a tablespoon of plant food granules on to the surface and work into the top layer of compost.

DAFFODIL

WALLFLOWER

GARDENER'S TIP

To save the bulbs for next year, allow the leaves to die right back and then dig up and store in a cool dry place.

PLANT BULBS IN THE AUTUMN OR PLANTS IN BUD IN SPRING

Miniature spring garden

Terracotta pots filled with crocuses, irises and primroses
nestling in a bed of moss, make a delightful scaled-down spring
garden which would fit on the
smallest balcony
or even a window-sill.

IRIS

MOSS

CROCUS

PRIMROSE

MATERIALS

Terracotta seed tray
2 terracotta pots, 13 cm (5 in) high
Crocks
Compost
Bun moss

PLANTS

3 primroses
Pot of Iris reticulata
Pot of crocuses

1 Cover the drainage holes of
the seed tray and the two pots
with crocks.

2 Half-fill the seed tray with
compost. Before planting the
primroses, loosen the roots by
gently squeezing the rootball and
teasing the roots loose.

3 Arrange the primroses in the
seed tray and fill in with
compost around the plants,
pressing down around the plants
to ensure they are firmly planted.

4 Arrange the bun moss around
the plants so that all the
compost is hidden.

5 Remove the irises from their
plastic pot and slip them into a
terracotta pot. Bed them in with a
little extra compost if necessary,
and then arrange moss around the
base of the stems.

6 Repeat this process with the
crocuses and then water all the
containers and arrange them
together.

GARDENER'S TIP

Once the irises and crocuses are past their best, hide them behind other pots to die down and dry out
before starting them into growth again in the autumn.

PLANT IN EARLY SPRING

Spring flowers in an instant

An arrangement of pots of
spring flowers is surrounded
with bark to give the
appearance of a planted
window box. As soon as the
flowers are over, the pots can
be removed and left to die
back, and the container is
ready for its summer planting.

MATERIALS

*40 cm (16 in) terracotta window
box*
Bark chippings

PLANTS

Pot of daffodils
Pot of yellow tulips
*4 yellow pansies
in pots*

DAFFODIL

PANSY

TULIP

GARDENER'S TIP

Once the flowers have finished and
the pots have been removed
from the window box, the pots of
bulbs can be tucked away
in a corner of the garden ready to
flower again next year.

PLANT IN LATE WINTER OR
EARLY SPRING

1 Position the pot of daffodils at
the right-hand end of the
window box.

2 Position the pot of tulips at
the left-hand end of the
window box.

3 Fill the centre and around the
pots with bark chippings until
the window box is half-full.

4 Position the pansies between
the tulips and the daffodils,
and add bark until all the pots are
concealed. Water moderately and
stand in any position.

A spring display of auriculas

An old strawberry punnet carrier makes an attractive and unusual window box in which to display some beautifully marked auriculas planted in antique terracotta pots. A large flower basket or wooden trug would look just as good as this marvellous old wooden carrier.

MATERIALS

8 8–10 cm (3–4 in) old or antique-style terracotta pots
Crocks or other suitable drainage material
Compost
50 cm (20 in) wooden carrier

PLANTS

8 different auriculas (Primula auricula)

AURICULAS

GARDENER'S TIP

A window-sill is an ideal position to see auriculas at their best. It is difficult to admire the full drama of their markings if they are at ground level. When they have finished flowering, stand the pots in a shady corner or a cold frame.

PLANT IN EARLY SPRING

1 Place a crock over the drainage hole of a pot.

2 Remove an auricula from its plastic pot and plant it firmly with added compost.

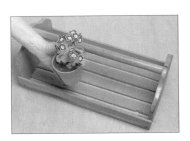

3 Stand the newly planted auricula in the wooden carrier.

4 Repeat the process for the other plants to fill the carrier. Water thoroughly and stand in light shade.

Display in a copper tub

A battered old washing boiler makes an attractive and characterful container for a display of white tulips, underplanted with purple violets and evergreen periwinkles.

MATERIALS

60 cm (24 in) copper boiler
20 cm (8 in) plastic pot
Compost

PLANTS

20 white tulip bulbs
or tulips in bud
5 purple violets
2 periwinkles
(Vinca minor)

VIOLET

TULIP

PERIWINKLE

GARDENER'S TIP

Lift the tulips when they have finished flowering and hang them up to dry in a cool airy place. They can be replanted late in autumn to flower again next year. Provided you pick off the dead heads the violets will flower all summer. For a summer display, lift the central violet and plant a standard white marguerite in the centre of the container.

PLANT BULBS IN AUTUMN OR PLANTS IN BUD IN SPRING. PLANT THE VIOLETS AND PERIWINKLES IN SPRING

1 Place the upturned plastic pot in the base of the tub before filling it with compost. This will save on the amount of compost used, and will not have any effect on the growth of the plants as they will still have plenty of room for their roots.

3 Do the underplanting in the early spring. The compost will have settled in the container and should be topped up to within 7.5 cm (3 in) of the rim. Remove the violets from their pots. Gently tweak the rootballs and loosen the roots to aid the plants' growth.

5 Plant a periwinkle on either side of the central violet, again loosening the rootballs.

2 If you are planting tulip bulbs, half-fill the container with compost, arrange the bulbs evenly over the surface and then cover them with a good 15 cm (6 in) of compost. This should be done in late autumn.

4 Plant one violet in the centre and four around the edges. Scoop out the soil by hand to avoid damaging the growing tips of the tulips beneath the surface.

6 If you are planting tulips in bud, the whole scheme should be planted at the same time, interplanting the tulips with the violets and periwinkles. Position in sun or partial shade.

Scented spring planter

Lilies-of-the-valley grow very well in containers and they will thrive in the shade where their delicate scented flowers stand out amongst the greenery. Surrounding the plants with bun moss is practical as well as attractive as it will stop the soil splashing back on to the leaves and flowers during fierce spring showers.

MATERIALS

Tinware planter
Clay granules
Compost
Bun moss

PLANTS

6–8 pots of
lily-of-the-
valley

LILY OF THE
VALLEY

1 Fill the bottom of the planter with 5 cm (2 in) of clay granules to improve drainage.

2 Cover the granules with a layer of compost and arrange the lily-of-the-valley plants evenly on the compost.

3 Fill in around the plants with more compost, making sure to press firmly around the plants so that they won't rock about in the wind. Now cover the compost with bun moss, fitting it snugly around the stems of the lily-of-the-valley, as this will also help keep the plants upright.

GARDENER'S TIP

If you want to bring your planter indoors to enjoy the scent of the flowers, use a container without drainage holes in the base, but be very careful not to overwater. Once the plants have finished flowering replant them in a pot with normal drainage holes or in the garden. They are woodland plants and will be quite happy under trees.

PLANT IN EARLY SPRING

Woodland garden

You do not need your own woodland area for this garden, just a shady corner and an attractive container to hold a selection of plants that thrive in damp shade. The plants are buried in bark chippings in their pots and will relish these conditions as they closely imitate their natural habitat.

MATERIALS

50 cm (20 in) glazed pot
Bark chippings

FERNS

BLUEBELL

ANEMONE
BLANDA

PLANTS

Pot of bluebells
3 hardy ferns
Pot of Anemone blanda

1 Fill the container three-quarters full with bark chippings. Plant your largest pot (in this case the bluebells) first. Scoop a hollow in the bark and position the pot so that the base of the leaves is approximately 5 cm (2 in) below the rim of the container.

2 Cover the pot with bark so that the plastic is no longer visible and the plant is surrounded by chippings.

3 Arrange the ferns so that they relate attractively to one another. Fill the spaces between the ferns with bark.

4 Add the *Anemone blanda* at the front of the container where its flowers will be seen to best advantage, and then top up the whole arrangement with bark. Stand the container in light shade and water.

GARDENER'S TIP

After the bluebells and anemones have finished flowering, lift them out of the container in their pots and set them aside in a shady corner to rest. They can be replaced by other woodland plants such as wild strawberries or periwinkle.

PLANT IN EARLY SPRING

A garland of spring flowers

Miniature daffodils, deep blue pansies, yellow polyanthus and variegated ivy are planted together to make a hanging basket that will flower for many weeks in early spring, lifting the spirits with its fresh colours and delicate woodland charm.

MATERIALS

30 cm (12 in) hanging basket
Sphagnum moss
Compost
Slow-release plant food granules

PLANTS

3 variegated ivies
5 miniature daffodil bulbs 'Tête-à-Tête' or similar, or a pot of daffodils in bud
3 blue pansies
2 yellow polyanthus

POLYANTHUS

IVY

PANSY

MINIATURE DAFFODIL

1 Line the lower half of the basket with moss.

2 Plant the ivies into the side of the basket by resting the rootballs on the moss, and guiding the foliage through the basket so that it will trail down.

3 Line the rest of the basket with moss and add a layer of compost to the bottom of the basket. Push the daffodil bulbs into the compost.

4 Fill the remainder of the basket with compost, mixing a teaspoon of slow-release plant food granules into the top layer. Plant the pansies, evenly spaced, in the top of the basket.

5 Plant the polyanthus between the pansies. Water the basket and hang in sun or shade. If planting daffodils in bud, remove them from the pot and place in the centre of the basket before arranging the ivies and filling with compost.

GARDENER'S TIP

When dismantling the arrangement, plant the variegated ivies in the garden. They look particularly good tumbling over walls, or threading their way through and linking established shrubs. Prune hard if they get out of hand and become too invasive.

PLANT IN AUTUMN IF GROWING DAFFODILS FROM BULBS; IN LATE WINTER OR EARLY SPRING FOR READY-GROWN DAFFODILS

A basket of contrasts

The deep green and burgundy foliage of *Fuchsia* 'Thalia' will be even more startling later in summer when the bright red pendant flowers stand out against the leaves and compete with the glowing colours of the nemesias. The yellow-green helichrysums provide a cooling contrast.

MATERIALS

30 cm (12 in) wall basket
Sphagnum moss
Compost
Slow-release plant food granules

PLANTS

3 Helichrysum petiolare 'Aureum'
Fuchsia 'Thalia'
4 nemesias in red, yellow and orange tones

NEMESIA

HELICHRYSUM

FUCHSIA

GARDENER'S TIP

Dead-head the nemesias regularly to ensure that they continue flowering throughout the summer.

PLANT IN LATE SPRING OR EARLY SUMMER

1 Line the back of the basket and the lower half of the front with moss. Fill the lower half of the basket with compost.

2 Plant two of the helichrysum plants into the side of the basket by resting the rootballs on the moss, and carefully feeding the foliage through the wires.

3 Line the rest of the basket with moss and top up with compost. Mix a half-teaspoon of slow-release plant food granules into the top layer of compost. Plant the fuchsia in the centre.

4 Plant the remaining helichrysum in front of the fuchsia. Plant two nemesias on each side of the central plants. Water the basket well and hang in full or partial sun.

Delicate summer flowers

CONVOLVULUS

BRACHYCOME

PANSIES

Pale orange pansies contrast beautifully with the lavender-blue convolvulus, and the pastel yellow brachycome daisies link the whole scheme together.

MATERIALS

30 cm (12 in) hanging basket
Sphagnum moss
Compost
Slow-release plant food granules

PLANTS

3 orange pansies
3 Brachycome 'Lemon Mist'
2 Convolvulus sabatius

1 Line the basket with moss and fill with compost, mixing a teaspoon of slow-release plant food granules into the top layer. Plant the pansies around the edge.

2 Plant the brachycome daisies between the pansies.

3 Place the convolvulus plants in the centre of the basket so that the tendrils can weave between the other plants. Water and hang in full or partial sun.

GARDENER'S TIP

Each time you water this basket be sure to remove any pansy flowers that are past their best. Once pansies start to set seed they quickly grow leggy and stop flowering.

PLANT IN SPRING

A mass of sweet peas

This large basket is filled with sweet peas surrounding a regal pelargonium. It is inter-planted with chives to provide a contrasting leaf shape and help deter pests. Their fluffy purple flowers will add a further dimension to the arrangement, and the leaves can be snipped off for use in the kitchen.

MATERIALS

40 cm (16 in) hanging basket
Sphagnum moss
Compost
Slow-release plant food granules

PLANTS

Regal Pelargonium 'Sancho Panza'
2–3 small pots or a strip of low-growing sweet peas such as 'Snoopea'
3 chive plants

SWEET PEAS

CHIVES

PELARGONIUM

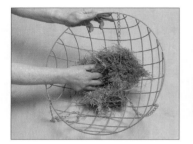

1 Line the basket with a generous layer of moss.

2 Fill the basket with compost and mix a teaspoon of slow-release plant food granules into the top layer. Plant the regal pelargonium in the centre of the basket.

3 Gently divide the sweet peas into clumps of about eight plants each.

4 Plant the sweet pea clumps around the edge of the basket.

5 Plant the chives between the sweet peas and the central pelargonium.

6 Fill any gaps with more moss. Water well and hang the basket in a sunny position.

GARDENER'S TIP

Sweet peas will bloom longer if you keep picking the flowers and be sure to remove any seed pods as they form. Similarly, the chives grow longer and are stronger if their flowerheads are removed before they seed.

PLANT IN LATE SPRING

Hot flowers in a cool container

Shocking-pink petunias and verbenas are the dominant plants in this window box which also features a softer pink marguerite and silver helichrysum. The dark green of the wooden window box is a pleasing foil for the vibrant flowers.

MATERIALS

76 cm (30 in) plastic window box with drainage holes
90 cm (3 ft) wooden window box (optional)
Compost
Slow-release plant food granules

PLANTS

Trailing pink marguerite (Argyranthemum *'Flamingo')*
2 bright pink verbenas, such as 'Sissinghurst'
3 shocking-pink petunias
4 Helichrysum petiolare microphyllum

MARGUERITE

VERBENA

PETUNIA

HELICHRYSUM

GARDENER'S TIP

To add height to this scheme, buy some 30 cm (12 in) green plant sticks. Push two into the soil behind each of the verbenas, and train them upwards.

PLANT IN LATE SPRING OR EARLY SUMMER

1 Fill the plastic window box with compost, mixing in 3 teaspoons of slow-release plant food granules. Plant the marguerite centre front.

2 Plant the verbenas in the back corners of the window box.

3 Plant one of the petunias behind the marguerite, and the other two on either side of it.

4 Plant one helichrysum on each side of the central petunia, and the other two in the front corners of the window box. Water well and lift into place. Stand in a sunny position.

A lime-green and blue box

MATERIALS

*76 cm (30 in) plastic window
 box with drainage holes*
Compost
Slow-release plant food granules

PLANTS

5 lime-green tobacco plants
2 scaevola
2 Helichrysum petiolare 'Aureum'
3 Convolvulus sabatius

Lime-green flowering tobacco and helichrysums contrast
beautifully with the blue scaevolas and convolvulus in this
window box of cool colours.

SCAEVOLA

TOBACCO

CONVOLVULUS

HELICHRYSUM

1 Fill the window box with
compost, mixing in 3
teaspoons of plant food granules.
Plant the tobacco plants along the
back of the window box.

2 Plant the two scaevolas
approximately 10 cm (4 in)
from each end, in front of the
tobacco plants.

3 Plant the two helichrysums on
either side of the centre of the
window box next to the scaevolas.

4 Plant two of the convolvulus
in the front corners of the box
and the third in the centre front.
Water thoroughly and position in
light shade or partial sun.

GARDENER'S TIP

At the end of the season pot up the
scaevolas and convolvulus. Cut
right back and protect from frost.

PLANT IN LATE SPRING

A miniature cottage garden

This basket derives its charm from its simple planting scheme. Pot marigolds and parsley are planted with bright blue felicias to create a basket which would look at home on the wall of a cottage or outside the kitchen door.

PARSLEY

FELICIA

POT
MARIGOLDS

MATERIALS

36 cm (14 in) hanging basket
Sphagnum moss
Compost
Slow-release plant food granules

PLANTS

5 parsley plants
3 pot marigolds (Calendula 'Gitana', or similar)
3 felicias

1 Line the lower half of the basket with moss.

2 Plant the parsley into the sides of the basket by resting the rootballs on the moss, and gently feeding the foliage through the wires.

3 Line the rest of the basket with moss, carefully tucking it around the roots of the parsley.

4 Fill the basket with compost, mixing a teaspoon of slow-release plant food granules into the top layer.

5 Plant the three pot marigolds, evenly spaced, in the top of the basket.

6 Plant the felicias between the marigolds. Water well and hang in full or partial sun.

GARDENER'S TIP

Regular dead-heading will keep the basket looking good, but allow at least one of the marigold flowers to form a seedhead and you will be able to grow your own plants next year.

PLANT IN SPRING

Foliage basket

An old basket makes an ideal container for this interesting group of foliage plants. The different leaf shapes and colours are emphasized when they are grouped together. Including flowers would detract from the architectural quality of the plants.

MATERIALS

30 cm (12 in) basket
Sphagnum moss
Loam-based compost
Slow-release plant food granules
Bark chippings

PLANTS

Phormium tenax
Mexican orange blossom
(Choisya ternata)
Carex brunnea 'Variegata'

PHORMIUM

MEXICAN ORANGE BLOSSOM

CAREX

GARDENER'S TIP

A planted basket makes an ideal gift for a friend, especially when you have chosen the plants yourself. Include a label, giving the names of the plants and how to care for them.

PLANT AT ANY TIME OF THE YEAR

1 Line the basket with moss. Place the phormium at the back and position the orange blossom next to it.

2 Add the carex and fill between the plants with compost enriched with a tablespoon of slow-release plant food granules.

3 Mulch around the plants with bark chippings. Water well and place in partial shade.

Layers of flowers

MATERIALS

36 cm (14 in) fibre window box
Drainage material
Compost
Slow-release plant food granules

PLANTS

2 white tobacco plants
Variegated Pelargonium
'l'Elégante'
2 pink busy Lizzies (impatiens)
3 white lobelias

This window box is unusual as the colours are in distinct layers, with upright white flowering tobacco above pink busy Lizzies, and tumbling white variegated pelargonium and lobelias. The fibre window box is concealed by a decorative twig container.

LOBELIAS

TOBACCO

PELARGONIUM

BUSY
LIZZIE

1 Put some drainage material in the base of the window box; fill with compost, mixing in 2 teaspoons of plant food granules. Plant the flowering tobacco near the back edge.

2 Plant the pelargonium at the front of the window box, in the centre.

3 Plant the busy Lizzies at each end of the window box.

4 Plant one of the lobelias between the flowering tobacco, and the other two on either side of the pelargonium.

GARDENER'S TIP

Somehow, rogue blue lobelias have appeared among the white plants. This sort of thing often happens in gardening and, as in this case, the accidental addition can turn out well.

PLANT IN SPRING

Full of cheer

Vivid red pelargoniums and verbenas are combined with cheerful yellow bidens and soft green helichrysums in this planter, which brightens the exterior of an old barn.

MATERIALS

76 cm (30 in) plastic window box
Compost
Slow-release plant food granules

PLANTS

3 *scarlet pelargoniums*
2 Bidens ferulifolia
2 *red trailing verbenas*
2 Helichrysum petiolare *'Aureum'*

HELICHRYSUM

VERBENA

PELARGONIUM

BIDENS

GARDENER'S TIP

Regular dead-heading and an occasional foliar feed will keep the pelargoniums flowering prolifically all summer.

PLANT IN SPRING

1 The easiest way to open the drainage holes in a plastic planter is with an electric drill.

2 Fill the window box with compost, mixing in 2 teaspoons of slow-release plant food granules.

3 Plant the pelargoniums, evenly spaced, in the window box.

4 Plant the two bidens on either side of the central pelargonium to spill over the front of the planter.

5 Plant the two verbenas on either side of the central pelargonium towards the back of the planter.

6 Plant the helichrysums in the front corners. Water thoroughly and stand the box in a sunny position.

An antique wall basket

This old wirework basket is an attractive container for a planting scheme which includes deep pink pansies, a variegated ivy-leaved pelargonium with soft pink flowers, a blue convolvulus and deep pink alyssum.

MATERIALS

30 cm (12 in) wall basket
Sphagnum moss
Compost
Slow-release plant food granules

PLANTS

5 rose-pink alyssum
Pelargonium 'L'Elégante'
3 deep pink pansies
Convolvulus sabatius

PELARGONIUM   ALYSSUM

CONVOLVULUS

PANSY

GARDENER'S TIP

Wall baskets look good among climbing plants, but you will need to trim the surrounding foliage if it gets too exuberant.

PLANT IN LATE SPRING OR EARLY SUMMER

1 Line the back of the basket and the lower half of the front with moss. Plant the alyssum into the side by resting the rootballs on the moss, and guiding the foliage through the wires.

2 Line the remainder of the basket with moss and fill with compost, mixing a half-teaspoon of plant food granules into the top layer. Plant the pelargonium at the front of the basket.

3 Plant the pansies around the pelargonium. Plant the convolvulus at the back of the basket, trailing its foliage through the other plants. Water well and hang in partial sun.

A cottage terracotta planter

Charming, cottage-garden plants tumble from this terracotta window box in a colourful display. The sunny flowers of the nemesias, marigolds and nasturtiums mingle with the cool, soft green helichrysums and blue-green nasturtium leaves.

MATERIALS

36 cm (14 in) terracotta window box
Crocks or other suitable drainage material
Compost
Slow-release plant food granules

PLANTS

3 pot marigolds (calendulas)
2 Helichrysum petiolare 'Aureum'
2 nasturtiums
2 Nemesia 'Orange Prince'

MARIGOLD

HELICHRYSUM

NASTURTIUM

NEMESIAS

1 Cover the base of the container with crocks and fill with compost, mixing in 2 teaspoons of plant food granules. Plant the marigolds along the back.

2 Plant the two helichrysums in the front corners of the window box.

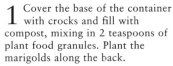

3 Plant the nasturtiums between the marigolds at the back of the container.

4 Plant the nemesias between the helichrysums. Water well and stand in partial sun.

GARDENER'S TIP

The golden-leaved helichrysum retains a better colour if it is not in full sun all day. Too much sun makes it looks rather bleached.

PLANT IN SPRING

A touch of gold

Yellow lantana and the yellow-flowered variegated-leaf nasturtium provide colour from early summer onwards, and later in the season the black-eyed Susan will be covered in eye-catching flowers. Hang this exuberant basket high on a sunny wall so that the trailing plants can make as much growth as they like.

NASTURTIUM

BLACK-EYED
SUSAN

LANTANA

MATERIALS

30 cm (12 in) hanging basket
Sphagnum moss
Compost
Slow-release plant food granules

PLANTS

3 Alaska nasturtiums
Yellow lantana
3 black-eyed Susans (Thunbergia alata)

1 Line the lower half of the basket with moss.

2 Plant the nasturtiums into the side of the basket by resting the rootballs on the moss, and carefully guiding the leaves through the wires.

3 Line the rest of the basket with moss. Fill the basket with compost, mixing a teaspoon of slow-release plant food granules into the top layer.

4 Plant the lantana in the centre of the basket.

5 Plant the black-eyed Susans around the lantana. Water well and hang in a sunny position.

GARDENER'S TIP

Save some of the nasturtium seeds for next year's baskets and pots – they are among the easiest of plants to grow and some of the seeds are quite likely to find their own way into nearby cracks and crevices.

PLANT IN LATE SPRING OR EARLY SUMMER

A wild one

Native plants are those that have grown naturally in the countryside for thousands of years. Some of the most colourful ones are cornfield flowers, but many are quite rare now. To enjoy them this summer, sow a pot full of wild flowers to stand on your doorstep.

MATERIALS

Pebbles
Very large flower pot
Garden soil

PLANTS

Packet of wild flower seeds

FLOWER POT

WILD FLOWER SEEDS

PEBBLES

GARDEN SOIL

1 Put a few pebbles in the base of the pot for drainage.

2 Fill the pot with garden soil, taking out any bits of roots or large stones.

3 Make sure the surface is level, then sprinkle a large pinch of flower seeds evenly on top.

4 Cover the seeds lightly with soil, just so you can't see them any more, and water them in with a gentle sprinkle.

GARDENER'S TIP

Remember to keep watering as the flowers grow!
Pots need much more watering than beds because the water drains away.

PLANT IN EARLY SPRING

A pastel composition

Pure white pelargonium blooms emerge from a sea of blue felicias, pinky-blue brachycome daisies and verbenas in this romantic basket.

PELARGONIUM

MATERIALS

36 cm (14 in) hanging basket
Sphagnum moss
Compost
Slow-release plant food granules

PLANTS

2 pink verbenas
2 Brachycome 'Pink Mist'
Blue felicia
White pelargonium

VERBENA

BRACHYCOME

FELICIA

1 Line the basket with moss and fill with compost, mixing a teaspoon of slow-release plant food granules into the top layer.

2 Plant the verbenas opposite each other at the edge of the basket, so that the foliage will tumble over the sides.

3 Plant the brachycome daisies around the edge of the basket. Plant the felicia off-centre in the middle of the basket.

4 Plant the pelargonium off-centre in the remaining space in the middle of the basket. Water thoroughly and hang in a sunny position.

GARDENER'S TIP

White pelargonium flowers discolour as they age; be sure to pick them off to keep the basket looking at its best.

PLANT IN LATE SPRING OR EARLY SUMMER

Daisy chains

The soft yellow of the marguerites' flowers and foliage is emphasized by combining them with bright blue felicia in this summery basket.

MARGUERITE

HELICHRYSUM

FELICIA

MATERIALS

40 cm (16 in) hanging basket
Sphagnum moss
Compost
Slow-release plant food granules

PLANTS

3 variegated felicias
3 yellow marguerites
  (argyranthemums)
3 Helichrysum petiolare 'Aureum'

GARDENER'S TIP

Pinch out the growing tips of the marguerites regularly to encourage bushy plants.

PLANT IN LATE SPRING OR
EARLY SUMMER

1 Line the lower half of the basket with moss. Plant the felicias into the sides of the basket by resting the rootballs on the moss, and carefully guiding the foliage through the wires.

2 Line the rest of the basket with moss. Fill with compost, mixing a teaspoon of slow-release plant food granules into the top layer. Plant the marguerites in the top of the basket.

3 Plant the helichrysums between the marguerites, angling the plants to encourage them to grow over the edge of the basket. Water well and hang in full or partial sun.

Begonias and fuchsias

Fuchsias are wonderful hanging basket plants as they flower prolifically late into the autumn. By the end of summer, when the other plants may start to look a bit straggly, the fuchsia will be at its best with a glorious display of colour.

MATERIALS

36 cm (14 in) hanging basket
Sphagnum moss
Compost
Slow-release plant
    food granules

PLANTS

2 Diascia *'Ruby Field'*
3 Helichrysum microphyllum
Fuchsia *'Rose Winston'* or
    similar soft pink
3 deep pink begonias

BEGONIA

DIASCIA

HELICHRYSUM

FUCHSIA

1 Line the lower half of the basket with moss and arrange the diascias and helichrysums in the basket to decide where to plant each one. Ensure they do not become tangled in the wires.

2 Plant the two diascias into the sides of the basket by resting the rootballs in the moss, and gently feeding the foliage through the wires.

GARDENER'S TIP

If some of the plants in the basket begin to look straggly in comparison with the fuchsia, cut them right back and give a liquid feed – they will grow with renewed vigour and provide a wonderful autumn show.

PLANT IN LATE SPRING OR EARLY SUMMER

3 Line the rest of the basket with moss, partly fill with compost and plant the three helichrysums into the side of the basket near the rim.

4 Fill the basket with compost. Mix a teaspoon of slow-release plant food granules into the top layer of compost. Plant the fuchsia in the centre of the basket.

5 Finally, plant the three begonias around the fuchsia. Water well and hang the basket in full sun or partial shade.

Pot of sunflowers

Sunflowers grow very well in pots provided you are not growing the giant varieties. Grow your own from seed; there are many kinds to choose from, including the one with double flowers used here.

MATERIALS

30 cm (12 in) glazed pot
Polystyrene or similar
 drainage material
Equal mix loam-based compost
 and container compost
Slow-release plant
 food granules

PLANTS

3 strong sunflower seedlings,
approximately 20 cm (8 in) tall

SUNFLOWER
SEEDLING

GARDENER'S TIP

Allow at least one of the sunflower heads to set seed. As the plant starts to die back, cut off the seedhead and hang it upside-down to ripen. Reserve some seeds for next year and then hang the seedhead outside for the birds.

PLANT SEEDS IN SPRING
AND SEEDLINGS IN SUMMER TO
FLOWER IN LATE SUMMER

1 Line the base of the pot with drainage material and fill with the compost mix. Scoop out evenly spaced holes for each seedling and plant, firming the compost around the plants.

2 Scatter 1 tablespoon of plant food granules on the surface of the compost. Place in a sunny position, out of the wind, and water regularly.

Alpine sink

An old stone sink is a perfect container for a collection of alpine plants. The rock helps to create the effect of a miniature landscape and provides shelter for some of the plants. The sink is set up on the stand of an old sewing machine so that the plants can be admired easily.

MATERIALS

Stone sink or trough 76 x 50 cm (30 x 20 in)
Crocks or other suitable drainage material
Moss-covered rock
Loam-based compost with 1/3 added coarse grit
Washed gravel

PLANTS

Achillea tomentosa
Veronica peduncularis
Hebe
Ivy
Sedum ewersii
Aster natalensis
Alpine willow (Salix alpina)
Arabis ferdinandi-coburgi *'Variegata'*

HEBE

SEDUM

ACHILLEA

VERONICA

IVY

1 Cover the drainage hole of the sink with crocks or other suitable drainage material. Position the rock. It is important to do this before adding the soil to create the effect of a natural rocky outcrop. Pour the compost into the sink.

2 Plan the position of your plants so that the end result will have a good balance of shape and colour. If the sink is very shallow you will need to scoop out the soil right to the base before planting but alpine plants are used to shallow soil. Make sure that the bottom leaves of low-growing plants are level with the soil. Too low and they will rot; too high and they will dry out.

3 When all the plants are in place, carefully pour washed gravel all around them to cover the whole soil area. Water and place in full or partial sun.

Flowers for late summer

Although this window box is already looking good, towards the end of the summer it will really come into its own – by then the vibrant red and purple flowers of the pelargonium, salvias and lavenders will be at their most prolific.

MATERIALS

60 cm (24 in) wooden planter, stained black
Polystyrene or other suitable drainage material
Compost
Slow-release plant food granules

PLANTS

Pelargonium *'Tomcat'*
2 *Lavenders* (Lavandula pinnata)
2 Salvia *'Raspberry Royal'*
2 *blue brachycome daisies*
Convolvulus sabatius
6 *rose-pink alyssum*

ALYSSUM

CONVOLVULUS

BRACHYCOME

LAVENDER

SALVIA

PELARGONIUM

1 Line the base of the container with polystyrene or similar drainage material. Fill the window box with compost, mixing in 3 teaspoons of slow-release plant food granules. Plant the pelargonium at the back of the window box, in the centre.

2 Plant the two lavenders in the rear corners of the box.

3 Plant the salvias at the front on either side of the pelargonium.

4 Plant the brachycome daisies in the front corners of the window box.

5 Plant the convolvulus in the centre, in front of the pelargonium.

6 Fill the spaces with the alyssum. Water well and place in a sunny position.

GARDENER'S TIP

Both the lavenders and the salvias are highly aromatic, so if possible position this box near a door or a path, so that you can enjoy the fragrance as you brush against the plants.

PLANT IN EARLY SUMMER

Autumn hanging basket

Towards the end of the season the colours of summer hanging baskets do not always marry happily with the reds and golds of autumn. This is the time to plant a richly coloured hanging basket for winter.

MATERIALS

30 cm (12 in) hanging basket
Plastic pot
Sphagnum moss
Equal mix loam-based compost
   and container compost
Slow-release plant food granules

PLANTS

4 winter-flowering pansies
3 variegated ivies
Euonymus fortunei ('Emerald
   and Gold' was used here)
2 dahlias

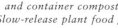

PANSY

DAHLIA

IVY

EUONYMUS

GARDENER'S TIP

Although special composts with water-retaining gel are a boon for summer baskets, they can get waterlogged in the cooler months. Mix equal parts of loam-based and container composts for autumn and winter planting.

PLANT IN SPRING OR SUMMER
TO FLOWER IN AUTUMN

1 Support the hanging basket on a pot. Unhook the chain from one fixing point so that it hangs down one side of the basket. Line the base and bottom half of the basket with a generous layer of sphagnum moss.

2 Pour in compost until it is level with the top of the moss. Plant your first layer of three pansies and three ivies, passing the foliage through the wire of the basket, so that the rootballs of the plants are resting on the compost.

3 Line the rest of the basket with moss and top up with compost, firming it around the roots of the ivies and pansies. Then plant the remaining plants in the top of the basket, with the euonymus in the centre and the remaining pansy and dahlias surrounding it. Scatter a tablespoon of slow-release plant food granules on to the compost and water the hanging basket well. Re-attach the chain and hang the basket in full or partial sun.

Heather window box

This is a perfect project for an absolute beginner as it is extremely simple to achieve. The bark window box is a sympathetic container for the heathers, which look quite at home in their bed of moss.

MATERIALS

30 cm (12 in) bark window box
Crocks or other suitable drainage
  material
Ericaceous compost
Bun moss

PLANTS

Heathers

HEATHERS

GARDENER'S TIP

Do not be tempted to use ordinary compost as it contains lime which, with a very few exceptions, is not suitable for the majority of heathers.

PLANT IN AUTUMN

1 Put a layer of crocks or other suitable drainage material in the bottom of the box.

2 Remove the heathers from their pots and position them in the window box.

3 Fill the gaps between the plants with the compost, pressing it around the plants. Water in well.

4 Tuck the bun moss snugly around the plants so that no soil is visible. Place in full or partial sun.

Evergreens with extra colour

They may be easy to look after but all-year-round window boxes can start to look a bit lifeless after a couple of seasons. It does not take much trouble to add a few seasonal flowers and it makes all the difference to a display.

MATERIALS

76 cm (30 in) plastic window box
Compost
Slow-release plant food granules

PLANTS

Hebe *'Baby Marie'*
Convolvulus cneorum
Potentilla *'Nunk'*
Variegated ivies
2 Diascia *'Ruby Field'*
Pink marguerite (Argyranthemum *'Flamingo')*

IVY

CONVOLVULUS

POTENTILLA

MARGUERITE

DIASCIA

HEBE

1 Check the drainage holes are open in the base and, if not, drill or punch them open. Fill the window box with compost, mixing in 3 teaspoons of slow-release plant food granules. Plant the hebe in the centre.

2 Plant the convolvulus near one end of the window box.

3 Plant the potentilla near the other end of the window box.

4 Plant the two ivies at the front corners of the window box.

5 Plant the diascias on either side of the hebe at the front of the window box.

6 Plant the marguerite between the hebe and the convolvulus at the back. Water well and stand in full or partial sun.

GARDENER'S TIP

At the end of the summer, remove the diascias and marguerite, feed the remaining plants with more granules, and fill the spaces with winter-flowering plants such as pansies or heathers.

PLANT IN SPRING

Classic topiary

MATERIALS

4 large terracotta pots
Bark chippings
Crocks or other suitable drainage
  material
Equal mix loam-based compost
  and container compost
Slow-release plant food granules

PLANTS

4 box trees (Buxus sempervirens)
in different topiary shapes

BOX TREES (*BUXUS SEMPERVIRENS*)

The clean lines of the topiary are matched by the simplicity of the terracotta pots. Since the eye is drawn to the outlines of the box plants, decorated pots would be a distraction.

1 If the plant has been well looked after in the nursery it may not need potting on yet. In this case simply slip the plant in its pot into the terracotta container.

2 To conserve moisture and conceal the plastic pot, cover with a generous layer of bark chippings.

3 To repot a box tree, first place a good layer of crocks or other drainage material in the bottom of the pot. Remove the tree from its plastic pot and place it in the terracotta container. Surround the rootball with compost, pushing it well down the sides.

4 Scatter a tablespoon of plant food granules on the surface of the compost and top with a layer of bark chippings. Water well and position in sun or partial shade.

GARDENER'S TIP

Don't get carried away when you trim topiary. Little and often, with an ordinary pair of scissors, is better than occasional dramatic gestures with a pair of shears.

**PLANT AT ANY
TIME OF THE YEAR**

Trug of winter pansies

Winter pansies are wonderfully resilient and will bloom bravely throughout the winter as long as they are regularly dead-headed. This trug may be moved around to provide colour wherever it is needed, and acts as a perfect antidote to mid-winter gloom.

MATERIALS

Old wooden trug
Sphagnum moss
Compost
Slow-release plant
   food granules

PLANTS

15 winter-flowering pansies
(violas)

PANSIES

1 Line the trug with a generous layer of sphagnum moss. Fill the moss lining with compost.

2 Plant the pansies by starting at one end and filling the spaces between the plants with compost as you go. Gently firm each plant into position and add a final layer of compost mixed with a tablespoon of plant food granules around the pansies. Water and place in a fairly sunny position.

GARDENER'S TIP

Not everyone has an old trug available, but an old basket, colander, or an enamel bread bin could be used instead. Junk shops and flea markets are a great source of containers that are too battered for their original use, but fine for planting.

PLANT IN AUTUMN TO FLOWER IN WINTER

Evergreen garden

Evergreen plants come in many shapes, sizes and shades. Grouped in containers they will provide you with year-round interest and colour.

MATERIALS

Terracotta pots of various sizes
Crocks or similar drainage material
Equal mix loam-based compost and container compost
Plant saucers
Gravel
Slow-release plant food granules

PLANTS

*False cypress (*Chamaecyparis lawsoniana *'Columnaris';* C. pisifera *'Filifera Aurea')*
Berberis darwinii
Berberis thunbergii *'Atropurpurea Nana'*
Pachysandra terminalis
Bergenia

FALSE CYPRESS   BERGENIA

BERBERIS   PACHYSANDRA

GARDENER'S TIP

Include some golden or variegated foliage amongst your evergreens and choose contrasting leaf forms to make a striking group.

PLANT AT ANY
TIME OF THE YEAR

1 Large shrubs, such as this conifer, should be potted into a proportionally large container. Place plenty of crocks or similar drainage material at the base of the pot. If the plant is at all potbound, tease the roots loose before planting in its new pot. Fill around the rootball with compost, pressing it down firmly around the edges of the pot.

2 Smaller plants, like bergenia, should be planted in a pot slightly larger than the existing one. Place crocks in the base of the pot, position the plant and then fill around the edges with compost. Repeat with the remaining plants.

3 Plants will stay moist longer if they are stood in saucers of wet gravel. This group of plants will do well positioned in partial shade. Water regularly and feed with slow-release plant food granules in the spring and autumn.

Year-round window box

In the same way that a garden has certain plants that provide structure throughout the year, this window box has been planted so that there is always plenty of foliage. Extra colour may be introduced each season by including small flowering plants, such as heathers.

MATERIALS

90 cm (3 ft) wooden window box, preferably self-watering
Equal mix loam-based compost and container compost
Slow-release plant food granules
Bark chippings

PLANTS

Skimmia reevesiana *'Rubella'*
2 Arundinaria pygmaea
2 Cotoneaster conspicuus
2 *periwinkles* (Vinca minor *'Variegata'*)
6 *heathers*

PERIWINKLE

COTONEASTER

SKIMMIA

ARUNDINARIA

HEATHER

1 If you are using a self-watering container, feed the wicks through the base of the plastic liner. Slip the liner into the wooden window box.

2 Before you start planting, plan the position of the plants so that the colours and shapes look well balanced. Remove the plants from their pots, tease loose their roots if they look at all potbound and position in the window box. Top up with compost.

3 Once the structure plants are in place you can add the colour; in this case, the heathers. Scoop out a hole for each heather and then plant, pressing firmly around each one. Scatter two tablespoons of plant food granules over the surface.

4 Top-dress the window box with a layer of bark chippings; this will help to conserve moisture. Water thoroughly.

GARDENER'S TIP

Plants do not need watering in winter, unless they are sheltered from the rain. Even then they should be watered sparingly and not in frosty weather. Self-watering containers should be drained before winter to prevent frost damage.

PLANT AT ANY TIME OF THE YEAR

Winter cheer

Many window boxes are left unplanted through the winter, but you can soon brighten the house or garden during this season with an easy arrangement of pot-grown plants plunged in bark.

MATERIALS

40 cm (16 in) glazed window box
Bark chippings

PLANTS

2 miniature conifers
2 variegated ivies
2 red polyanthus

POLYANTHUS

IVY

CONIFER

1 Water all the plants. Place the conifers, still in their pots, at each end of the window box.

2 Half-fill the window box with bark chippings.

3 Place the pots of polyanthus on the bark chippings between the two conifers.

4 Place the pots of ivy in the front corners of the box. Add further bark chippings to the container until all the pots are concealed. Water only when plants show signs of dryness. Stand in any position.

GARDENER'S TIP

When it is time to replant the window box, plunge the conifers, still in their pots, in a shady position in the garden. Water well through the spring and summer and they may be used again next year.

PLANT IN EARLY WINTER

Classic winter colours

Convolvulus cneorum is an attractive small shrub with eye-catching silver-grey leaves, which last through winter, and white flowers in spring and summer. Planted with ice-blue pansies, it makes a softly subtle display from autumn to spring.

MATERIALS

30 cm (12 in) hanging basket
Sphagnum moss
Compost

PLANTS

8 silver/blue pansies (Viola 'Silver Wings', or similar)
Convolvulus cneorum

CONVOLVULUS

PANSIES

1 Half-line the basket with moss and fill with compost to the top of the moss. Plant four of the pansies into the side of the basket by placing their rootballs on the compost, and gently guiding the leaves through the side of the basket.

2 Line the rest of the basket with moss and top up with compost. Plant the convolvulus in the centre of the basket.

GARDENER'S TIP

At the end of the winter cut back any dead wood or straggly branches on the *Convolvulus cneorum*, and give a liquid feed to encourage new growth. Small shrubs such as this may be used in hanging baskets for one season, but will then need planting into a larger container or the border.

PLANT IN AUTUMN

3 Plant the remaining four pansies around the convolvulus. Water well and hang in sun or partial shade.

Gothic ivy

Twisted willow branches set into a chimney pot offer an attractive support for ivy, and will provide welcome interest in the winter.

MATERIALS

Chimney pot
Compost
90 cm (3 ft) wire netting

PLANTS

4–5 branches of twisted willow
Large ivy (Hedera helix var. hibernica was used here)

IVY

1 Place the chimney pot in its final position (in shade or half-shade) and half-fill with compost. Fold or crumple the wire netting and push down into the chimney pot so that it rests on the compost.

2 Arrange the willow branches in the chimney pot, pushing the stems through the wire netting.

3 Rest the ivy, in its pot, on the wire netting amongst the willow branches. Fill the chimney pot with compost to within 10 cm (4 in) of the rim. Cut loose any ties and remove the cane.

4 Arrange the stems of ivy over the willow branches and water. To start with it may look rather contrived, but as the ivy settles into its new surroundings it will attach itself to the willow.

GARDENER'S TIP

You may find that some of your twisted willow branches take root in the compost. Plant a rooted branch in the garden where it will grow into a tree. It will eventually be quite large so do not plant it near the house.

PLANT AT ANY
TIME OF THE YEAR

Golden Christmas holly

Evergreen standard holly trees are splendid container plants. This golden holly in a gilded pot has been dressed up for Christmas with bows and baubles.

HOLLY

MATERIALS

40 cm (16 in) terracotta pot
Gold spray-paint
Crocks or similar drainage
   material
Composted manure
Loam-based compost
Pine cones
90 cm (3 ft) wired ribbon
Tin Christmas decorations

PLANTS

Golden holly

1 Spray the pot with gold paint and leave to dry. Place a good layer of crocks or similar drainage material in the base. Cover with a 7.5 cm (3 in) layer of composted manure and a thin layer of loam-based potting compost. Remove the holly from its existing container and place in the gilded pot.

2 Surround the rootball with compost, pressing down firmly to ensure that the tree is firmly planted, and cover the surface with pine cones.

GARDENER'S TIP

In the autumn, plant some corms of *Iris reticulata* or similar small bulbs in the compost surrounding the tree for a delightful spring display.

PLANT IN AUTUMN, WINTER OR SPRING

3 Tie the ribbon into a bow around the trunk of the tree. Spray the decorations gold and hang in the branches. Water the tree to settle it in, but do not do this on a frosty day.

An evergreen wall basket

Pansies will flower throughout the winter. Even if they are flattened by rain, frost or snow, at the first sign of improvement in the weather their heads will pop up again to bring brightness to the dullest day. They have been planted with ivies to provide colour from early autumn through to late spring.

MATERIALS

30 cm (12 in) wall basket
Sphagnum moss
Compost

PLANTS

2 golden variegated ivies
2 copper pansies (viola)
Yellow pansy (viola)

PANSIES

IVY

GARDENER'S TIP

Winter baskets do not need regular feeding and should only be watered in very dry conditions. To prolong the flowering life of the pansies, dead-head regularly and pinch out any straggly stems to encourage new shoots from the base.

PLANT IN AUTUMN

1 Line the basket with moss. Three-quarters fill the basket with compost and position the ivies with their rootballs resting on the compost. Guide the stems through the sides of the basket so that they trail downwards. Pack more moss around the ivies and top up the basket with compost.

2 Plant the two copper pansies at either end of the basket.

3 Plant the yellow pansy in the centre. Water well and hang in shade or semi-shade.

Edible collections

What could be nicer than reaching out of the kitchen window to gather fresh herbs from the window-sill, or eating succulent tomatoes or strawberries grown on the balcony? If you don't have room for a vegetable patch, even if you don't have a garden at all, you can still enjoy home-grown produce if you plant it in containers. Go for compact varieties of beans and tomatoes, and choose lettuces such as 'Salad Bowl' so that you can pick just what you need and leave the plants to go on growing. You will be able to grow a wide range: you could even try a few early potatoes in a pot, for the first and most delicious crop of the year.

Kitchen-garden containers can be beautiful, too. Alpine strawberries are both decorative and delicious tumbling out of a hanging basket, and you can grow herbs for their looks as well as their flavour, choosing variegated mints, red-leaved basil or purple sage to contribute to the visual feast.

ABOVE: *Herbs thrive on a sunny windowsill.*

Herbs in the shade

Although the Mediterranean herbs need lots of sunshine, there are many others which prefer a cooler situation to look and taste their best. This window box, ideal for just outside the kitchen door or window, has an interesting variety of mints, sorrel, chives, lemon balm and parsley.

LEMON BALM

MINTS

CHIVE

SORREL

PARSLEY

MINT

MATERIALS

50 cm (20 in) terracotta window box
Polystyrene or other suitable drainage material
Compost
Slow-release plant food granules, pelleted chicken manure, or similar organic plant food

PLANTS

Lemon balm
3 mints (black peppermint, silver mint and curly spearmint were used here)
Sorrel
Chives
Parsley

1 Line the base of the container with polystyrene or similar drainage material. Top up with compost, mixing in 3 teaspoons of slow-release plant food granules or organic alternative.

2 Plant the lemon balm and two of the mints along the back of the window box.

3 Plant the third mint, the sorrel and the chives along the front. Finally, plant the parsley in the centre. Position the box in light shade and water thoroughly.

GARDENER'S TIP

Use the freshly picked mint to make refreshing teas. Pour hot boiled water over a few washed leaves and infuse for five minutes.

PLANT IN EARLY SPRING

Vital ingredients

A lovely present for an enthusiastic cook, this window box contains chervil, coriander, fennel, garlic, purple sage, French tarragon, savory, origanum and basil.

MATERIALS

45 cm (18 in) wooden window box
Crocks or other suitable drainage material
Compost
Slow-release plant food granules, pelleted chicken manure, or similar organic plant food

PLANTS

French tarragon
Chervil
Garlic
Coriander
Purple sage
Basil
Fennel
Savory
Origanum

FENNEL
GARLIC
SAVORY
BASIL
ORIGANUM
CORIANDER
CHERVIL
FRENCH TARRAGON
PURPLE SAGE

GARDENER'S TIP

There are now various kinds of basil seed available (some specialists sell at least 12), with varieties ranging from Greek to Indonesian. The key point when growing them is to remove the flower buds the moment they appear as the leaves will quickly lose their flavour once the flowers open.

PLANT IN SPRING

1 Line the base of the container with crocks or other suitable drainage material. Fill the window box with compost, mixing in a teaspoon of slow-release plant food granules or an organic alternative.

2 Before planting the herbs, arrange them in the window box in their pots.

3 Plant the back row of herbs in the window box first.

4 Plant more herbs at the front of the window box. Water well and stand in a sunny position.

Wine case herb garden

Add a coat of varnish to an old wine case to make an attractive and durable container for a miniature herb garden. The container can be placed near the kitchen door or on a balcony.

MATERIALS

Wooden wine case
Pliers
Sandpaper
Paintbrush
Light oak semi-matt varnish
Crocks or similar drainage
  material
Compost with ⅓ added coarse
  grit
Slow-release plant food granules
  or pelleted chicken manure
Bark chippings

PLANTS

Selection of 7 herbs, such as sage, chives, parsley, mint, tarragon, lemon thyme and creeping thyme

SAGE

PARSLEY

CHIVES

1 Remove any wire staples from around the edges of the box and sand down the rough edges. Apply two coats of varnish on the inside and outside of the box, allowing the varnish to dry thoroughly between coats. When dry, cover the base of the box with a layer of crocks or similar drainage material.

GARDENER'S TIP

Some herbs like cool, partial shade while others like hot, dry, free-draining soil. A mixed herb garden will thrive for only one growing season.

PLANT IN SPRING

2 Before planting, decide how you are going to arrange the plants in the container to achieve a pleasing balance of colour, height and shape.

3 Fill the box with gritty compost and plant from one end of the box to the other. Loosen the rootballs, as this will help the plants to root into the surrounding compost.

4 When the planting is complete, scatter 2 tablespoons of plant food granules or pelleted chicken manure on the surface of the compost. Firm in the plants and mulch with bark chippings to retain moisture. Water well.

The good life

This window box will not exactly make you self-sufficient, but it is surprising how many different vegetables can be grown in a small space. It is perfect for anyone who likes the taste of home-grown vegetables but does not have a garden to grow them in.

MATERIALS

76 cm (30 in) plastic window box
Compost
Slow-release plant food granules, pelleted chicken manure or similar organic plant food

PLANTS

Garlic
3 Chinese leaves
4 plugs of beetroot (see Gardener's Tip)
Pepper plant
3 dwarf French beans
3 plugs of shallots

1 Check the drainage holes are open in the container's base. Fill the window box with compost, mixing in 2 teaspoons of slow-release plant food granules or an organic alternative. Start planting from one end.

2 Starting at the right-hand end of the window box, first plant the garlic. Next plant the Chinese leaves.

3 Follow these with the plugs of beetroot.

4 Plant the pepper plant next, just to the left of the centre.

BEETROOT   CHINESE LEAVES

GARLIC

FRENCH BEAN

PEPPER

SHALLOTS

5 Now plant the three dwarf French bean plants.

6 Finally, plant the shallot plugs in the left-hand corner. Water well and stand in full or partial sun.

GARDENER'S TIP

It is now possible to buy plugs of small vegetable plants at garden centres. There is no need to separate the plants provided there is sufficient room between the clumps.

PLANT IN SPRING

A taste for flowers

It is often said that something "looks good enough to eat", and in this instance it is true. All the flowers in this window box may be used for flavour and garnishes.

MATERIALS

36 cm (14 in) terracotta window box
Crocks or other suitable drainage material
Compost
Slow-release plant food granules, pelleted chicken manure or similar organic plant food

PLANTS

Chives
2 nasturtiums
2 pansies (viola) with well-marked "faces"
2 pot marigolds (calendula)

CHIVE

NASTURTIUM

PANSY

MARIGOLDS

GARDENER'S TIP

To keep all the plants producing flowers, dead-head regularly. Once a plant has set seed it considers its work done and will produce fewer and fewer flowers.

PLANT IN EARLY SPRING

1 Cover the base of the window box with a layer of crocks or similar drainage material. Fill with compost, mixing in 2 teaspoons of slow-release plant food granules or an organic alternative. Plant the chives in the right-hand corner.

2 Plant one of the nasturtiums in the left-hand corner and the other centre-front.

3 Plant one pansy at the back next to the chives, and the other at the front to the left of the central nasturtium.

4 Plant one of the marigolds at the back between the pansy and nasturtium, and the other one just behind the central nasturtium.

A hanging garden of herbs

A basket of herbs is both decorative and useful, especially when hung near the kitchen door or window. Herbs benefit from regular picking to encourage the plants to produce lots of tender new shoots throughout the summer. Some herbs can be very vigorous so be sure to choose compact varieties for your hanging basket.

MATERIALS

30 cm (12 in) hanging basket
Sphagnum moss
Compost
Slow-release plant food granules

PLANTS

5 parsley
French tarragon
Sage
Rosemary (prostrate form)
2 basil

PARSLEY

FRENCH
TARRAGON

BASIL

ROSEMARY

SAGE

GARDENER'S TIP

Fortunately, the strongly aromatic nature of most herbs does dissuade pests, but if you should have any problems be sure to use a safe organic pesticide. Soapy washing-up water can be used against greenfly.

PLANT IN SPRING

1 Line the lower half of the basket with moss. Plant the parsley, resting the rootballs on the moss and feeding the leaves through the sides of the basket.

2 Line the rest of the basket with moss and fill with compost. Mix a teaspoon of slow-release plant food granules into the top. Plant the tarragon.

3 Plant the sage. Plant the prostrate rosemary, angling it slightly to encourage it to grow over the side of the basket.

4 Finally, plant the two basil plants and water well before hanging in partial sun. A regular liquid feed is recommended.

Butler's tray kitchen garden

Not many of us have the space or time to maintain a kitchen garden, but this table-top selection of plants will give you a taste of the delights to be had, and might even inspire you to try the real thing.

MATERIALS

Terracotta pots of various sizes
Crocks or other suitable drainage material
Compost
Butler's tray
Thick plastic sheet
Clay granules

PLANTS

Selection of kitchen garden plants, such as pot marigolds (calendula), basil, nasturtium, miniature tomato, strawberry and French tarragon

STRAWBERRY

TARRAGON

TOMATO

NASTURTIUM

BASIL   MARIGOLD

1 If the plants have well-developed root systems, like this marigold, they will benefit from being planted in a larger pot. Place crocks in the bottom of the pots for drainage. Gently tease loose some of the roots before you repot the plant.

2 You may be able to divide a single basil plant when repotting, enabling you to fill two pots. The miniature tomato and the strawberry should be planted in larger pots to allow plenty of room for root development.

3 Nasturtiums flower better in poor soil. Once you have planted them, leave them to their own devices. Give them a little water but no plant food or you will get lots of leaves and very few flowers.

4 Line your tray with a thick plastic sheet and cover it with clay granules. These retain moisture and create a damp micro-climate for the plants. Arrange your plants on the tray, place in a sunny position and water and feed (except the nasturtiums) regularly.

Beans and parsley in a basket

A hanging basket planted with dwarf beans and parsley can be surprisingly productive and will outwit all but the most acrobatic of snails.

MATERIALS

36 cm (14 in) hanging basket
Sphagnum moss
Compost
Slow-release plant food granules

PLANTS

7 parsley plants
3 dwarf bean plants

PARSLEY

DWARF BEAN

1 Line the lower half of the basket with moss and half-fill with compost.

2 Plant the parsley into the sides of the basket, resting the root-balls on the compost and feeding the leaves through the wires.

3 Gently separate the bean plants from one another.

4 Line the upper half of the basket with moss and add more compost. Mix a teaspoon of slow-release plant food granules into the top layer. Plant the beans in the compost. Water the basket thoroughly and hang in partial sun.

GARDENER'S TIP

Fruit and vegetable hanging baskets need quite a lot of attention to crop well. They should be kept moist at all times and need a liquid feed once a week. If you are going to be away, move the basket into the shade, where it will not dry out so quickly.

PLANT IN SPRING

Wild strawberry basket

Wild strawberries can be grown in a basket and enjoyed anywhere, whether in the countryside or a small city garden.

MATERIALS

30 cm (12 in) square wire basket
Sphagnum moss
Equal mix loam-based compost
* and container compost*
Slow-release plant food granules
* or organic plant food*

PLANTS

4 alpine
strawberry plants

ALPINE
STRAWBERRY

1 Line the base and sides of the basket with a generous layer of sphagnum moss.

2 Fill the lined area with compost. Scoop out a hollow for each strawberry plant, and press the compost firmly around the rootball as you plant.

3 Scatter a tablespoon of plant food granules on the surface of the compost.

4 Tuck more moss around the edges and under the leaves to conserve moisture and stop the fruit touching the soil. Water and place in full or partial sun.

GARDENER'S TIP

Propagate strawberry runners by pinning the plantlets into small pots of compost. A loop of wire or a hairpin placed on either side of the plantlet will hold it firmly in place until it has rooted. Then simply cut the runner and you have a new strawberry plant.

PLANT IN SPRING TO FRUIT IN SUMMER

Good enough to eat

All the plants in this basket bear an edible crop: the tomato fruit, nasturtium flowers and parsley leaves. You could even impress your family or guests with a "hanging basket salad", using all three together.

MATERIALS

36 cm (14 in) hanging basket
Sphagnum moss
Compost
Slow-release plant food granules

PLANTS

6 parsley plants
3 trailing nasturtiums
3 'Tumbler' tomatoes, or similar

PARSLEY

TRAILING
NASTURTIUM

TOMATO

GARDENER'S TIP

If you would prefer to grow your plants organically, plant this basket using an organic compost and use natural plant foods such as pelleted chicken manure or a liquid seaweed feed.

PLANT IN LATE SPRING OR EARLY SUMMER

1 Line the lower half of the basket with moss.

2 Plant three parsley plants into the side of the basket by resting the rootballs on the moss, and feeding the leaves through the side of the basket.

3 Line the basket to just below the rim and fill with compost. Mix a teaspoon of slow-release plant food granules into the top of the compost. Plant three nasturtium plants into the side of the basket, just below the rim.

4 Finish lining the basket with moss, being careful to tuck plenty of moss around the nasturtiums.

5 Plant the tomato plants in the top of the basket.

6 Plant the remaining three parsley plants amongst the tomatoes in the top of the basket. Water well and hang in a sunny position. Liquid feed regularly.

Summer fruits

The red of ripening strawberries is matched by vibrant red pelargonium flowers in this unusual arrangement. Alpine strawberry plants make a good contrast, with their delicate fruit and tendrils.

STRAWBERRY

ALPINE STRAWBERRY

PELARGONIUM

MATERIALS

36 cm (14 in) hanging basket
Sphagnum moss
Compost
Slow-release plant food granules
  or organic plant food

PLANTS

3 'Maxim' strawberry plants, or
  similar
Pelargonium 'Miss Flora', or
  similar
3 alpine strawberry plants

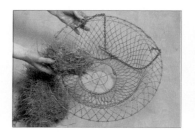

1 Line the basket with moss.

4 Plant the alpine strawberries in between the larger strawberry plants. Water well, and hang in partial or full sun.

GARDENER'S TIP

After the large strawberries have fruited, cut back all their foliage to encourage the formation of next year's flowers. The pelargonium and alpine strawberries will stop the basket looking too bare while the new foliage is growing.

PLANT IN SPRING

2 Fill the basket with compost. Mix a teaspoon of slow-release plant food granules into the top layer of compost. Plant the strawberry plants around the side of the basket.

3 Plant the pelargonium in the centre of the basket.

Home-grown salads

These compact but heavy-fruiting tomato plants have been specially bred to be grown in containers. Teamed with lettuce, radishes, chives and parsley, they provide all the ingredients for a fresh garden salad.

MATERIALS

76 cm (30 in) plastic window box
Compost
Slow-release plant food granules, pelleted chicken manure or similar organic plant food

PLANTS

3 'Tumbler' tomatoes
Chives
4 lettuces, 'Little Gem' or 'Corsair'
2 'Salad Bowl' lettuces
4 parsley plants
Radish seed

TOMATO

LETTUCE

CHIVES

LETTUCE

PARSLEY

1 Check the drainage holes are open in the base of the window box and, if not, drill or punch them open. Fill with compost, mixing in 2 teaspoons of slow-release plant food granules or organic alternative. Plant the tomatoes, evenly spaced, along the centre.

2 Plant the chives in front of the middle tomato plant. Plant the 'Little Gem' or 'Corsair' lettuces diagonally to one another between the tomato plants.

3 Plant the 'Salad Bowl' lettuces in the front corners. Plant the parsley plants diagonally opposite one another alongside the 'Little Gem' or 'Corsair' lettuces.

4 Scatter radish seed between the plants and gently rake into the soil. Water thoroughly and stand in a sunny position.

Scented collections

Scent gives a lovely extra dimension to container planting schemes, especially for planters that are sited at "nose" level, such as window boxes. On warm days the aromas will drift in through open windows. Use plants with scented leaves for a really lasting effect: herbs such as lavender and mint are invaluable foils for larger-flowered plants and will fill the air with fragrance. The scented-leaf pelargoniums are perfect container plants and you can choose from a wide variety of lovely variegations and leaf shapes as well as perfumes that range from lemon and mint to rose. Their charming pink flowers are an added bonus. Put scented plants in containers near paths and doorways, where their rich fragrances will be released each time you brush past them. A fragrant plant in a pot by the front door makes a special welcome for visitors.

ABOVE: *Lavender is always a favourite for its delightful scent. Here it is combined with scaevolas and trailing convolvulus.*

Scented window box

The soft silvers and blues of the flowers and foliage beautifully complement this verdigris window box. The scent of the lavender and petunias will drift magically through open windows.

MATERIALS

60 cm (24 in) window box
Gravel or similar drainage material
Equal mix loam-based compost and container compost
Slow-release plant food granules

PLANTS

2 lavenders
2 pale blue petunias
4 deep blue petunias
4 Chaenorhinum glareosum (or lilac lobelia)
6 Helichrysum petiolare

PETUNIA

CHAENORHINUM

HELICHRYSUM

LAVENDER

GARDENER'S TIP

To keep a densely planted container like this looking its best it is necessary to feed regularly with a liquid feed, or more simply to mix slow-release plant food granules into the surface of the compost to last the whole summer. Cut back the lavender heads after flowering to ensure bushy flowering plants again next year.

PLANT IN LATE SPRING OR EARLY SUMMER

1 Fill the bottom 5 cm (2 in) of the window box with drainage material and half-fill with compost. Position the lavender plants, loosening the soil around the roots before planting, as they will establish better this way.

2 Now arrange the flowering plants around the lavender, leaving spaces for the helichrysums between them.

3 Finally, add the helichrysums and fill between the plants with compost, pressing firmly so that no air gaps are left around the roots. Place in a sunny position and water regularly.

A nose-twitcher window box

One of the French country names for the nasturtium means 'nose-twitcher' and refers to the peppery smell of the plant. It has been planted here with the equally aromatic and colourful ginger mint and pot marigold.

MATERIALS

25 cm (10 in) terracotta window box
Crocks or other suitable drainage material
Compost
Slow-release plant food granules

PLANTS

Variegated ginger mint
Nasturtium, Tropaeolum *'Empress of India',*
*   or similar*
Pot marigold (Calendula 'Gitana', or similar)

MARIGOLD

NASTURTIUM

GINGER
MINT

1 Cover the base of the window box with a layer of crocks or similar drainage material. Fill the container with compost, mixing in a half-teaspoon of slow-release plant food granules.

2 Plant the ginger mint on the right of the container.

3 Plant the nasturtium in the centre.

GARDENER'S TIP

A small window box like this one can double as a table-centre for an outdoor meal.

PLANT IN SPRING

4 Plant the marigold on the left of the container. Water well and stand in full or partial sun.

Sweet-smelling summer flowers

Scented pelargonium and verbena are combined with heliotrope and petunias to make a window box that is fragrant as well as a visual pleasure.

MATERIALS

40cm (16 in) terracotta window box
Crocks or other suitable drainage material
Compost
Slow-release plant food granules

PLANTS

Scented-leaf Pelargonium 'Lady Plymouth'
3 soft pink petunias
Heliotrope
2 Verbena 'Pink Parfait'

HELIOTROPE

PETUNIA

VERBENA

PELARGONIUM

GARDENER'S TIP

At the end of the summer the pelargonium can be potted up and kept through the winter as a houseplant. Reduce the height of the plant by at least a half and it will soon send out new shoots.

PLANT IN LATE SPRING OR EARLY SUMMER

1 Cover the base of the window box with a layer of crocks. Fill with compost, mixing in 2 teaspoons of slow-release plant food granules. Plant the pelargonium to the right of centre, towards the back of the window box.

2 Plant a petunia in each corner and one in the centre at the front of the window box.

3 Plant the heliotrope to the left of the pelargonium.

4 Plant one verbena behind the heliotrope and the other in front of the pelargonium. Water well and place in a sunny position.

Sweet-scented lavender

In this large basket an unusual lavender is planted amongst *Convolvulus sabatius* and the fan-shaped flowers of scaevola in cool, toning shades of blue. Underplanting with trailing plants ensures that the flowers cascade down the sides of the basket.

MATERIALS

40 cm (16 in) hanging basket
Sphagnum moss
Compost
Slow-release plant food granules

PLANTS

3 Convolvulus sabatius
2 scaevolas
2 lavenders (Lavandula dentata *var.* candicans)

LAVENDER

CONVOLVULUS

SCAEVOLA

1 Line the lower half of the basket with moss.

2 Plant two of the convolvulus into the side of the basket by resting the rootballs on the moss, and carefully guiding the foliage between the wires.

3 Plant one of the scaevolas into the side of the basket in the same way.

4 Line the rest of the basket with moss, taking care to tuck it around the underplanting.

5 Fill the basket with compost, mixing a teaspoon of slow-release plant food granules into the top layer. Plant the lavenders opposite one another in the top.

6 Plant the remaining convolvulus and scaevola plants in the spaces between the lavenders. Water thoroughly and hang in a sunny position.

GARDENER'S TIP

If you are unable to obtain *Lavandula dentata*, the varieties called 'Hidcote' or 'Munstead' are readily available and make suitable substitutes.

PLANT IN SPRING

Scented pelargoniums

There is a wonderful variation in leaf size, shape and colouring, as well as an incredible diversity of scents, amongst the *Pelargonium* family. Choose the fragrances you like best and put the plants where you will brush against them to release their fragrance.

MATERIALS

40 cm (16 in) terracotta window box
Crocks or other suitable drainage material
Compost
Slow-release plant food granules

PLANTS

4 scented-leaf pelargoniums

PELARGONIUMS

GARDENER'S TIP

During the summer, pick and dry the leaves of these pelargoniums for use in pot-pourri or in muslin bags to scent linen. If you have a greenhouse or conservatory, move the window box inside for the winter and water sparingly until spring.

PLANT IN SPRING

1 Cover the base of the window box with a layer of crocks or other suitable drainage material. Fill with compost, mixing in 2 teaspoons of slow-release plant food granules. Plant the first pelargonium at the right-hand end of the container.

2 Choose a plant with contrasting leaf colour and shape, and place this next to the first pelargonium towards the front edge of the window box.

3 Plant the third pelargonium behind the second.

4 Finally, plant the fourth pelargonium at the left-hand end of the container. Water well and position in full or partial sun.

A butterfly garden

We should all do our bit to
encourage butterflies into our
gardens and this window box
filled with sedum, marjoram,
thyme and origanum should
prove irresistible. All these
plants are perennials and can
be over-wintered in the
window box.

MATERIALS

60 cm (24 in) stone window box
Crocks or other suitable drainage
  material
Compost
Slow-release plant food granules

PLANTS

Sedum *'Ruby Glow'*
Marjoram
*Lemon thyme (*Thymus
  citriodorus*)*
*Common thyme (*Thymus
  vulgaris*)*
Origanum

LEMON THYME

ORIGANUM

MARJORAM

COMMON THYME

SEDUM

GARDENER'S TIP

You can imitate the look of an old
stone window box by painting a
new one with a dilute mixture of
liquid seaweed plant food and water.
This encourages moss to grow and
ages the stone.

PLANT IN SPRING

1 Cover the base of the window
box with a layer of crocks or
other suitable drainage material.
Fill with compost, mixing in 3
teaspoons of slow-release plant
food granules.

2 Plant the sedum off-centre to
the left of the window box and
the marjoram to the left of the
sedum.

3 Plant the lemon thyme in the
centre front and the common
thyme in the back right-hand
corner of the container.

4 Plant the origanum in the
front right-hand corner of the
window box. Water well and place
in a sunny position.

Star-jasmine in a villandry planter

The soft, seductive scent of the star-jasmine makes this a perfect container to place by the side of a door where the scent will be appreciated by all who pass through.

STAR-
JASMINE

MATERIALS

50 cm (20 in) villandry planter or similar, preferably self-watering
Equal mix loam-based compost and standard compost
Slow-release plant food granules
Bark chippings

PLANTS

Star-jasmine (Trachelospermum jasminoides)

GARDENER'S TIP

Use a plastic liner inside all large planters. It is easier to remove the liner when replanting rather than dismantle the entire container.

PLANT IN LATE SPRING OR EARLY SUMMER

1 Feed the wicks through the holes in the base of the liner.

2 Fill the water reservoir in the base of the planter to the top of the overflow pipe, and place the liner inside the planter.

3 Fill the bottom of the liner with compost while pulling through the wicks so that they reach the level of the roots.

4 Remove the jasmine from its pot, gently tease the roots loose and stand it in the planter.

NOTE *Steps 1–3 are for self-watering planters only.*

5 Add compost and firm it around the rootball of the jasmine. Scatter 2 tablespoons of plant food granules on the surface, and gently work them into the top layer of compost with the trowel.

6 Mulch around the plant with a layer of bark chippings, then water. Check the reservoir of the self-watering container once a week and top up if necessary. Conventional pots should be watered daily in the early morning or evening during hot weather.

Difficult situations

A shady pathway or a bare corner of the patio may cry out for plants to enliven it,
but it can be hard to know what to grow there. The areas near the house
walls are usually very dry, and may be in shade for most of the day. On the other hand,
paved areas can be so hot and sunny that many plants would not be able to
survive without scorching. Here are some solutions to furnishing the more difficult parts
of the garden. With imaginative use of dramatic foliage and careful
choice of shade-tolerant flowering plants, you can light up the darkest areas
with exciting and colourful arrangements. It really is possible to achieve a flower-filled
hanging basket on a north-facing wall. For windy corners, choose varieties with
wiry stems, such as bidens, that will not suffer from being blown about, and for hot
spots go for sun-lovers like osteospermum or mesembryanthemum.

ABOVE: *Ferns thrive in shady spots and can add a burst of colour to even
the darkest corner of the garden.*

Busy Lizzies in bloom

There are not many shade-loving plants as colourful and prolific as the busy Lizzie. These plants will very happily bloom all summer long in a hanging basket on a north-facing wall, or in any shady or partially shaded position.

LOBELIA

MATERIALS

30 cm (12 in) hanging basket
Sphagnum moss
Compost
Slow-release plant food granules

PLANTS

6 rose-pink lobelias
3 pale pink busy Lizzies
   (impatiens)
3 white busy Lizzies
3 dark pink busy Lizzies

BUSY LIZZIES

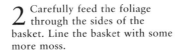

1 Line the lower half of the basket with moss and plant three lobelias through the side of the basket near the bottom.

2 Carefully feed the foliage through the sides of the basket. Line the basket with some more moss.

3 Plant one busy Lizzie of each colour. Line the rest of the basket with moss and partly fill with compost, mixing in a teaspoon of plant food granules. Plant the remaining three lobelias into the side of the basket near the top edge. Add more compost.

4 Plant the remaining busy Lizzies in the top of the basket. Water thoroughly and hang in partial or full shade.

GARDENER'S TIP

In wet or windy weather, busy Lizzies can look a bit battered, but once the weather improves, five minutes spent removing dead or damaged flowers will soon restore the basket to its former glory.

PLANT IN LATE SPRING OR EARLY SUMMER

Shady characters

All the plants used in this window box are perfectly happy in the shade. A periwinkle with variegated leaves and blue spring flowers is planted with blue-leaved hostas and summer-flowering busy Lizzies in a window box that will brighten a gloomy corner for many months.

MATERIALS
....
45 cm (18 in) fibre window box
Crocks or other suitable drainage material
Compost
Slow-release plant food granules

PLANTS
....
Variegated periwinkle (Vinca minor
  'Aureovariegata')
3 Hosta 'Blue Moon'
5 white busy Lizzies (impatiens)

HOSTA

BUSY LIZZIE

PERIWINKLE

1 Cover the base of the window box with a layer of drainage material. Fill the window box with compost, mixing in 2 teaspoons of slow-release plant food granules.

2 Plant the periwinkle in the centre of the window box.

3 Plant two of the hostas in the back corners of the window box and the third in front of, or slightly to one side of, the periwinkle.

4 Plant the busy Lizzies in the remaining spaces.

GARDENER'S TIP

To keep the busy Lizzies looking their best, pick off the dead flowers and leaves regularly or they will stick to the plant and spoil its appearance.

PLANT IN LATE SPRING

Full of ferns

A damp shady corner is the perfect position for a basket of ferns. Provided they are regularly fed and watered, and the ferns are cut back in late autumn, this basket will give pleasure for many years. These are hardy ferns, but the idea can be adapted for a conservatory or bathroom using less hardy plants such as the maidenhair fern.

MATERIALS

36 cm (14 in) hanging basket
Sphagnum moss
Compost
Slow-release plant food granules

PLANTS

4 different ferns (dryopteris, athyrium, Matteuccia struthiopteris *and* Asplenium scolopendrium *'Crispum')*

FERNS

1 Line the basket with moss.

2 Fill the basket with compost. Mix a teaspoon of slow-release plant food granules into the top of the compost.

3 Before removing the ferns from their pots, arrange them in the basket to ensure that you achieve a balanced effect. Plant the ferns and water well.

GARDENER'S TIP

Strange as it may seem, finely chopped banana skins are a favourite food of ferns. Simply sprinkle around the base of the stems and watch the ferns flourish.

PLANT IN SPRING

Bronze and gold winners

Bronze pansies and mimulus and golden green lysimachias take the medals in this striking arrangement, with richly coloured heuchera adding to the unusual mixture of tones. This arrangement will work most successfully in a partially shaded situation.

MATERIALS

40 cm (16 in) hanging basket
Sphagnum moss
Compost
Slow-release plant food granules

PLANTS

Heuchera *'Bressingham Bronze'*
3 bronze-coloured pansies (viola)
3 bronze-coloured mimulus
3 Lysimachia nummularia 'Aurea'

LYSIMACHIA

MIMULUS

HEUCHERA

PANSY

1 Line the basket with moss.

2 Fill the basket with compost, mixing a teaspoon of plant food granules into the top layer of compost.

3 Plant the heuchera in the middle of the basket.

4 Plant the pansies, evenly spaced around the heuchera.

5 Plant the three mimulus between the pansies.

6 Plant the lysimachias around the edge of the basket. Water well and hang in light shade.

GARDENER'S TIP

At the end of the season the heuchera can be planted in the border or in another container. It will do best in partial shade, as full sun tends to scorch and discolour the leaves.

PLANT IN SPRING

Shady corner

Shady corners are often thought of as problematical, when in fact there is a wealth of wonderful plants that thrive in these situations, such as the hosta, hydrangea and fern used in this arrangement.

MATERIALS

3 terracotta pots of various sizes
Crocks or other suitable drainage
  material
Composted manure
Equal mix standard compost and
  loam-based compost

PLANTS

Hosta sieboldiana elegans
Variegated hydrangea
Polystichum fern

HYDRANGEA

POLYSTICHUM

HOSTA

GARDENER'S TIP

The hosta is a beautiful foliage plant much loved by slugs and snails which chew unsightly holes in the leaves. To prevent this, smear a broad band of petroleum jelly below the rim of the container and the leaves will remain untouched.

PLANT AT ANY TIME
OF THE YEAR

2 Plant the fern in a terracotta pot slightly larger than its existing pot. It should not need transplanting for 2–3 years.

1 Plant the hosta in a pot large enough for its bulky root system, and with space for further growth. The pot used here nicely echoes the shape of the leaves. Place crocks at the bottom of the pot and then put in a layer of manure before adding the potting compost. Follow this procedure with the hydrangea as well.

3 The hydrangea makes a great deal of growth during the summer and could get very top-heavy. Plant in a sturdy pot with plenty of space for root growth.

A space in the sun

Since osteospermum, portulaca and diascia are all sun-lovers this is definitely a basket for your sunniest spot, where the plants will thrive and the colours will look their best.

PORTULACA

DIASCIA

OSTEOSPERMUM

MATERIALS

36 cm (14 in) hanging basket
Sphagnum moss
Compost
Slow-release plant food granules

PLANTS

6 peach portulaca
Osteospermum *'Buttermilk'*
3 Diascia *'Salmon Supreme', or similar*

1 Line the lower half of the basket with moss. Plant three portulaca by resting the rootballs on the moss, and guiding the foliage between the wires.

2 Add more moss to the basket, tucking it carefully around the portulaca.

3 Partly fill the basket with compost, mixing a teaspoon of slow-release plant food granules into the top layer. Plant the remaining three portulaca just below the rim of the basket.

4 Line the rest of the basket with moss. Plant the osteopermum centrally. Plant the diascias around the osteospermum. Water thoroughly and hang in a sunny spot.

GARDENER'S TIP

Keep pinching out the growing tips of the osteospermum to ensure a bushy plant.

PLANT IN LATE SPRING OR EARLY SUMMER

A dazzling display

The succulents in this window box will provide a vivid splash of colour throughout the summer, and will cope very well on a hot dry window-sill. Mesembryanthemum, kalanchoe and portulaca all love the sunshine and will grow happily in this small window box.

PORTULACA

MESEMBRYANTHEMUMS

MATERIALS

36 cm (14 in) plastic window box
Compost
Slow-release plant food granules

PLANTS

Kalanchoe
2 portulaca
3 mesembryanthemum

KALANCHOE

1 Check the drainage holes are open in the base and, if not, drill or punch them open. Fill the window box with compost, mixing in a teaspoon of slow-release plant food granules.

2 Plant the kalanchoe in the centre of the window box.

3 Plant the two portulaca in the front corners of the window box.

4 Plant one mesembryanthemum in front of the kalanchoe and the other two behind the two portulaca. Water well and stand in a sunny position.

GARDENER'S TIP

Since mesembryanthemum flowers open in response to direct sunlight, it is essential to place them in a position where they are in full sun for as long as possible every day.

PLANT IN LATE SPRING OR EARLY SUMMER

Desert belles

An attractively weathered window box is the container used for this dramatic collection of succulents. With their architectural leaf shapes and wonderful range of colouring they would look particularly good in a modern setting.

MATERIALS

40 cm (16 in) terracotta window box
Crocks or other suitable drainage material
Compost
Gravel
Slow-release plant food granules

PLANTS

Aloe
Crassula ovata
Echeveria elegans
Sansevieria trifascia

ECHEVERIA

CRASSULA

SANSEVIERIA

ALOE

GARDENER'S TIP

Move the window box to a conservatory or frost-free greenhouse for the winter. Water sparingly only if plants show signs of shrivelling.

PLANT IN LATE SPRING OR EARLY SUMMER FOR OUTDOOR USE, OR ANY TIME OF YEAR FOR A CONSERVATORY

1 Place a layer of crocks or other suitable drainage material in the base of the container. Fill with compost, mixing in a teaspoon of slow-release plant food granules. Plant the aloe at the right-hand end of the window box.

2 Plant the crassula next to the aloe, the echeveria at the back of the window box, and the sansevieria in front.

3 Surround the plants with a layer of gravel. Water well to establish and thereafter water sparingly. Place in full sun.

Inspirational containers

Sometimes a container is so characterful it dictates its own planting scheme. A wooden tub with an oriental feel, for example, is a perfect container for a delicate Japanese maple – a restrained yet stunning combination. Or the shape of the pot may echo that of the flowers, such as lilies planted in a curvaceous urn. Old wooden boxes and trugs call for cottage-garden mixtures to enhance their old-fashioned charm. If you can find striking and original containers like these, seek out plants that suit them and show them to their best advantage.

There are also ideas here for truly dramatic effects; a plunging cascade of variegated foliage, a black-and-white pot with black and white flowers to match, ivy trained into a formal topiary shape and a fountain of fuchsias.

ABOVE: *Ivy trained around a shaped hoop adds height and interest to this pot of petunias.*

Old favourites

Dianthus, violas and candytuft are delightful cottage-garden plants that make a pretty display during late spring and early summer. Although by the time we took our photograph the candytuft was over, the other flowers were still putting on a good show.

MATERIALS

40 cm (16 in) painted wooden window box
Crocks or other suitable drainage material
Compost
Slow-release plant food granules

PLANTS

Dianthus
Candytuft (iberis)
2 violas

DIANTHUS

CANDYTUFT

VIOLAS

GARDENER'S TIP

Once the flowers are over, cut back the plants and plant them out in the garden. There is still time to replant the window box with summer plants.

PLANT IN EARLY SPRING

1 Cover the base of the container with a layer of drainage material. Fill with compost, mixing in a teaspoon of slow-release plant food granules.

2 Plant the dianthus slightly to the right of the centre of the window box.

3 Plant the candytuft to the left of the centre of the window box beside the dianthus.

4 Plant a viola at each end. Water well and stand in a mixture of sun and shade.

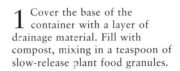

Colourful evergreens

Evergreen cordyline with its dramatic red spear-shaped leaves, a green hebe and a golden conifer have been mixed with blue-green hostas in a permanent planting, which is given seasonal interest by the addition of red-flowered New Guinea impatiens.

MATERIALS

76 cm (30 in) plastic window box
Compost
Slow-release plant food granules

PLANTS

Red cordyline
Golden conifer Chamaecyparis pisifera *'Sungold'*
Hebe *'Emerald Green'*
Hosta *'Blue Moon'*
Golden grass Hakonechloa *'Aureola'*
2 red-flowered New Guinea impatiens

CORDYLINE

HOSTA

IMPATIENS   HEBE

CONIFER

GOLDEN GRASS

GARDENER'S TIP

At the end of the summer replace the impatiens with pansies, polyanthus or heathers.

PLANT IN SPRING

1 Check the drainage holes are open in the base and, if not, drill or punch them open. Fill the window box with compost, mixing in 3 teaspoons of slow-release plant food granules. Plant the cordyline left of centre and the conifer at the right-hand end.

2 Plant the hebe in the centre of the window box. Plant the hosta between the hebe and the conifer.

3 Plant the golden grass at the left-hand end of the window box. Plant the impatiens between the golden grass and the cordyline, and next to the hosta. Water well and stand in partial sun.

A trough of alpines

A selection of easy-to-grow alpine plants is grouped in a basket-weave stone planter to create a miniature garden. The mulch of gravel is both attractive and practical as it prevents soil splashing on to the leaves of the plants.

MATERIALS

40 cm (16 in) stone trough
Crocks
Compost
Slow-release plant food granules
Gravel

PLANTS

Sempervivum
Alpine aquilegia
White rock rose (helianthemum)
Papaver alpinum
Alpine phlox
Pink saxifrage
White saxifrage

SEMPERVIVUM

PAPAVER
ALPINUM

SAXIFRAGES

ALPINE PHLOX

ROCK ROSE

ALPINE AQUILEGIA

1 Cover the base of the trough with a layer of crocks. Fill the container with compost, mixing in a teaspoon of slow-release plant food granules and extra gravel for improved drainage.

2 Arrange the plants, still in their pots, in the trough to decide on the most attractive arrangement. Complete the planting, working across the trough.

3 Scatter a good layer of gravel around the plants. Water thoroughly and stand in a sunny position.

GARDENER'S TIP

Tidy the trough once a month, removing dead flowerheads and leaves, adding more gravel if necessary. A trough like this will last a number of years before it needs replanting.

PLANT IN SPRING

The apothecary's box

Many plants have healing qualities and, while they should always be used with caution, some of the more commonly used herbs have been successful country remedies for centuries.

CHAMOMILE

FENNEL

MATERIALS

Wooden trug
Crocks or other suitable drainage
  material
Compost
Pelleted chicken manure

MARIGOLD

LAVENDER

ROSEMARY

FEVERFEW

PLANTS

Lavender – for relaxation
Rosemary – for healthy hair
  and scalp
Chamomile – for restful sleep
Fennel – for digestion
Feverfew – for migraine
3 pot marigolds (calendula) –
  for healing

1 Place drainage material in the trug and fill with compost, mixing in 2 teaspoons of fertilizer. Plant a central lavender.

2 Plant the rosemary in the front right-hand corner of the trug.

3 Plant the chamomile in the back left-hand corner.

4 Plant the fennel in the back right-hand corner.

5 Plant the feverfew in the front left-hand corner.

6 Plant the marigolds in the remaining spaces. Water well and stand in full or partial sun.

GARDENER'S TIP

Herbs should not be used to treat any medical condition without first checking with your medical practitioner.

PLANT IN THE SPRING

Daring reds and bold purples

The colour of the fuschia's flowers is echoed by the deep purple and crimson petunias. The stark white window box provides the perfect contrast to make a bold display.

GARDENER'S TIP

At the end of the season the catmint plants can be trimmed back and planted in the garden. The fuchsia and campanulas can be cut back and potted up to be overwintered in a frost-free greenhouse.

PLANT IN SPRING

MATERIALS

76 cm (30 in) plastic window box
90 cm (3 ft) wooden window box (optional)
Compost
Slow-release plant food granules

PLANTS

Fuchsia *'Dollar Princess'*
*2 low-growing catmint (*Nepeta mussinii)
2 white-flowered Campanula isophylla
2 crimson petunias
2 purple petunias

CAMPANULA

CATMINT

PETUNIAS

FUCHSIA

1 Check the drainage holes are open in the base and, if not, drill or punch them open. Fill the window box with compost, mixing in 3 teaspoons of slow-release plant food granules. Plant the fuchsia in the centre.

2 Plant a catmint at each end of the window box. Plant the campanulas next to the catmint.

3 Plant the crimson petunias on either side of the fuchsia at the back and the purple one in front.

4 Water thoroughly and allow to drain. Lower the plastic window box into place inside the wooden window box, if using. Stand in a sunny position.

Chinese water garden

In China, glazed pots are frequently used as small ponds in courtyards.
This pot contains a water lily, a flowering rush and an arum lily.

FLOWERING RUSH

WATER LILY

ARUM LILY

MATERIALS

Water lily basket
Piece of hessian
Aquatic compost
Large bucket
70 cm (28 in) glazed pot
Putty (optional)
Bricks

PLANTS

Compact water lily
(Nymphaea tetragona)
Flowering rush
(Butomus umbellatus)
Arum lily (Zantedeschia
aethiopica)

1 Line the basket with hessian, insert the water lily and top up with aquatic compost. Lower the basket into a bucket of water to settle the compost.

2 If the glazed pot has a drainage hole, plug it with putty and leave to harden overnight. Use bricks to create platforms for the two potted plants.

3 Before filling the pot with water, position the rush so that its pot will be fully submerged and the arum lily so that the pot will be half-submerged.

4 Fill the pot with water and gently lower the water lily into position – its leaves should float on the surface. This water garden will do best in a sunny position.

GARDENER'S TIP

This arrangement is not recommended for anyone with small children; they can drown in a surprisingly small amount of water.

PLANT IN LATE SPRING OR EARLY SUMMER

Colourful cooking pot

Junk shops are a rich source of old pots and pans which can make characterful containers for plants when their kitchen days are over.

MATERIALS

30 cm (12 in) cooking pot
Gravel
Equal mix loam-based
  compost and
  container compost
Slow-release plant food granules

IVY

PLANTS

Ceratostigma plumbaginoides
Inula *'Oriental Star'*
Golden ivy

CERATOSTIGMA

INULA

GARDENER'S TIP

These plants are all perennials. When the ceratostigma and inula have finished flowering, plant them in a border where they will flower again next year.

PLANT IN SPRING OR EARLY SUMMER

1 Make one or two drainage holes in the base of the pot and add a 5 cm (2 in) layer of gravel.

2 Remove the ceratostigma from its pot and plant it at one side of the container.

3 Add the inula and the ivy, and fill in between the plants with compost, firming them in position as you work. Scatter a tablespoon of plant food granules over the surface of the compost. Water and place in a sunny position.

Black-and-white arrangement

Linking the colour of the container with the plants creates a harmony of design, which is given extra dramatic impact when the colours used are black and white.

MATERIALS

Terracotta pot, 30 cm (12 in) high
Masking tape
Paint brush
Matt white and black paint
Crocks or other suitable
  drainage material
Compost
Slow-release plant food granules
Fine gravel

BLACK
GRASS

VIOLA

OSTEOSPERMUM

PLANTS

White osteospermum
Black grass (Ophiopogon planiscapus *'Nigrescens')*
3 Viola *'Molly Sanderson'*

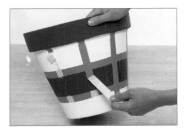

1 Mark out a checkered pattern on the pot with masking tape.

2 Paint the top and bottom row of checks white and the rim and the middle row black. Remove the tape.

3 Cover the drainage holes at the bottom of the pot with crocks and half-fill with compost. Plant the osteospermum at the back of the container.

4 Place the black grass next to the osteospermum and top up the container with compost. Plant the three violas in a group.

5 Scatter a tablespoon of plant food granules on the surface of the compost and mulch with fine gravel. Water and stand in a sunny position.

GARDENER'S TIP

Experiment with other colourful themes. You could try a sky blue-and-white check container planted with a morning glory, or a bright red and green pot planted with a red pelargonium.

PLANT IN SPRING OR
EARLY SUMMER

Topiary ivy with white petunias

Use wire topiary frames (available at most garden centres) to train ivy or other climbing plants into interesting shapes. The ivy will take some months to establish a strong outline; in the meantime, miniature white petunias complete the picture.

MATERIALS

45 cm (18 in) oval terracotta window box
Crocks or other suitable drainage material
Compost
Slow-release plant food granules
Wire topiary frame
Pins made from garden wire
Plant rings

PLANTS

2 variegated ivies
4 miniature white petunias

IVIES

PETUNIA

1 Place a layer of drainage material in the base of the window box. Fill the window box with compost, mixing in 2 teaspoons of slow-release plant food granules.

2 Plant the two ivies, one in front of the other in the centre of the window box.

3 Position the topiary frame in the centre of the window box and use pins to hold it in place.

4 Wrap the stems of ivy around the stem of the frame, and then around the frame itself.

5 Cut away any straggly stems and use plant rings to secure the ivy to the frame.

6 Plant the petunias around the topiary ivy. Water thoroughly and stand in light shade.

GARDENER'S TIP

Maintain the shape of the ivy with regular trimming and training – 5 minutes once a week will create a better shape than 15 minutes once a month.

PLANT IVY AT ANY TIME OF YEAR, PETUNIAS IN SPRING

Dramatic foliage

GROUND IVY

NEMESIA

BEGONIA

BLACK GRASS

VIOLA

Viola 'Bowles' Black' is combined with black grass – ophiopogon – and the dramatically coloured *Begonia rex*. Pale pink nemesias and variegated ground ivies provide an effective contrast.

MATERIALS

36 cm (14 in) hanging basket
Sphagnum moss
Compost
Slow-release plant food granules

PLANTS

Begonia rex
Black grass (Ophiopogon planiscapus 'Nigrescens')
2 variegated ground ivies (Glechoma hederacea 'Variegata')
2 Nemesia denticulata 'Confetti'
2 Viola 'Bowles' Black'

1 Line the basket with moss and fill it with compost, mixing a teaspoon of plant food granules in the top layer of compost. Plant the begonia at the back of the basket. Plant the black grass in front of the begonia.

2 Plant the ground ivies at either side of the basket, angling the plants so that the foliage tumbles down the sides of the basket.

3 Plant the nemesias on either side of the begonia. Plant the violas on either side of the black grass. Water the basket well and hang in light shade.

GARDENER'S TIP

At the end of the season the begonia can be potted up and kept indoors as a houseplant and the black grass can be planted in an outdoor container.

PLANT IN LATE SPRING OR EARLY SUMMER

Foliage wall pot

The bushy growth of *Fuchsia magellanica* 'Alba Variegata' is ideal for displaying as a crown of leafy hair in a head-shaped wall pot. This copy of an ancient Grecian head will add a classical touch to a modern garden.

MATERIALS

*Grecian head wall pot
Expanded clay granules*

PLANTS

Fuchsia magellanica *'Alba Variegata'*

FUCHSIA

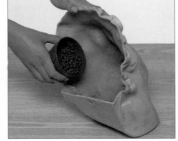

1 Check that the wall pot has a hook or can be hung up. The hanging point will need to be sufficiently strong to carry the weight of a moist pot.

2 Add expanded clay granules to the base of the wall pot to lift the top of the plant to the right level.

3 Place the plant in its pot inside the wall pot.

4 Arrange the foliage to make a convincing leafy crown of hair for the head.

GARDENER'S TIP

Check the base of the pot for drainage holes. If there are no holes, you will need to remove the pot each time you water it, allowing the compost to drain before replacing it.

PLANT AT ANY TIME OF YEAR

Filigree foliage

The purply-black leaves of this heuchera are all the more stunning when surrounded by the delicate silver-and-green filigree foliage of senecio, the tender *Lavendula pinnata* and the soft lilac-coloured flowers of the bacopa and the brachycome daisies. The plants are grown in a white plastic planter which is concealed inside an elegant wooden window box.

MATERIALS

76 cm (30 in) plastic window
  box
Compost
Slow-release plant food granules
90 cm (3 ft) wooden window box
  (optional)

PLANTS

Heuchera *'Palace Purple'*
2 *Lavenders*
2 *blue brachycome daisies*
3 *Senecio cineraria 'Silver Dust'*
2 *blue bacopa*

SENECIO

LAVENDER

BRACHYCOME

BACOPA

HEUCHERA

1 Check drainage holes are open in the base of the planter and, if not, drill or punch them out. Fill the window box with compost, mixing in 2 teaspoons of slow-release plant food granules. Plant the heuchera in the centre.

2 Plant the two lavenders on either side of the heuchera.

3 Plant the two brachycome daisies at each end of the window box.

4 Place the three senecios at the front of the box between the brachycomes.

5 Plant the two bacopa between the senecio and the heuchera.

6 Water thoroughly and lift into place in the wooden window box, if using. Place in full or partial sun.

GARDENER'S TIP

Wooden window boxes can be assembled so they are self-watering where access is difficult for daily watering. A variety of self-watering containers are available and come with full instructions for their use.

PLANT IN SPRING

Fuchsia wall fountain

A dry terracotta wall fountain makes a lovely innovative planting pot. *Fuchsia* 'Daisy Bell' is particularly suited to growing in such a fountain or in a hanging basket. Its growth is trailing, lax and self-branching, and it produces numerous flowers freely throughout the summer.

MATERIALS

Terracotta wall fountain
Bricks
Clay granules
Peat-free compost

PLANTS

3 Fuchsia *'Daisy Bell'*

FUCHSIA

1 Prop the wall fountain securely upright using the bricks. Make sure that the planting bowl is held straight, so that you can create a balanced arrangement.

2 Fill with expanded clay granules and peat-free compost. Add a water-retaining gel if you are concerned about the rapid water-loss from terracotta.

3 Arrange the plants while still in their pots.

4 Plant them when you are satisfied with your arrangement, adding extra compost to cover the rootballs. Finally, add a layer of clay granules to the top of the compost as a mulch to prevent excessive water loss through evaporation.

GARDENER'S TIP

When planting a wall pot, avoid using a fuchsia cultivar that needs regular stopping to encourage branching. Choose a variety like 'Daisy Bell' which is naturally abundant and bushy.

PLANT IN EARLY SPRING OR EARLY SUMMER

Illusions of grandeur

A small plastic window box takes on unexpected grandeur when filled with rich, velvety purples and pinks, and placed in a stylish setting.

MATERIALS

30 cm (12 in) plastic window box
Compost
Slow-release plant food granules

Dead-head the violas regularly to keep them flowering, and pinch out any straggly stems.

PLANT IN SPRING

PLANTS

Heliotrope
2 Viola 'Bowles' Black'
Blue verbena
4 lilac lobelias

HELIOTROPE

VERBENA

VIOLA

LOBELIA

1 Check the drainage holes are open in the base and, if not, drill or punch them open. Fill the container with compost, mixing in a teaspoon of slow-release plant food granules. Plant the heliotrope in the centre at the back.

2 Plant the violas at either end of the window box in the back corners. Plant the verbena centrally in front of the heliotrope.

3 Plant two of the lobelias on either side of the verbena and the others between the heliotrope and the violas. Water thoroughly and stand in partial shade.

Mediterranean garden

The brilliant colours of the Mediterranean are recreated with these painted pots. While the plants thrive in the climate of the Mediterranean, they also perform perfectly in less predictable weather.

MATERIALS

4 terracotta pots of various sizes
Paint brush
Selection of brightly coloured emulsion paints
Masking tape
Crocks
Loam-based compost with 1/3 added grit
Gravel

PLANTS

Prostrate rosemary
Aloe (optional)
Golden thyme
Large red pelargonium

ROSEMARY

ALOE

PELARGONIUM

1 Paint the pots with solid colours or with patterns using two coats if necessary. The terracotta absorbs the moisture from the paint, so they will dry very quickly.

2 Paint the rim of one pot with a contrasting colour.

3 Create a zig-zag pattern using masking tape and painting alternate sections.

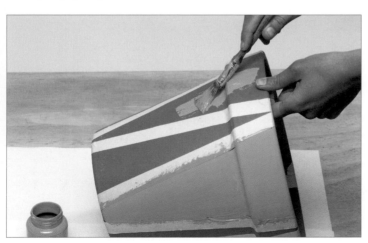

4 Place crocks in the bottom of the pots and then position the plants, firming them in place with extra compost. The compacted roots of this rosemary will benefit from being teased loose before planting.

5 The aloe does not need a large pot. Plant it in a pot just slightly larger than the one you bought it in.

6 Plant the thyme and pelargonium in separate pots. Finish the plants with a top-dressing of gravel, water well and place in a sheltered sunny corner.

GARDENER'S TIP

For commercial reasons the plants you buy will probably have been grown in a peat compost, although they prefer a loam-based compost. Gently loosen the peat around their roots and mix it with the loam-based compost before potting up in the new mixture.

PLANT IN LATE SPRING OR EARLY SUMMER

Japanese-style planter

A wooden apple barrel makes an inexpensive container for this Japanese maple. The tree is surrounded by moss and stones to create the effect of a Japanese garden. This planted container is designed to be very lightweight and would be ideal for a roof terrace or balcony.

MATERIALS

Apple barrel or similar wooden tub
Plastic saucer to fit the bottom of
  the container
Slow-release plant food granules
Perlite or polystyrene packing material
Bun moss
Large stones

JAPANESE
MAPLE

PLANT

Japanese maple (Acer palmatum *var.* dissectum)

GARDENER'S TIP

The tree should be checked annually to see if it needs repotting. If roots are showing through the base of the pot this is a sure sign that the tree should be moved into a larger one. If weight is not a consideration use clay granules instead of perlite or polystyrene.

PLANT AT ANY TIME OF THE YEAR

1 Place the plastic saucer in the base of the container.

2 Stand the tree in its pot in the saucer. Scatter half a tablespoon of slow-release plant food granules on the surface of the compost. Fill the area around the pot with perlite or polystyrene.

3 Cover the surface of the perlite or polystyrene with bun moss interspersed with stones. Place in full or partial sun and water regularly.

Regency lily urn

The shape of this urn is based on the shape of the lily flower, so it makes an appropriate container for this lovely mix of lilies, lavenders, pink marguerites and helichrysums.

MATERIALS

Suitably shaped urn
Gravel
Loam-based compost
  with 1/3 added grit
Slow-release plant
  food granules

PLANTS

2 *white lilies*
2 *Lavenders* (Lavandula *'Hidcote')*
2 *pink marguerites* *(argyranthemums)*
3 Helichrysum petiolare

LILY
LAVENDER
MARGUERITE
HELICHRYSUM

1 Place a 5 cm (2 in) layer of gravel at the bottom of the urn and half-fill with compost. Place the lilies in the centre.

2 Arrange the lavenders and marguerites around the lilies.

3 Plant the helichrysums around the edge of the urn so that they cascade over the rim as they grow. Fill between the plants with additional compost enriched with a tablespoon of slow-release plant food granules. Water well and place in a sunny position.

GARDENER'S TIP

Cut back the lavender heads when they have finished flowering, leave the lilies to die down naturally, and dead-head the marguerites regularly to keep them flowering all summer. The helichrysums and marguerites are not frost hardy, but the lavenders and lilies should bloom again next year.

PLANT IN SPRING

Standard fuchsia

Fuchsia 'Tom West' is an excellent hardy variety which was raised in 1853. Here, underplanted with variegated ivy, and benefiting from the large Chinese-style glazed pot, the display has a very modern chic appeal.

MATERIALS

Large glazed pot, at least 70 cm (28 in) diameter
Crocks
Peat-free compost
Slow-release plant food granules

PLANTS

1 half-standard Fuchsia *'Tom West'*
6 variegated ivies

FUCHSIA

IVY

1 Cover the drainage hole in the base of the pot with the crocks. This prevents it from becoming blocked and facilitates the free drainage of excess water from the compost.

2 Almost fill the pot with peat-free compost. Add slow-release plant food granules to the compost.

3 Remove the half-standard fuchsia from its pot, and lower it gently on to the compost so that the top of its rootball is slightly lower than the lip of the pot.

4 Add more compost. Plant the variegated ivies around the base of the fuchsia. Fill in the gaps between the rootballs, and tease the ivies' stems and foliage across the compost surface. Water to settle the compost.

GARDENER'S TIP

The variegated foliage of 'Tom West' develops a lovely rich pink colouring when grown in a sunny position. The best foliage colour is on the young growth, so regular pinching out of new stem tips will ensure a colourful plant.

PLANT IN EARLY SPRING OR EARLY SUMMER

Galvanized-bath garden

An old tin bath makes an ideal planter; it is large and deep enough to take quite large plants. Here, foxgloves and euphorbias are underplanted with violets, making an attractive early summer display.

EUPHORBIA

FOXGLOVE

VIOLET

MATERIALS

Tin bath, 60 cm (24 in) wide
Gravel or similar drainage material
Equal mix loam-based compost and
  standard compost
Slow-release plant food granules

PLANTS

3 foxgloves (digitalis)
2 euphorbia
3 violets (viola)

1 If the bath does not have drainage holes, you should make some in the base, and then cover it with a 10 cm (4 in) layer of gravel or similar drainage material. Half-fill the bath with the compost mix, and position the foxgloves.

2 Next add the euphorbia, teasing loose the roots to enable growth if they are at all potbound. Fill between the plants with compost, pressing down firmly around the rootballs.

3 Finally, plant the violets around the edges, where they can tumble over the sides as they grow. Water and place in a shady position.

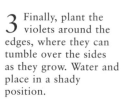

GARDENER'S TIP

Buy your foxgloves before they have formed their flower spikes; they will transplant better and you will have the pleasure of watching them grow. Do not cut the stems down after flowering; when you can hear the seeds rattling, simply shake them over any corner of the garden where you would like foxgloves to grow.

PLANT IN AUTUMN OR SPRING

Chimney pot clematis

It is well known that clematis love to have their heads in the sun and their roots in the shade. A chimney pot creates the perfect environment as it provides exactly these conditions. Ideally, the clematis should be planted in soil with the chimney pot placed over it, but with a little care, pot-grown plants will do well for a few years.

MATERIALS

2 x 20 cm (8 in) plastic pots
Gravel or other suitable drainage material
Equal mix loam-based compost and container compost
Slow-release plant food granules
60 cm (24 in) chimney pot

PLANTS

Clematis 'Prince Charles'

CLEMATIS

1 Fill one of the plastic pots with gravel.

2 Plant the clematis in the other plastic pot, filling around the rootball with the compost mix. Scatter a tablespoon of plant food granules over the surface of the compost. (The two pots will be positioned one on top of the other inside the chimney pot, as shown.)

3 Place the chimney pot over the pot of gravel and then carefully lower the clematis into position. It will need a sunny position and regular watering.

GARDENER'S TIP

Clematis can suffer from clematis wilt: suddenly whole stems will start to wilt and die. Cut all affected growth away from the plant and spray the remaining plant fortnightly with a product containing Benolyl.

PLANT IN SPRING

A topiary planting

BOX PYRAMID

BOX BALL

BACOPA

Topiary box plants remain in their pots in this window box. A mulch of bark conceals the pots and retains moisture, and small pots of white bacopa add another dimension to the sculptured design.

MATERIALS

64 cm (25 in) terracotta planter
Bark chippings

PLANTS

Box pyramid in 5 litre (9 in) pot
2 box balls in 5 litre (9 in) pot
5 pots white bacopa

1 Water all the plants thoroughly. Stand the box pyramid in its pot in the centre of the container.

2 Stand the box balls on either side of the pyramid.

3 Fill the container with bark chippings to hide the pots.

4 Plunge the pots of bacopa in the bark at the front of the container. Stand in light shade. Water regularly.

GARDENER'S TIP

Provided the box plants are not root-bound they will be quite happy in their pots for a year. If the leaves start to lose their glossy dark green colour, it is a sign that they need a feed. Sprinkle a long-term plant food on the surface of the pots and boost with a liquid feed.

PLANT BOX AT ANY TIME OF THE YEAR,
AND BACOPA IN SPRING

The young container gardener

Most children become enthusiastic gardeners as soon as they have a patch of soil they can really call their own, and this applies equally to containers. What is more, if they can make or decorate their container before planting it up, they'll get a real sense of achievement. These projects use easily available plants and seeds that can be bought with pocket money and are reliable and free-flowering, given a little care and attention. There are suggestions for easy-to-grow vegetables and a small pond made from a toy-box that will quickly become a haven for wildlife. Youngsters will have every reason to be proud of the results.

ABOVE: An old pair of boots can make a fun container for brightly coloured flowers.

Watering can planter

An old watering can makes an attractive container, especially when it is painted and stencilled. When planted with an evergreen plant, such as the ivy used here, it will provide an eye-catching year-round display.

MATERIALS

Old watering can
Paintbrush
Eggshell paint, for the base coat
Stencil design
Masking tape
Stencil brush
Stencil paints, for the decoration
Fine paintbrush
Bark chippings
Slow-release plant food granules

PLANT

Ivy

1 Paint the watering can with the base colour. Apply two coats if necessary and leave each coat to dry thoroughly before painting the next.

2 Fasten the stencil design in place with masking tape. When stencilling, the brush should not hold much paint; dab it on newspaper to get rid of the excess. Use two or three colours to give your design a more three-dimensional effect.

GARDENER'S TIP

Other galvanized tin containers such as tin baths and buckets may also be painted and used.

PLANT AT ANY TIME OF THE YEAR

3 Use the fine paintbrush to paint the rim of the can. You could pick out additional detailing if you wish.

4 When all the paint is quite dry, fill the watering can with bark chippings.

5 Scoop out a hollow in the chippings and plant the ivy in its pot. Scatter some slow-release plant food granules on the surface. Arrange the tendrils so that they trail over the handle and spout of the watering can. Water, pouring any excess water out through the spout. Place the watering can in a shady spot or hang it from a hook in a cool corner.

Seaside garden

Even if you live miles from the sea you can create your own garden in
a sunny corner with some seashells, succulents and driftwood.

MATERIALS

Seashells
Self-hardening clay
4 terracotta pots of various sizes
Loam-based compost with
  ⅓ added grit
Gravel
Driftwood

PLANTS

Gazania
3 mesembryanthemum
2 crassula
Upright lampranthus
2 trailing lampranthus

GAZANIA

LAMPRANTHUS

1 Fill the shells with clay,
leaving some unfilled to cover
the compost.

2 Press the shells onto the
terracotta pots and leave the
clay to harden overnight.

3 Plant the gazania in one of the
larger pots.

4 Plant the three
mesembryanthemums as a
group in one pot.

5 Plant the crassulas together in
a fairly small pot. These plants
grow naturally in poor soils and
do not mind overcrowding.

6 The upright and trailing
lampranthus have similar
colour foliage and flower but quite
different shapes so they make an
interesting contrast when planted
together. Cover the compost in
each pot with a layer of gravel and
then add seashells and pieces of
driftwood. Group together in a
sunny position.

Small is beautiful

Not everyone has room for a large hanging basket, especially when the plants have reached maturity, but there is sure to be space for a small basket like this one which will flower cheerfully all summer long.

MATERIALS

25 cm (10 in) hanging basket
Sphagnum moss
Compost
Slow-release plant food granules

PLANTS

4 nasturtiums
2 Lysimachia nummularia 'Aurea'
3 pot marigolds (calendula)

NASTURTIUM

LYSIMACHIA

MARIGOLDS

GARDENER'S TIP

Small baskets dry out very quickly so be sure to water frequently. To give a really good soak you can immerse the basket in a bucket of water, but be careful not to damage the trailing plants.

PLANT IN SPRING

1 Line the lower half of the basket with moss. Plant three of the nasturtiums into the side of the basket by resting the rootballs on the moss and carefully guiding the leaves through the sides of the basket.

2 Line the rest of the basket with moss and fill with compost, mixing half a teaspoon of slow-release plant food granules into the top layer. Plant the lysimachia opposite one another at the edge of the basket.

3 Plant the pot marigolds in the top of the basket.

4 Plant the remaining nasturtium in the middle of the basket. Water well and hang the basket in a sunny position.

Terrific tyres

Old car tyres get a new and completely different lease of
life with a lick of paint. They make perfect containers for
all sorts of plants and are ideal for a first garden.

MATERIALS

Coloured emulsion paints
Paintbrush
2 car tyres
Compost and garden soil
Newspaper

PLANTS

Selection of bedding plants
such as cosmea
pelargoniums, pansies
(viola), and pot marigolds
(calendula)

1 Use ordinary emulsion to paint
the tyres – any colours look
good, the brighter the better.

2 Put one tyre on top of another
and fill with potting compost
or equal quantities of garden
soil and compost. To cut down on
the amount of compost, stuff
newspaper into the tyres.

3 Put the tallest plants in first –
this is a cosmea. Surround it
with smaller plants like
pelargoniums, pansies and
marigolds.

4 Plant some delicate trailing
plants to grow over the edge.
Start your tyre garden off by
giving it a lot of water. Keep
watering through the summer and
do not let it get too dry.

GARDENER'S TIP

You can get old tyres for free at most
garages. For something cheap and
fast-growing, try growing pumpkin
plants. A ring of lobelia will grow
happily if planted between two tyres.

Blooming old boots

This is a blooming wonderful way to recycle an old pair of boots, the bigger the better. It just goes to show that almost anything can be used to grow plants in, as long as it has a few holes in the bottom for drainage. Try an old football, a sports bag, or even an old hat for plant containers with lots of character.

MATERIALS

Knife
Old pair of working boots
Compost

PLANTS

Selection of bedding plants such as impatiens, pelargoniums, verbenas, pansies and lobelias

BEDDING PLANTS

1 Using a knife very carefully, make some holes in between the stitching of the sole for drainage. It helps if there are holes there already.

2 Fill the boots with compost, pushing it down right to the toe so there are no air spaces.

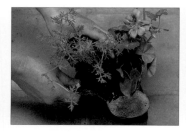

3 Plant flowers like pelargoniums, that can cope with hot dry places, and verbenas which will trail over the edge.

4 Squeeze in a pansy with a contrasting flower colour and a trailing lobelia plant. Lobelia grows in the smallest of spaces and will delicately tumble over the edge.

5 The boots need watering every day in the summer, and bloom even better if some plant food is mixed into the water once a week.

SAFETY NOTE

Children should always be supervised when using any sharp objects.

PLANT IN SPRING

A watery world

No garden is complete without the sight and sound of water. Great for toe-dipping on a hot sunny day, this mini-pond is too small for fish but a welcome watering spot for thirsty birds. Any large container can be used to make a mini-pond, as long as it is watertight. A toy-tidy, like this one, is ideal.

MATERIALS

Large, wide container
Gravel
Lead from a wine bottle top
Flower pot

PLANTS

2 aquatic plants such as golden
*   sedge and monkey flower*
Strands of oxygenating weed
Small floating plants
*   such as water lettuce*
*   and floating ferns*

AQUATIC PLANTS

OXYGENATING   FLOATING
WEED   PLANTS

GARDENER'S TIP

Keep shallow containers in a semi-shady area to avoid excess evaporation. Plant up an adjoining mix of tulips and alliums for a spring and early summer display.

PLANT IN SPRING

1 Put a layer of gravel in the bottom of a large, wide container and fill with water almost to the top.

2 Lower the aquatic plants (which should be in net pots when you buy them) gently into the water around the edge.

3 Bend a piece of lead around the base of pieces of oxygenating weed to weigh them down. Pot the bunch into a flower pot and put a layer of gravel on the surface.

4 Lower the pot into the mini-pond, then add a few floating plants. Sink the pond into a hole in the garden so that it keeps cool.

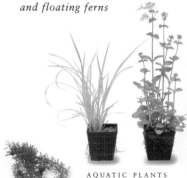

Good enough to eat!

You do not need a large garden to grow fruit and vegetables – it is possible to grow some in just a window box. Strawberries and bush or trailing tomatoes are small enough, so are radishes and lettuces. Nasturtium leaves and flowers are edible, with a hot, peppery taste. They look lovely in a salad.

MATERIALS

76 cm (30 in)
  plastic window box
Compost

PLANTS

2 tomato plants
2 strawberry plants
Radish seeds
Lettuce seeds
Nasturtium seeds

STRAWBERRY PLANTS

LETTUCE SEEDS

NASTURTIUM SEEDS

TOMATO PLANT

RADISH SEEDS

1 Fill the window box with compost to just below the rim. Plant the tomatoes in the back corners of the window box.

2 Plant the strawberries, about 30 cm (12 in) away from the tomatoes.

4 Sow some nasturtium seeds in the corners so that they can grow up and trail over the edge. Water thoroughly.

3 Sow radish and lettuce seeds 1 cm (½ in) apart. After the young radishes have been harvested, the lettuces can grow into their space.

GARDENER'S TIP

To get a plant out of a pot, turn it upside down with the stem between your fingers. With the other hand, firmly squeeze the bottom of the pot to release the rootball.

PLANT IN SPRING

Garden with a buzz

To encourage beautiful butter-flies and buzzing bees into the garden, grow a few of their favourite plants to tempt them in from miles around. Many butterflies are now becoming scarce, so every butterfly-friendly plant that you can grow will help them to survive. Bees and butterflies like lots of sunshine so put the barrel or planter in a sunny spot.

MATERIALS

Pebbles
Large planter or half barrel
Compost or equal quantities of
garden soil and compost

PLANTS

Selection of suitable plants such
as phlox, aster, lavender,
verbena, blue lobelia, scabious

PLANTS

GARDENER'S TIP

Other excellent plants are broom, catmint, delphinium, nasturtium, ox-eye daisy, petunia, primrose, stock, sweet William and thrift.

PLANT IN SPRING

1 Put a few pebbles in the bottom of the barrel or planter for drainage, then fill with compost or an equal mixture of soil and compost.

2 Plant phlox and aster in the middle because they will grow the tallest.

3 Plant lavender and verbena around the edge.

4 Plant blue lobelia in the front, so it tumbles over the edge. Water the container.

Fuchsias for tots

Several fuchsia cultivars are excellent plants for children to grow. These fuchsias can be bought at the start of the summer in small pots or in polystyrene trays. Transferred to small, brightly painted pots on a window-sill, or in a light corner in the children's room, they will flower continuously through the summer.

FUCHSIA

MATERIALS

7.5 cm (3 in) terracotta pots
Paintbrush
Bright acrylic or emulsion paints
Crocks
Compost

PLANTS

Fuchsia 'Happy' and F. 'Tom Thumb'

1 Paint the pots with bright primary colours in stripes or bold patterns. The paints used here are thick and water-resistant. If you use ordinary emulsion, you may need a couple of coats to achieve a bold effect. To achieve geometric patterns, use masking tape to mask out specific areas before painting. Let the paint dry before you continue.

2 Place small crocks in the bottom of the pots to cover the drainage hole and facilitate quick drainage.

3 Remove the fuchsias from their plastic pots and place one in each terracotta pot. Add more compost down the sides of the pot.

4 Use the blunt end of the paintbrush to ease the compost into the gap between the plant's rootball and the pot. Tamp down the compost firmly but not too tightly. Water the pots and allow to drain.

PLANT IN EARLY SPRING,
OR EARLY SUMMER

Spring into action

On misty, autumn days spring might seem a long time away, but young gardeners have to think ahead. If you want a cheerful pot of flowers to greet you early next year, now is the time to get planting. There are hundreds of different types of spring-flowering bulbs to choose from, and mixed and matched with forget-me-nots, daisies, pansies or wallflowers, you cannot go wrong.

MATERIALS

Large flower pot
Small stones
Compost

PLANTS

Tulip bulbs
Wallflowers
  (cheiranthus)
Forget-me-nots,
  daisies or   FORGET-ME-NOT
  pansies (violas)

TULIP BULBS

WALLFLOWERS

GARDENER'S TIP

The plants will not need heavy watering over the autumn and winter, but they will need an occasional drink so keep an eye on the pot in case it dries out.

PLANT IN AUTUMN

1 Use the biggest pot that you have got and put a few stones over the hole in the bottom for drainage. Fill the pot two-thirds full with compost.

2 Plant about 5 tulip bulbs. Cover the bulbs with handfuls of compost.

3 Using your hands to make holes, plant three wallflowers evenly spaced out. If you dig up a tulip bulb by mistake, just pop it back in again.

4 Fill any gaps with forget-me-nots, daisies or pansies, or a mixture. Give all the plants a good watering.

Cactus garden

Planting a bowl of cacti may take a little care and patience, but it is worth the effort since children love cacti. Once planted, the cacti ask nothing more than benevolent neglect.

MATERIALS

25 cm (10 in) terracotta bowl
Cactus compost
Newspaper
Cactus gravel

PLANTS

Euphorbia submammilaris
Rebutia muscula
*Rose pincushion (*Mammilaria
 zeilmanniana)
Cheiridopsis candidissima
Astrophytum ornatum
Prickly pear (Opuntia)

REBUTIA   EUPHORBIA   PRICKLY
                         PEAR

CHEIRIDOPSIS

ASTROPHYTUM

ROSE PINCUSHION

GARDENER'S TIP

If there are young children in your household be sure to choose the site of your cactus garden with care. If cacti are too aggressive for you, plant succulents instead: they require the same treatment, but are free of thorns.

PLANT AT ANY TIME OF THE YEAR

1 Fill the bowl with cactus compost to within 5 cm (2 in) of the rim. Prepare a thickly folded strip of newspaper to help you handle the cacti.

2 Before planting, decide on your arrangement of the plants by standing them, in their pots, in the bowl.

3 Ease the plants from their pots, surround them with a newspaper collar and lift into place. Handle more ferocious plants carefully, and leave the really prickly cacti until last or you will stab yourself on them as you are planting the rest.

4 Fill in around the plants with extra compost if needed. Add a finishing touch with a top-dressing of fine cactus gravel. Stand in good light and water sparingly.

Indoor containers

*Plants do furnish a room, and the same considerations apply to the effective use of
containers indoors as in the garden: find containers that suit their surroundings and the
plants you have chosen for them; plant them imaginatively and group them for impact.
Foliage plants will form the backbone of most arrangements, rather as trees
and shrubs do in the garden. Flowering plants won't be so long-lasting indoors, but are
always the centre of attraction while they are in bloom.
Decorative pots intended to go outdoors can be used very successfully indoors too.
Baskets make good plant holders if you line them with plastic. Your indoor plants will
appreciate good light (although direct sunlight through glass is too powerful
for most species) and a moist atmosphere: stand the pots in saucers of wet gravel and
give them a daily misting to help keep them looking their best.*

ABOVE: *Introduce flowering plants to your indoor collections to brighten
up your home.*

Indoor table-top garden

Many indoor plants have dramatically coloured flowers and foliage. In this arrangement the purple flowers of the African violet are echoed by the velvety leaves of the gynura. The delicate fronds of the maidenhair fern and the dark green foliage of the button fern add interest with their contrasting shape and colour.

MATERIALS

30 cm (12 in) terracotta seed
tray
Crocks
Houseplant compost
Slow-release plant food granules
Clay granules

PLANTS

Maidenhair fern (adiantum)
African violet (saintpaulia)
Gynura
Button fern (Pellaea rotundifolia)

AFRICAN VIOLET

MAIDENHAIR
FERN

GARDENER'S TIP

Terracotta transmits moisture and will mark a table-top if it is in direct contact with it.
Cut 2.5 cm (1 in) sections from a cork and glue them to the four corners of the seed tray.
A plastic tray smaller than the seed tray can then be slipped underneath it to catch any drips.

PLANT AT ANY TIME
OF THE YEAR

1 Cover the drainage holes in the bottom of the seed tray with crocks.

2 Arrange the plants before removing them from their pots. Plant the tallest plant first, then add the others around it.

3 Fill any gaps with compost and scatter a tablespoon of plant food granules on the surface. Mulch between the plants with clay granules to help retain moisture. Water and place in a light position, but out of direct sunlight. Spray regularly with water.

Bottle it up

Bottle gardens are great fun to make, and if you choose a stoppered bottle you will probably be able to grow some of those tricky plants that demand very high humidity. Don't worry too much about choosing the right plants, however. If you are prepared to replace plants when they outgrow their space, just concentrate on the plants that please you. You will have to improvise tools for your bottle garden by lashing old pieces of cutlery to garden canes.

SMALL FOLIAGE PLANTS

MATERIALS

Large glass bottle with cork
Fine gravel
Paper or thin cardboard
Charcoal
Compost
Knife, fork, spoon and
   cotton reel attached to canes

PLANTS

Small foliage plants

1 Place some fine gravel in the bottom of the bottle. If the neck is narrow you can make yourself a funnel from paper or thin cardboard to scatter it evenly over the base.

2 Add a thin layer of charcoal. This will help to absorb impurities and reduce the risk of the bottle smelling if there is too much moisture.

3 Spread a layer of compost over the base, and level it. Using your improvised trowel, make a hole for the plant.

4 Firm each plant in well. If you can't reach with your hand, use a cotton reel pushed on to the end of a cane to tamp down the compost.

5 Work around the whole bottle until it is fully planted. Then mist the plants. Aim the spray at the sides of the bottle if compost is clinging to the glass and spoiling the effect. Leave the plants and compost moist but not soaking wet.

6 If using a stoppered bottle you will have to balance the atmosphere over a week or two. You may need to keep inserting or removing the cork for periods (see opposite).

GARDENER'S TIP

Place the cork firmly in position and leave it for a day or two. Some misting of the glass, especially in the morning,
is quite normal – but if it never clears there is too much moisture, so leave the cork off for a day and try again.
If no condensation appears at all, it is probably too dry – mist again, then return the cork. It will take trial and error at
first, but once the atmosphere is balanced you can leave the bottle for months without attention, although you will have
to prune or remove plants that become too large.

PLANT IN SPRING

Palm court

Palms look graceful and elegant. They usually look best in isolation or among other palms, rather than in a group of mixed plants. Display them so that their classic shape can be appreciated. Allow these aristocrats space to make a statement.

MATERIALS

Decorative pot with drainage hole
Polystyrene or other suitable drainage material
Compost (loam-based if the plant is large)
Bark chippings

PLANT

Palm, appropriate for size of pot

PALM

1 Unless your palm is small (a few never grow large in the home), choose a large pot. As it will be conspicuous, choose an attractive, decorative one that does the plant justice. Start by placing a layer of polystyrene or other drainage material in the bottom.

2 Stand the palm in the pot and surround the rootball with container compost, pressing it firmly around the plant. Scatter a tablespoon of plant food granules on the surface.

3 Cover the compost with a layer of bark and water. Place in a position that receives good light, but no more than a couple of hours of direct sunlight each day. Water regularly during growing season, but allow the compost to dry out between waterings during the winter.

GARDENER'S TIP

Palms can look splendid in isolation, but they usually look more impressive in a collection. Display plants of different sizes to add interest, and place small ones on pedestals in front of taller ones in large pots. Like most houseplants, the palm will benefit from being stood outside during warm summer rain. A good soaking shower removes dust from the leaves and gives the plant the benefit of a drink of untreated water.

PLANT IN SPRING

Colourful kitchen herbs

Make a bright cheerful statement by using painted tins as containers for your kitchen herbs, often now available in pot from most supermarkets.

PARSLEY

CORIANDER

BASIL

MATERIALS

Empty food tins
White spirit
Masking tape
Paintbrush
Gloss paint

PLANTS

Dill
Chives
Parsley
Coriander
Basil

GARDENER'S TIP

Large painted tins make colourful planters in the garden. Ask your local restaurant or school for some of the catering size tins that they normally throw away.

PLANT AT ANY TIME OF THE YEAR

1 Thoroughly wash and dry the tins. Use white spirit to remove any residual spots of glue. Wrap masking tape round the lips of the tins so that half of it protrudes above the rims.

2 Fold the protruding masking tape inside the rims of the tins.

3 Paint the tins and leave them to dry.

4 Depending on the colours you choose, some of them may need more than one coat. Leave to dry completely.

5 Place each plant, pot and all, in a separate tin. Stand in a light position and water if the compost dries out.

Sweet scents for a conservatory

This simple, very informal planting would thrive in a conservatory. A pretty combination of scented-leaf pelargonium, deep blue miniature petunias, purple trailing verbenas and exuberant tumbling ground ivies.

VERBENA

GROUND IVY

MATERIALS

30 cm (12 in) plastic window box
Compost
Slow-release plant food granules

PLANTS

Scented-leaf Pelargonium 'Lady Plymouth'
2 variegated ground ivies (Glechoma hederacea 'Variegata')
2 deep purple trailing verbenas
2 deep blue 'Junior' petunias

PETUNIA

PELARGONIUM

1 Check drainage holes are open; if not, drill or punch them out. Fill the window box with compost, mixing in a teaspoon of slow-release plant foot granules. Plant the pelargonium in the centre.

GARDENER'S TIP

If the ground ivy gets too rampant, cut it back. Root some pieces and plant out in the spring to run wild over a wall.

PLANT IN SPRING

2 Plant the ground ivies at each end, and the two verbenas at the back of the box between the pelargonium and ground ivies.

3 Plant the petunias between the pelargonium and ground ivies at the front of the box. Water thoroughly and stand in a sunny position.

Water-loving plants

The sweet flag is a marsh plant which loves the moist conditions in most bathrooms. Planted in gravel in a stylish glass pot or vase, it is easy to see when the water needs topping up.

MATERIALS

20 cm (8 in) glass vase or pot
Gravel

SWEET FLAG

PLANTS

1 large or 2 small sweet flags
(Acorus gramineus 'Variegatus')

1 Fill the bottom half of the container with gravel.

2 Take the plants out of their existing pots and place them on the gravel.

3 Fill the pot with gravel to the base of the leaves and half-fill the container with water. Place on a light window-sill and never allow the plants to dry out.

GARDENER'S TIP

The umbrella plant (*Cyperus alternifolius*) will also thrive in these conditions.

PLANT AT ANY TIME OF THE YEAR

Combined effects

Displaying houseplants in groups creates a humid microclimate, which the plants prefer to the dry atmosphere of most homes. The humidity is increased by standing the pots in saucers of wet gravel kept moist by regular watering. Choose plants of contrasting shapes and sizes for the most striking effect.

MATERIALS

4 pots of various sizes with saucers
Crocks
Compost
Gravel

PLANTS

Lilies
Maidenhair fern (adiantum)
Cretan fern
Variegated creeping fig (Ficus pumila)

LILY

MAIDENHAIR FERN

CREEPING FIG

CRETAN FERN

1 Place the crocks in the bottom of the pots. Check the proportion of pot to plant.

2 Remove the lilies from their plastic container and position in the pot.

3 Fill gaps around the rootballs with compost, pressing down firmly to avoid any air spaces.

4 Remove the foliage plants from their containers and plant in the other pots, topping up with compost.

5 Water the plants thoroughly. Fill the saucers with gravel. Stand the pots in their saucers and position the plants in good light, but away from direct sun. Keep the gravel in the saucers damp, and water the plants when the compost dries out.

GARDENER'S TIP

Bear in mind the background of your display when choosing your plants. Large architectural leaves and strong plain colours won't get lost against a busy wallpaper, whereas lots of variegations and colour are better against a plain background.

PLANT AT ANY TIME OF THE YEAR

Beautiful baskets

A basket is a great way to display a small group of houseplants. You don't need a lot of plants to make a superb show, and when one is past its best you can just remove it and pop in a replacement.

MATERIALS

Basket
Plastic sheet
Compost
Sphagnum moss or
  fresh moss

PLANTS

5–6 small plants such as saintpaulia (African violet), chlorophytum, adiantum, exacum, and impatiens

ADIANTUM   IMPATIENS

SAINTPAULIA   CHLOROPHYTUM   EXACUM

1 To protect the basket (and your furniture) from the effects of moisture, line it with a piece of plastic cut to size.

2 Add a layer of compost to retain moisture, and provide a humid atmosphere around the plants.

3 Remove the plants from their pots and place in the basket. It may be necessary to remove some compost from the bottom, or add a little more to bring each plant to the right height.

4 Make sure you are entirely happy with the arrangement of the plants, then trickle a little more compost between them to fill in the gaps.

5 Use dried or fresh moss to fill any spaces between the plants.

GARDENER'S TIP

You could leave the plants in the individual pots for convenience.

PLANT AT ANY TIME OF YEAR

Indoor topiary

Proper topiary is not practical indoors, but you can cheat a little and achieve a similar effect by training ivy over a frame. Start with an easy shape like the lollipop shown here, and once you are proficient you can experiment with all kinds of imaginative shapes. Buy a wire frame or make your own.

MATERIALS

Pot large enough to accommodate frame
Crocks or bark chippings
Compost
Wire frame

PLANTS   IVY

2–3 small-leaved variegated ivies

1 Place crocks or large pieces of bark chippings over the drainage hole and cover with a layer of compost.

2 Insert the wire frame, making sure it is placed centrally, and top up with more compost to secure it.

3 Insert the ivies around the edge of the pot. The more plants you use, the more quickly the frame will be covered.

4 Leave a few shoots to trail over the edge of the pot, but thread the rest through the frame. Within a few months the frame will probably be completely hidden by the new growth. Thread new shoots through bare areas, and pinch back any that are too long. Regular pinching back of long shoots will help to retain the shape once the frame has been covered.

GARDENER'S TIP

Once you have mastered this lollipop shape, try making an animal (teddy bear or rabbit). If you can't find a ready made template, then make your own wire shape. Alternatively, try something more ambitious like a large cup and saucer, or even a tennis racket.

PLANT IN EARLY SPRING

Terrarium display

FOLIAGE AND
FLOWERING
PLANTS

Terrariums are similar to bottle gardens and come in a variety of shapes. Many of them are not sealed, so the atmosphere is less humid. They provide a more ornamental way to display plants. If access is easy, you may want to consider a few flowering plants to provide colour.

MATERIALS

Terrarium
Expanded clay granules
Gravel
Compost

PLANTS

Selection of small
plants

1 Place a layer of expanded clay granules, followed by gravel, in the base to reduce the risk of the compost becoming water-logged. Use either gravel or clay granules if you cannot get both.

2 Add the compost, making the layer several centimetres deep if possible. If this is not practical because of the design of the terrarium, you will need to reduce the depth of the rootballs.

3 If your centrepiece plant is too large, try a little judicious pruning with scissors.

4 You should be able to plant and firm the plants by hand. Plant the back, or the least accessible area first.

5 Place the plants most likely to require regular pruning or pinching back in the most accessible positions.

6 Plant your centrepiece, firming it in well.

GARDENER'S TIP

Be sure that you select slow-growing small-leaved plants, or what began as an airy, well-presented display could end up as a miniature jungle.

PLANT IN EARLY SPRING

Orchid basket

MILTONIA

PLANTS

Miltonia or phalaenopsis orchid

Orchids are no longer the rare exotic plants that they used to be and most garden centres now stock some. A few inexpensive materials and a little time will create a stylish container to show these lovely flowers at their very best.

MATERIALS

Plastic-lined twig basket, 15 cm (6 in) diameter
Gravel
Sphagnum moss
3 x 40 cm (16 in) canes
Raffia

1 Pour a 2.5 cm (1 in) layer of gravel into the base of the basket and line with moss.

2 Slip the orchid (still in its pot) into the basket.

3 Push the canes into the moss at the edge of the basket so that they are held firmly in place.

4 Tie a length of raffia between each cane, finishing off with a neat knot.

GARDENER'S TIP

Orchids do not like to stand in water, but they do like a humid atmosphere. A layer of gravel underneath the pot acts as a reservoir for excess water which creates humidity. The orchid will also benefit from being sprayed with water.

PLANT AT ANY TIME
OF THE YEAR

Plant crazy

These highly decorative and unusual planters are enhanced by the careful choice of plants which provide the royal head-dresses. The queen's tresses float delicately above the crown, whilst the king's tumble downwards.

MATERIALS

2 decorative pots
Gravel
Compost

CREEPING FIG

PLANTS

Chandelier plant
(Kalanchoe
tubiflora)
Creeping fig
(Ficus pumila)

CHANDELIER
PLANT

1 Pour a 5 cm (2 in) layer of gravel into the bottom of the pots.

2 Place the chandelier plant into the planter; if there is any space around the rootball, fill with compost and gently firm the plant in position.

3 After you have planted the creeping fig in the other planter, arrange the sprays of leaves so that they resemble hair. As the plant grows it will need an occasional haircut to keep it under control. Water regularly and stand in a light position.

GARDENER'S TIP

If you are going away for a few days during the summer months, give your houseplants a holiday in the garden. Stand them on a tray lined with a thick layer of damp newspaper, positioned in a shady corner, where they will not dry out.

PLANT AT ANY TIME
OF THE YEAR

Period fuchsias

Fuchsias were first cultivated in Europe in the 1780s. Many cultivars bred in the 1800s can still be found in cultivation today. Fuchsia 'Bland's New Striped' was first seen in cultivation in 1872, and 'Claire de Lune' in 1880. Growing plants from a particular period will add an exciting historic flavour to any collection.

MATERIALS

Victorian copper pot
Expanded clay granules
Victorian-style planter
Crocks
Compost

PLANTS

Fuchsia 'Claire de Lune'
Fuchsia 'Bland's New Striped'

1 Put a layer of expanded clay granules into the base of the Victorian copper pot. This will help to create a humid atmosphere around the plants.

2 Place the *Fuchsia* 'Claire de Lune' in the copper pot, arranging the branches and foliage to fall around the sides.

3 Cover the drainage hole in the bottom of the Victorian-style planter with terracotta crocks.

4 Fill the pot with compost.

5 Remove *F.* 'Bland's New Striped' from its pot. The network of fresh, healthy roots shows that the plant is strong and vigorous.

6 Plant in the compost. Cover the rootball and firm the compost with your hands.

GARDENER'S TIP

Orange flowers are often considered to be a modern advance in fuchsia cultivars, but 'Lye's Unique' has salmon-orange flowers, and originated in 1886. Other old varieties to look out for include 'Charming', a hardy bush which was developed in 1877.

PLANT IN EARLY SPRING OR EARLY SUMMER

Copper-bottomed begonia

The stunningly marked leaves of this begonia are shown to great advantage in this old copper pot. The pot was an inexpensive purchase from a flea market, and was cleaned before use.

MATERIALS

Copper pot, 20 cm (8 in) diameter
Lemon
Slow-release plant food granules
Clay granules

PLANT

Begonia

BEGONIA

1 Rub the tarnished pot with half a lemon. The acidity of the juice will quickly clean the pot, but don't overclean it or it will look brand new and lose some of its character.

2 Place the begonia, in its plastic pot, in the copper container. Scatter a teaspoon of plant food granules on the surface of the compost.

3 Surround the plant with clay granules. Place in a light, but not sunny, position and water regularly.

GARDENER'S TIP

Other houseplants recommended for this treatment are streptocarpus, gynura and cyclamen.

PLANT AT ANY TIME OF THE YEAR

Dramatic datura

The angel's trumpet or *Datura* (strictly speaking, it should now be known as *Brugmansia*), a popular conservatory plant, will grow enormous in time, provided it is planted in a large container and given regular food and water. The plant will benefit from a period outdoors during the summer, but will grow indoors for the rest of the year.

MATERIALS

Deep planter, at least 40 cm (16 in) diameter
Polystyrene or similar drainage material
Gloves
Equal mix loam-based compost and container compost
Slow-release plant food granules

PLANTS

Angel's trumpet (Brugmansia suaveolens)
4 white busy lizzies (impatiens)

ANGEL'S TRUMPET

BUSY LIZZIE

1 Fill the base of the container with lightweight polystyrene or similar drainage material. Wear gloves to lift the angel's trumpet into the container.

2 Pour compost round the edges of the plant, pressing down firmly around the rootball. Scatter 2 tablespoons of plant food granules on the surface.

3 Plant the busy Lizzies around the base of the angel's trumpet, and remember to water frequently.

GARDENER'S TIP

All parts of the angel's trumpet are poisonous, and it should be handled with care. Standing it outside in summer is recommended as the scent of the flowers can have a narcotic effect in confined spaces. It is not recommended in households with small children. While it is sensible to be cautious, it is also a fact that many commonly cultivated plants are poisonous. For example, with the exception of its tubers, the potato plant is poisonous, as are dieffenbachia and oleander.

PLANT IN SPRING

Success with Houseplants

Discovering houseplants • Caring for
houseplants • Simple multiplication
• Trouble-shooting • Creative displays
• A–Z directory of houseplants

Introduction

Some use houseplants purely as decorations, like ornaments or paintings on the wall, others treat them almost as botanical specimens, choosing examples of the native flora from every continent. However, if you want to get the best out of your houseplants, you need to appreciate them as plants as well as decorations and some understanding of the different plant groups will help you to display them appropriately and grow them more successfully. In the first chapter, *Discovering Houseplants,* you will find advice on how to recognize and use all the major plant groups around the home, along with tips on selecting the best plants for different positions.

However, be prepared to experiment with plants, accept that there will be failures, and look beyond the commonplace to discover the range of interesting or more unusual plants that you can grow in the home. Growing houseplants will then become an even more stimulating hobby.

The second chapter, *Caring for Houseplants,* will give you the advice and guidance you need to keep your plants in tip-top condition. Houseplants do, of course, demand time and attention. If you forget to water them, few will forgive the lapse. If you don't feed them, most will look weak and starved. None of this should deter anyone from growing them, for there are always plants and techniques that you can choose to suit the time you can devote to your plants.

For example, if watering is something you just can't remember to

OPPOSITE: *A large specimen plant, such as this majestic palm, will make a statement in any home.*

RIGHT: *Plant groupings, such as these ferns displayed in a basket, create a stronger visual impact than single plants dotted around a room.*

think about every day, or business or pleasure travel takes you away from home and there's nobody to plant-sit for you, there are simple solutions: concentrate on cacti and succulents that are naturally adapted to this kind of deprivation, or grow ordinary houseplants in special containers. Self-watering planters are ideal for groups of plants and you only need to top up the reservoir every week or so. Hydroculture is another excellent option if you want to minimize the watering chore. Feeding is also easy with modern fertilizers. There are now slow-release tablets and sticks that you can push into the compost (potting soil) to release nutrients over a long period.

All these aids for the busy person are extremely useful, but caring for

your plants can be a pleasurable part of growing them. By grooming them occasionally you not only notice whether pests are about to launch an attack, you also get to know your plants better, and often you will see things that would otherwise go unnoticed. If you do no more than slosh a bit of water onto your aspidistra you will soon take it for granted. But if you groom it by removing a dying leaf, or wiping the leaves over with a moist cloth to bring back the sparkle and gloss, you may suddenly notice a curious-looking purple flower sitting at compost level, a gem that you would otherwise miss. Houseplants are full of surprises, many of which only reveal themselves when you *really* care for them.

Raising your own houseplants from seeds or cuttings can be extremely rewarding, and the third chapter, *Simple Multiplication,* offers clear advice on a whole range of different propagation techniques. Most houseplants can be raised from simple cuttings but, unlike hardy plants, the majority require warmth and humidity to root rapidly, so a propagator is a good investment. Apart from its use for cuttings, it will enable a whole range of seedlings to be started off in spring for both home and garden.

Lack of a propagator is only a restriction and not a bar to successful propagation. Seeds can be germinated in any warm location (provided that they are moved into a light position *without delay* as soon as the first ones have germinated). You can make a mini propagator by covering a pot with a clear plastic bag. Alternatively, a sheet of glass placed over a seed tray or a small cardboard box containing

cuttings, can often work wonders with quite tricky plants.

Some people find propagation so fascinating that it becomes a hobby itself – with a constant search for new plants to try from cuttings or seed. Friends and neighbours are usually happy to spare a shoot or leaf from a plant that you take a fancy to, and looking through the seed catalogues for interesting houseplants to try is a pleasurable pastime.

Chapter 4, *Trouble-shooting,* is devoted to the problems you may experience in caring for your houseplants. Pests and diseases will undoubtedly occur from time to time. However, it should not be necessary to reach for potent sprays or to take drastic action such as discarding your plants as a first step. If a watch is kept for early signs of trouble when you groom the plants on a regular basis, pests like aphids can be eliminated before they breed and multiply. For example,

ABOVE: *Nurseries and garden centres often offer a good selection of the more popular houseplants and some specialize in particular plants such as cacti and succulents.*

BELOW LEFT: *Collecting cacti and succulents can be a fascinating hobby. The examples shown here are, from left to right:* Echinocactus grusonii, Euphorbia milii *(syn.* E. splendens*) and* Opuntia vestita.

OPPOSITE LEFT: *Some plants, such as codiaeums, can be quite difficult to rear, but the challenge is worth pursuing.*

OPPOSITE RIGHT: *Bathrooms can be quite tricky locations for many plants, so be sure to select those that enjoy humidity.*

many leaf diseases can be contained or eliminated simply by picking off any affected parts as soon as the disease is noticed. This will often prevent the disease from spreading and, more importantly, from releasing spores that will affect other parts of the plant or its neighbours.

While fast action is commendable, the overkill approach that resorts to a chemical armoury first is not always appropriate. If you want to avoid the use of chemicals completely, you can try a combination of good hygiene, vigilant hand picking and natural

predators. You can buy predatory insects that parasitize pests such as whitefly, and although intended for use primarily in the greenhouse can be used indoors. They are useful in a conservatory, but natural control is not without problems: you have to accept a low level of pest infestation otherwise the predator dies out, and if you try to knock out the insects not controlled by the predator using insecticides that kill a broad range of pests, you will again upset the natural control cycle.

Sometimes plants fall sick for other reasons, such as nutritional deficiencies or physiological reasons. Plants that are pot-bound will look sick, and even too much feeding will cause symptoms of collapse that could be mistaken for pests or diseases affecting the roots.

In the final chapter, *Creative Displays,* you will find lots of ideas for using houseplants imaginatively, with suggestions for different rooms, and for ways in which you can use plants together so that one enhances the other. By using houseplants as ornaments, focal points and as integrated decorations in the home, you will derive even more pleasure from your plants than you would by regarding them merely as botanical specimens.

Although plants are constantly changing – they grow, die, or simply alter their shape – this very lack of stability can be turned to your advantage. Unlike any other decorative element that you can place and forget, and eventually even take for granted, plants have a dynamic existence. You have to move them, rearrange them, even repot them into different containers, all of which gives them an extra dimension and vitality that other kinds of ornaments lack. Flowering plants usually make a transient impact, but their use in internal design is no less powerful than that of the aristocratic yucca or tall ficus. You can choose flowers and backgrounds that blend or contrast, to complement the mood you are trying to create.

Plants not only need to look good in a setting, they have to be happy there too. No matter how grand a plant looks in a rather gloomy corner of the room, it won't thrive, or even survive, if it needs good light. Plants that demand a humid atmosphere might survive in a kitchen but not in a living-room.

The creative displays used here should provide plenty of inspiration, but be prepared to experiment with your own ideas, to suit *your* tastes and *your* home. Above all, houseplants should please you and express your own personal tastes.

Discovering houseplants

GROWING HOUSEPLANTS SHOULD BE
A VOYAGE OF DISCOVERY, NOT ONLY ABOUT
THE TYPES OF PLANTS THAT WILL OR WON'T
GROW WELL IN YOUR HOME, BUT ALSO AN
EXPLORATION OF THE PLANT KINGDOM IN
ALL ITS DIVERSE MANIFESTATIONS. YOU
WILL GET A LOT MORE OUT OF YOUR HOUSE-
PLANTS IF YOU INVESTIGATE THE POTENTIAL
OF THE VARIOUS TYPES OF PLANTS, AND
HOW THEY CAN BE USED IN THE HOME.

Dependable evergreens

CHOOSE SOME OF THE EASIEST AND MOST DEPENDABLE EVERGREENS AS THE

BACKBONE OF YOUR DISPLAYS. MANY OF THEM ARE TOUGH ENOUGH FOR

THE MORE DIFFICULT POSITIONS AROUND THE HOME, AND MOST OF THOSE

SUGGESTED HERE ARE BOLD ENOUGH TO BE FOCAL POINT PLANTS TOO.

The glossy evergreens such as dracaenas, fatsias, ficus, scheffleras, palms and philodendrons generally make excellent stand-alone plants, but they can also be used as the framework plants for groups and arrangements. They will be far more robust than plants with thin or papery leaves, feathery and frondy ferns, or even those with hairy leaves. You need these other leaf textures, as well as flowering plants, to add variety of shape and form, and a touch of colour, but it makes sense to use the toughest evergreens as the basis of your houseplant displays.

Indoor 'trees'

Even the plainest room can be brought to life and given a sense of design and character with a large specimen plant that has the stature of a small tree. Some houseplants grow into real trees in their natural environment, but indoors you need plants that are in proportion with the dimensions of your room, and that won't quickly outgrow their space.

Large palms are ideal for this purpose, but many of the ficus family do just as well. The common *Ficus elastica,* once so popular, but now often passed by as unexciting, is a good choice, and there are many excellent variegated varieties that are far from dull. If you want an all-green one (and these have the merit of growing more quickly than the variegated kinds), 'Robusta' is a good variety to choose. If you don't like the upright and

TOP: Ficus elastica *was once a very popular houseplant, and is still well worth growing. The variety usually grown is 'Robusta', an improvement on the species that used to be grown years ago.*

ABOVE: Ficus lyrata *is a bold 'architectural' plant that can easily reach ceiling height.*

FAR LEFT: Philodendron scandens *is effective both as a trailing plant and grown up a moss pole, as here.*

LEFT: Yucca elephantipes *is a justifiably popular houseplant. It makes a bold focal point and is a really tough plant that should survive for years.*

sometimes leggy appearance of this plant, cut out the tip when it is about 1.5–1.8m (5–6ft) feet high, to stimulate low branching.

Other ficus to look for are *F. lyrata* (very large leaves with a distinctive shape), *F. benghalensis* (though the downy appearance of the leaves can make it a dull-looking plant), and the widely available *Ficus benjamina*. This is especially beautiful because it grows tall with a broad crown and arching branches. There are also beautiful variegated varieties of this species such as 'Starlight'.

Bushy plants that will give height and spread include *Schefflera arboricola* (syn. *Heptapleurum arboricola*) and *Schefflera actinophylla*. Both have finger-like leaflets radiating from a central point.

When a tough plant is needed

If you need a tough, glossy evergreen for a cold or draughty spot, perhaps for a hallway or near the back door, consider using some of the hardy foliage plants that have to cope with frost and gales when planted outdoors!

Fatsia japonica is another glossy evergreen with fingered foliage, rather like the palm of a hand (look for a variegated variety if you don't like the plain green leaves). Closely related is × *Fatshedera lizei*, a bigeneric hybrid between *Fatsia japonica* and an ivy. Grow it as a shrub by pinching out the growing tips each spring, or let it show its ivy parentage and grow more upright.

Others to look for are variegated varieties of *Aucuba japonica*, and *Euonymus japonicus* varieties such as 'Mediopictus', 'Microphyllus Albovariegatus' and 'Microphyllus Aureovariegatus'.

Ivies are ideal if you need a tough climber or trailer, and there are lots of varieties to choose from, with a wide choice of leaf shape, size and colour.

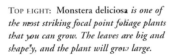

Philodendrom scandens

P. 'Blue Mink'

P. 'Xanadu'

P. bipinnatifidum

P. 'Pink Prince'

Philodendron leaves

Some genera have species and varieties with very different leaves, and they can make an interesting collection. The five philodendron leaves shown here are typical of the variation you can find within one group of plants.

TOP RIGHT: Monstera deliciosa *is one of the most striking focal point foliage plants that you can grow. The leaves are big and shapely, and the plant will grow large.*

ABOVE: **Scindapsus aureus,** *often sold under its other name of* Epipremnum aureum, *is a useful climber or trailer. This is the golden variety 'Neon'.*

ABOVE RIGHT: *Radermachera combines tough glossy leaves with a 'loose' and almost ferny appearance; a refreshing change to most of the glossy evergreens.*

RIGHT: **Aspidistra elatior** *is a tough plant that seems to tolerate all kinds of neglect. If you look after it properly, however, you will have a fine foliage plant. There is also a variegated variety.*

Elegant palms

PALMS ARE THE EPITOME OF ELEGANCE AND WILL ADD A TOUCH OF SOPHIS-

TICATION TO YOUR HOME. THEY BRING TO MIND IMAGES OF A TINKLING

PIANO IN THE PALM COURT OF A GRAND HOTEL, YET SOME CAN LOOK JUST AS

ELEGANT AND IMPOSING IN AN ULTRA-MODERN HOME INTERIOR.

Many palms are slow-growing, and, consequently, large specimens are often expensive. But don't be deterred from trying palms; if you provide the right conditions, even small plants will gradually become impressive specimens.

Not all palms grow large, and many are compact enough for a table-top or for pride of place on a pedestal. Some are even small enough to use in a bottle garden while young. The box opposite will help you choose a suitable palm for a particular position.

How to grow healthy palms

The most common mistake is to regard all palms as lovers of hot sunshine and desert-dry air. They often have to cope with both in countries where they grow outdoors, but as houseplants you want them to remain in good condition with unblemished leaves.

- Keep cool in winter, but not less than 10°C (50°F).
- Keep out of direct sunshine unless you know that your palm revels in sunshine (a few do).
- Use a loam-based compost (potting soil) and ensure that the drainage is good (poor drainage is sure to cause problems).
- Only repot when absolutely essential as palms dislike root disturbance. Always ensure that the new compost is firmly compacted if you do repot.
- Water liberally in spring and summer, sparingly in winter.
- Mist the plants frequently with water and sponge the leaves occasionally with water.
- Do not use an aerosol leaf shine.

WHAT WENT WRONG

❧ **Brown leaf tips** are usually caused by dry air. Underwatering and cold are other likely causes.

❧ **Brown spots on the leaves** are probably caused by a disease, encouraged by overwatering or chills. Cut off all affected leaves.

❧ **Yellowing leaves** are most likely to be caused by underwatering, though they could also indicate that the plant needs feeding.

❧ **Brown leaves** are nothing to worry about if they are few in number and only the lowest ones are affected.

LEFT: *Washingtonia palms have fan-like leaves that create a striking effect.*

CHOOSING A PALM

❧ Tall and tough

Chamaerops humilis Can be grown outdoors where frosts are only mild; suitable for a cold position indoors. *Howeia forsteriana* (syn. *Kentia forsteriana*) and *H. belmoreana* (syn. *K. belmoreana*) Associated with the old palm courts. Will survive in a dark situation, but growth is very slow. *Phoenix canariensis* This one enjoys full sun (but beware of leaf scorch through glass) and can sit on the patio for the summer. Keep in a cool room – minimum about 7°C(45°F) – in winter.

❧ Table-top and easy

Chamaedorea elegans (syn. *Neanthe bella*) Can be used in a bottle garden when small. Insignificant flowers often appear on young plants.

❧ Difficult but worth the effort

Cocos nucifera This is the coconut palm, and it is usually grown as a novelty with the large nut clearly visible at the base. Even a young plant can be 1.8m (6ft) tall, and it is difficult to keep in the home. *Cocos weddeliana* A slow-grower. Can be used in a bottle garden.

Dealing with brown leaves

It is natural for the lower leaves on palms to turn brown and die in time. To keep the plant looking smart, cut these off close to the point of origin (top). Secateurs (floral scissors) are adequate for most palms, but a saw may be required for specimens with very tough leaves. If the tips of the leaves turn brown, trim them off with scissors, but avoid actually cutting into the healthy leaf (above).

ABOVE RIGHT: Howeia belmoreana *is sometimes sold under its other name of* Kentia belmoreana.

RIGHT: Cocos nucifera *is a big palm that is quite difficult to keep in the home.*

FAR RIGHT: Chamaedorea elegans *is a palm to choose if you want one that is easy and dependable. It will remain compact enough to use on a table-top.*

Variegated plants

VARIEGATED FOLIAGE PLANTS WILL BRING COLOUR AND A TOUCH OF THE EXOTIC INTO A DULL CORNER OR BRIGHT WINDOWSILL, DEPENDING ON THE TYPE. UNLIKE FLOWERING PLANTS, MOST REMAIN COLOURFUL FOR TWELVE MONTHS OF THE YEAR.

Variegation has evolved for several reasons, and the two main ones are important to understand if you want to grow healthy-looking plants with good variegation.

Many variegated houseplants are derived from forest-floor dwellers in which variegation is useful where they occur in lighter areas, such as on the edge of clearings, because it reduces the area of functional leaf. This type of variegation is frequently white and green, the white areas cutting down the area that is reactive to sunlight. This group of plants often has the best variegation when positioned away from direct light.

Others are light-demanding species and have acquired colours and patterns for other reasons. Red and pink leaves are able to absorb light from different parts of the spectrum to green leaves, for example, and many different colours in the one leaf may make it more efficient. The variegation on these plants is often better if positioned in good light.

A few plants have colourful leaves to attract pollinators. The common poinsettia (*Euphorbia pulcherrima*), and bromeliads such as neoregelia, are able to change the colour of the leaves that surround the insignificant flowers from green to bright colours such as reds and pinks.

There are other reasons for variegation, such as a being a warning to predators, so there can be no simple rules that apply to all colourful foliage plants. Some, such as coleus and crotons (codiaeums) need bright light;

others like fittonias, with their white or pale pink variegation, must be kept out of direct sun.

Potential problems

Some plants lose their strong variegation if the light is too strong, others if it is too weak. If the plant seems unhappy, move it to a lighter or shadier position as appropriate.

If any isolated, all-green shoots appear on an otherwise satisfactorily variegated plant, cut them back to the point of origin. Some plants will 're-vert' and the all-green part of the plant will eventually dominate unless you remove the offending shoots.

Coloured bracts (the modified leaves that frame a cluster of flowers) will lose their colour or intensity of colour outside the flowering period. You can do nothing about this.

Begonia rex leaves
Although they are unlikely to be labelled as specific varieties, you can collect a whole range of *Begonia rex* with different variegations. Two other types of foliage begonias are shown here: *B. masoniana* (top left) and, to the right of this, *B.* 'Tiger'.

GOING FOR A COLLECTION

🙠 There are so many variegated houseplants that some people like to start a collection of a particular group of them. This makes it easy to provide the right conditions for all of them, and the searching out of new species or varieties to add to the collection adds another dimension to the hobby.

Good plants to collect are begonias (there are many variations among *B. rex*, but lots of other begonias have interesting variegation), caladiums (if you like a challenge), codiaeums, dracaenas and cordylines, marantas and calatheas, and pileas. Named varieties of vegetatively propagated coleus are difficult to obtain, but a packet of seeds will give you an amazing range of colours and variegation from which to select those to keep.

OPPOSITE TOP: **Begonia rex** *varies in leaf colouring from one plant to another, but all are attractively variegated and make bold foliage plants.*

OPPOSITE LEFT: **Cordyline terminalis**, *also sold as Dracaena terminalis, comes in many varieties, the difference being in the colouring and variegation.*

OPPOSITE RIGHT: **Dracaena marginata** *is a popular houseplant, and there are varieties with attractively variegated leaves.*

TOP LEFT: **Ficus benjamina** *'Starlight' is an outstanding houseplant with brightly variegated leaves on a plant that will eventually make a tall specimen with attractively arching shoots.*

TOP RIGHT: *Ivies (varieties of* **Hedera helix**) *are versatile plants that can be used as climbers or trailers.*

RIGHT: *Codiaeums, also known as crotons, can be demanding to grow well, but they make spectacular plants. Leaf hue and shape vary greatly according to variety, but all are bright and colourful.*

Graceful ferns

FERNS ARE FASCINATING PLANTS THAT WILL ADD A SPECIAL CHARM TO ANY
ROOM IN WHICH YOU WANT TO CREATE A FEELING OF COOL TRANQUILLITY
AND GREEN LUSHNESS. THEY BESTOW A RELAXED ATMOSPHERE IN CONTRAST
TO THE VIVID COLOUR OF BRIGHTER FOLIAGE PLANTS AND THE BRASHNESS OF
SOME FLOWERS.

Ferns are grown mainly for the grace and beauty of their fronds, and their elegance compensates for their lack of flowers.

The majority of ferns will thrive in shade or partial shade, conditions that are easily provided in any home. Unfortunately they also require lots of moisture and high humidity, both of which are in short supply in the average living-room. If you want ferns to thrive, you will have to choose easy and tolerant varieties (see the *Fern Selector* above right) or provide them with the humidity and moisture that is so vital. Although most of the ferns

sold as houseplants come from tropical regions and benefit from warmth, central heating spells death to many of them unless you counteract the dry air by taking measures to increase the humidity, at least immediately surrounding the plants.

The ideal place for ferns is in a conservatory, porch or garden room where it is easier to establish a moist atmosphere.

Not all ferns need coddling, however, and some have adapted to dry air or cool temperatures. There are sure to be some ferns that you can grow successfully, and if you are determined to

FERN SELECTOR

🌿 **Good for beginners**
Asplenium nidus
Cyrtomium falcatum (syn. *Polystichum falcatum*)
Nephrolepis exaltata
Pellaea rotundifolia

🌿 **For the more experienced**
Adiantum capillus-veneris
Platycerium bifurcatum
Polypodium aureum
Pteris cretica (and its varieties)

🌿 **Difficult but interesting**
Asplenium bulbiferum
Davallia fejeenis

grow the delicate types with thin, feathery fronds, you can try planting them in a bottle garden or terrarium where they will thrive.

Starting with ferns
If you haven't grown ferns before, start with the easy ones. As you gain experience, add some of the more exotic and difficult species.

The commonest ferns are inexpensive, and even the more unusual kinds are usually cheap if you choose small specimens.

Florists and garden centres sell the most popular houseplant ferns, but you may have to buy the less common ones from a specialist nursery.

Propagating ferns
The simplest way to increase your ferns is to divide a large clump, or to remove offsets. Some, like *Davallia fejeenis,* send out rhizomes that root and can be used to grow new plants,

LEFT: *Most of the aspleniums are much easier to care for than the ferns with very thin and finely divided leaves.* Asplenium nidus *(left) has broad leaves that radiate from a central well or 'nest' and is a particularly good houseplant.*

others produce small bulbils or even plantlets on the leaves (*Asplenium bulbiferum* is one). These will usually root into moist compost if pressed into the surface. These are interesting and fun ways to grow more ferns.

Growing your own ferns from spores is possible but slow, and you may find it difficult to obtain fresh spores of houseplant species with good germination.

Don't be deceived!

Many plants commonly regarded as ferns simply masquerade under that name. Some, like the selaginellas, are also primitive plants, other such as asparagus 'ferns' are more evolved flowering plants that simply have fine, feathery-looking foliage – an attribute associated with ferns. The asparagus fern is in fact a member of the lily family, though you would hardly recognize the connection from its insignificant flowers.

Selaginellas are pretty, low-growing plants that like the same conditions as indoor ferns: damp shade and moderate warmth. They will happily grow alongside ferns in a bottle garden.

Several asparagus ferns are available as houseplants, all of them tougher and more tolerant of neglect than the majority of true ferns.

Mounting a stag's horn

The *Platycerium bifurcatum* is a native of Australia and unlike most ferns it does not mind a dry atmosphere. One of the most spectacular ways to display it is mounted on bark. Keep the root-ball damp and mist the plant regularly.

1. Find a suitably sized piece of bark. Cork bark is ideal and you can usually buy this from a florist or aquarium shop. Start with a small plant and remove it from the pot. If necessary, remove some of the compost to reduce its bulk, then wrap the roots in damp sphagnum moss. Secure the moss with wire.

2. Bind the mossy root-ball to the cork bark, using florists' wire or plastic-covered wire to hold it securely.

ABOVE Adiantum capillus-veneris, *like most of the maidenhair ferns, demands a humid atmosphere to do well. However, this is a truly graceful species.*

ABOVE RIGHT: Cyrtomium falcatum *is the one to choose if you find ferns generally too demanding. This one will tolerate a much drier atmosphere than most, and does not need a lot of warmth.*

RIGHT: Nephrolepsis exaltata *is one of the best ferns for a pedestal or table-top display. There are several varieties, with variation in leaf shape, some being more 'ruffled' than others.*

Cacti and succulents

SOME PEOPLE ARE FASCINATED BY CACTI AND THEY BECOME A PASSIONATE

HOBBY, OTHERS DISMISS THEM AS BEING NOT QUITE 'REAL' HOUSEPLANTS.

WHATEVER YOU THINK OF THEM, CACTI AND SUCCULENTS ARE SOME OF THE

EASIEST PLANTS TO LOOK AFTER AND MAKE THE IDEAL CHOICE IF YOU OFTEN

HAVE TO LEAVE YOUR HOUSEPLANTS UNATTENDED.

Cacti can be very beautiful in flower, and a huge epiphyllum bloom can be almost breath-takingly beautiful, but you will probably decide whether or not to grow cacti depending on whether you like or dislike their overall shape and form. It has to be admitted that a few, like the epiphyllum just mentioned, can be ungainly and unattractive when out of bloom, but the vast majority are neat, compact and in the eyes of most people have a fascinating beauty of their own. There are species that creep and cascade, others which have hairy or cylindrical spiny columns, some with flat jointed pads, and others with globular or candelabra shapes.

Succulents are just as diverse: some are grown for their flowers, others for shape or foliage effect. There are hundreds of them readily available, and many more can be found in specialist nurseries.

Flowers of the desert

These need minimal water between mid-autumn and early spring, but plenty of sunshine at all times. As a rule, keep them cool in winter (about 10°C/50°F) to encourage flowering. Repot annually when young, but later only repot when really necessary as a small pot also hastens flowering.

Not all cacti will flower when young, so if you want some that flower freely on young plants, look for species of echinopsis, lobivia, mammillaria, notocactus, parodia and rebutia.

Forest cacti

The forest cacti, which have flattened, leaf-like stems, are the most popular type of cacti. To keep them flowering well each year remember not to treat them like ordinary cacti, and follow these basic guidelines.

Exact treatment depends on the species, but they will require a resting period, when they are kept cool and watered only infrequently, usually mid-autumn to mid-winter or late winter to early spring, followed by a period of warmth when they are watered freely. They will also benefit from spending the summer in a shady spot outdoors.

LEFT: *Cacti often look better in small groups rather than as isolated specimens. In the group shown here, a grafted cactus (to the left of the arrangement) has been used to add additional interest.*

BELOW: *Epiphyllums have huge flowers and are among the most spectacular cacti in bloom. Unfortunately they look ugly and ungainly out of flower, so for most of the year you will want to relegate them to an inconspicuous spot.*

Succulents

Succulents vary enormously in their requirements – some, such as sempervivums, are tough and frost-tolerant, others are tender and temperamental. Always look up the specific needs for each plant, but as a rule they need very good light and little water in winter.

Displaying and collecting

Few cacti and succulents make good focal point plants – though a large epiphyllum in a porch can be a real stunner – and they are generally best displayed as groups in dish gardens (shallow planters) or troughs. Cascading cacti, however, like the forest cacti already mentioned, are almost always displayed in isolation and look good on a pedestal while they are in bloom. But if you have a conservatory, you can try planting several of them in a hanging basket.

Cacti are very collectable, and you can grow literally hundreds of them in a modest-sized home. A frost-free greenhouse widens the scope considerably, and you can rotate the plants with those indoors, to maintain variety and interest.

Handling cacti

Repotting a cactus can be a prickly job. Make it easier on your hands by folding up a strip of newspaper or brown paper (top). Wrap this around the plant leaving enough paper at each end to form a handle (above).

CACTUS OR SUCCULENT?

Succulent simply means a plant that has adapted to dry conditions and can retain moisture with minimal loss from its leaves, which are often plump and fleshy. Cacti are also succulents, but in all except a few primitive species the leaves have become modified to spines or hairs and the stems have taken over the function of leaves – being thick, fleshy and with the ability to photosynthesize.

Although most cacti have their natural home in warm, semi-desert regions of America, some grow as epiphytes on trees in the forests of tropical America. Some of these, such as zygocactus, schlumbergera and rhipsalidopsis, have produced hybrids and varieties that are popular flowering houseplants in winter and spring.

ABOVE: Crassula ovata, *like most succulents, is undemanding and will thrive with just a modicum of care.*

FAR LEFT: Euphorbia trigona *is an easy-to-grow succulent with distinctive three- to four-sided branches.*

LEFT: Sansevieria trifasciata *'Laurentii' is an attractive variegated plant that is really tough and needs minimal attention.*

Bromeliads

BROMELIADS ARE STRANGE PLANTS. SOME HAVE LEAVES THAT FORM WATER-HOLDING VASES, OTHERS HAVE BRIGHTLY COLOURED LEAVES THAT MAKE A SUBSTITUTE FOR COLOURFUL FLOWERS, AND A FEW ACTUALLY GROW ON AIR AND NEED NO SOIL.

Some bromeliads – aechmeas, vrieseas and guzmanias for example – are grown for their attractive flower heads as well as for their foliage. A few – billbergias, for example – have individual flowers that are both strange and beautiful. The vast majority are best considered as foliage plants. Some, such as neoregelias, form a rosette of leaves that becomes brightly coloured in the centre when the plants flower, others like cryptanthus are prettily variegated. The pineapple is the best-known bromeliad, but it is the variegated forms such as *Ananas comosus* 'Variegatus' that are generally grown as houseplants.

Air plants
A large group of tillandsias are known as air plants because they grow without soil. In nature they drape themselves over branches or even wires, or cling to rocks. One of the most attractive ways to display them is on a bromeliad tree (see opposite), but you can buy them displayed in shells, baskets, or even attached to a mirror with glue. You can also improvise with any suitable containers that you have around the house.

• Mist the plants regularly, especially from spring to autumn. This is the only way that they can receive moisture if the air itself is not sufficiently humid.
• Feed by adding a very dilute liquid fertilizer to the misting water, perhaps once a fortnight, when the plants are actively growing.

CARING FOR BROMELIADS

🐾 Bromeliads need special care. The following advice applies to most kinds, but see the separate instructions for air plant tillandsias.

🐾 Most kinds need only moderate warmth (about 10°C/50°F), but some need 24°C/75° to flower.

🐾 Give them good light, out of direct sun (a few, such as cryptanthus and pineapples, will tolerate full sun).

🐾 Grow in small pots as they don't need much compost (potting soil), and water only when the compost becomes almost dry.

🐾 Use a peat-based compost rather than one with loam, and if possible mix in perlite or sphagnum moss.

🐾 For those that form a 'vase', keep this topped up with water (rainwater in hard-water areas).

🐾 Mist the leaves in summer, and add a foliar feed occasionally. Vase types can have a one-third strength fertilizer added to the vase water every couple of weeks.

ABOVE LEFT: *Most tillandsias are popularly known as air plants because they do not need planting in compost (potting soil). They are very ornamental when mounted on a piece of bark or driftwood.*

LEFT: **Neoregelia carolinae** *is typical of the 'vase' bromeliads. The central leaves colour when the small flowers appear in the central vase formed by the rosette of leaves.*

OPPOSITE LEFT: **Ananas bracteatus striatus** *is a variegated version of the pineapple that makes a striking houseplant.*

OPPOSITE RIGHT: *Most guzmanias, like G. lingulata, have long-lasting flower heads.*

BELOW: *Aechmea fasciata has weird but beautiful flowers, set off by bold, greyish foliage.*

MAKE A BROMELIAD TREE

🔖 The size and shape of your 'tree' will depend on the space that you have available, a suitable container, and the size of your branch. Choose a forked branch from a tree and saw it to size.

Anchor the branch in the container with stones, bricks or beach pebbles – this will add weight and stability as well as holding the branch upright. Then pour in plaster of Paris or a mortar or concrete mix, to within a couple of centimetres (an inch) of the top of the container. You can set a few empty pots into the plaster or concrete to allow for planting into the base later.

When the plaster or concrete has set, wire your bromeliads to the tree. Remove most of the compost (potting soil) from the roots, and pack some sphagnum moss around them. Secure the roots to the tree with plastic-covered or copper wire. Make sure that you take advantage of any forks in the branch to hold an attractive bromeliad.

Air plant tillandsias such as *T. usneoides* can simply be draped over the branches; other species may have to be wired or glued on.

Flowering houseplants

FLOWERING HOUSEPLANTS ARE USUALLY SHORT-LIVED IN THE HOME, BUT
THEY BRING A SPLASH OF COLOUR AND VIBRANCY THAT NOT EVEN COL-
OURED FOLIAGE CAN ACHIEVE. THEY ALSO ADD AN ELEMENT OF SEASONAL
VARIATION THAT FOLIAGE PLANTS LACK.

The most rewarding flowering houseplants are those that grow bigger and better each year, with each subsequent blooming crowning another year of good cultivation and care. Flowers that you should be able to keep growing in the home from year to year include beloperones, bougainvilleas, *Campanula isophylla,* clivias, gardenias, hoyas, *Jasminum polyanthum, Nerium oleander,* pelargoniums, saintpaulias, spathiphyllums and streptocarpus.

The disposables
Many flowering pot plants are difficult to keep permanently in the home and are best discarded when flowering has finished (or in some cases placed in a greenhouse if you have one). They are no less valuable indoors, and should be

regarded rather like long-lasting cut flowers. A lot of them are annuals and can, therefore, be inexpensively raised from seed: try browallias, calceolarias, cinerarias and exacums, which are all bright and cheerful, inexpensive to buy and not difficult to raise from seed yourself.

Annuals die after flowering and have to be discarded, but others are just not worth the effort of trying to

LEFT: **Begonia elatior** *hybrids can be in flower for most months of the year, but plants like the dwarf narcissus 'Tete-a-Tete' are especially welcome because of their seasonal nature.*

BELOW LEFT: *Varieties of* **Kalanchoe blossfeldiana** *are available in flower the year round.*

BELOW: *Pot-grown lilies make striking houseplants, but it is usually better to buy them in flower rather than try to grow your own from bulbs. Commercial growers can ensure that suitable dwarf varieties are used, and chemicals are often employed to keep the plants compact. Plant them in the garden to flower in future years.*

save in home conditions. Impatiens are often leggy if saved, and easy to raise or cheap to buy. Hiemalis begonias quickly deteriorate and are difficult to keep healthy. Furthermore, they are so cheap to buy that it's hardly worth taking up valuable space with them once flowering is over. Garden bulbs like hyacinths may bloom beautifully if forced for early flowering, but they will fail to give an acceptable repeat performance and are therefore best put out in the garden to recover and give a garden display in future years.

Hardy border plants such as astilbes are sometimes sold as pot plants. They look magnificent in flower, but the pot of large leaves left afterwards is hardly attractive, and the plant is almost sure to deteriorate if kept indoors. By planting it in the garden after flowering you will have enjoyed plumes of beauty for a few weeks after purchase, then years of pleasure in the garden afterwards.

Tricked into flowering

Some plants are tricked into flowering at a particular time, or into blooming on compact plants. You won't be able to reproduce these conditions in the home. Year-round chrysanthemums are made to bloom every month of the

RIGHT: *Saintpaulias are among the most popular flowering plants, and there are so many variations in flower shape, size and colour that you can easily form an interesting collection of them.*

BELOW LEFT: *Hydrangeas make attractive houseplants if bought in flower, but they do not make easy long-term residents in the home. Try planting them in the garden when they have finished flowering.*

BELOW RIGHT: *Impatiens have always been popular houseplants, but the New Guinea types have bolder foliage than the older types usually grown. Some also have striking variegated leaves, as a bonus to the pretty flowers.*

year by having their day length adjusted by special lighting and by blacking out the greenhouse. They will probably be blooming on compact plants because they have been treated with dwarfing chemicals, the effects of which gradually wear off. If you manage to keep them going, they will become taller and probably flower at a different time. Try planting them in the garden – some varieties will thrive as garden plants if the winters are not too severe.

The poinsettia (*Euphorbia pulcherrima*) is another plant that is controlled by manipulating day length and in which height is also chemically controlled. Some people keep them successfully for future years, but they become taller plants, and the colourful bracts are produced at a different time of year unless their day length is controlled. This can be done by covering with a black polythene bag for fourteen hours a day for eight weeks. It is much easier to buy new plants.

Kalanchoes are also induced to flower outside their normal period by adjusting day length in the same way.

BRIGHT BERRIES

Don't overlook plants with bright berries. These will often remain attractive for much longer than flowers; some of the most popular ones are easily raised from seed and are relatively inexpensive if you have to buy them. Annual peppers (*Capsicum annuum*) have cone-shaped fruits in shades of yellow, red, and purple. *Solanum capsicastrum* has orange or red berries shaped like small tomatoes – and with luck you can keep the plant going for another year, placing it outdoors for the summer. Remember to keep the air humid by misting periodically to prevent berries dropping prematurely.

OPPOSITE ABOVE: *Year-round chrysanthemums make excellent short-term houseplants. They are best bought in bud or flower then enjoyed for a few weeks before being discarded.*

OPPOSITE BELOW: *Berries can be as bright as flowers, and often last for much longer. Those of* Solanum capsicastrum *and* S. pseudocapsicum *and their hybrids look like cherry-sized tomatoes. The plants are usually discarded after flowering but can be kept for another year.*

TOP LEFT: Beloperone guttata *is easy to grow, long-lasting in flower, and you should be able to keep it from year to year.*

TOP RIGHT: Primula obconica *is a delightful houseplant when it is in flower. However, some people have an allergic reaction to the leaves.*

CENTRE RIGHT: *The azalea most commonly sold as a pot plant, and sometimes called* Azalea indica, *is botanically* Rhododendron simsii.

RIGHT: Euphorbia pulcherrima, *the so-called poinsettia, has insignificant true flowers, but really spectacular and colourful bracts to surround them.*

GARDEN ANNUALS

☙ If you have a few spare plants after planting out the summer bedding, it might be worth potting some of them up into larger pots to use indoors. Among those that can make attractive short-term houseplants if the position is light enough are ageratums, lobelias, salvias and French marigolds.

Scent in the air

SCENT ADDS ANOTHER DIMENSION TO YOUR PLANTS, AND IT'S NOT ONLY
FLOWERS THAT ARE FRAGRANT. TAKE ANOTHER JOURNEY OF DISCOVERY
WITH SOME OF THE AROMATIC HOUSEPLANTS THAT WILL MAKE YOU WONDER
WHY YOU EVER USED CHEMICAL AIR FRESHENERS.

ABOVE: *The flowers of* Gardenia
jasminoides *are pure white in full bloom,
darkening to a creamy-yellow with age,
and are richly fragrant.*

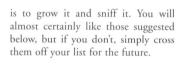

BELOW LEFT: **Datura suaveolens** *(syn.*
Brugmansia suaveolens*) is a large and
magnificent plant, with huge bell-like
flowers and a strength of scent that matches
the size of the blooms. This variety is
'Grand Marnier'.*

Perception of scent is an individual experience, and one that is more developed in some individuals than in others. Our ability to detect scents can be affected by the way in which our scent receptors are genetically determined. Some people are scent blind in the same way in which some people are colour blind. They can detect most smells but have a deficiency in certain types: someone who can smell a rose or a sweet pea might be unable to appreciate the equally potent perfume of the freesia. This makes it difficult to recommend specific plants to others without qualification: the plants suggested here have a smell readily de-

tected by most people, but you may find a particular scent weak or even indiscernible.

Scent is further complicated by individual reactions to a scent when it is detected. Sometimes this may be for biochemical reasons, but it may even be that some scents are associated with pleasant or unpleasant experiences. There are scented-leaved geraniums (pelargoniums) that might remind one person of the tangy fragrance of lemons while another may detect a thymol smell in them that reminds them of an earlier visit to a dentist.

The only way to discover whether you like the scent of a particular plant

is to grow it and sniff it. You will almost certainly like those suggested below, but if you don't, simply cross them off your list for the future.

Placing scented plants

Plants that have a delicate fragrance, which you have to sniff at close quarters, such as an exacum, need to be positioned where sniffing is easy – perhaps on a table or shelf that you pass in the hall, or as a centrepiece for the dining table.

Plants with a dominant scent, like gardenias and hyacinths, can be so potent that one plant will fill the whole room with scent. It doesn't matter where you place these in the room, but avoid other fragrant plants that may conflict with them; place these in another room where you can appreciate their own distinct fragrances in isolation.

ABOVE: Stephanotis floribunda *is a very fragrant climber that can be grown as a pot plant while young.*

ABOVE CENTRE: *A bowl of hyacinths will fill a room with scent. Although they are at their best for perhaps a week, by planting different varieties, and using ordinary bulbs and those specially treated for early flowering, you can enjoy them over a period of months.*

ABOVE RIGHT: *Scented-leaved geraniums (pelargoniums) usually have insignificant flowers. Grow them for their aromatic foliage and position them where you might accidentally brush against them, or can touch the leaves to release their pungent fragrance. This is* Pelargonium graveolens, *with a scent reminiscent of lemons.*

BELOW: *Oranges make superb conservatory plants, and can be brought into the house for short spells.*

FRAGRANT FOLIAGE

Some of the best plants to grow for fragrant foliage are the scented-leaved geraniums (pelargoniums). These are just of few of them:
P. capitatum (rose-scented)
P. crispum (lemon-scented)
P. graveolens (slightly lemony)
P. odoratissimum (apple-scented)
P. tomentosum (peppermint-scented)

Plants that you have to touch or brush against to release the scent, like scented-leaved geraniums (pelargoniums), should be placed where you might come into contact with them accidentally, or intentionally, as you pass: alcoves or windows by a flight of stairs and on the kitchen table or worktop, for example.

SCENTED FLOWERS

Citrus (fragrant flowers, citrus-scented foliage and fruit)
Datura suaveolens
Exacum affine
Hyacinths
Hymenocallis × festalis, H. narcissiflora
Jasminum officinale
Narcissus 'Paperwhite'
Stephanotis floribunda

Orchids and other exotics

ADD A TOUCH OF CLASS TO YOUR COLLECTION OF HOUSEPLANTS BY GROWING
A FEW ORCHIDS, ALONG WITH OTHER EXOTICS, SUCH AS STRELITZIA, THE
'BIRD OF PARADISE FLOWER'.

Orchids have a reputation for being difficult to grow and, consequently, many people are deterred from trying them as houseplants. If you choose the right types, however, they are relatively undemanding and should make larger and more impressive clumps each year.

The drawback to orchids is the contrast between the beauty of their exotic flowers and the rather ungainly foliage with which you have to live for the other ten or eleven months of the year. The best way to grow them is to stand the plants in a sheltered and partially shaded spot in the garden during the summer – or better still in a conservatory if you have one – and then to bring them indoors for the winter or when they are coming into flower.

Easy orchids

The best orchids to start with are cymbidium hybrids, which are easy to grow, readily available and inexpensive to buy if you are not fussy about a particular variety.

Miltonias are a better choice if you want a more compact plant. The large, flat, pansy-like flowers come in a range of brilliant colours, and will often last for a month.

Cypripediums (paphiopedilums) are another group of distinctive and easy orchids to try. Sometimes called slipper orchids, the bottom petals form a slipper-shaped pouch.

Other orchids can be grown indoors, especially if you are able to create a special area for them, perhaps with artificial light, but it is best to gain experience first with the easy genera described above.

Other exotics

Try some of the following exotic-looking flowering plants that will bring some of the brilliance and flamboyance of the tropics to your home.

Anthuriums have vivid pink, red or orange 'flowers' that will never be ignored. The 'flower' is actually a spathe and it is the curly tail-like spadix that contains the true flowers. The 'flowers' are long-lasting and the foliage is attractive too.

Bougainvilleas are at their best climbing into the roof of a conservatory, but you could try one in a porch or light window. The bright 'flowers' are actually papery bracts. Prune after flowering and keep cool but frost-free for the winter.

Grooming orchids
With age, orchid leaves often become blemished. If the damage is towards the end of the leaf, try cutting it away. Angle the cut to make the end a more natural shape than if cut at right-angles.

Daturas are big plants, really at their best in a conservatory, although you can use small plants indoors. The huge bell-like flowers are usually white, pink or yellowish, depending on the species and variety. The heady scent matches the magnificence of the blooms, and even a single flower can almost fill a small house with scent in the evening.

Hibiscus rosa-sinensis grows into quite a large shrub but can be bought as a small plant. The blooms are big and beautiful: 10cm (4in) or more across, in shades of red, yellow and almost orange.

Strelitzias are sometimes called 'bird of paradise flowers' because the orange and blue flowers are thought to resemble the head of an exotic-looking bird. The leaves are often 1m (3ft) or more tall, and a large plant is truly spectacular.

HOW TO GROW ORCHIDS

🍃 It is best to check the specific requirements for each species, but the following rules apply to most:

🍃 Place them in a very light position, but not in direct, strong sunlight.

🍃 Provide plenty of humidity. Stand the pots on a gravel tray, or mist regularly. Small plants do well in an enclosed plant case.

🍃 Avoid draughts, but provide plenty of ventilation. Move them away from a cold window at night.

🍃 Repot only when the pot is full of roots. Always use a special potting mixture recommended for orchids (you may have to buy it from a specialist nursery).

🍃 Feed regularly during the summer.

🍃 Stand the plants outdoors in a sheltered position for the summer if you don't have a conservatory to put them in.

🍃 Water only when the compost (potting soil) is almost dry.

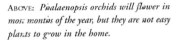

OPPOSITE TOP: **Strelitzia reginae**, *the 'bird of paradise flower', never fails to impress with its flamboyant flowers.*

OPPOSITE CENTRE: *The red or pink 'petals' that surround the insignificant proper flowers of the striking anthuriums are in fact modified leaves.*

TOP: *Bougainvilleas have a really exotic look, and although they are climbers can be used as a houseplant while small. Larger plants are best in a conservatory.*

ABOVE: *Phalaenopsis orchids will flower in most months of the year, but they are not easy plants to grow in the home.*

ABOVE RIGHT: *Cymbidiums are among the easiest orchids to grow in the house, but even so they usually benefit from a spell outdoors or in the greenhouse during the summer months.*

RIGHT: **Hibiscus rosa-sinensis** *blooms are big, bold and bright; they seldom fail to attract attention.*

Fun plants

SOME PLANTS ARE ENTERTAINING OR EDUCATIONAL RATHER THAN BEAUTI-

FUL. THEY ARE A GOOD WAY TO INSTILL CHILDREN WITH AN APPRECIATION

OF PLANTS, BUT SOME OF THEM MAKE INTERESTING HOUSEPLANTS TOO.

Carnivorous plants always fascinate children. Few of them are beautiful, though some have quite pretty flowers. *Pinguicula grandiflora* has pretty pink flowers like violets on long stalks that seem to last for weeks. Most have uninteresting flowers, however, and their attraction lies solely in the various forms of trap.

Some cannot be grown satisfactorily in the home, but the following are worth trying: *Dionaea muscipula* (a snap trap), *Drosera capensis* (an adhesive trap), *Pinguicula grandiflora* (a 'fly paper' trap), and *Sarracenia flava* (a pitfall trap). Enthusiasts grow dozens of different kinds, but these represent four different types of trap and all make quite acceptable houseplants, though they must be treated with care if they are not to be short-lived.

Sensitive plants

Several plants are sensitive to touch, collapsing on contact. The most widely available one is *Mimosa pudica,* which makes quite a pretty plant with its sensitive leaflets and attractive flowers like pink balls. It's easy to raise from seed if you can't find plants in local nurseries or garden centres.

Leaves that bear 'babies'

Some plants have the ability to produce small plantlets on the leaves, which eventually fall and root (or you can speed things up by removing them and potting them up).

Two that are quite widely available are *Kalanchoe daigremontiana* (syn. *Bryophyllum daigremontianum*), which has miniature plants all around the edge of the leaf, and *K. tubiflora* (syn.

Bryophyllum tubiflorum), which produces them in clusters at the ends of the leaves.

Other widely available plants that produce ready-made 'babies' are the fern *Asplenium bulbiferum* and *Tolmiea menziesii* (young plantlets form at the base of mature leaves).

Bulbs that flower without soil

For a novelty, try flowering colchicums 'dry'. You can just stand them on the windowsill after purchase, but for stability it is best to place them on a saucer of sand. Usually within weeks, the large crocus-like flowers emerge from the dry bulb.

An unusual bulb called *Sauromatum venosum* (syn. *S. guttatum*) is sometimes sold as a novelty for flowering 'dry' (treat like the colchicums). The tube-like flower that eventually emerges is a sinister greenish-purple. This strange flower will soon make its presence known by the awful stench of carrion – fascinating for children, but not something to have in your living-room for long!

OPPOSITE ABOVE: **Colchicum autumnale** *can be grown 'dry'. Either stand the corms directly on a windowsill or place them in a saucer of sand or pebbles for stability, and wait just a few weeks for the large crocus-like flowers to emerge.*

OPPOSITE BELOW: **Dionaea muscipula** *is a carnivorous plant with a snap trap that quickly closes over its prey.*

TOP RIGHT: **Sarracenia flava** *is a carnivorous plant with a pitfall trap.*

CENTRE RIGHT: **Drosera capensis** *is an example of an adhesive trap, and makes an interesting addition to a collection of carnivorous plants.*

LEFT AND ABOVE: **Kalanchoe daigremontiana** *(syn.* Bryophyllum daigremontianum*) produces plantlets along the edges of its leaves (left). These often* fall and root into the compost (potting soil) around the parent plant, but you can easily remove them to pot up for a supply of plants to give to friends (above left).*

CARING FOR CARNIVOROUS PLANTS

🌿 Don't use an ordinary potting compost. It needs to be acidic and low in soluble minerals. A suitable compost (medium) usually includes peat (peat moss), sand, sphagnum moss, and sometimes perlite or finely chipped bark.

🌿 Grow a collection of them in a plant case or old aquarium. Cover it if possible, to create a humid environment.

🌿 Provide good light.

🌿 Stand the pots on trays of gravel filled with water to provide humidity if not in an enclosed environment.

🌿 Some species prefer a constantly wet compost and you can stand these in a saucer that is kept topped up with water (not advisable for normal houseplants).

🌿 Only ever use soft water (distilled or deionized would do, but rain-water is best).

🌿 It is best not to use a fertilizer. Most may be harmful, and if you think the plants really do need feeding, try misting them with a foliar feed made up at quarter strength, about once a fortnight during the period of active growth.

🌿 These plants catch prey to obtain nutrients, but indoors the number of insects available to them will be limited. Some people release fruit flies near them or feed them with fly maggots (often available from fishing tackle shops).

Caring for houseplants

IF YOU WANT YOUR HOUSEPLANTS TO THRIVE, THEY NEED CARING FOR AND NURTURING. YOU HAVE TO CHOOSE AND BUY WISELY, UNDERSTAND THE NEEDS OF INDIVIDUAL PLANTS AND MAKE GROOMING A REGULAR JOB, JUST LIKE WATERING AND FEEDING.

Shopping for houseplants

SHOPPING FOR NEW AND INTERESTING HOUSEPLANTS CAN BE FUN, BUT BE WARY ABOUT WHERE AND WHEN YOU BUY. A PLANT THAT HAS BEEN POORLY TREATED BEFORE YOU BUY IT MAY ONLY REVEAL THE ILL-TREATMENT AFTER YOU GET IT HOME.

Choosing houseplants requires as much thought and care as the purchase of anything else for the home. Indeed, some plants will be with you for much longer than many household items.

You can buy a plant simply because you like the look of it, then try to find a suitable spot; or decide what you need to fill a particular niche in the home, before going out to buy an appropriate plant. The latter is undoubtedly the theoretical ideal, but it overlooks reality.

Except for the most common house-plants, the chances of finding a particular plant, even over several shopping trips, is not great and, more importantly, you may overlook a beautiful plant that you hadn't previously considered. Part of the fun of growing plants is to come across unexpected discoveries, plants that you've never seen before. Although advance planning is desirable, never be deterred from the impulse buy of something interesting or unusual, especially if you are prepared for a few failures along the way.

Where to buy

For everyday houseplants, a garden centre is often the best place to buy: there is likely to be a reasonable selection of 'basic' houseplants, and usually at least a few uncommon kinds. Most importantly, they will almost certainly be in conditions similar to a greenhouse: good light, warmth (ventilated in summer), with a buoyant and humid atmosphere. Staff are also

ABOVE: *Try to buy your houseplants from a nursery or garden centre where they have excellent growing conditions in good light.*

GETTING THEM HOME

🌿 Buy your plants last, immediately before you go home.

🌿 Don't put plants in a hot car boot (trunk), especially if you don't plan to drive straight home, or if the drive is a long one.

🌿 Make sure that they are wrapped in a protective sleeve if carrying them home by public transport. This will protect them from cold and wind, and guard against knocks.

usually knowledgeable, but beware of assuming that part-time or temporary staff know more than you do!

Florists also sell pot plants but, except for the very largest shops, the range is inevitably limited and conditions are seldom good. Some florists have pavement displays outside the shop, in which they include pot plants as well as cut flowers. Avoid these: you run the same risks as with market stalls (outdoor stands), where at least the price is usually cheaper.

Some large stores sell a limited range of plants. At the best of them the quality is excellent, with the plants well looked after and removed from sale if not bought within a certain time. In others they can languish in poor light and with inadequate care, slowly deteriorating until they reach the point of death. The quality and condition of plants sold by ordinary shops or home-improvement stores vary enormously. Go through the *Buyer's checklist* below carefully before buying from these sources.

Market stalls often sell plants at very competitive prices, and they are usually sold quickly, so it is possible to obtain quality plants cheaply if you don't mind the limited range. Beware of buying in cold weather – especially in winter. The chill plants receive, having come out of hot-house conditions, may not be obvious until a few days after you get them home, when the leaves start to drop. Even in the summer, houseplants displayed outdoors can suffer a severe check to growth if the weather is cold or windy.

Buyer's checklist

- Check the compost (potting soil). If it has dried out the plants have been neglected. Don't buy.
- Lift and check the base of the pot. If lots of roots are coming out of the bottom, the plant should have been repotted sooner. A few small roots through the bottom of the pot is not a sign of neglect, and is normal where the plants have been grown on capillary matting.

- If buying a flowering plant, make sure that there are still plenty of buds to open, otherwise the display may be brief.
- Look critically at the shape. If growth is lop-sided, or the plant is bare at the base, choose another.
- Make sure the plant is labelled. A label should tell you how to care for the plant, and unlabelled plants suggest a lack of concern for plants and customers.
- Avoid plants with damaged or broken leaves.
- Don't be afraid to turn the leaves over. Look for signs of pests and diseases. If you find any, leave them in the shop!
- If the plants are displayed in a protective sleeve, don't buy unless you can remove your potential purchase for inspection. Display sleeves can hide all kinds of horrors, such as rots and diseases, pests, and even a sparse or poorly shaped plant.

Root check

It is natural for a few roots to grow through the bottom of the pot, especially if a capillary watering system has been used (which is normal in plant nurseries), but a mass of roots growing through the pot is probably a sign that the plant needs repotting.

Flowering plants

When buying a flowering plant, make sure that there are plenty of buds still to open. A plant in full flower may be more spectacular initially, but the display will be shorter.

Pests and diseases

Examine the undersides of a few leaves to make sure they are free of pests and diseases before you buy.

Pot sizes

Houseplants look better, and will grow better, if they are in a pot of an appropriate size. The plant in the picture at the top of the page is in a pot that's too large – it dominates the plant. The one shown above is in a pot that's too small; not only is it top-heavy and unstable, but the amount of compost (potting soil) in the pot is unlikely to be sufficient to sustain the plant.

Protective sleeves

These can be useful: they help to get the plant home with minimum damage and offer some protection from cold winds in winter. But make sure they don't hide damaged or diseased leaves. Be prepared to remove the sleeve to examine a plant if they are displayed in this way.

Creating the right environment

IT'S IMPOSSIBLE TO RECREATE THE ATMOSPHERE OF A SOUTH AMERICAN

RAINFOREST OR THE SEMI-DESERT CONDITIONS OF THE WORLD'S MORE ARID

REGIONS IN OUR HOMES. YET WE EXPECT ORCHIDS AND BROMELIADS TO

THRIVE ALONGSIDE CACTI AND SUCCULENTS, PLANTS FROM THE WORLD'S

WARMEST REGIONS TO COEXIST WITH HARDY PLANTS SUCH AS IVIES AND

AUCUBAS. CREATING THE RIGHT CONDITIONS TO SUIT SUCH A DIVERSITY OF

PLANTS, WHILE KEEPING A HOME THAT'S ALSO COMFORTABLE TO LIVE IN,

CALLS FOR INGENUITY AND A DASH OF COMPROMISE.

Use the advice on labels and in books as a guide to the best conditions in which to keep your plants. In reality you may not be able to accommodate all the conditions listed as desirable, but most plants will still survive even if they do not thrive. Take recommendations for humidity seriously: a plant that requires very high humidity is likely to die soon in very dry air. Recommendations regarding light and shade are important but if you get this slightly wrong the consequence is more likely to be poor variegation, perhaps scorch marks on the leaves, or drawn and lanky plants, rather than dead ones. You can usually correct the problem by moving the plant.

Temperature is the most flexible requirement, and most plants will tolerate a wide fluctuation above or below the suggested targets.

Temperature

Treat with caution advice in books and on labels that gives a precise temperature range. Most plants will survive temperatures much lower than the ones normally recommended, and, in winter when the light is poor, a high temperature may stimulate growth that can't be supported by the light levels. Upper temperature figures are meaningless unless you have air conditioning. In summer the outside temperature often rises above those recommended for particular plants, and unless you have some way of cooling the air, the plants will have to suffer the heat along with you. They will almost certainly come to no harm if shaded from direct sun and provided that the humidity is high enough.

Once the temperature drops towards freezing, however, most houseplants are at risk. Even in a centrally heated home, temperatures can drop very low if heating is turned off at night.

Light and shade

The best position for most plants is in good light but out of direct sun. Even plants that thrive in sun outdoors may resent the strongly magnified rays through glass, which will often scorch the leaves. Be especially wary of positioning plants behind patterned glass in full sun: the pattern can magnify the sun's rays.

Only plants that normally grow in deserts, on steppes, high mountains and barren moors grow in areas devoid of shade. And even these may not like the sun's rays intensified through glass. If possible, fit shades that you can use for the hottest part of the day. Even net curtains are useful in screening out some of the strongest rays.

The so-called shade plants do not like any direct sun, but that does not necessarily mean that they will grow in gloom. The eye is deceptive when it comes to judging light levels. Use a camera fitted with a light meter, and measure the light in different parts of the room. You might discover that the light is as poor immediately above or below a window as it is in the centre of the room. If the windows are high, experiment with the light meter to see how much better the light might be if

Effects of heat

Leaf scorch (brown marks or blotches that leave the areas looking thin and papery) is a common problem on plants placed on a very sunny windowsill. Unless they are adapted to this kind of intense heat, the tissue of the leaves can be damaged. The problem is most likely if drops of water are left on the foliage in bright sunlight (the water acts like a magnifying glass) or where patterned glass intensifies the sun's rays as it acts like a lens.

you raised a plant on a pedestal or positioned it on a low table.

Humidity

Humidity – or the amount of moisture present in the air at a given temperature – is important to all plants, but especially those with thin or delicate leaves, such as ferns, selaginellas and caladiums. Grow those plants that need a very humid atmosphere in a bottle garden or plant case, or mist the plants frequently (at least once a day, more often if possible).

For less demanding plants that still need high humidity, grow them in groups to create a microclimate or stand the plants on gravel, pebbles or marbles in a shallow dish containing water. Provided that the bottom of the pot is not in direct contact with the water the air will be humid without the compost becoming waterlogged. Misting is still desirable, but if the plants are in flower shield the blooms while you do so, otherwise the petals may become marked or begin to rot.

Simple humidity trays to place over radiators are inexpensive and help to create a more buoyant atmosphere for houseplants.

ABOVE: *Plants like schizanthus and cinerarias will make a super show if you can provide good light and humid conditions.*

Increasing humidity
It can be difficult to create a humid environment in the home, but a small microclimate can be created around the plant. Standing the plant over a dish containing water will increase the humidity, but the pot must be stood on small pebbles or marbles to keep it above water level and avoid waterlogged compost (potting soil).

Misting foliage plants
The majority of houseplants will benefit from misting with water. If you can do it daily the plants will almost certainly grow better. Delicate ferns that need a very high humidity may need misting several times a day for really good results.

Misting flowering plants
Although the foliage benefits from misting, water can damage delicate flowers. Simply protect the blooms with a piece of paper or cardboard if the plant is in flower.

Windowsill plants

WINDOWSILLS ARE A FAVOURITE POSITION FOR HOUSEPLANTS, BUT YOU
NEED TO CHOOSE PLANTS APPROPRIATE TO THE ASPECT. NOT ALL PLANTS
APPRECIATE A BAKING IN THE SUNSHINE.

ABOVE: Hoya carnosa *is a pretty climber or trailer for a sunny position. It is usually grown for its white flowers, but the variegated 'Tricolor' also makes an attractive foliage plant.*

It is a good idea to analyse the amount of direct light coming through each window before deciding on the best spots for various plants with different light needs. Large windows obviously let in most light, but it will still be less than outdoors, and the larger the area of glass, the more rapidly temperatures drop at night.

The majority of plants flourish best when placed in good light in a position that is shaded from the direct rays of the sun. There are bound to be some rooms that receive little direct light, but most will receive some sun at least in the morning or evening. Except for shade lovers that are particularly vulnerable to direct sun, the majority of plants will benefit from this as the strength of the sun is generally weaker in the early morning and evening, so leaf scorch is less likely. The compost (potting soil) is also less likely to dry out rapidly if the sun has moved around before its midday peak.

Very sunny windows can still be packed with interest if you select the plants carefully, but be prepared to keep the compost well watered in warm weather. Avoid splashing the leaves when the sun is on them, however, as the droplets of water can act like a further magnifying glass and scorch the leaves.

The lists of suggested plants given here are not definitive, but an example of what can be grown. Be prepared to experiment with many more, especially on a light windowsill that does not receive fierce direct sun.

Where only the genus is mentioned, all the widely available species sold as houseplants should be successful.

You will find some plants listed in more than one group. Many plants will grow in sun or partial shade and a few will do well in both direct sun and indirect light.

Plants for a very sunny window
Ananas, cacti, ceropegia, chlorophytum, coleus, geraniums (pelargoniums), regal, zonal, scented-leaved, gerbera, hippeastrum, *Hoya carnosa,* hypocyrta, impatiens, iresine, *Kalanchoe blossfeldiana* and hybrids, nerium, *Plectranthus fruticosus,* sansevieria, setcreasea, stapelia, succulents (most), yucca and zebrina.

Plants for a window that receives early or late sun
Aechmea, aglaonema, anthurium, aphelandra, begonia, beloperone, billbergia, caladium, calathea, capsicum, chlorophytum, chrysanthemum, cocos, codiaeum, coleus, *Cordyline terminalis* (syn. *C. fruticosa*) and varieties, crossandra, cuphea, ficus (most), gardenia, gynura, hoya, impatiens, maranta, nertera, *Plectranthus oertendahlii,* rhipsalidopsis, saintpaulia, sansevieria, sinningia, solanum, spathiphyllum, tolmiea, tradescantia, zebrina.

Plants for a light window out of direct sunlight
Adiantum, aglaonema, anthurium, asparagus, aspidistra, asplenium, billbergia, calathea, chlorophytum, clivia, dieffenbachia, dracaena, ferns, *Ficus deltoidea, Ficus pumila,* hydrangea, maranta, orchids, saintpaulia, sansevieria, selaginella, soleirolia (syn. helxine), spathiphyllum.

ABOVE: Aphelandra squarrosa *needs good light but not direct summer sun. Grow it where it just receives early or late sun in the summer and in the best light possible in winter.*

ABOVE: *Gerberas will tolerate a very sunny position, but if you plan to discard the plant after flowering you can use it to brighten up dull spots too.*

ABOVE: Mammillaria elongata, *like most cacti, will thrive in a hot, sunny position.*

ABOVE: Aglaonema 'Silver Queen' *grows well in semi-shade or bright light, but avoid direct midday sun.*

ABOVE: Sansevieria trifasciata 'Laurentii' *is one of those tough plants that will do well on any windowsill, in shade or full sun.*

ABOVE: Yucca elephantipes *benefits from as much light as possible. It will enjoy a hot, sunny position.*

BELOW: Zygocactus (Schlumbergera) *hybrids are forest cacti, best grown in good light shaded from direct sunlight.*

RIGHT: Kalanchoe blossfeldiana *hybrids do well on a sunny windowsill.*

ABOVE: Calathea zebrina *is best in a light position that receives early or late sun, but not direct midday sun.*

ABOVE: Aechmea fasciata *is grown mainly for its fascinating flower spike. Because it grows naturally in trees, it is not adapted to life on a very hot, sunny windowsill. Position it where it receives early or late sun.*

Shady spots

PLANTS THAT TOLERATE SHADE ARE PARTICULARLY USEFUL, ESPECIALLY IF YOU NEED FOCAL POINT PLANTS FOR DIFFICULT POSITIONS WITHIN THE ROOM. LARGE SPECIMEN PLANTS ARE USUALLY TOO LARGE FOR A WINDOW-SILL SO THESE HAVE TO COMBINE SIZE WITH SHADE TOLERANCE.

It is a mistake to position a plant purely for decorative effect, and you should always choose a spot that the plant will at least tolerate even if it doesn't thrive. For really inhospitable corners where it's just too dark even for shade lovers, use disposable flowering plants, or even ferns if you are prepared to discard them after a couple of months.

In winter, plants are unlikely to tolerate a light intensity less than 1,000 lux, and 5,000 lux in summer is about the minimum for foliage plants such as aspidistras and *Cissus rhombifolia* (syn. *Rhoicissus rhomboidea*). These are meaningless figures unless you have a way of measuring light, but fortunately there is a simple rough-and-ready way that can be used. Two methods of judging light levels are described in *How to Assess Light* (opposite).

ARTIFICIAL LIGHT

Artificial light can be used to highlight plants in dull spots, and can also be used to help plants thrive where natural light is inadequate.

Even ordinary light bulbs can help plants to grow by providing localized warmth and a degree of increased illumination. However, fluorescent tubes are better for plant growth and, because they generate less heat, they can be used closer to the plant. Light sources need to be close, and if possible the tubes should be specially balanced for plant growth (you can buy these at some gardening shops and also at aquarium suppliers). Otherwise use the tubes in pairs with one 'daylight' and one 'cool white' used together.

ABOVE: Aglaonema *'Silver Queen' is undemanding and useful for low-light areas.*

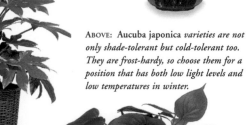

ABOVE: Aucuba japonica *varieties are not only shade-tolerant but cold-tolerant too. They are frost-hardy, so choose them for a position that has both low light levels and low temperatures in winter.*

ABOVE: Ficus pumila *is a low-growing trailer that would soon die on a sunny window. The variegated varieties are more attractive than the all-green species.*

ABOVE: Fatsia japonica *is a garden shrub hardy enough to grow outside except in very cold regions, but indoors the variegated form is more attractive. Choose it for a low light area where temperatures also drop in the winter.*

ABOVE: Philodendron scandens *is a useful trailer for a low-light area.*

ABOVE: Helxine soleirolii, *also sold as* Soleirolia soleirolii, *is a tough carpeter that will tolerate low light and cool temperatures (it will even stand some frost). There are green, silver and golden forms.*

ABOVE: Ivies (*varieties of* Hedera helix) *grow happily in the wild in sun or shade, and they will do the same in the home. If possible provide bright conditions in winter and avoid direct sunlight in summer.*

ABOVE: Fittonia verschaffeltii *is one of the more difficult foliage plants to try. It will be short-lived in direct sunlight.*

ABOVE: Pellaea rotundifolia *does not demand such a humid atmosphere as most ferns; a light window out of direct sunlight is ideal.*

ABOVE: Adiantum capillus-veneris *will not tolerate a hot, sunny position for long. It will be much happier in a humid and shaded conservatory.*

ABOVE: Scindapsus aureus, *also sold as* Epipremnum aureum, *is a trailer or climber that will do well in low-light areas. This golden form is particularly bright, but in time the leaves become more green and less colourful.*

ABOVE: Asplenium nidus *is one of the easiest ferns to grow.*

HOW TO ASSESS THE LIGHT

Use a camera with a built-in light meter, and set it to a 100 ISO (ASA) film speed and 1/125 second shutter speed. Take the reading at about midday on a bright day in late spring or early summer. Position the camera where you want to place the plant, and point it towards the window.

Read off the aperture setting then use the following as a rough guide to the light level:

f16 or more = Strong light, suitable for those plants that need the best light.

f8–11 = Equivalent to screened daylight, and suitable for those plants that like good light but not strong direct sunlight.

f4–5.6 = Poor light, only suitable for those plants adapted to shade.

f2.8 = Suitable for only the most shade-tolerant species, and plants may not survive in the winter months.

Another test is to try reading a newspaper where you plan to position the plant. Assuming that you have good eyesight, the position is too dark for plants if you can't read the newspaper comfortably.

Plants for poor light

Aglaonema, araucaria, asplenium, aspidistra, aucuba, bulbs (such as hyacinths), but keep in good light until flowering starts, *Cissus rhombifolia* (syn. *Rhoicissus rhomboidea*) × Fatshedera, fatsia, ferns (most), *Ficus pumila*, fittonia, *Hedera helix* (ivy), palms (most), *Philodendron scandens*, pteris, sansevieria, *Scindapsus aureus* (syn. *Epipremnum aureum, Rhaphidophora aurea),* but be prepared for it to lose most of its variegation, *Soleirolia soleirolii* (syn. *Helxine soleirolii).*

Watering

NO PLANT CAN SURVIVE WITHOUT WATER, YET MORE PLANTS PROBABLY DIE FROM OVERWATERING THAN FROM UNDERWATERING. GETTING TO GRIPS WITH THIS APPARENTLY SIMPLE PROCEDURE IS ONE OF THE ESSENTIALS OF GOOD PLANT CARE.

Compost (potting soil) check
If you use a clay pot, it will ring with a hollow sound if you tap it with a cotton reel on a cane or pencil and the compost is dry. If the compost is still moist the sound will be duller. With a little experience you will be able to detect the difference.

Meters and indicator strips that are pushed into the compost help to put some kind of measurement to the amount of moisture available in the compost, but are impractical if you have a lot of houseplants. You will soon tire of pushing a probe into each pot or reading indicators left in each one. These devices are best used by beginners still gaining experience of how to judge the moisture content by other means.

How much water?
There are no fixed rules about watering. How much a plant needs, and how often, depends not only on the plant but also the kind of pot (clay pots need watering more often than plastic ones), the compost (potting soil), (peat-based composts retain more water than loam-based), and the temperature and humidity.

Watering is an acquired skill, and one that needs to be practised on an almost daily basis, otherwise it is best to switch to self-watering containers or hydroponically grown plants.

Useful techniques
Examine the pots daily if possible, using whichever of the following techniques you find the most convenient:

• Appearance alone can be a guide. Dry, loam-based composts (potting soils) look paler than when they are moist. A dry surface does not mean that the compost is dry lower down, but if it looks damp you know that you don't need to

water. If the plant is placed in a saucer, see if there is any standing water. Apart from bog plants, never add more water if there is any trace still left in the saucer.
• The touch test is useful for a peat-based compost. Press a finger gently into the surface – you will know immediately if it feels very dry or very wet.
• The bell test is useful for clay pots, especially large ones containing specimen plants and that hold a large volume of compost. Push a cotton reel onto a short garden cane

Watering from above
A small watering-can is still the most popular way to water houseplants. Choose one that is well-balanced to hold and with a long, narrow spout that makes it easy to direct the water to the compost (potting soil) rather than over the plant.

and tap the pot: a dull thud indicates moist compost (although it could also indicate a cracked pot!), a clear ring suggests dry compost. This doesn't work well with peat-based composts, and not at all with plastic pots.
• With practice you can tell when the compost is dry simply by lifting the pot slightly: a pot with dry compost will feel much lighter than one with moist compost.

How to water

When you water, fill the pot to the brim – dribbles are not sufficient. If the root-ball has completely dried out, water may run straight through, down the inside of the pot, in which case stand the pot in a bucket of water until the air bubbles stop rising.

After watering, always check whether surplus water is sitting in the saucer or cache-pot. This will not matter if there are pebbles or marbles to keep the bottom of the pot out of contact with the moisture, but otherwise you must tip out the extra water. *Failure to tip out standing water is the most common cause of failure.* With just a few exceptions, if you leave most ordinary houseplants standing in water for long, they will probably die.

A long-necked watering-can is the most convenient way to water the majority of houseplants. The long neck makes it easy to reach among the leaves, and a narrow spout makes it easier to control the flow, which is also less forceful and unlikely to wash the compost (potting soil) away.

Watering with a can means that you may wet the leaves and crown of ground-hugging plants such as saint-paulias, and unless you are careful this can encourage rotting. For plants like this you may prefer to stand them in a bowl with a few centimetres (inches) of water in the bottom. Remove and allow to drain as soon as the surface of the compost becomes moist. You will probably find it less trouble, however, to be careful with a long-necked watering-can, getting the spout beneath the leaves.

Special needs

Tap water is far from ideal, but the vast majority of houseplants will tolerate it. If the water is hard (has a high calcium or magnesium content), however, you need to make special arrangements for plants that react badly to alkaline soil or compost. These include aphelandras, azaleas, hydrangeas, orchids, rhododendrons and saintpaulias. Rain-water is usually recommended for these plants, but a good supply is not always available throughout the year, and in some areas it can be polluted.

If your tap water is only slightly hard, simply filling the watering cans the day before and allowing the water to stand overnight may be sufficient. For harder water, try boiling it: part of the hardness will be deposited in the form of scale, and you can use the water once it has cooled.

Many water softeners work on a principle that unfortunately does not help the plants: if you want to benefit the plants, a demineralization system is necessary, which removes all the minerals and leaves distilled water. However, it is only worth the expense if you have a lot of plants.

Underwatering

If a plant wilts or collapses like this (top) it can usually be revived by standing the pot in a bow of water for a few hours, then leaving it in a cool, shady position for a day. By the next day it will probably be as perky as before (above). Always make sure that the compost (potting soil) is dry before doing this, as an overwatered plant will also wilt.

Watering the outer pot
Just a few plants tolerate standing with their roots in water, like this cyperus. With these you can add water to the saucer or outer container, but never do this unless you know the plant grows naturally in marshy places.

Self-watering pots
If you find watering a chore, self-watering pots may be the answer. The moisture is drawn up into the compost (potting soil) through wicks from a reservoir below, and you will need to water much less frequently.

Overwatering
Before an overwatered plant reaches the stage of collapsing, it will probably begin to look sickly. The plant on the left has been overwatered, the one on the right has received the correct amount of water.

Feeding

FEEDING CAN MAKE THE DIFFERENCE BETWEEN A PLANT THAT SIMPLY EXISTS AND SEEMS TO 'STAND STILL', AND ONE THAT LOOKS HEALTHY AND VIGOROUS AND REALLY FLOURISHES. MODERN FERTILIZERS HAVE MADE FEEDING REALLY EASY, AND NOW IT ISN'T EVEN A CHORE THAT YOU HAVE TO REMEMBER ON A REGULAR BASIS.

Houseplants are handicapped simply by being contained in a pot. The volume of soil or compost that the roots can explore is strictly limited, and sometimes we expect the same compost to support a large plant for many years.

With a few exceptions, your plants will look better if you feed them. You can buy special fertilizers for flowering plants, foliage plants and even special groups such as saintpaulias, but if you want to keep things simple and use one type of feed for all your plants they will still respond better than if they hadn't been fed at all.

When to feed
If in doubt about a particular plant, check the label or look it up in a book. As a general rule, however, plants should be fed only when they are growing actively and when light and temperature are such that they can actually take advantage of the additional nutrients. This generally means between mid-spring and mid-autumn, but there are exceptions – notably with winter-flowering plants.

Cyclamen are fed during the winter as well as before, and the winter- and spring-flowering forest cacti are fed during the winter but rested in summer. The rule of 'active growth' is more important than the time of year.

Controlled-release fertilizers (see top right) are useful for houseplants, but bear in mind that they are influenced by temperature, so they won't stop releasing nutrients in winter as they would outdoors.

How often to apply
Some trial and error is inevitable. Books and plant labels often give advice like 'feed once a fortnight' or 'feed weekly', but with so many different formulations available such advice may be inappropriate. It assumes a typical liquid houseplant feed. Do not follow this advice too closely if you use one of the other types.

Controlled- and slow-release fertilizers
These are widely used commercially, especially for outdoor container-grown plants, and also for pot plants to keep them healthy until sale. Unlike ordinary fertilizers, the nutrients are released slowly over a period of months, so a couple of applications in a year is all that most plants require.

Controlled-release fertilizers are most useful for outdoor plants because they release the nutrients only when the soil temperature is high enough for the plants to make use of them.

Slow-release fertilizers are most useful for houseplants as a compost (potting soil) additive when potting up an established plant.

Why feed?
These two *Rhoicissus rhomboidea* are the same age and were the same size when bought. The plant on the left has been fed regularly and repotted once; the one on the right has not been fed and shows typical signs of starvation.

Slow-release fertilizers
Slow-release fertilizers are worth adding to the compost (potting soil) because they sustain the plants over a period of perhaps six months. The nutrients in many peat-based (peat-moss based) or peat-substitute composts may become depleted within weeks or perhaps a couple of months.

Liquid feeds
Liquid fertilizers are quick-acting, and useful when a plant needs an immediate boost. Strengths and dilutions vary, so *always follow the manufacturer's advice* for rate and frequency of application. Some are weak and designed to be used at almost every watering, others are very strong and should be applied less frequently.

Pellets and sticks
There are various products designed to take the chore out of regular feeding. These will save you a lot of time and trouble in comparison with liquid feeds, although they may work out more expensive in the long run. Some

---

DON'T OVER-FEED

🐾 Because some feeding is good does not mean that more feeding is better. Do not apply more than the manufacturer recommends, otherwise you might kill your plants. Salts build up in the compost (potting soil) and can affect the intake of water and nutrients which, coupled with an over-stimulation of the plant, can end in collapse.

Fertilizer sticks and pellets

Pot-plant fertilizers are also available in sticks (top) and pellets (above) that you push into the compost (potting soil). Many people find these more convenient to use than having to mix and apply liquid feeds.

are tablet-shaped, others stick-shaped, but the principle is always the same: you make a hole in the compost (potting soil), push in the fertilizer stick or pellet, then leave it to release its nutrients slowly over a period of a month or so (check the instructions).

Slow-release sachets
Slow-release fertilizers are available in sachets that you place inside the pot at the bottom. These are most appropriate when repotting.

Soluble powders
These work on the same principle as liquid feeds, but you simply dissolve the powder in water at the appropriate rate. They often work out less expensive than ordinary liquid fertilizers.

Granular fertilizer
If you have to add a granular or powder fertilizer to the compost (potting soil), use a fork to stir it into the surface, then water it in thoroughly.

Benefits of feeding

To appreciate the benefits of feeding try starting with two plants of the same age and size, then feed just one of the plants regularly. The two *Pilea cadierei* (top) are the plants as bought. The same plants (above) show the effect a couple of months later after the one on the right was given just one dose of slow-release fertilizer.

Choosing a compost

YOUR PLANTS WILL ONLY BE AS GOOD AS THE COMPOST THEY GROW IN. FEEDING WILL HELP TO OVERCOME NUTRITIONAL DEFICIENCIES, BUT THE STRUCTURE OF THE COMPOST IS ALSO IMPORTANT IF THE ROOTS ARE TO GET THE RIGHT BALANCE BETWEEN MOISTURE AND AIR, SO VITAL FOR HEALTHY GROWTH. COMMERCIALLY, COMPOSTS ARE CHOSEN THAT MAKE CAPILLARY WATERING EASY, AND THAT ARE LIGHT TO TRANSPORT, BUT IN THE HOME THEY MAY NOT BE THE MOST APPROPRIATE GROWING MEDIUM.

Compost (potting soil) does more than simply anchor the plant. It also acts as a reservoir for nutrients and, if the structure is right, it achieves the right balance between moisture and air. A good compost also acts as a host to many beneficial micro-organisms.

Earlier generations of gardeners used to formulate their own special potting mixtures for different types of plant. Nowadays, however, composts are available that suit the majority of plants, and only a few types have any special requirements.

The main choice is between loam-based composts and those based on peat (peat moss) or a peat substitute. Most plants will grow well in either type, but there are pros and cons that may make one more or less appropriate for a particular plant.

Loam-based composts
This type of compost uses sterilized loam as its main ingredient, with added sand and peat to improve the structure, as well as fertilizers to supplement the nutrients already present in the loam.

Loam composts have weight, which is a useful attribute for a large plant with a lot of top growth, such as a big palm, since the weight provides stability to the pot.

Peat-based composts
These are light and pleasant to handle, and many plants thrive in them. Sand or other materials are sometimes added, but all of them depend on the addition of fertilizers to support plant growth. Often the fertilizers present in the compost run out quickly, and the plants will almost certainly suffer unless you begin supplementary feeding as soon as the plants show signs of poor growth.

Peat composts are very easy to manage on a commercial scale, with automatic watering systems, but in the home they demand more careful watering than loam composts. They can dry out more completely and become difficult to re-wet, and they are also more easily overwatered.

Some gardeners are reluctant to use peat-based composts on the grounds of depleting wetland areas where peat is excavated. For that reason many alternative products are now being introduced, including composts based on coir (waste from coconuts) and finely pulverized bark. Some use a mixture of materials. Results from these alternative composts can be very variable, depending on the make and formulation. Try a number of plants in several different makes – potting up the same types of plants in each – then decide which is best.

SPECIAL MEDIUMS

A few plants have particular needs that make a general-purpose compost (potting soil) inappropriate. Lime-hating plants, such as azaleas, many begonias, ericas and saintpaulias, are the most common group, and they will grow poorly in ordinary composts. Even peat-based (peat-moss) composts are generally alkaline, because they have lime added to make them suitable for the majority of houseplants. For lime-hating plants you need an 'ericaceous' compost widely available at garden centres.

Bromeliads, cacti and orchids are other groups that have special needs, and you can buy specially formulated composts suitable for these from many specialist nurseries and good garden centres.

Perlite

Gravel

Expanded clay granules

Sphagnum moss

Water-absorbing crystals

Controlled-release fertilizer

Cactus compost

Ericaceous compost

Peat-based compost

Loam-based compost

Orchid compost

Coir-based compost

ADDITIVES

❧ There are traditional compost (potting soil) additives such as perlite and vermiculite, which keep the compost open and admit plenty of air around the roots while still retaining moisture. These are sometimes used alone to root cuttings, but they contain no significant nutrients. Their contribution is purely structural. You can add them to ordinary composts to make them more moisture-retaining or to keep the compost open so that roots have plenty of oxygen.

Super-absorbent polymers (water-absorbing crystals) have become popular, especially for outdoor containers such as hanging baskets, and by adding them to the compost you will increase the amount of moisture that it will hold. They are no substitute for regular watering, however, and their use for houseplants is fairly limited.

Pots and containers

POTS NEEDN'T JUST BE PRACTICAL, THEY CAN BE PRETTY OR INTERESTING
TOO. BUT WHATEVER TYPE YOU CHOOSE, THEIR SIZE AND PROPORTION IN
RELATION TO THE PLANTS CONTAINED WILL AFFECT HOW THEY ARE PER-
CEIVED, AND THE POT CAN MAKE OR MAR A PLANT.

ABOVE: *This zinc container creates just the right atmosphere for an old-fashioned kitchen setting. If a container is large enough, try using a couple of compatible plants, like the adiantum and pellaea ferns used here.*

Ordinary clay or plastic pots lack visual appeal, and most people hide them in a more decorative cache-pot that is slightly larger. If you do this, put gravel, expanded clay granules or a few pebbles in the base to keep the bottom of the pot from contact with the surplus water that collects in the base. Alternatively, pack the space between the inner and outer pots with peat (peat-moss) to absorb most of the moisture, at the same time helping to create a more humid microclimate around the plant. Only use the latter method if you are very methodical about watering and are unlikely to overwater or leave stagnant water sitting at the base of the container. It will be difficult to detect and tip out once the space between the two pots has been filled.

Some plants do look good in clay pots, especially cacti and some succulents. But half-pots are often more appropriate as cacti do not have a large root system, and a shallower pot will usually look more in proportion to the plant. Half-pots have the same diameter as a full pot, but stand only about half the height. Seed pans, which are uncommon now, are similar but shallower; although intended for seed-sowing they can also be used for low or prostrate plants.

Many other plants look better in a half-pot, including azaleas, most begonias, saintpaulias and the majority of bromeliads. Be guided by the type of pot the plant is in when you buy it: if it's a shallow one, use another half-pot when you need to repot.

Some of the better quality plastic pots are coloured and come with a matching saucer, and these can look as attractive as a cache-pot, especially if you choose a colour that is co-ordinated with the room.

You can decorate ordinary clay or plastic pots by painting them freehand or using a stencil. For clay pots use masonry paint (the colours are limited, but you can compensate with a strong design), for plastic pots use acrylic artists' paints.

Square pots are more often used in the greenhouse than indoors, but they are space-saving if you have a collection of small plants such as cacti.

ABOVE: *Rush baskets can be very effective for small spring bulbs or compact plants like saintpaulias. Always line them or use them simply as a cache-pot.*

PLASTIC OR CLAY?

The vast majority of the plants on sale are grown in plastic pots: evidence that commercial growers find them satisfactory. Plastic pots are clean, light, easy to handle, remain largely free of algae and are inexpensive. They retain moisture better and the compost (potting soil) is less likely to dry out.

Perhaps surprisingly, clay pots will usually last longer than plastic ones. Plastic pots become brittle with age and even a slight knock is sometimes sufficient to break them. A clay pot won't break unless you actually drop it onto a hard surface. The extra weight of a clay pot will also be of benefit if a plant is large and rather top-heavy.

ABOVE: *Ceramic pots look stylish, and so much more colourful than an ordinary clay or plastic pot.*

ABOVE: *Bark baskets look good for houseplants that you would normally associate with trees, such as an ivy.*

ABOVE: *In a modern setting you may want a stylish type of container, like this small zinc one. The purple gynura does not detract from the container, which is a feature in its own right.*

ABOVE: *Terracotta hanging pots look more attractive than the plastic versions for a semi-cascading plant like this nephrolepis fern.*

ABOVE: *This china cache-pot picks up the colour of the cyclamen flowers to create a co-ordinated look.*

ABOVE: *Moss baskets make a nice setting for a few spring plants like primroses, and crocuses. Do not plant directly into this type of container unless you can ensure the surface is protected from drips.*

ABOVE: *Keep an eye open for the unlikely or unexpected. This distinctive container is made from dried fungi! The plant in it is a variegated Ficus pumila.*

ABOVE: *Stoneware pots are appropriate for plants in a kitchen. This one has been planted with Helxine soleirolii (syn. Soleirolia soleirolii), which reflects the rounded shape of the pot.*

ABOVE: *Terracotta wall planters can be used indoors as well as out. This Philodendron scandens will have to be trimmed after a few months to retain the container as a feature.*

ABOVE: *This metal planter is the kind of container that would look stunning in the right setting. You can line it with moss, rather like a hanging basket.*

ABOVE: *Sometimes old hand-made clay pots can be used effectively. The white deposit that often appears on old pots adds to the impression of age. These have been planted with ivies.*

ABOVE: *Matching drip trays are useful, and this one is particularly attractive because it takes three ceramic pots.*

ABOVE: *All kinds of decorative cache-pots are available in stores and garden centres, so it should be easy to choose those that appeal to your own tastes.*

Potting plants

SOONER OR LATER MOST PLANTS NEED REPOTTING, AND IT CAN GIVE AN
AILING PLANT A NEW LEASE OF LIFE. BUT NOT ALL PLANTS RESPOND WELL TO
FREQUENT REPOTTING, AND SOME PREFER TO BE IN SMALL POTS. KNOWING
WHEN TO REPOT, AND INTO WHICH SIZED POT, IS A SKILL THAT DEVELOPS
WITH EXPERIENCE.

Never be in too much of a hurry to
pot on a plant into a larger
container. Plants do not appreciate
having their roots disturbed, and any
damage to them will result in some
check to growth.

Repotting should never simply be
an annual routine. It's a job to be
thought about annually, but not
actually done unless the plant needs it.

Young plants require potting on
much more frequently than older ones.
Once a large specimen is in a big pot it
may be better to keep it growing by
repotting into another pot of the same
size, by topdressing, or simply by
additional feeding.

When repotting is necessary

The sight of roots growing through
the base of the pot is not in it itself a
sign that repotting is necessary. If the
plants have been watered through a
capillary mat, or the pot has been
placed in a cache-pot, some roots will
inevitably grow through the base to
seek the water.

If in doubt, knock the plant out of
its pot. To remove the root-ball easily,
invert the pot and knock the rim on a
hard surface while supporting the
plant and compost (potting soil) with
your hand. It is normal for a few roots
to run around the inside of the pot,
but if there is also a solid mass of roots
it's time to pot on.

There are several ways to repot a
plant, but the two described here are
among the best.

When to repot

A mass of thick roots growing through the
bottom of the pot (top) is an indication that
it's time to move the plant into a large one.
Equally, a mass of roots curled around the
edge of the pot (above) is another sign that
it's time for a larger container.

Pot-in-pot method

1. Prepare the new pot as described in the
Traditional method, if using a clay pot.
However, don't cover the drainage hole at all
if using a plastic pot and you intend using a
capillary watering mat.

POTTING ON, POTTING UP, REPOTTING

🐾 Although some of these terms are
commonly used interchangeably,
their true meanings are specific:

🐾 **Potting up** is what happens the
first time a seedling or cutting is
given its own pot.

🐾 **Potting on** is the action of
replanting the root-ball in a larger
pot.

🐾 **Repotting** is sometimes taken to
mean replacing the plant in a pot of
the same size, but with most of the
compost replaced. This is only
necessary if the plant cannot be
moved into a larger pot.

2. Place a little dampened compost (potting soil) over the base material then insert the existing pot (or an empty one the same size), ensuring that the level of the soil surface will be about 1cm (½in) below the top of the new pot when filled.

3. Pack more compost firmly between the inner and outer pots, pressing it down gently with your fingers. This creates a mould when the inner pot is removed.

4. Remove the inner pot, then take the plant from its original container and drop it into the hole formed in the centre of the new compost. Gently firm the compost around the root-ball, and water thoroughly.

Traditional method

1. Prepare a pot that is one or two sizes larger than the original and, if the pot is a clay one, cover the drainage hole with a piece of broken pot or a few pieces of chipped bark.

2. Make sure that the plant has been watered a short time beforehand, and knock the root-ball out of the old pot. Sometimes you can remove it by pulling gently on the plant, otherwise invert the pot and tap the rim on a hard surface.

3. Place a small amount of compost (potting soil) in the base of the new pot, then position the root-ball so that it is at the right height. If too low or too high, adjust the amount of compost in the base.

4. Trickle more compost around the sides, turning the pot as you work. It's a good idea to use the same kind of compost – peat- (peat-moss) or loam-based – as used in the original pot.

5. Gently firm the compost with the fingers. Make sure there is a gap of about 1–2.5cm (½–1in) between the top of the compost and the rim of the pot, to allow space for watering. Water thoroughly.

TOPDRESSING

🔹 Once plants are in large pots, perhaps 25–30cm (10–12in) in diameter, continual potting on into a larger pot may not be practical. Try removing the top few centimetres (inches) of compost (potting soil), loosening it first with a small hand fork. Replace this with fresh potting compost of the same type. This, plus regular feeding, will enable most plants to be grown in the same pot for many years.

Pruning and grooming

GROOMING YOUR PLANTS OCCASIONALLY NOT ONLY KEEPS THEM LOOKING GOOD, IT ALSO ENABLES YOU TO CHECK THEM FOR EARLY SIGNS OF PESTS AND DISEASES BEFORE THESE BECOME A PROBLEM.

Some pruning and grooming tasks simply keep the plants looking fresh and tidy, others actually improve them by encouraging bushier growth or promoting further flowering.

Apart from picking off dead flowers, which is best done whenever you notice them, grooming is only a once-a-week task. Most jobs need doing less frequently than this, but by making a routine of tidying up your plants you will almost certainly detect pest, disease and nutritional problems that much earlier. One also learns to appreciate the plants more by close examination, so you will benefit as well as the plants.

Deadheading

This keeps the plant looking tidy, and in many cases encourages the production of more flowers. It also discourages diseases: fungus infections often start on dead or dying flowers, before spreading to the leaves.

Plants with masses of small flowers, such as fibrous-rooted begonias (*B. semperflorens*) are difficult to deadhead often enough, but unless you make some effort the flowers that fall often make a mess of the furniture or sill that they fall on, as well as spoiling the appearance of the plant itself.

Apart from where the flowers appear in a spike, remove the flower stalks as well as the flowers. Sometimes the stalks are most easily removed by hand, using a pulling and twisting motion at the same time.

If the flowers appear in spikes or large heads, such as a hydrangea, cut the whole head or spike back to just above a pair of leaves when the last blooms have finished.

Leaves

Dust and dirt accumulate on leaves as well as on furniture, but this is not always obvious unless the foliage is naturally glossy. This accumulation not only implies neglect, it also harms the plant slightly by cutting down on the amount of light falling on the leaf and thereby hindering photosynthesis, the process by which the plant produces energy for growth.

Wipe smooth leaves with a soft, damp cloth. Some people add a little milk to the water to produce a shine on glossy foliage. The alternative is to use a commercial leaf shine. Some leaf cleaners come as aerosols or sprays, others as impregnated wipes. If you are using an aerosol, follow the manufacturer's instructions carefully and pay particular attention to the recommended spraying distance.

Cloths and sprays are no use for cleaning hairy leaves. Instead, use a small paintbrush as a duster. You can dust cacti in the same way.

Removing leaves
Sooner or later all plants have a few dead leaves. Even evergreens drop old leaves from time to time. Don't let them spoil the appearance of the plant; most are easily removed with a gentle tug, but tough ones may have to be cut off.

TOOLS FOR THE JOB

🌿 Most of the equipment you need in order to care for houseplants you will probably already have around the home. You might want to try commercial leaf shines or buy secateurs (floral scissors), but a sponge or soft cloth and kitchen scissors will usually do the job just as well.

It is worth keeping a small grooming kit handy, perhaps in a small box that you can carry around during grooming sessions. It should contain:

🌿 Sharp, pointed scissors, or a small pair of secateurs or flower-gathering scissors.

🌿 A supply of split canes for supports.

🌿 A ball of soft garden string, preferably green, or metal split rings. For some jobs, a reel of green plastic-covered wire is useful.

🌿 A sponge for wiping glossy leaves.

🌿 A small paintbrush for cleaning hairy leaves.

Leaf wipes
You might find commercial leaf wipes more convenient to use. They leave large, glossy leaves looking shiny and bright.

Deadheading
Removing dead flowers will keep the plant looking smart, and reduce the chance of dead petals encouraging the growth of moulds and other diseases. Some plants also make a mess of the table or windowsill if the flowers are simply allowed to drop.

Immersing foliage
If the plant is small enough to handle conveniently, try swishing the foliage in a bowl of tepid water. Do not do this if the plant has hairy or delicate leaves.

Brushing leaves
Plants with hairy leaves, like this saintpaulia, should not be sponged or cleaned with a leaf wipe. Instead, brush them occasionally with a soft paintbrush.

Sponging
Glossy-leaved plants like this ficus will look smarter if you wipe over the foliage with slightly soapy water occasionally. The plants also benefit because dust can reduce the amount of light received and also clog some of the pores through which the plant 'breathes'.

Pinching out
If you want a bushy rather than a tall or sprawling plant, pinch out the growing tips a few times while it is still young. This will stimulate the growth of sideshoots that will produce a bushier effect. Most plants will respond to this treatment, but beware of doing it to slow-growing plants.

Compact non-flowering plants that don't have hairy leaves – aglaonemas for example – can be cleaned by swishing the foliage in a bowl of tepid water. But make sure that the plant dries off out of direct sunlight, otherwise the leaves may be scorched.

Shaping and training
You can improve the shape of many houseplants by pinching out the growing tips to prevent them from becoming tall and leggy. Removing the tips of the shoots makes the plant bushier. Impatiens, hypoestes, pileas and tradescantias are among the many plants that benefit from this treatment. Start when the plants are young, and repeat it whenever the growth looks too thin and long. This is especially useful for trailers such as tradescantias: a dense, bushy cascade about 30cm (1 ft) long will look much better than thin, weedy-looking shoots of twice the length.

If any all-green shoots develop on a variegated plant, pinch or prune them back to the point of origin.

Climbers and trailers need regular attention. Tie in any new shoots to the support, and cut off any long shoots that spoil the shape.

Holiday care

HOLIDAYS ARE GOOD FOR US, BUT NOT FOR PLANTS. UNLESS YOU HAVE A
FRIENDLY NEIGHBOUR WHO CAN PLANT-SIT FOR YOU, YOU WILL HAVE TO
DEVISE WAYS OF KEEPING YOUR PLANTS WATERED WHILE YOU ARE AWAY.

Most houseplants will survive in winter for a few days, or even a week, if they are well watered beforehand, especially if the central heating is turned down. In hot summer weather, special arrangements will have to be made for your plants if you are leaving them for anything more than a long weekend.

If you can't arrange for a neighbour to pop in every couple of days to water your houseplants, take the following precautions:

- If it is summer, stand as many as possible outdoors. Choose a shady, sheltered position, and plunge the pots up to their rims in the soil. Then apply a thick mulch of chipped bark or peat over the pots to keep them cool and to conserve moisture. Provided that they are watered well before you leave, most plants will survive a week like this, even without rain.
- Move those that are too delicate to go outdoors into a few large groups in a cool position out of direct sunlight.
- Stand as many as possible on trays of gravel, watered to just below the level of the pot bases. Although this will not moisten the compost (potting soil), the humid air will help to keep the plants in good condition.
- Ensure that all of the most vulnerable plants have some kind of watering system.

Proprietary watering devices
Many kinds of watering devices can be bought, and new ones – usually variations on an old theme – appear each year. Most work on one of the following principles:

Porous reservoirs are pushed into the compost (potting soil) and filled with water. The water slowly seeps though the porous walls over a period of a few days to a week. These are useful for one or two pots for a short period of time, but as you need one for each pot and the reservoir is small, their use is limited.

Ceramic mushrooms work on a similar principle, but the top is sealed and there is a connecting tube for insertion into a large reservoir of water (such as a bucket). As the water seeps through the porous shaft, the pressure in the sealed unit drops and fresh water is drawn from the reservoir. This simple but effective device will keep a plant happy for a couple of weeks, but again, you need one for each pot!

Wicks are sold for insertion into the base of the pot, which is then stood above a reservoir of water. This is a good method if you only have a handful of plants, otherwise too tricky to set up.

Drip feeds, sold for greenhouse and garden use, are a good solution. They can be expensive, and if you use a portable bag reservoir they are not very elegant for the home – but that will not matter while you are away.

Improvising
Two reliable systems use the kitchen sink or bath and capillary matting, which is available at all good garden centres and home improvement stores.

For the sink, cut a length of matting that fits the draining area and is

Short-term holiday care
If you have to leave your plants unattended for a while, try grouping them together in a large container. Place them on wet capillary matting and make sure the compost (potting soil) is moist too. If leaving them for more than a few days, you may need to arrange a system to keep the mat moist.

Improvised wicks
Make your own porous wicks by cutting capillary matting into strips. Make sure the wicks and compost (potting soil) are moist before you leave, and that the wick is pushed well into the compost.

Conserving moisture
Placing a plant in an inflated plastic bag like this will conserve the moisture for quite a long time, but if left too long there is a risk of leaves rotting. Try to keep the bag out of contact with the leaves if possible.

long enough to dip into the basin part. You can fill this with water as a reservoir, or leave the plug out but let the tap drip onto the mat to keep it moist. If you leave the tap dripping, have a trial run beforehand to make sure that it keeps the mat moist without wasting water.

You can set up a similar arrangement in the bath, but if you want to leave water in the bath, place the mat and plants on a plank of wood supported on bricks, to leave space beneath for the water.

Bear in mind that compost (potting soil) in clay pots with broken pots over

the drainage holes will not be able to benefit from the capillary action efficiently (though you could insert small wicks though the holes, cut from scraps of the matting). The system works best for houseplants kept in plastic pots, with nothing placed over the drainage holes.

Hardy plants
Many of the tougher houseplants can stand outdoors with their pots plunged in the ground. Choose a shady spot, water the plants thoroughly and cover the tops of the pots with a thick layer of chipped bark.

Porous irrigators
Porous irrigators can be useful if you only leave your plants for a few days. Make sure the compost (potting soil) is moist then fill the irrigators with water.

Porous wicks
Use a large needle to pull the wicks through the compost (potting soil) and out of the drainage hole at the base of the pot.

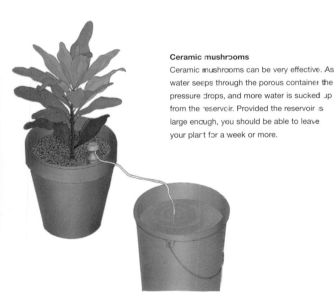

Ceramic mushrooms
Ceramic mushrooms can be very effective. As water seeps through the porous container the pressure drops, and more water is sucked up from the reservoir. Provided the reservoir is large enough, you should be able to leave your plant for a week or more.

Using the bath
The bath is a good place to keep plants moist on capillary matting; you can also stand the plants on *porous* bricks without the mat. Have a trial run to make sure the plug retains the water without seepage.

Hydroculture

HYDROCULTURE – ALSO KNOWN AS HYDROPONICS – IS A METHOD OF
GROWING PLANTS WITHOUT SOIL OR COMPOST (POTTING SOIL). WATERING IS
NORMALLY ONLY NECESSARY EVERY COUPLE OF WEEKS, AND FEEDING IS ONLY
A TWICE-YEARLY TASK. HYDROCULTURE WILL GIVE YOU SUCCESSFUL PLANTS
WITH THE MINIMUM OF ATTENTION.

Starting off a new plant

1. Choose a young plant and wash the roots free of all traces of compost (potting soil), being careful not to damage them. Then place the plant in a container with slatted or mesh sides.

Hydroponics can be a highly scientific way to cultivate plants, with nutrient solutions carefully controlled by expensive monitoring equipment. However, the system usually used in homes by amateurs – and generally referred to as hydroculture – is designed to be simple and can be used successfully even by the complete beginner.

You can buy plants that are already growing hydroponically, and these are the best way to start as you would in any case have to buy suitable containers, clay granules and a special fertilizer. But once you realize how easy hydroculture plants are to look after, you will probably want to start off your own plants from scratch.

Routine care

Wait until the water indicator registers minimum, *but do not water immediately.* Allow an interval of two or three days before filling again. Don't keep topping up the water to keep it near the maximum level – it is important that air is allowed to penetrate to the lower levels.

Always use *tap* water because the special ion-exchange fertilizer depends on the chemicals in tap water to function effectively.

Make sure that the water is at room temperature. Because there is no compost (potting soil), cold water has an immediate chilling effect on the plant, and this is a common cause of failure with hydroculture plants.

🍂 Plants can grow different kinds of roots: ground roots and water roots. If you root a cutting in water it will produce water roots, but once you pot it into compost (potting soil) it almost has to start again by producing ground roots. This makes the transition between compost and water cultivation tricky in either direction. But once the plant has passed through the transitional phase, a hydroculture plant can draw its moisture and nutrients from the solution at the base of the container, while those above can absorb the essential oxygen.

The level of the nutrient solution is crucial. If you fill the tank with too much water there will not be enough air spaces left for the roots to absorb sufficient oxygen and the plant will die.

5. Pack with more clay granules to secure the inner pot and water indicator.

Make a note of when you replace the fertilizer, and renew it every six months. Some systems use the fertilizer in a 'battery' fitted within the special hydroculture pot, but otherwise you can just sprinkle it on to be washed in with a little water.

Just like plants in compost, hydroculture plants gradually grow larger. Because the roots do not have to search for moisture and nutrients the root system is usually smaller than for a comparable plant in compost, but in time the plant will need repotting, especially if the top growth looks out of proportion with the container.

Remove the plant as carefully as possible. It may be necessary to cut the inner container to minimize damage to the roots, but sometimes you can leave the plant in the inner container and just use a larger outer one. If a very large and tangled root system has formed, some judicious pruning may be called for. Both roots and top growth can often be trimmed back

2. Pack expanded clay granules around the roots, being careful to damage them as little as possible.

3. Insert the inner pot into a larger, watertight container, first placing a layer of clay granules on the base to raise the inner pot to the correct level of about 1cm (½ in) below the rim.

4. Insert the water level tube. If you cannot find one specially designed to indicate the actual water level, use one that indicates how moist the roots are – those designed for other systems using aggregates are suitable.

6. Sprinkle the special hydroculture fertilizer over the clay granules.

7. Wash the fertilizer down as you water to the maximum level on the indicator. If the indicator does not show an actual level, add a volume of water equal to one-quarter the capacity of the container – and only water again when the indicator shows dry. Always fill with tap water.

8. A few months on and the houseplant is flourishing.

successfully, but much depends on the type of plant.

Suitable plants

Not all plants respond well to hydroculture, so some experimentation may be necessary. The range is surprisingly wide, however, and includes cacti and succulents (with these it is essential to ensure an adequate 'dry period' before topping up with more water, and not to let the water level rise too high), as well as orchids.

As a starting point, try some plants from the following list, or be guided by what you see planted in commercially-produced hydroculture units. Then experiment further as you gain more experience – *Aechmea fasciata,* aglaonema, amaryllis, anthurium, asparagus, aspidistra, beaucarnea, *Begonia manicata, Begonia rex,* cacti*, cissus, clivia, cociaeum, dieffenbachia, dizygotheca, dracaena, *Euphorbia pulcherrime,* ficus, gynura, hedera, hibiscus, hoya, maranta, monstera, nephrolepis, philodendron, saintpaulia, sansevieria, schefflera, *Spathiphyllum wallisii,* stephanotis, streptocarpus, tradescantia, *Vriesea splendens,* yucca.

* Most cacti can be grown hydroponically, but it is essential that the water level is regulated carefully. If the water level is too high the plants will soon die.

Simple multiplication

A PLANT THAT YOU HAVE RAISED YOURSELF, FROM SEED OR A CUTTING, ALWAYS SEEMS MORE SPECIAL THAN ONE THAT YOU HAVE BOUGHT. PROPAGATION IS ONE OF THE MOST DEEPLY SATISFYING ASPECTS OF GARDENING, AND ONCE YOU HAVE ENOUGH PLANTS FOR YOUR OWN NEEDS YOU WILL STILL HAVE PLENTY TO EXCHANGE WITH FRIENDS.

Growing from seed

IT CAN BE PARTICULARLY GRATIFYING TO TELL ADMIRING FRIENDS THAT

YOU RAISED YOUR ABUTILON OR VENUS FLY TRAP FROM SEED, BUT PEREN-

NIALS CAN BE QUITE A CHALLENGE AND, IN THE CASE OF MIXTURES, NOT

ALL THE PLANTS WILL BE AS GOOD AS NAMED VARIETIES. ANNUALS, ON THE

OTHER HAND, ARE VERY EASY TO GROW AND SELDOM DISAPPOINT.

If you haven't grown houseplants from seed before, start with easy annuals, which will bring quick and reliable results. This spurs most people to try the trickier or more interesting plants like cacti, cycads and ferns (which are actually grown from spores and not true seeds), as well as favourites like saintpaulias.

As a general rule, those houseplants offered by seed merchants that normally deal in the more common and 'everyday' plants are likely to be the

How to sow in a tray

1. Fill the tray loosely with a seed compost (medium) – loam- and peat-based (peat-moss based) are equally satisfactory for the majority of seeds. Do not use a potting compost as the higher level of nutrients these contain can inhibit germination.

2. Level off the compost, using a piece of wood or rigid cardboard, then firm it gently with a 'presser' or piece of wood that will fit within the tray. Make sure that the compost is still level.

3. Sprinkle the seeds as carefully and as evenly as possible over the surface. A good way to do this with small seeds is in a folded piece of paper that you tap gently with a finger as you move it over the surface.

4. Unless the seed is very fine, or the packet says that the seeds should be left exposed to light, sprinkle a little more compost over the top of the seeds. As a guide, cover with a layer of compost that is about the thickness of the seeds themselves. Use an old kitchen sieve to sift the compost over. This keeps back large pieces and makes it easier to spread evenly.

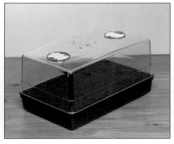

5. Water carefully, using a watering-can fitted with a very fine rose (fine-mist head) – take the tray outdoors to do this. Otherwise stand it in a bowl of water as described for pots opposite. Place the tray in a propagator, or cover it with a sheet of glass. Follow the instructions on the seed packet regarding the required level of light or darkness, and temperature.

SOWING VERY FINE SEED

🞂 Some seeds are very tiny, almost like dust, making them difficult to sow evenly. Mix seed that is this small with a little silver sand in the palm of one hand, then use the finger and thumb of the other to sprinkle the mixture over the surface of your seed tray. If the seed and sand have been well combined, distribution of the seed should be even, especially as the sand will help you judge how evenly you are sowing the seed.

easiest to grow. Those offered by seed merchants specializing in the uncommon or unusual are often more difficult to germinate, but the very fact that they are demanding explains part of their appeal to many enthusiasts.

Many perennial houseplants can be slow to germinate and they may take a couple of years to reach a respectable size. If you have a heated greenhouse or conservatory it makes sense to grow them on in there until they are large enough to be used for indoor display.

Sow in trays if you need a lot of plants, otherwise use pots, as these take up less space.

Pricking out

As soon as the seedlings are large enough to handle, prick them out, either into individual pots or into seed trays, to grow on until large enough for their own pots.

Use a potting compost (medium) for this, and always lift the seedlings carefully by their leaves rather than by the fragile stem.

AVOID THE CONDENSATION PROBLEM

🐾 Condensation will form inside a propagator or on the sheet of glass covering the tray or pot. If this is so heavy that drips start to fall on the germinating seedlings, ventilate the propagator or wipe the glass.

How to sow in a pot

1. Fill the pot with a seed compost (medium), but this time use a round presser to firm and level it gently. Make a presser from wood, or simply use a jam-jar.

3. Water by the immersion method. Stand the pot in a bowl of water, making sure that the water level remains below the top of the compost. Remove the pot to drain once the surface of the compost has become moist. Using this method, even the smallest seeds will not be disturbed.

2. Sow the seeds as evenly as possible. The easiest way to sow over the small area of a pot is to sprinkle the seeds between finger and thumb as you might sprinkle salt. Sprinkle more compost over the sown seeds unless they are very fine, or the instructions on the packet advise otherwise. Most seeds should be covered with approximately their own depth of compost.

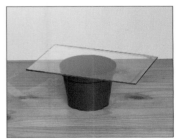

4. Place in a propagator or cover with a sheet of glass.

RIGHT: **Exacum affine** *is one of the easiest houseplants to try raising from seed. Sow in spring to flower in summer and autumn, or in autumn to flower the following spring.*

Stem cuttings

MOST HOUSEPLANTS CAN BE RAISED FROM STEM CUTTINGS, AND SOME ARE SO

EASY THAT THEY WILL EVEN ROOT IN WATER. OTHERS ARE MORE CHALLENG-

ING, REQUIRING ROOTING HORMONES AND A PROPAGATOR.

Most houseplants can be prop-agated from softwood cuttings taken in spring, and many of the shrubby plants root from semi-ripe cuttings taken later in the year.

Softwood cuttings
This method of taking cuttings is similar to semi-ripe cuttings, but choose the ends of new shoots. Take softwood cuttings after the first flush of spring but before the shoots have become hard. Now follow the same procedure as for semi-ripe cuttings.

Cuttings in water
Softwood cuttings can often be rooted in water, especially easy ones like coleus and impatiens.

Almost fill a jam-jar with water and fold a piece of wire-netting (chicken wire) over the top, or use a piece of aluminium foil with holes pierced in it. Take the cuttings in the normal way but, instead of inserting them into compost (potting soil), rest them on the netting or foil, with the end of the stem in water.

Top up the water as necessary. When roots have formed, pot the cut-tings up into individual pots using a sandy potting compost. Keep the plants out of direct sunlight for at least a week to give them a chance to become established in the pot.

Impatiens
Impatiens are often grown from seed, but they root readily from softwood cuttings. As

old plants often lose their compact shape, take a few cuttings periodically.

Geraniums
Geranium (pelargonium) softwood cuttings root readily. You can use this technique for

zonal geraniums, regal geraniums like these, and scented-leaved geraniums.

HORMONES HELP ROOTING

❧ Some plants, such as impatiens and some tradescantias, root readily even without help from a rooting hormone. Others, and especially semi-ripe cuttings, will benefit from the use of a rooting hormone. Rooting hormones are available as powders or liquids, and their use usually results in more rapid rooting and, in the case of the trickier kinds of plants, a higher success rate.

How to take semi-ripe cuttings

1. Fill a pot with a cuttings compost (medium) or use a seed compost, and firm it to remove large pockets of air.

2. Make the cuttings 10–15cm (4–6in) long (they may have to be shorter on very compact plants), choosing the current season's growth after the first flush of growth but before the whole shoot has become hard. They should be firm yet flexible, and offer some resistance when bent.

3. Trim the cutting just below a leaf joint, using a sharp knife, and remove the lower leaves to produce a clear stem to insert into the compost.

4. Dip the cut end of the cutting into a rooting hormone. If using a powder, moisten the end in water first so that it adheres.

5. Make a hole in the compost with a small dibber or a pencil, and insert the cutting so that the bottom leaves are just above the compost. Firm the compost gently around the stem to remove large air pockets. You can usually insert several cuttings around the edge of a pot

6. Water the cuttings (adding a fungicide to the water will help to reduce the risk of the cuttings rotting), then label and place in a propagator. If you don't have a propagator, cover the pot with a clear plastic bag, making sure it does not touch the leaves. Keep in a light place, but *out of direct sunlight.*

If a lot of condensation forms, reverse the bag or ventilate the propagator until excess condensation ceases to form. Do not allow the compost to dry out.

Pot up the cuttings individually once they have formed a good root system.

Leaf cuttings

LEAF CUTTINGS ALWAYS SEEM MORE FASCINATING TO ROOT THAN STEM

CUTTINGS, AND THERE ARE PLENTY OF HOUSEPLANTS THAT YOU CAN PROP-

AGATE THIS WAY. THE TECHNIQUES ARE EASY AS WELL AS FUN, AND SOME

OF THE MOST POPULAR PLANTS, SUCH AS SAINTPAULIAS, FOLIAGE BEGONIAS,

STREPTOCARPUS AND SANSEVIERIAS, CAN BE RAISED FROM LEAF CUTTINGS.

Square leaf cuttings

1. First cut the leaf into strips about 3cm (1¹/4in) wide, in the general direction of the main veins, using a sharp knife or razor-blade.

There are several types of leaf cuttings described here. For leaf petiole cuttings you need to remove the leaves with a length of stalk attached. Some leaves form new plants from the leaf blades, especially from points where the veins have been injured. For square leaf cuttings, instead of placing a whole leaf on the compost (medium), you can cut it into squares and insert these individually. With leaf midrib cuttings, the long, narrow leaves of plants such as streptocarpus can simply be sliced into sections and treated like square leaf cuttings.

Leaf petiole cuttings

1. Use only healthy leaves that are mature but not old. Remove the leaf with about 5cm (2in) of stalk, using a sharp knife or razorblade.

2. Fill a tray or pot with a suitable rooting compost (medium), then make a hole with a dibber or pencil.

PLANTS TO GROW FROM LEAF CUTTINGS

🌣 **Leaf petiole cuttings**
Begonias (other than *B. rex*)
Peperomia caperata
Peperomia metallica
Saintpaulia

🌣 **Leaf blade cuttings**
Begonia rex

🌣 **Leaf midrib cuttings**
Gesneria
Sansevieria*
Sinningia speciosa (gloxinia)
Streptocarpus

* If you use this method for the variegated *S. trifasciata* 'Laurentii' the plantlets will not be variegated.

3. Insert the stalk into the hole, angling the cutting slightly, then press the compost gently around the stalk to firm it in. The base of the blade of the leaf should sit on the surface of the compost. You should be able to accommodate a number of cuttings in a seed tray or large pot. Water well, preferably with a fungicide, and allow surplus moisture to drain.

4. Place the cuttings in a propagator, or cover with a clear plastic bag. Make sure that the leaves do not touch the glass or plastic, and remove condensation periodically.

Keep the cuttings warm and moist, in a light place out of direct sunlight. Young plants usually develop within a month or two, but leave them until they are large enough to be handled easily.

2. Next cut across the strips to form small squares of leaf.

3. Fill a tray with a rooting compost (medium), then insert the squares on edge, making sure that the edge that was nearest to the leaf stalk faces downwards.

4. After a month or two you should have plenty of young plants that have grown from the leaf squares. Once these are well established, pot them up individually.

Leaf midrib cuttings

1. Remove a healthy, undamaged leaf from the parent plant, ideally one that has only recently fully expanded.

> ### LONGITUDINAL LEAF CUTTINGS
>
> ✍ An alternative method of propagating streptocarpus:
>
> ✍ Lay the leaf on a hard surface, and cut it twice along the length of the leaf, on both sides of the main vein. Discard the main vein.
>
> ✍ Insert these halves into the compost, so that they stand on edge with about one-third in the compost.

2. Place the leaf face down on a firm, clean surface, such as a sheet of glass. Cut the leaf into strips, no wider than 5cm (2in).

3. Fill a tray or large pot with a rooting compost (medium), and insert the cuttings into this about 2.5cm (1in) apart. Insert the end that was nearest the stalk into the compost. About one-third of the cutting should be in the compost.

Young plants will eventually appear from the compost. Pot these up individually when they are large enough to handle safely.

Leaf blade cuttings

1. Select a healthy leaf, and sever it close to the base of the main stalk.

2. Cut off the attached stalk close to the blade.

3. Cut across the main and secondary veins on the underside of the leaf, using a sharp knife or razor-blade. Make the cuts about 2.5cm (1in) apart.

4. Fill a seed tray with a rooting compost (medium), then peg the leaf so that the back is in contact with the compost. Make several small U-shaped 'staples' from pieces of galvanized wire, to act as anchors.

5. Alternatively, instead of using wire staples, you can hold the leaf in contact with the compost by using small stones as weights.

6. Keep in a propagator, or in a warm place, in a light position but out of direct sunlight. Do not allow the compost to become dry.

New plants will eventually grow, and once these look well established, pot them up individually. Often the old leaf has disintegrated by this time, but if not, just cut the new plants free of the old leaf.

LEFT: **Begonia rex** *should be propagated using leaf-blade cuttings, rather than other methods.*

Easy division

DIVISION IS THE QUICKEST AND EASIEST OF ALL METHODS OF PROPAGATION. THE RESULTS ARE INSTANT, AND MOST PLANTS WITH A CROWN OR THAT FORM A CLUMP CAN BE PROPAGATED THIS WAY.

Many ferns can be divided, including adiantum, phyllitis, and *Pteris cretica*. Marantas, and related genera such as calathea, also form a clump and lend themselves to division. Other popular houseplants to try are anthuriums and aspidistras.

Water the plant about an hour before you divide it. If the roots are thick and fleshy, have a sharp knife handy to cut though them.

Dividing a plant

1. Knock the plant out of its pot. If the plant is large and the pot full of roots, you may need to invert the pot and tap the rim on a hard surface. Place a hand over the root-ball to catch it as it falls free.

2. Pull away some of the compost (potting soil) from the bottom and sides, freeing some of the roots in the process.

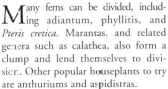

3. Try pulling the plant apart with your hands, first into two pieces, and then into smaller ones if you need a lot of new plants.

4. Sometimes the tough or fleshy roots make this difficult: chlorophytums are an example. If this is the case, prise the roots apart with a hand fork and separate the clump into smaller pieces with a sharp knife.

5. Replant healthy young pieces of the root clump, using a smaller pot and a good potting compost (medium). It may be necessary to trim back some of the largest roots with a knife, but try to leave the small, fibrous ones intact.

After watering, keep the plants in good light but out of direct sun, at least until they have become established and started to grow again.

Layering

LAYERING IS A USEFUL TECHNIQUE IF YOU REQUIRE JUST A FEW EXTRA OR REPLACEMENT PLANTS. ORDINARY LAYERING IS ONLY PRACTICAL FOR A FEW PLANTS INDOORS, BUT AIR LAYERING IS A POPULAR WAY TO IMPROVE AN OLD FICUS THAT HAS BECOME BARE AT THE BASE.

Ordinary layering is most appropriate for climbers or trailers with long and flexible shoots that can easily be pegged down into pots close to the parent plant. Ivies and *Philodendron scandens* are plants that readily lend themselves to this form of propagation.

Air layering is most often used for large ficus, such as *F. elastica,* but the method can also be used for other plants, such as dracaenas. Normally plants are air layered on an area of bare stem just below the leafy part, but if a few old leaves are in the way cut these off flush with the stem.

Ordinary layering

1. Fill a few small pots with a seed or cuttings compost (medium), and position them close to the parent plant.

2. Choose long, healthy shoots with young growth, and untangle them from the rest of the plant so that they can be pegged down into the pots.

3. Use pieces of bent wire to hold the stem in contact with the compost where there is a leaf joint. It does not matter if the stem is slightly covered by the compost.

4. When the roots have formed – usually after about four weeks – and new shoots begin to grow, sever the new plant from its parent. Keep the newly severed plant in a light position out of direct sunlight, and pay special attention to watering, until it is well established and obviously growing away strongly.

ABOVE: **Philodendron scandens** *is one of the few plants which you can successfully propagate by ordinary layering.*

ABOVE: *Try air layering a leggy* Ficus elastica *'Robusta' and you will once more have a plant like this.*

Air layering

1. Make a sleeve out of a piece of clear plastic and secure it below the point where the layer is to be made, using a plastic-covered twist-tie or adhesive tape. Then, using a sharp knife or blade, make an upward-facing cut about 2.5cm (1in) long, finishing just below a leaf joint. Make sure that you do not cut more than about one-third of the way through the stem, otherwise the top may break.

2. Brush inside the wound with a rooting hormone. A small paintbrush is useful for this. To hold the wound open, insert some moist sphagnum moss into the incision, or use a small piece of matchstick.

3. Pack plenty of moist sphagnum moss around the area, then bring up the plastic sleeve to hold it in place.

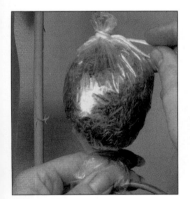

4. Secure the top of the sleeve with another twist-tie or some adhesive tape.

5. Check the moss occasionally to make sure that it is still moist, and to see if any roots have formed.

6. Once new roots are visible through the sleeve, cut off the stem just below the root-ball. Loosen the ball of moss slightly, but do not attempt to remove the moss when you pot up the plant. As the root system will still be small at this stage, it may be necessary to provide a stake for a few weeks.

Offsets and plantlets

OFFSETS AND PLANTLETS PROVIDE YOU WITH NEW PLANTS FOR THE MINIMUM
OF EFFORT – AND YOU DON'T HAVE TO SACRIFICE THE PARENT PLANT.

A few plants obligingly grow 'babies' on their leaves – just waiting to root when they come into contact with the compost (potting soil). Others produce plantlets on runners and raising new plants from these is as simple as pegging them down. Many plants – such as bromeliads – produce new shoots clustered around the old ones. These are easily detached and potted up.

Plantlets

Two succulents popularly grown as curiosities carry baby plants on their leaves: *Kalanchoe daigremontiana (syn. Bryophyllum daigremontianum)* and *K. Tubiflora* (syn. *B. tubiflorum*). The plantlets often fall off and can be found growing in the compost (potting soil) at the base of the parent plant. Just lift these up carefully after loosening the compost, and pot them up individually. Alternatively, re-move the largest of the plantlets from the leaves before they fall, and gently press them into the surface of a cut-tings compost (medium). Other vivi-parous plants like this, such as *Asple-nium bulbiferum,* can be treated in the same way.

Tolmiea menziesii has young plant-lets at the base of its leaves. Just detach a parent leaf, cut off the sur-plus leaf blade around the plantlet, and bury it just below the compost, with the plantlet still visible.

Runners

Some popular houseplants, such as *Saxifraga stolonifera,* produce plantlets on long runners, others, like *Chlor-ophytum comosum,* produce them at the ends of arching stems. All of these are very easy to propagate.

Place small pots filled with a cut-tings compost (medium) around the parent plant and peg down the plant-lets into them using pieces of bent wire or hairpins, to hold them in close contact with the compost. Keep well watered and sever the plantlets from the parent plant once plenty of roots have formed and the new plant has started to grow.

Offsets

Some plants produce offsets – new growth close to the old that can be separated and grown on independently – and this is normal with bromeliads.

Bromeliad offsets

1. Bromeliads produce offsets around the edge of the main flowering part of the plant, which later dies. Pot up these offsets when they are about a third the height of the parent plant.

Runners

1. *Chlorophytum comosum* is easy to propagate from plantlets produced at the ends of long, arching stems.

2. Peg the plantlets down into small pots, using pieces of bent wire to hold them in position.

3. Sever the plants from their parent once they have rooted well and are growing strongly.

2. They can usually be pulled away easily, but if necessary cut them away with a knife.

3. Pot the offsets up individually.

4. Firm the plants in, then water and keep in a warm, humid position, out of hot direct sunlight, until they show signs of new growth.

Many epiphytic bromeliads (those that in nature grow in trees or on rocks) have flowering rosettes that die after blooming. Before these plants die, they produce plenty of offsets around the old mature rosette. Leave these on until they are about one-third of the size of the parent plant, then detach them and pot up individually. Most can simply be pulled off by hand, but the tough ones will have to be severed with a sharp knife.

Some terrestrial bromeliads, such as ananas, produce offsets on stolons (short horizontal stems). Remove the plant from its container and cut off the offsets without causing too much damage to the parent.

Pot up the offsets without delay, and keep moist. Position them in good light but out of direct sunlight. They will soon start to grow independently and should then be treated normally.

Propagating from plantlets

1. *Kalanchoe tubiflora* (syn. *Bryophyllum tubiflorum*) produces plenty of plantlets at the ends of its leaves. Remove the plantlets with a gentle tug, and avoid holding the roots.

2. Plant them in a free-draining cuttings compost (medium), where they will soon grow away as young plants.

3. *Kalanchoe daigremontiana* (syn. *Bryophyllum daigremontianum*) produces plantlets around the edges of its leaves. Treat like the previous species, or simply peg down a whole leaf.

4. The ensuing plantlets can be potted up singly when they are larger.

Sometimes cacti are grafted for fun, or to make them flower more quickly than they would on their own roots, but a few that have stem colours other than green, such as some orange-red gymnocalycium species and varieties, have to be grafted onto a green stem because they are incapable of supporting themselves without the green chlorophyll found there. For these, flat grafting is the easiest method.

Some orchids, such as cymbidiums, have back-bulbs (a kind of bulb that sits on the surface of the compost). These can be removed and potted separately to produce new plants. Orchids can also be propagated using the division technique.

Fern spores can be used to propagate new plants; they resemble dust-like seeds, but they are not the equivalent of seeds. The fern plant is just an asexual stage in the life cycle, and the spores are another asexual stage. When they germinate they produce the sexual stage, the prothallus, which is green and prostrate or scale-like and carries both male and female organs. When fertilization takes place, the fern as we know it begins to grow.

Propagating orchids

1. Orchids can produce large clumps and may need dividing. Remove growth from the outer edge to repot. Some produce back-bulbs (old bulbs without leaves) that can be used for repotting.

2. Pot up individually, and always use a special orchid compost (medium). Back-bulbs (which may have no leaves) are treated in the same way. Plant to one side of the pot, as new growth will expand in front of the old growth.

Grafting cacti

1. Slice the top off the rootstock using a sharp knife to produce a flat surface.

2. Slightly bevel the edges of the cut with a knife.

3. Slice off the part to be grafted onto the rootstock, again cutting it cleanly.

4. Place the two parts together and hold in place with a couple of elastic bands looped over the top of the grafted cacti and under the bottom of the pot.

5. Label and keep in a warm, light place. The elastic bands can be removed as soon as new growth is noticed. The grafted cactus on the left is *Gymnocalycium* 'Black Cap'.

Ferns from spores

1. Fill a shallow pot with a peaty compost (peat-moss potting soil). Some people then sprinkle a thin layer of brick dust over the top. Firm it gently so that it is lightly compacted and level.

2. Sprinkle the spores over the surface as evenly as possible.

3. Cover the pot with a piece of glass and stand it in a saucer of water (rain or soft water is best). Keep in a warm, shaded position, and make sure that there is some water in the saucer.

BELOW: *Fern spores are usually sold to amateurs as mixtures of either hardy or tropical species. This* Asplenium nidus *is one fern that a mixture might include, but if you want to propagate a particular species it is worth saving and sowing the spores from your own plants.*

4. In about a month the tiny prothalli will start to grow and gradually cover the surface. It is essential that the compost remains moist at this stage. It is also worth keeping the glass over the pot.

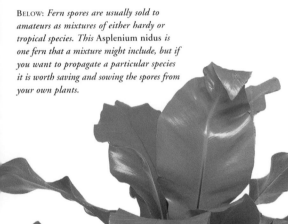

5. A month or two later the ferns proper should begin to appear. At this stage, remove the glass but still keep out of direct hot sunlight. When large enough to handle, prick out the little clumps of ferns into a seed tray.

When the small ferns are large enough to handle easily and a suitable size for their own pot, prick them out into individual pots.

Trouble-shooting

No matter how circumspect you are in selecting new plants, how carefully you check them for signs of ill-health, or how well you care for them, pests and diseases arrive unannounced. However, they should never be allowed to spoil your enjoyment of houseplants and with a little vigilance most should be easily kept under control.

Eliminating pests

EVERYONE GETS PESTS ON THEIR HOUSEPLANTS: BEGINNERS, EXPERTS AND

EVEN PROFESSIONALS. SOME, LIKE APHIDS, READILY ATTACK A WHOLE RANGE

OF PLANTS, OTHERS ARE MORE SELECTIVE AND TEND TO BE A PROBLEM ONLY

ON CERTAIN TYPES OF PLANT, OR IN PARTICULAR CONDITIONS. ALL NEED TO

BE DEALT WITH QUICKLY AND EFFECTIVELY.

Red spider mites
Red spider mites are so small that you can
hardly see them without a magnifying glass,
but, as this sick *Fatsia japonica* shows, an
infestation can be serious.

Aphids
Aphids are perhaps the most common and
troublesome pest, but are relatively easy to
control provided you act as soon as they are
detected.

Whitefly
Whitefly look like tiny white moths that often
rise up like a cloud when the plant is moved.
Although tiny, they gradually weaken the
plant, as this radermachera shows.

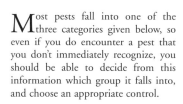

Mealy bugs
Mealy bugs are slow-moving and multiply less
rapidly than aphids, but they still weaken the
plant and can spread diseases.

Most pests fall into one of the three categories given below, so even if you do encounter a pest that you don't immediately recognize, you should be able to decide from this information which group it falls into, and choose an appropriate control.

Sap-suckers
The ubiquitous aphids are the biggest problem, and even if you win the first battle when you realize that an attack is under way, never let your guard down because there will always be new armies of aphids to take their place.

Aphids, and all sap-sucking insects, are important not only for the immediate damage they do, but also because of the long-term health risk to your plants. When aphids cluster on buds or the tips of shoots, leaves and flowers will often be distorted when they open, and because they tap into

the veins and 'blood' supply of the plant, they can easily transmit virus diseases from one plant to another. Always take aphids seriously, and take action before the population rapidly increases, as they can reproduce at a phenomenal rate.

Whitefly look like tiny moths and rise up in a cloud when disturbed. The nymphs (immature insects) are green to white and scale-like, turning yellow before emerging as an adult fly.

Red spider mites are tiny and the actual insects are easily missed, but you will notice their fine webs and yellowing, mottled leaves.

Control: almost all houseplant insecticides will control aphids, so choose one that is convenient to use, and has the right persistence taking into account your personal views on garden chemicals. You can buy some insecti-

cides that kill only aphids and leave beneficial insects unharmed, but in the home this is of marginal benefit. You don't have to worry about pollinating insects or natural predators as you might outdoors. Many strong insecticides are not suitable for use indoors, but you can take your plant outside to spray it. Alternatively, use one of the milder and less persistent ones – often based on natural substances like pyrethrum – more often.

Systemic insecticides that you water into the soil, or that are contained in impregnated sticks pushed into the compost, are easy to use indoors and protect the plant for weeks.

Pests like whitefly need repeated spraying with ordinary contact insecticides, so don't give up too soon.

Red spider mites dislike a humid atmosphere Once you've used the chemical control, regular misting to

Caterpillar damage
Caterpillars can be a problem on indoor
plants as well as in the garden. Here one has
attacked a pereskia.

Biological controls
A predatory mite – *Phytoseiulus persimilis* –
can be used for red spider mite as a
biological control. Here a leaf containing the
parasite is being placed on a houseplant.

Nematode weevil control
There is now a natural control for vine weevil
grubs – a microscopic parasitic nematode.
Mix the culture with water and apply to the
plants. Here a cyclamen is being dosed.

Vine weevil grubs
Vine weevil grubs are particularly
troublesome because they eat the roots and
the first you may know of the problem is
when the plant collapses.

Using systemic insecticides
These special 'pins' release a systemic
insecticide that is absorbed by the plant's
roots, making the plant toxic to sap-sucking
insects for weeks.

Controlling aphids
You may be able to reduce the population of
insects such as aphids simply by swishing the
plant in water.

create a humid atmosphere will please
the plants and deter the mites

Mealy bugs and other relatively
stationary sap-sucking insects can be
treated by dabbing them with a cotton swab dipped in alcohol. This will
penetrate the waxy coat that protects
them from most contact insecticides.
Otherwise try using a systemic insec-
tide that will be carried in the sap.

Leaf eaters
Leaf eaters give themselves away soon
after arrival, by the tell-tale chunks
missing from leaves. Fortunately,
most of the these pests are large and
easily seen, and on the whole control is
relatively simple.

Control: large pests that remain on the
plant, such as caterpillars, slugs and
snails, can usually be picked off by
hand (remove the whole leaf if in-
fested). Chemical control is hardly
ever necessary indoors, but in a conservatory you may want to use slug
bait (protect it under pieces of broken
pot if you have pets).

Those insects that feed at night and
hide during the day, such as earwigs,
present a bigger problem. Most
household crawling insect powders
and sprays will control these if you use
them around the area where the plants
are. If you don't want to use an
insecticide, leave small traps made
from matchboxes, left slightly open
and filled with litter such as chopped
straw. Check these each morning and
destroy any pests that you find.

Root chewers
The problem with root pests is that
you are unlikely to know of their
existence until the plant collapses,
by which time it's often too late.

A number of pests affect the roots,
from some types of aphids to the grubs
of insects such as weevils. If a plant
looks sick, fails to grow properly, or
starts to collapse, and there is no
obvious cause such as overwatering or
underwatering, remove the plant from
its pot and shake off the compost
(potting soil). Examine the roots: if
there are grubs or other pests, that's
the likely cause; if you find none but
the roots are sparse or rotting, a fungus disease is the more likely cause.

Control: if you have taken the plant
out of its pot for examination, shake
the compost off the roots and dip
them into an insecticidal solution before repotting in fresh compost. Your
plant may then recover. Drench the
compost in nearby pots with an insecticidal solution as a further precaution, though results may be variable.

Dealing with diseases

PLANT DISEASES CAN BE DISFIGURING AND EVEN FATAL, SO ALWAYS TAKE
THEM SERIOUSLY. IF YOU CAN'T CONTROL THEM BY PICKING OFF THE
AFFECTED LEAVES, RAPID RESORT TO A FUNGICIDE MAY BE THE BEST SOLU-
TION. IF A VIRUS STRIKES, IT MAY BE BETTER TO SACRIFICE THE PLANT TO
THE BIN RATHER THAN RISK THE INFECTION SPREADING TO OTHER PLANTS.

Leaf spot
Leaf spots are quite common, and are
caused by various fungi. If just a few leaves
are affected, pick them off then spray the
rest of the plant as a precaution.

Fungus diseases are often difficult to identify accurately and many different species of fungi can cause similar symptoms. Fortunately, a scientific identification of the exact fungus is not necessary in order to go about controlling it. The chemicals used to control each main group of diseases are largely effective against all the organisms likely to be responsible – but don't assume that all fungicides are equally effective against all fungus diseases. Always read the label to check what disease a particular chemical is most effective against.

Leaf spots
Various fungi and bacteria cause leaf spots. If tiny black specks can be seen on the affected surface, they are likely to be the spore-bearing bodies of a fungus, so a fungicide is likely to be effective. If no specks can be detected it might be a bacterial problem, though a fungicide might still be of some help.

Control: prune off and destroy the affected leaves. Water with a systemic fungicide, and avoid misting too frequently. Increase ventilation if the weather permits.

Root rots
The first sign of a root rot is usually the sudden collapse of a seemingly healthy plant. The leaves turn brown or black, and curl up. The entire plant may wilt. This is almost always the result of overwatering.

Control: if the plant has not already deteriorated too far, try drying it out. However, there is usually little that can be done at this stage.

Sooty mould
The fungus covers the leaves, often the back but sometimes the front, with a black growth that looks like soot. It does not directly harm the plants but looks unsightly.

Fungal diseases
The protective sleeve of this newly purchased saintpaulia disguised the fact that it is infected with *Botrytis cinerea*. This grey-brown mould develops on dead or damaged plants, and can be caused by lack of ventilation.

Sooty mould

Sooty mould is a fungus that grows on the sugary substance excreted by aphids and other sap-suckers. If you control the pests you will eliminate the disease, which is unsightly but not particularly harmful.

Mildew

Various kinds of mildew affect houseplants, and begonias are particularly prone to them. Control is difficult once the disease is well established, but various fungicides are useful for early and preventative treatment.

Control: sooty mould is a fungus that lives on the 'honeydew' (excrement) left by aphids and whitefly. When this food disappears so will the sooty mould, so eliminate the insects that are the prime cause.

Mildews

There are various kinds of mildew, the powdery types being the most common. Evidence of the disease is seen as a white, powdery deposit, almost as if the leaf has been sprinkled with flour. The problem starts in one or two areas but quickly radiates out and can soon engulf the whole leaf. Some plants, such as begonias, are more prone to mildew than others.

Control: pick off the affected leaves at an early stage, then use a fungicide to limit its spread. Increase ventilation, and reduce the humidity around the plant – at least until the disease is under control.

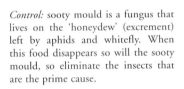

Using fungicides

If you need to use a fungicide, you can use those developed for outdoor plants by mixing a small amount and using it in a hand-pumped mister.

Viruses

The main symptoms of virus diseases are stunted or distorted growth, irregular yellow blotches on foliage and streaked petals on flowering plants. They are easily transmitted by sap-sucking insects such as aphids, and can even be carried on the knives used to take cuttings.

There is no effective control and, apart from the rare cases where the plants are cultivated for the variegation caused by the virus, the plants are best destroyed.

Disorders and deficiencies

NOT ALL TROUBLES ARE CAUSED BY PESTS AND DISEASES. SOMETIMES PHY-

SIOLOGICAL PROBLEMS SUCH AS CHILLS AND COLD DRAUGHTS, OR NUTRI-

TIONAL DEFICIENCIES, CAN BE THE CAUSE.

Tracking down a physiological problem calls for a bit of detective work. The descriptions of some common problems described here will help to pinpoint some potential causes, but be prepared to look for anything that has disturbed the usual routine – has the plant been moved, watered more or less heavily, has the weather become much colder, have you turned the central heating on but not increased humidity or ventilation? By piecing together the various clues you can often deduce probable causes, and thereby work out what you can do to avoid a repetition.

Temperature
Most houseplants will tolerate cool but frost-free temperatures if they have to. It is sudden changes of temperature or icy draughts in a warm room that cause most problems.

If leaves drop it may be due to low temperature. This often happens with newly bought plants that have been on display outdoors or chilled on the way home. Leaves that look shrivelled and slightly translucent may have been touched by frost.

Hardy plants like *Euonymus japonicus* may drop their leaves if kept too warm in winter. Berries are also likely to fall prematurely if the temperature is kept too high.

Light and sun
Plants that need a high light intensity will become elongated and drawn if the illumination is poor, and leaves and flower stalks will be drawn to-wards the window. Lop-sided growth is another indication of inadequate

Neglect
This plant is clearly showing signs of stress and lack of nutrients. It may be best to discard a plant in this state.

Sun scorch
Plants that are not adapted to grow in very strong light are easily scorched by strong sunlight intensified by a glass window. This dieffenbachia is suffering from scorch.

light. If you can't move the plant into a lighter position, try turning the pot round by 45 degrees each day (put a tiny mark on the pot as a reminder of whether you've turned it).

Light is usually a good thing, but direct sunlight, intensified through glass, will often scorch leaves – the effect will be brown, papery areas on the leaf. Patterned glass is a particular problem as it can act like a magnifying glass, causing dry brown patches where the rays have been concentrated.

Humidity
Dry air can cause leaf tips to go brown and papery on vulnerable plants.

Watering
Too little water is the most likely cause of wilting and collapse, if the compost (potting soil) feels very dry to the touch. If the plant collapses and the compost feels very wet, or water is standing in the saucer or cache-pot, suspect overwatering.

Feeding
Pale leaves and short, stunted growth may be due to lack of fertilizer in the

Effects of overwatering
Yellowing lower leaves are often a sign of overwatering, but may also be due to a chill if it happens in winter. This is a *Fatshedera lizei* beginning to show signs of overwatering.

Aerosol scorch

A plant can also be damaged by aerosol sprays (even one containing an insecticide intended for houseplants). This dieffenbachia has dropped many of its leaves, and others are scorched, because an insecticidal aerosol was used too close to the plant.

Effects of dry air

Dry air is a particular problem for most ferns. This adiantum is showing the signs of low humidity.

compost (potting soil). Try liquid feeding for a quick boost. Specific plants, such as citrus fruits and rhododendrons, may show signs of iron deficiency (yellowing leaves) if grown in an alkaline compost. Feed with a chelated (sequestered) iron and next time you repot use an ericaceous compost (specially developed for lime-hating plants).

Bud drop

Bud drop is often caused by dry compost (potting soil) or dry air, but sometimes it is due to the plant being moved to a different position or turned once the buds have formed. (Zygocactus is an example of a plant that resents having to re-orientate its buds to light from a different direction.)

Dehydration

This thunbergia shows the classic symptoms of a dehydrated plant. The very dry compost (potting soil) is confirmation of the cause. The best treatment is to stand the pot in a bowl of water for several hours, until the compost is thoroughly wet. Peat (peat moss) composts are particularly difficult to rewet once they have dried out completely, but a few drops of mild household detergent added to the water will help to rewet it.

Bud drop

Bud drop is often caused by dry root, overwatering, or by moving a plant once the flower buds have formed.

Wilting and worse

WHEN A PLANT WILTS OR APPEARS TO COLLAPSE, IT'S TIME TO TAKE DRASTIC

ACTION. THE FIRST PRIORITY IS TO DECIDE WHAT'S WRONG, THEN, IF

POSSIBLE, TO APPLY FIRST AID MEASURES WITHOUT DELAY TO BRING THE

PLANT BACK TO HEALTH.

First aid for a dry plant

1. If the leaves of a plant have started to wilt like this, the compost (potting soil) is probably too dry. Feel it first – overwatering also causes wilting.

2. Stand the pot in a bowl or bucket of water and leave it until the air bubbles have ceased to rise.

3. It will take some hours for the water to revive the plant. In the meantime, help the plant further by misting the leaves with water from time to time.

4. Once the plant has revived, remove it from the bowl and stand it in a cool place out of direct sunlight for at least a day.

Wilting and collapse are a signal that something is drastically wrong. If you ignore this warning, you may lose the plant. Plants usually wilt for one of three reasons:

- Too much water.
- Too little water.
- Insects or a disease affecting the roots.

The first two will usually be obvious: if the compost (potting soil) is hard and dry, underwatering is the likely cause: if there is water standing in the cache-pot or saucer, or if the compost oozes water, overwatering is almost certainly the cause.

If the compost seems neither overwatered nor underwatered, check the base of the plant just above compost level. If the stem looks black or rotten, a fungus disease is the likely cause and the plant is best discarded.

If none of the above symptoms are present, remove the plant from its pot and shake off some of the soil. If many of the roots are soft or black and decaying, a root disease is the likely cause. Look also for grubs or other insects around the roots. The larvae of beetles such as weevils can sometimes cause a plant to collapse.

First aid for root pests or diseases
It will be very difficult to revive a plant with a severe root rot, but you can try drenching the compost with a fungicide, then after a couple of hours letting it dry out on absorbent paper. If the root system is badly damaged it may be worth repotting it in sterilized compost first, after removing as much of the old soil as possible.

Some soil pests, such as root aphids, can be controlled if drenched with an insecticide. Wine weevil grubs and other serious soil pests are not so easy to control. Try shaking the old soil off the roots, dusting them with an insecticidal powder, then repotting in fresh, sterilized compost. If the damage is not too extensive the plant may survive once it has had time to make new growth.

First aid for a wet plant

1. Knock the plant out of its pot. If it does not come out easily, invert the plant while holding the compost (potting soil) in with one hand, and knock the rim of the pot on a hard surface.

2. Wrap the root-ball in several layers of absorbent paper.

3. Stand the plant in a warm place, out of direct sunlight, with more absorbent paper wrapped around the root-ball. Change the paper periodically if it is still drawing moisture from the compost.

OTHER POSSIBLE CAUSES OF COLLAPSE

🍃 Plants may collapse for physiological reasons:

🍃 Cold air at night, especially in winter, may cause some plants to collapse, especially if they have been kept warm during the day.

🍃 Strong, hot sunshine through glass will make many plants wilt. Usually they recover when given cooler, shadier conditions.

🍃 Hot, dry air will have a similar effect on some plants, such as the more delicate ferns.

🍃 Poor light will eventually cause a plant to exhaust itself. But this is likely to be a gradual process, much less rapid than collapse caused by watering problems or pests.

4. Continue until the compost has dried out, but do not let it become completely dry. Repot and water only very cautiously for the next week.

Creative displays

WHETHER YOU COLLECT HOUSE-PLANTS AS A PHILATELIST COLLECTS STAMPS, OR WHETHER YOU CHOOSE THEM IN THE SAME WAY AS AN INTERIOR DESIGNER SELECTS A PAINTING, YOU HAVE TO FIND POSITIONS THAT WILL NOT ONLY PLEASE THE PLANT, BUT ALSO SUIT THE DÉCOR.

Interior design

THE WAY IN WHICH YOU FURNISH AND DECORATE YOUR HOME IS AN EXPRESSION OF YOUR OWN PERSONALITY. YOU MAY NOT BE ABLE TO INFLUENCE THE WORLD OUTSIDE, OR EVEN YOUR WORKPLACE, BUT IN YOUR OWN HOME YOU CAN MAKE THE KIND OF STATEMENTS THAT PLEASE YOU PERSONALLY. HOUSEPLANTS CAN HELP YOU TO CREATE YOUR CHOSEN IMAGE: WHETHER WARM AND 'COTTAGEY', BOLD AND CLINICAL, STYLISH AND ELEGANT, OR SIMPLY PROVOCATIVE. IT DOES NOT MATTER WHETHER YOU HAVE A COUNTRY COTTAGE, CITY FLAT, OR SUBURBAN HOUSE, YOU CAN USE PLANTS TO COMPLEMENT YOUR CHOSEN DÉCOR.

A room without plants is rather like a meal without any seasoning. It serves its purpose and can even look good, but it lacks spice and that extra ingredient that would make it interesting. Not everyone wants to be strangled by an over-exuberant ivy as they mount the stairs, or grapple with a monstera in order to place a coffee cup on the sideboard, but a few well-chosen plants will transform a bare or dull room into something special in the same way as a carefully chosen picture or ornament.

Plants can also serve a functional purpose when used to screen off part of a room in a natural and much less obtrusive way than furniture or normal room dividers.

Establishing a style

Decide on the image and style that you intend to create, then buy plants that will help you to achieve it. Be prepared to invest in one or two really good specimens if necessary: they may cost no more than half a dozen mediocre plants yet will have far more impact. To create an old-fashioned cottage atmosphere, however, a collection of traditional plants on the win-

dowsill and a large aspidistra or sansevieria in an attractive cache-pot are more likely to achieve the right ambience than some big, bold 'architectural' plants that would create a strong statement in a large modern room, office, or foyer.

Groups or single specimens?

Most plants prefer to grow in groups as they benefit from the microclimate produced, and three or five quite ordinary houseplants grouped in a large container will make a far greater impact than they would if dotted around the room individually. Grouping plants usually means you have to use a large container rather than ordinary plant pots, and this also adds to the sense of purpose and design.

Large plants can usually be used in isolation, and many of the tall-

ABOVE AND LEFT: *A good way to learn about the best ways to arrange plants in the home is to place the same plants in different containers or groups to see the very different effects you can create with the same plants. Here three cyclamen have been placed in separate containers (above) then grouped together in a single cache-pot (left). Both displays look elegant, but strikingly different.*

growers, such as yuccas, philo-dendrons, and ficus such as *F. benjamina* and *F. lyrata,* often have enough presence to stand alone as focal point. If they become rather tall and bare at the base, however, you could try planting some flowering plants, or even small trailing ivies, in the same container to hide the stem.

Backgrounds and backdrops

Most plants are best viewed against a plain background. If you have a highly patterned wall covering, especially if it includes leaves or floral motifs, the plants you choose need to have big, bold foliage. This is where plain green has a definite advantage over varie-gated foliage: visual chaos will result from a boldly coloured and variegated plant placed against a brightly deco-rated wall covering.

Making the most of height

If all your plants are on tables or windowsills, they will look attractive but predictable. Use a few large speci-mens on the floor, or consider hanging containers in light corners of the room that seem devoid of decoration at a higher level. Use trailers from the

TOP: *Plants usually make a bolder feature if grouped, and they benefit from the microclimate produced. Here, the plants have been graded in height to provide an attractive foliage screen between the eating and working areas of the kitchen.*

ABOVE: *A disused fireplace can become a focal point if used to frame plants. Use taller plants in the hearth and smaller plants and trailers on the mantelpiece.*

mantelpiece if you do not use the fireplace, and make the most of pedes-tals for attractive containers with trail-ers like *Scindapsus aureus,* spiky up-right plants like dracaenas or arching plants like nephrolepsis ferns.

Choosing containers

Containers should never dominate, but they can make a mediocre plant look special, and many are ornaments in their own right. Try using an attractive ornament as a cache-pot for a plant, or if you have an interesting container, like an old kettle or coal-scuttle, plant it up with a flowering or foliage plant that makes a happy mar-riage and which does not dominate the container.

A question of scale

The relationship between the size of the plant and its required function in the room should not be overlooked. A solitary saintpaulia, even if it is set on an attractive table, will make no im-pact in the overall composition; like-wise, a large *Ficus benjamina* in a tiny room in a cottage will certainly be noticed, but not for its contribution to the interior design.

Table-top displays

A BEAUTIFUL FLOWERING PLANT OR AN ARRANGEMENT OF FOLIAGE PLANTS MAKES A SUPERB CENTREPIECE FOR A TABLE, WHETHER YOU USE IT AS A FOCAL POINT ON A BARE TABLE OR AS THE CROWNING GLORY TO A TABLE-SETTING FOR A DINNER PARTY. UNFORTUNATELY SUCH POSITIONS SUIT FEW PLANTS, MOST OF WHICH PREFER A LIGHTER SPOT NEAR THE WINDOW, SO CHOOSE YOUR PLANTS CAREFULLY AND BE PREPARED TO CHANGE THEM FREQUENTLY.

Flowering plants
Give your table display a designer look by choosing a flowering plant that is colour co-ordinated with the table-cloth. This can look particularly pleasing if you are using the plant as part of a table-setting for a meal, and even a small plant will look effective if it appears to have been chosen and displayed with care.

A cloth can be used to good effect on a table used purely for display, especially if the table itself is mediocre. By choosing a patterned or plain cloth that is light in colour, you can draw attention to the feature, and make even more of a focal point with your plant. A cyclamen may look nice but uninspiring if placed on a bare table. But if you put it on a pink tablecloth to match the shade of the flower, it becomes something special.

Try positioning a bright flowering plant with blooms on long stems, such as a gerbera, on a side table with a mirror behind. It will reflect the tall blooms and appear to multiply the number of flowers.

Gerberas are good examples of flowering pot plants that are suitable for a table display. They are usually sold in bloom and are difficult to keep for more than one year, so you might treat them like a long-lasting display of cut flowers. It will not matter that

the light is poor if the plant is to be discarded after flowering, which should continue for weeks.

Other flowering pot plants that will bring colour and cheer to a dull corner and that are usually discarded after flowering include year-round chrysanthemums, cinerarias, *Erica* × *hyemalis* and *E. gracilis,* and small annuals like *Exacum affine.* In winter and spring, bowls of bulbs such as hyacinths can be used if you keep them in good light until they come into flower and do not try to force them to flower indoors the following year.

Foliage plants
It is among the foliage plants that the most shade-tolerant types are to be found, but most are unsuitable for table-tops. Most species of ficus, for example, grow too large, while others, such as ivies, have a sprawling habit. Choose something tough and variegated, with a neat shape, such as *Sansevieria trifasciata gigantea* 'Laurentii', or variegated aglaonemas.

For a cool position, such as an unheated bedroom, or a hall that is not too stuffy, varieties of *Aucuba japonica* are useful.

Pot-et-Fleur

A *pot-et-fleur* arrangement makes an ideal centre piece, giving plenty of scope for artistic presentation. Anyone keen on floral art will find plenty of scope for expressing their talent.

To make a classic *pot-et-fleur* arrangement, choose an attractive planter (some self-watering pots are suitable), and plant a group of three or five foliage plants (you can plant more but the container needs to be large). As you plant them, insert a glass tube or metal florist's tube into the compost (potting soil), either at the centre of the arrangement or a little to one side.

Fill the tube with water and insert a few cut flowers (and cut foliage if you want). You won't need many flowers, yet they will bring a touch of colour to the arrangement, and because you have to replace them regularly the composition will be constantly changing. If one or two of the foliage plants begin to deteriorate in time, just replace them with fresh ones.

Opposite above: *Colour co-ordinate your plants for a really tasteful effect. Here a pink cyclamen harmonizes with the tablecloth and wallpaper border.*

Opposite left: *Try placing a plant, like this gerbera, in front of a mirror where the reflection can make even a small plant look larger and more imposing.*

Right: *This* pot-et-fleur *arrangement uses floral foam to hold the cut flowers, which makes it particularly flexible in the way you can arrange the blooms. Lilies, freesias, cut fern leaves and ivies were used to create the arrangement, here displayed in a hearth.*

Creating a pot-et-fleur with foam

1. If using a basket like this, line it first to ensure that it is waterproof.

2. Position your foliage plants first, preferably in shallow pots.

3. Cut floral foam to size to pack between the pots.

4. Insert your flowers (and additional cut foliage if wished) into the moist floral foam.

Pedestals and hanging pots and baskets

HANGING AND CASCADING PLANTS ARE ESPECIALLY USEFUL IF YOU WANT TO MAKE THE MOST OF A VERTICAL SPACE OR CREATE A FEELING OF LUSHNESS IN A GARDEN ROOM. WHERE SPACE IS LIMITED AND THE FLOOR ALREADY HAS ITS BURDEN OF PLANTS, HANGING CONTAINERS CAN MAKE THE MOST OF THE AVAILABLE SPACE. USE THEM TO CREATE CASCADING CURTAINS OF FOLIAGE.

Pedestals

Many pedestals are extremely ornate, and make focal points in themselves. If you have an attractive pedestal, don't cover it with long trailers that mask its beauty. Use short trailers that will cascade over the pot but won't completely hide the pedestal under a curtain of leaves. Good plants to choose for this effect include *Asparagus densiflorus* 'Sprengeri', *Campanula isophylla* and flowering hybrids of zygocactus and rhipsalidopsis.

Plants with an arching rather than a cascading habit are also ideal for a pedestal where you want to show off both pot and pedestal: chlorophytums

ABOVE: *Chlorophytums look good displayed on a pedestal or in a hanging basket, where the arching effect can be seen to advantage. Hanging baskets are much more successful in a conservatory than indoors.*

LEFT: *The nephrolepis fern is a popular choice for a pedestal, as it makes a neat mound of growth with enough 'droop' to take the eye down to the pedestal. Here an attractive table has been used, and the opportunity taken to place another fern on the shelf beneath.*

OPPOSITE LEFT: *Hanging baskets should always be placed in a bright position, as the light near the ceiling is almost always poorer than lower down the window. This one contains a rhoicissus.*

and nephrolepis ferns are especially attractive used in this way.

For a pedestal that is functional rather than decorative, go for tumbling curtains of growth, with plants like ivies, *Plectranthus oertendahlii* and *P. coleoides* 'Marginatus', or a golden *Epipremnum aureum* 'Neon' (syn. *Scindapsus aureus*).

Hanging pots and baskets

Ordinary hanging baskets are unsuitable for using indoors, although you can of course use them in a conservatory. Unless you are prepared to take great care with the watering, and take precautions to avoid drips over your carpets and furniture, choose a hanging pot with a drip tray, or a specially designed indoor 'basket' (in effect a basket-shaped pot, sometimes with a water reservoir).

Hanging containers are difficult to position: they shouldn't be hung where they can be a hazard to anyone walking by, and in addition many plants suitable for baskets need to be near good light. If the room is not large enough for hanging baskets, try the same plants in half baskets or wall pots. Many trailing or arching plants look magnificent when positioned against the background of a plain or pale wall.

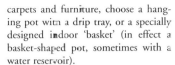

PRACTICAL POINTS

❧ Pedestals are far more practical than hanging pots. The plants will usually be in better light (because sunlight generally shines downwards, the upper part of the room is generally gloomier than the lower part), and watering is much easier if the plants are grown in ordinary pots. Baskets are difficult to water, and need to be hung where the baskets and their trailing contents do not cause an obstruction to anyone walking by.

TRAILERS AND CASCADERS TO TRY

❧ **Flowering plants**

Aeschynanthus, *Aporocactus flagelliformis*, *Campanula isophylla*, columnea, *Rhipsalidopsis gaertneri* and *Zygocactus truncatus*.

❧ **Foliage plants**

Asparagus densiflorus 'Sprengeri', *Chlorophytum comosum* 'Variegatum', *Epipremnum aureum* (syn. *Scindapsus aureus*), *Hedera helix* (ivies), small-leaved varieties, plectranthus and *Rhoicissus rhomboidea* (syn. *Cissus rhombifolia*).

Planting a pedestal arrangement

1. A wide, shallow container, which is more stable and detracts less from the pedestal itself, has been chosen here.

2. Choose a mixture of flowering and foliage plants for a spectacular display. You can try them for position while still in their pots, until you are happy with the arrangement.

3. Remove them from their pots for final planting. Try setting those at the edge at a slight angle so that they tend to grow outwards and tumble over the side.

RIGHT: *Don't just think of single specimens when choosing plants for a pedestal. A group can be arranged rather like a hanging basket, but planted in a pot.*

Grouping large plants

SOMETIMES A LARGE PLANT IS BEST VIEWED IN ISOLATION: ITS VERY SIZE AND IMPORTANCE WILL THEN BE EMPHASIZED. MORE OFTEN, HOWEVER, THEY LOOK BETTER WHEN POSITIONED AS PART OF A GROUP, PERHAPS WITH SMALLER PLANTS IN FRONT.

Group plants together in places that might otherwise look bare. A disused fireplace can be improved with perhaps a single, elegant fern, provided that it is large enough. The whole fireplace and hearth area can be the ideal place for a group of plants – tall ones positioned mantelpiece height at the back, smaller ones in front at the bottom of the hearth, and arching or trailing plants sitting on the mantelpiece.

If you have a really magnificent plant, perhaps a yucca 1.8m (6ft) tall or more, or a beautiful variegated *Ficus benjamina* that almost reaches the ceiling, show it off in splendid isolation. These plants deserve to act as focal points in their own right. Less imposing plants usually look better arranged in small groups, where they will make a greater impact than they would individually. You can create the effect of a garden brought indoors by positioning plants in this way. Plants standing shoulder to shoulder always look more convincing than those dotted around the room wherever there seems to be space to put a plant.

Small plants are easily grouped in a large planter, but this is not suitable for large specimens. The huge planters used in offices and hotel foyers are not practical for the home, and the plants are best left in their own pots and arranged in close proximity with the largest at the back and smaller ones in front.

The majority of large houseplants are grown for their foliage, but many are variegated or boldly coloured. It's a good idea to mix a few plants with coloured or variegated foliage among the greens, although you may sometimes need an all-green group to produce a cool, tranquil effect. Variegated plants also require higher light levels than all-green ones because a smaller area of the leaf is able to photosynthesize with what light is available, so it's best to avoid these for plant groupings in the darkest parts of the home.

Group policy

The natural way to group large house-plants is with the tallest at the back, with bushier, lower ones at the front. Take into account their position in the room. If the group is placed halfway down a long room with windows at each end, so that the plants act almost as a divider, include more plants in the arrangement, with smaller ones at each side and the tallest in the centre. In a corner of a room, a group of plants consisting of a single big specimen at the back, with smaller ones spilling forwards to fill out the corner, can look quite stunning.

If the plants in your group lack sufficient variation in height, try standing some on a low table or raise them in some other way.

To protect the floor, stand each pot on a saucer – those designed to match the pot look good and are perfectly practical. It is difficult to water plants at the back of a group, so the risk of a little water overflowing will be that much greater.

COMPATIBLE NEEDS

Wherever practical, group together those plants with similar needs. Yuccas and palms will tolerate a dry atmosphere and will be happy together, but most philodendrons and dracaenas prefer a humid atmosphere. For the short term you can mix any plants together, but if you plan to keep them in good condition, it's worth grouping plants with similar requirements so that they receive the most appropriate care.

OPPOSITE: *Plants often look better in groups, but choose ones appropriate to the setting. A group of small plants would look out of proportion in this hearth. The large specimens used here fill the space and give the setting a sense of design.*

TOP: *If this nephrolepis fern on a pedestal had been displayed on its own, it would probably have looked too isolated. By using it with other plants it looks interesting yet integrated.*

ABOVE: *Add one or two flowering plants to a group. Even a little colour will draw the eye.*

ABOVE: *Tall plants are always impressive, but they can look bare towards the base. By surrounding them with smaller bold plants in front, you can create a well-planned group. A selection of all-green and variegated plants with a wide array of leaf size and shape have been selected here for maximum visual interest.*

Grouping small plants

SMALL PLANTS CAN BE DISPLAYED MORE CREATIVELY THAN JUST IN INDI-
VIDUAL POTS. PLANT THEM IN GROUPS IN PLANTERS OR SELF-WATERING
POTS. YOU CAN EVEN CREATE MINIATURE GARDENS.

Grouping plants together often makes them easier to care for, and they usually look more attractive as an arrangement rather than as individual plants.

The overall effect of a group is usually bolder than that of individual specimens, and by placing taller ones at the back of the arrangement the effect is more 'landscaped'. Small-leaved prostrate plants such as *Ficus pumila* and *Helxine soleirolii* (syn. *Soleirolia soleirolii*) assume a new role in a group and are less insignificant than when they are grown as prostrate plants in an individual pot. In a group they become ground-cover plants, which is their natural state. Another advantage of grouping plants is that you can get away with less than perfect specimens: a plant with lop-sided growth, or one that is bare at the base, can be arranged so that its defects are hidden by other plants.

Grouped plants benefit from the microclimate created when plants are grown together. The local humidity is likely to be a little higher as the leaves tend to protect each other from drying air and cold draughts, and it is easier to keep the compost (potting soil) evenly moist in a large container than a small one. Groupings are ideal for self-watering containers and for plants grown hydroponically, and simply ensuring a steady and even supply of moisture almost always produces better growth.

Group styles

There are no hard and fast rules about how to group plants – whatever pleases you is right provided that the plants are also happy (avoid placing together plants with totally different needs). The suggestions for grouping styles described here work well for most plants, and generally look attractive, but be prepared to experiment. A group of plants arranged in an old coalscuttle in the hearth, for example, may look more attractive than any of the more traditional styles if the setting is right.

Collections of pots have the advantage of being infinitely flexible. You can rearrange and remove plants at will, and use transient flowering plants such as chrysanthemums and poinsettias more easily than in a permanent planting. A group of five or six plants in their individual pots will look cheery and bold if you mix different types of foliage plants (stiff and upright, arching, feathery or trailing) with a couple of flowering plants. You can space them out as necessary to fill the space, but make sure that they are close enough to overlap a little and look like a group.

Pebble trays are ideal for plants that like a lot of humidity. Use a tray

---

Grouping plants in a planter

1. A bowl without drainage holes will protect the table, but place a drainage layer at the bottom and be *very* careful not to overwater.

2. Place a little compost (potting soil) in the bowl first, then insert the plants. Try to achieve a good balance between flowering and foliage plants.

3. Firm the plants in, and pack more compost around the roots if necessary. Water, but be careful not to waterlog the compost.

ABOVE: *Pot up several plants in a bowl to make an attractive group; a* **Begonia rex,** *a cyclamen and ivies were used here.*

that will fit on a table or windowsill, and fill it with pebbles. Stand the pots on the pebbles. It does not matter if water stands in the tray provided that the bottoms of the pots are not in direct contact with it.

Planters and self-watering pots will usually accommodate at least three plants if you choose a suitable size. These look elegant, and are ideal if you find regular watering difficult. Choose plants that will not need frequent repotting or removing, and plant directly into the compost (potting soil).

WATCH OUT FOR PROBLEMS

Growing plants in groups has some drawbacks. Pests and diseases can spread more easily and rapidly, and you may be less likely to notice the early symptoms on leaves that are hidden by other plants. If grooming is a regular routine, however, this should be only a minor drawback, and one that is easily overcome.

ABOVE: *Grouping small plants is particularly effective if you need to use them in a low position, where they are viewed from above. Add some flowering plants (here gerberas and begonias) to bring a foliage group to life.*

TOP: *Small plants benefit from grouping as much as large ones. You can often group small plants in one large container, but by keeping them in individual containers you can ring the changes more easily. This is especially important if you use flowering plants that may look attractive for only a relatively short time.*

ABOVE: *Grouping plants in a shallow dish keeps them happy and looks good too. Because these plants are raised on expanded clay granules (you could use small gravel), some water can be kept in the bottom without waterlogging the compost (potting soil) – providing invaluable humidity for the ferns.*

Garden rooms and conservatories

WITH A GARDEN ROOM OR CONSERVATORY YOU CAN GROW ALMOST ANY HOUSEPLANT SUCCESSFULLY, AS WELL AS MANY MORE FOR WHICH YOU WOULD NORMALLY NEED A GREENHOUSE. HOWEVER, YOU WILL HAVE TO RESOLVE THE CONFLICT BETWEEN THE NEEDS OF PLANTS AND HUMANS, FOR WHAT IS A COMFORTABLE ENVIRONMENT FOR TROPICAL PLANTS MAY NOT BE COMFORTABLE FOR YOU. WITH CAREFUL PLANNING, HOWEVER, YOU CAN MAKE THE GARDEN ROOM AN EXTENSION OF THE LIVING AREA, WHERE YOU CAN ENJOY HOUSEPLANTS AT THEIR VERY BEST.

Many conservatories and garden rooms are built on as a home extension or a sun room where the garden can be enjoyed when the weather is pleasant but not warm, and in which the plants are merely decorative accessories. You can, however, create a veritable jungle atmosphere, with plants from floor to roof, and hot and humid air to match.

Mainly for people

If a sun room or conservatory is to be a comfortable place to sit for long periods and enjoy the view of the garden, a few attractive chairs, a coffee table and a few elegant pot plants dotted around are all that's required. It just becomes another room.

Paint the back wall white or cream, plant a bougainvillea against it, buy a few big palms and add one or two flowering shrubs such as *Nerium oleander,* and perhaps an orange or lemon in an attractive tub, and you will have a room with instant charm.

Mainly for plants

If your conservatory was bought mainly to increase the number and type of houseplants that you can grow, treat it like a greenhouse. Indeed the distinction between some modern lean-to greenhouses and garden rooms can be a little blurred.

Make the most of climbers; these will clothe the wall and cover the roof space if you secure galvanized wires at about 30–60cm (1–2ft) intervals for support. The roof cover will provide welcome shade in the summer, and if you choose deciduous climbers such as a grapevine or a passiflora, the other inhabitants will receive full light at the time of year when they most need it. Even so, climbers such as grapes may still need to be cut back periodically during the summer to prevent them from dominating and casting too much shade.

Plant climbers and wall shrubs in the ground if possible, by lifting the paving and making planting pits. Use special display shelves, or improvise your own. Don't just arrange plants around the edge of the structure, create islands of plants, or use them as a backdrop for seats, which can be almost surrounded with plants.

Hanging baskets should thrive, so use plenty of them and be adventurous with what you plant. Although traditional bedding plants can be used in a conservatory, cascading fuchsias or curtains of columneas are usually much more spectacular.

For healthy houseplants, lay a floor that won't come to harm if you splash water about. Use a humidifier if possible, so that the air is aways moist in warm weather, and provide heating for the winter. A minimum of 7°C (45°F) is sufficient to keep most houseplants alive, while the majority of tender types will survive the winter at 13°C (55°F) minimum.

ABOVE: *Bold, tall plants, like this palm, can be used as an eye-catching feature in a conservatory. It also emphasizes the vertical line of the magnificent wrought-iron staircase.*

OPPOSITE: *Citrus fruits, such as oranges, do not do well indoors, but they make excellent conservatory plants. Try painting your conservatory wall white to reflect light and to make an attractive backdrop against which to view your plants.*

TOP RIGHT: *By keeping most of the planting around the edge, and using plenty of hanging baskets, you can give the impression of lush plant growth while still retaining an attractive sitting area.*

ABOVE RIGHT: *Make the most of available space. Plant climbers against the house wall and use hanging baskets, which will do much better in the improved light than indoors.*

RIGHT: *Plants should thrive in a conservatory and you can use bold all-green foliage groups like this. With a tiled floor you can provide plenty of moisture and humidity without worrying about drips or splashed water.*

Bottle gardens

BOTTLE GARDENS, CREATED IN SEALED BOTTLES WITH MOISTURE RECIRCU-

LATING AS IT CONDENSES AND RUNS DOWN THE GLASS, MAKE AN IDEAL HOME

FOR MANY SMALL BUT DEMANDING PLANTS THAT ARE DIFFICULT TO KEEP IN

A NORMAL ROOM ENVIRONMENT. THEY ALSO MAKE A VERY DECORATIVE WAY

OF DISPLAYING PLANTS AND ONE THAT IS SURE TO BECOME A TALKING POINT

WITH VISITORS.

The still, protected and humid environment of a sealed bottle garden makes it possible to grow many small jungle and rain forest type plants that would soon die in a dry living-room. Yet if you leave the top off and water very carefully, a bottle garden can also be a pretty way to display those that enjoy less humid conditions. Even flowering plants can be used if you are careful to deadhead them regularly to prevent the rotting flowers becoming a source of diseases.

Sealed bottles will thrive for months without attention, and you can go on

How to plant a bottle garden

1. Place a layer of charcoal and gravel or expanded clay granules in the bottom of a thoroughly clean bottle, then add compost (potting soil). Use a funnel or cone made from thick paper or thin cardboard as a guide.

2. Use small plants, and if necessary remove some of the compost to make insertion easier. Unless the neck is very narrow you should be able to insert the plants without difficulty.

3. After tamping the compost around the roots (use a cotton reel on the end of a cane if necessary), mist the plants and compost. If necessary, direct the spray to remove compost adhering to the sides.

LEFT: *An open-topped bottle like this will require regular careful watering, but as it contains some quick-growing plants the ready access makes routine grooming and pruning much easier.*

holiday confident that even tricky ferns and selaginellas will be safe until you return. Unsealed containers require careful watering, and if you use flowering or fast-growing plants in them, regular grooming and pruning are essential.

Bottle gardens can be difficult to display. The plants need good light, and if you choose a bottle with coloured glass (many of those readily available are green) it is important to remember that much of the useful light will be filtered out. A sunny window is as undesirable as a gloomy corner: temperatures can soar as the sun's rays penetrate two layers of glass. The best place is by a window that does not receive direct sunlight, or on a table just below a sunny window, where it will receive good light but little direct sun.

Metal display stands make more of a feature of a bottle that would otherwise be placed on the floor, and help by raising it a little towards the light.

Sealed or open?

If you have a container with a stopper, a sealed environment will mean that you can leave it for months without watering, *once the atmosphere has been balanced*. But these are not suitable for plants with flowers, or fast-growing foliage plants. Any plant used in a sealed bottle must be able to tolerate constantly damp, humid conditions, and poor light.

Tip
If you can't get your hand into the bottle, use a spoon tied to a cane to make the planting hole, and a fork tied to another one to hold the plant while you lower it into position.

BALANCING A SEALED BOTTLE

❧ If you add too much water to a sealed bottle, the plants may rot and condensation on the glass will be a constant problem. If you add too little, the plants will not grow. You can only achieve the correct balance by trial and error.

❧ If the compost (potting soil) looks or feels too wet, leave the stopper off for a few days until it begins to dry out.

❧ It is normal for the bottle to mist up inside when the outside temperature drops, so a 'steamed up' bottle in the morning is not abnormal. If the condensation does not clear during the morning, the compost is too moist (leave the stopper off for a day). If there is no condensation when the room temperature drops significantly, the compost may be too dry.

ABOVE LEFT: *A large kitchen jar makes an interesting bottle garden. This one contains a miniature saintpaulia. Open the jar regularly to remove dead flowers, which will otherwise start to decay and cause the other plants to rot.*

FAR LEFT AND LEFT: *Bottle gardens can be used to display a variety of foliage plants, such as selaginella, variegated ivy and a colourful dracaena (far left). A collection of just one kind of plant, such as three different pileas (left), can also make an interesting group.*

Terrariums and other plant cases

TERRARIUMS AND PLANT CASES ARE USUALLY USED AS A DECORATIVE ORNA-
MENT, PERHAPS ON A SIDE TABLE WITH ADEQUATE ARTIFICIAL LIGHTING TO
SHOW OFF THE CONTAINER AND TO STIMULATE PLANT GROWTH, OR ON A
TABLE IN FRONT OF A WINDOW. KEEP THE PLANTS SIMPLE AND UNCLUT-
TERED IF YOU WANT TO MAKE THE MOST OF AN ATTRACTIVE CONTAINER;
CONCENTRATE ON A LUSH PLANTING IF THE CASE IS PRACTICAL RATHER
THAN PLEASING.

Terrariums and plants cases encompass those containers that are not bottles, but the advantages and challenges are exactly the same as for a bottle garden. With a terrarium you can let your imagination roam wider in search of suitable containers. The old-fashioned Wardian cases (now rare and expensive, though replicas can be found) are especially attractive, but a second-hand aquarium will do just as well and you may be able to obtain one quite cheaply as it does not even have to be watertight.

Some glass cases can be sealed, in the same way as a bottle garden, but most are left open. The plants are protected from draughts on all sides, and this helps to keep the atmosphere warm and moist around the plants.

SUITABLE CONTAINERS

❧ Elaborate terrariums are available from garden centres and shops, but you can sometimes buy kits to make your own. Designs vary from plain to ornate, but most are assembled with glass cut to shape and held together with strips of lead. Inexpensive, improvised containers are often just as successful if your interest lies in the plants rather than in the container.

❧ **Aquariums** offer plenty of scope for 'landscaping'. On the one hand they can be used without a top and kept fairly dry for a cactus garden, complete with a suitably arid setting of stones and stone chippings; on the other they will make an ideal home for delicate ferns if you create a humid atmosphere by covering with a glass top. You can buy aquarium covers that include a light, enabling you to make a feature of it even in a dark corner. But be sure to use the type of fluorescent tube sold for aquariums, as these are balanced to produce a quality of light that is suitable for plant growth.

❧ **Goldfish bowls** can be used for just one or two plants. A single plant like a saintpaulia will look good, or choose a spreading small-leaved carpeter such as *Helxine soleirolii* (syn. *Soleirolia soleirolii*) that will gradually creep up the sides and then spill over the rim.

❧ **Specimen jars,** originally used to preserve biological specimens, can be attractive, but they are more difficult to obtain (try a laboratory equipment supplier).

LEFT: *Miniature kalanchoes and miniature saintpaulias can be depended on to provide colour in any terrarium, but a contrasting foliage plant, like the selaginella in this one, will improve the arrangement.*

Planting a terrarium

1. Always place a drainage layer at the bottom of the terrarium. Use gravel and charcoal or expanded clay granules to counter the effects of standing water.

2. Plants that are a little too tall for the terrarium, such as this palm, can be trimmed to size, but do not use fast-growing plants that would quickly dominate the smaller specimens.

3. If necessary, remove some of the compost (potting soil) from the root-ball and firm the plant in well.

Many containers used for terrariums have more room than bottles or preserving jars, so larger plants can be grown, and you don't have to worry so much if a vigorous member of the group tries to pop its head above the rim. Long or deep containers, such as an aquarium, also offer much more scope for 'landscaping', with small rocks, even miniature pools.

Follow the watering advice for bottle gardens and take care with preparation and planting:

- Place a layer of charcoal and gravel at least 1cm (½in) thick on the bottom.
- Use a sterilized potting or seed compost (medium), but avoid feeding or using a compost high in nutrients, otherwise the plants will soon outgrow their space.
- Add small rocks or pebbles if you want to 'landscape' the terrarium, but avoid wood as this may rot and encourage diseases.
- Cover the container with a sheet of close-fitting glass if appropriate, and if you want to create an enclosed environment.

ABOVE: *An attractive terrarium like this can be expensive to buy, but some people make their own, and you may be able to buy one in kit form to assemble yourself.*

RIGHT: *Saintpaulias are a good choice for a container with easy access for removing dead flowers. They benefit from the protected and humid atmosphere. Instead of planting them alone, use them with a carpet of moss or low-growing selaginellas.*

Specimen plants

EVERY HOME NEEDS AT LEAST A COUPLE OF SPECIMEN PLANTS TO PROVIDE
ATTRACTIVE FOCAL POINTS. THEY DO NOT NEED TO BE LARGE SPECIMENS
LIKE SMALL TREES, PROVIDED THAT THEY ARE IMPOSING. A WELL-
ESTABLISHED CLIMBER THAT FORMS PART OF A ROOM DIVIDER, OR A REALLY
LARGE ASPIDISTRA OR *NEPHROLEPIS EXALTATA* ON A PEDESTAL, FOR EXAM-
PLE, WILL SERVE THE SAME PURPOSE AS A LARGE *FICUS BENJAMINA* THAT
ALMOST TOUCHES THE CEILING.

The purpose of a specimen plant is to catch the eye and be admired. This can be achieved by a really well-grown chlorophytum in a hanging container with cascading shoots carrying their small plantlets, as effectively as by an large, expensive palm. It just needs to be a superb example of the plant, well displayed, against a suitable background.

A large plant with a bold profile or outline, often called an 'architectural' plant, will transform a bare wall in a large room, add character to an otherwise uninspiring hallway, or give a sense of design and purpose if placed at the end of a long passage. If necessary, use spotlights to highlight the plant. If you use lights balanced for good plant growth the plant will benefit too. It is difficult to grow such large specimens yourself simply by starting with a small plant. It may take years and in the poor light and dry atmosphere indoors it will be extremely difficult to grow a plant to a large size without blemishes. Large specimens are expensive, however, so be sure that you can provide conditions that will maintain your investment.

Background and lighting
A bold plant requires a suitable background to show off its size and shape to advantage. A plain background is

usually best, and a light-coloured wall will make most plants look good. If the background is colourful or confused, choose a plant with bold plain green leaves, such as a *Ficus lyrata.*

Once natural light fails, use spotlights to draw attention to key plants, but make sure that the bulbs are not so close that the heat generated damages the plant.

Containers
Choose a container that does justice to the plant. An ordinary large plastic or clay pot will let down a magnificent palm or large weeping fig. If you want an ordinary terracotta pot, choose one that is large and ornately decorated (you don't have to worry about whether it is frostproof for indoors). If the décor demands something more modern, there are many very attractive planters and coloured plastic plant holders available.

Make sure that the colour of your chosen container goes with your décor and that the size is in proportion to the plant. A pot that is too large or too small will mar the effect.

OPPOSITE: *A single plant may be all that you need in a room if it's bold enough, like this majestic spathiphyllum.*

TOP LEFT: *You don't need to buy expensive or exotic plants for a specimen with real impact. The commonplace chlorophytum is so easy to grow and propagate that many plants are acquired as gifts from friends with surplus plants. If you keep a young plant for long enough, repot it annually, and are generous with the feeding and watering, you can end up with a magnificent specimen.*

ABOVE LEFT: Monstera deliciosa *is a firm favourite as a specimen plant, and this picture shows why. Here the clever use of a mirror not only makes the most of an attractive clock, but also reflects the bold leaves of the monstera.*

ABOVE RIGHT: *A large window or patio door with no sill needs a big floor-standing plant to create instant impact. Yuccas, and palms like this one, are ideal.*

PLANTS TO TRY

❧ Architectural plants
Araucaria heterophylla (syn. *A. excelsa*), *Fatsia japonica*, *Ficus benjamina*, *Ficus elastica* varieties, *Ficus lyrata*, palms, *Philodendron bipinnatifidum* and yucca.

❧ Climbing plants
Cissus antarctica, *Monstera deliciosa* and *Philodendron domesticum* (syn. *P. hastatum*).

Choosing a container

BESIDES FULFILLING AN ESSENTIAL FUNCTION, CONTAINERS CAN ALSO BE DECORATIVE IN THEIR OWN RIGHT AND FORM PART OF THE ROOM DÉCOR JUST LIKE A VASE OR ORNAMENT. THE RIGHT CONTAINER WILL ENHANCE AN ATTRACTIVE PLANT AND CAN OFTEN COMPENSATE FOR A MEDIOCRE ONE. THE CHOICE OF CONTAINER CAN DEMONSTRATE YOUR ARTISTIC FLAIR AND EVEN YOUR SENSE OF HUMOUR.

Ordinary plant pots have a place in the greenhouse, but not in the home. Some plants, especially large palms, benefit from the weight of a large clay pot, which gives them stability if filled with a loam-based compost (potting soil), but indoors an ornate one with an attractive pattern will always look nicer than a plain one. As a general rule, all other houseplants look better in especially designed indoor containers.

Cache-pots

Repotting into a new container is not always necessary. A cache-pot (an outer container in which you hide the pot containing the plant) creates the right illusion and avoids the need to repot. This technique is especially useful for flowering plants that will probably only be in the home for a short time, and for fast-growing plants that are likely to need frequent repotting.

Any decorative container can be used as a cache-pot. Attractive ones are available in shops and garden centres, but a search around the home often provides something suitable. Even old kitchenware, such as a teapot or copper saucepan, can look appropriate for a plant in the kitchen.

If you are an amateur potter, making your own cache-pots can be particularly rewarding, and the plants provide a good opportunity to display your talents around the home.

OPPOSITE ABOVE: *Sometimes a container that blends in with the background, like this fern-leaf basket, is as effective as one that contrasts with it.*

OPPOSITE BELOW: *If you don't have matching decorative containers for a group arrangement, improvise. Ordinary plastic pots and saucers have here been wrapped in strips of white cotton fabric for an eye-catching effect.*

ABOVE LEFT: *A metal container like this ornamental bucket adds to the crisp, clean look of a plant like* Asplenium nidus.

ABOVE CENTRE: *If you have a container with lots of character, like this antique 'self-watering' planter, choose a plant that does not detract from it. This* Asparagus plumosus *(syn.* A. setaceus*), has a feathery appearance that clothes the container without masking it.*

ABOVE RIGHT: *Containers like this decorative milk churn are great for kitchen herbs, such as parsley, but water very cautiously unless you can make drainage holes in the base.*

RIGHT: *This beautifully rounded container made from a hollowed-out pumpkin reflects the rounded shape and colour of the begonia it contains. As a finishing touch, moss has been draped around the plant and allowed to tumble over the rim of the container.*

Plastic and ceramic containers

A visit to any good garden centre will give you an idea of the huge choice of pretty yet practical containers that you can use. Whenever possible, choose one with drainage holes, otherwise you will have to treat it like a cache-pot or be *very* careful with watering. It is never a good idea to plant directly into any container without drainage holes. Even if you are careful about watering, sooner or later the roots will find themselves standing in water and, as a result of oxygen starvation, they will start to die

Don't dismiss modern plastic containers. Some of them are bright, clean-looking and appropriate for a modern décor, or perhaps an office setting. Otherwise the choice of material and design must reflect your own taste and home décor.

Planters and self-watering containers

Planters are generally taken to mean containers that are large enough to hold several plants rather than individual specimens. These are ideal for displaying a group of plants.

Some planters are self-watering, with a reservoir at the bottom. Plants will generally thrive in these, and you can leave them for a few days with no problem. Although more expensive than ordinary containers, they are strongly recommended if plastic containers do not look incongruous in your home.

Think small as well as big

Very small plants are sometimes difficult to display, and a prostrate plant such as *Nertera depressa* can look slightly ridiculous grown in a normal pot – you will see more of the pot than of the plant. Try growing plants like these in small, decorative or fun containers, such as a collection of ducks or hens with a planting space in their backs. If you have a group of perhaps three such containers, planted with

---

WARNING WORDS

🔹 Cache-pots usually lack a drainage hole. This means that you don't have to bother with a saucer beneath the pot, but the plant inside will be standing in water and will soon die unless you are very careful about watering.

🔹 Place a few pebbles or marbles in the bottom, to raise the inner pot off the bottom of the container. If a little surplus water drains through, the compost (potting soil) should not remain soaked. But always check that the bottom of the inner pot is clear of any standing water.

🔹 If planting in any container without drainage holes, be *extremely careful* when watering. It's almost impossible to know whether there is standing water in the bottom of a container. You may want to risk it for a short-term plant that you know will have to be discarded soon, otherwise just use the container as a cache-pot or choose a different one.

TOP LEFT: *Glass containers can look very stylish. A lining of moss will look more attractive than exposed compost (potting soil). Careful watering is essential if you plant straight into any container without drainage holes.*

CENTRE LEFT: *Ornamental cabbages and kales are usually sold for outdoor decoration, but you can use them indoors for a few weeks. For a table-top display, try wrapping the plastic pot in a crisp white napkin.*

BELOW LEFT: *Sometimes the colour of a variegated leaf can pick up and extend the colour of the container. Here a variegated ivy tumbles out of a white teapot.*

BELOW RIGHT: *Low, mound-forming or carpeting plants such as* Helxine soleirolii *(syn.* Soleirolia soleirolii*) need a small container in proportion to the plant.*

OPPOSITE ABOVE: *Moss baskets make unusual containers for the right plants. This spathiphyllum looks right because the flower is taller than the handle.*

OPPOSITE BELOW: *Use a bit of lateral thinking in the kitchen. Try displaying some of your fruit with the flowers. Here oranges and apples share an interesting wooden container with* Streptocarpus saxorum.

matching or different prostrate plants, they will bring a touch of humour to your home, and should not seem to be in poor taste.

Baskets

Many foliage and flowering plants look especially attractive in wicker and moss-covered baskets, but if using a basket not specifically intended for plants, be sure to line it with a protective sheet. If you simply place pots into the basket, or replant into compost (potting soil) placed directly into the basket, moisture will seep through, mar any surface beneath, and in time rot or damage the basket.

Line the basket with a sheet of flexible plastic or any other waterproof membrane (a large piece of kitchen foil will do if you have nothing more suitable to hand). The protective liner can be taped down and should not be visible once the basket has been filled with compost and planted.

Small plants can look especially pretty in a basket with a handle, but taller plants can look awkward if the plant is very leafy or its height coincides with the top of the handle.

Search out the unusual

The container that is just right for a particular plant, or a special position, may be one that you will only recognize when you see it. Part of the fun of growing houseplants lies in using them creatively, and displaying them with imagination. Searching out fun or interesting containers can become part of the hobby.

Garden centres often have a useful range of containers to start with, but for the more stylish plant holders you may have to visit the kind of shop that sells well-designed furniture, stores that specialize in modern home accessories, and even antique shops. But you might find something just as good, and far less expensive, in a junk shop or even a jumble or garage sale. One person's throw-away may be a source of inspiration to a flower arranger or houseplant enthusiast.

Porch plants

USE YOUR PORCH TO GROW THE TOUGHER HOUSEPLANTS THAT NEED PLENTY

OF SPACE AND GOOD LIGHT. YOU CAN EVEN MAKE IT LOOK LIKE A SMALL

CONSERVATORY.

A porch influences the visitor's first impression of your home, so one that is well clothed with plants rather than bare and bleak will make a warmer welcome. An enclosed porch can be awash with colour the year round, but with an open porch in an exposed or cold position you will have to be content with hardy foliage plants for the cold months.

Enclosed porches

An enclosed porch can be like a mini lean-to greenhouse, and you can enjoy lush foliage and colourful flowers every month of the year. However, try to avoid using plants that will resent the sudden, icy blasts of air that occur when the outer door is opened in cold weather. Intolerant plants will soon drop their leaves and probably die.

Choose mainly plants recommended for cool temperatures, such as primulas, bowls of bulbs such as hyacinths and tulips, or cyclamen and azaleas for the winter. During the summer, regal and zonal geraniums (pelargoniums) do well in the hot atmosphere of such a small enclosed space, and cacti and succulents usually thrive. Provided that the porch can be maintained above freezing temperature, most cacti and succulents will benefit from being left there during the winter. The majority of cacti flower better if they have experienced a cold period during the winter.

Make use of climbers against at least one of the walls: passifloras would do well, but are generally too rampant. Choose something that is more easily restrained, such as *Hoya carnosa* or *Jasminum polyanthum* (be prepared to

ABOVE: *Porches can be bright or gloomy, protected or exposed. Choose plants appropriate to the conditions. This large* Ficus benajamina *will be happy in this position for the summer months, but will have to be brought indoors once the weather turns cold.*

keep it cut back once well established), or even a bougainvillea. Or go for foliage effect with *Cissus antarctica* or *Rhoicissus rhomboidea* (syn. *Cissus rhombifolia*).

If the porch is large, you can use plenty of big plants in floor-standing pots, such as *Fatsia japonica* (a variegated variety will look brighter in a porch), or perhaps an oleander (*Nerium oleander*).

Shelves will be needed to display small plants. If there are no built-in shelves, use the small free-standing display units sold for greenhouses, or special plant stands.

Open porches

Even an open porch can be made attractive. Group plenty of pots of hardy evergreens such as *Aucuba japonica varieties, Fatsia japonica*, skimmias (most have attractive berries in winter), and ivies if you want a trailer or climber. If you have pot-grown camellias and rhododendrons, for example, you can bring them into the porch for extra colour when they are in bloom.

Erica × *hyemalis, E. gracilis, Solanum capsicastrum* and its hybrids, even year-round chrysanthemums, will all provide colour for weeks or even months before having to be discarded.

During the summer, many of the tougher indoor plants can be placed in your porch. Yuccas will do well, and the variegated chlorophytums are reliable, but you can use plants as diverse as the brightly coloured coleus and flowering bougainvilleas. Don't be afraid to add a few unusual hardy foliage plants, such as rhubarb, to create a talking point.

PRACTICAL PROBLEMS

Most houseplants will thrive in an enclosed porch if you avoid extremely high or low temperatures.

A small electric heater coupled to a thermostat will keep it frostproof at little cost, and a fan heater will warm the air rapidly when the door is open. But blasts of cold are hard to avoid, so don't persevere with plants that seem to resent the position.

Too much heat is the main problem in summer. Unlike a greenhouse or conservatory, ventilation is often inadequate. If the porch is in a position where it receives a lot of direct sun, be sure to fit at least one automatic ventilator and, whenever possible, open all the windows before the temperature rises. However, bear in mind that these solutions may affect the security of your property.

Shading will help, and you may find the shade offered by a climber more acceptable than blinds or shading paints.

OPPOSITE: *This large regal pelargonium is kept indoors as a houseplant, but moved to the porch in full flower so that it can be shared with passers-by.*

ABOVE: *This indoor yucca is happy to stand outdoors for the summer in a sheltered position, and it gives height and 'presence' to the rest of the group, which is made up of tough houseplants that will also tolerate cold conditions.*

RIGHT: *The porch is where indoor plants can rub shoulders with hardy plants. Here, a tender begonia has been used with hardy miniature daffodils grown in a pot, and a pot-grown rosemary. The miniature roses were bought as houseplants but will later be planted in the garden. The rhododendron is totally hardy.*

Living-rooms

THE LIVING-ROOM IS THE PLACE WHERE MOST PEOPLE GROW THEIR HOUSE-
PLANTS. IT IS LIKELY TO BE WARM AND LIGHT, WITH PLENTY OF SPACE TO
DISPLAY PLANTS CREATIVELY.

The living-room is probably the best room for houseplants. There are usually large windows – often ceiling to floor patio doors at one end – plenty of standing places such as windowsills, tables and ledges or alcoves, and usually ample space for large floor-standing specimens. It is also the room that most people make an effort to decorate attractively, and where they spend most of their leisure time.

Just as the appearance of a room can be changed by moving the furniture around, so the positioning of plants can radically alter how a room looks. This is especially true for large specimen plants that act as focal points, and for groups of large plants used to screen areas.

In living-rooms, the colour and texture of plants can play important roles, especially the way in which they blend or contrast with the background. Try to use the juxtaposition of contrasting forms, shapes and colours to emphasize the visual impact of the plants.

Colour always needs to be considered. A foliage or flower colour that blends with an accompanying pot or ornament will look tasteful, but the wall behind will look best if it is neutral, or plain and contrasting. But for a special effect you may want to blend the colours of your plants with a more decorative background – perhaps white daisy-like flowers with green ferns, and green-and-white dieffenbachia against white net curtains, all set off on a white table.

Texture adds variety. The long purple hairs of a gynura will be best emphasized by a smooth pale background, a prickly cactus may look more in keeping with the colour and texture of rough bricks behind. The papery, wing-like leaves of caladiums will need a colour behind that brings out the beauty of these exotic-looking leaves (as they vary from white and green to bright red, the best background depends on the variety). But above all, the leaves of caladiums need to be illuminated well, either from behind or in front, to show off their delicate texture. The puckered leaves of the *Begonia masoniana* have a texture that you want to touch, adding tactile to visual stimulation.

Shape will compensate for lack of colour. Most philodendrons have large and interestingly shaped leaves, like the fingered and fringed *P. bipinnatifidum* and the more deeply cut *P. selloum,* and among the large-leaved ficus, *F. lyrata* has enormous, waxy leaves the shape of an upside-down violin. Plants like this will create as much interest as those with bright flowers or brilliant foliage, and they do it in a restrained way that creates the right mood for an elegant and sophisticated living-room.

Making a mini cactus garden

1. Make sure there are adequate drainage holes. Cover these with pieces of broken pot.

2. Although a cactus compost (potting soil) is preferable, you can use an ordinary compost.

3. If you have a very prickly cactus to plant, hold it in a strip of folded paper like this.

LEFT: *Cacti and succulents often look best in small groups, and a half-pot or shallow clay container is particularly appropriate.*

ABOVE: *Living rooms are usually light and spacious. Plants like aglaonemas, which like bright light but not direct sunlight, often do well by a window with net curtains. White net curtains make an excellent backdrop for many plants.*

RIGHT: *The living room is where you might want to use an especially beautiful container as a cache-pot for an appropriately impressive plant, like this azalea. As the blooms on one flowering plant die, replace with another, so that your special corner of the room always looks fresh and colourful.*

FAR RIGHT: *Succulents like this crassula are undemanding provided you can give them a position near the window. As they lack colour, try using a bright pot.*

Kitchens

IN THE DAYS WHEN KITCHENS WERE DARK AND DINGY AND COOKING WAS DONE WITH COAL GAS, OR EVEN AN OPEN RANGE, THE KITCHEN WAS A PLACE FOR ONLY THE TOUGHEST OF PLANTS. MODERN KITCHENS ARE USUALLY LIGHT, BRIGHT AND RELATIVELY SPACIOUS. PLANTS SHOULD THRIVE HERE, AND THERE ARE PLENTY OF OPPORTUNITIES TO USE THEM.

As always, the windowsill is the first place to fill with plants. Here you can grow those that need good light, but if the room receives direct sun at the hottest part of the day you will be restricted to those that tolerate the sun's rays intensified by the glass, such as cacti and succulents, geraniums (pelargoniums) and tradescantias.

Make the most of the tops of cupboards near the window for trailing plants. Although watering can be difficult, and the light near the ceiling will be poor, as the plants trail and tumble they enter the zone of better light and most will thrive. If they become thin and straggly, keep pinching back the long shoots to keep the growth bushy and compact.

Avoid trailing or cascading plants on or near work surfaces or eating areas. Choose plants with upright growth that will not get in the way. *Sansevieria trifasciata* 'Laurentii', upright dracaenas, especially those on a mini trunk, clivias and aglaonemas are among the plants that look good and won't get in the way of normal kitchen activities.

Practical pot plants

Many cooks like the idea of having culinary herbs on hand to pluck straight from pot to pot. Unfortunately, if you use herbs a great deal in your cooking, your herb plants will not remain attractive for long! So don't

expect your indoor herbs to keep the kitchen supplied, but they will create the right mood and aromas, and you can raid the plants for a leaf or two in an emergency. Nearly all herbs need good light, and the best place for them is by a bright window.

You can place individual pots on the windowsill, but it is more effective, and better for the plants, if you stand them all on a tray covering the length of the window and filled with gravel on which to stand the pots. Some, such as basil and pot marjoram, will need turning regularly to even up the growth, and regular pinching out of the growing tips is essential for many herbs. Unless you pinch out the growing tip, and later subsequent main shoots, basil will grow tall, flower and then deteriorate before you can harvest much of a crop. Marjoram needs to be pinched back regularly to keep it compact: the flowers are pretty, but an untamed plant will be too big and bushy for a windowsill.

Young plants of shrubs such as sage *(Salvia officinalis)* and rosemary *(Rosmarinus officinalis)* are inexpensive to buy and are worth growing as young pot plants. They will deteriorate indoors long before they become the large shrubs that you see in gardens, but they will enhance the kitchen for a season. If they are still alive and healthy the following spring, plant them in the garden, and buy another small plant for indoors.

Planting a herb windowbox

1. For an inexpensive improvised windowbox, use a polystyrene (styrofoam) trough. You can paint it to suit the decor.

2. Always insert a layer of drainage material, such as gravel and charcoal or expanded clay granules, before filling with potting compost (medium).

3. Choose small, bushy plants wherever possible. Some will eventually grow too tall, but you can usually restrict the height by repeatedly pinching out the growing tips.

OPPOSITE ABOVE: *Windowsill space is often limited, but kitchen shelves provide scope for many more plants, and a white-painted wall will reflect the available light and encourage growth.*

OPPOSITE BELOW: *Use trailers like this* **Philodendron scandens** *where its cascading stems won't get in the way. Near working surfaces, choose compact plants like this variegated* Tolmiea menziesii.

CENTRE RIGHT: *An indoor or outdoor windowbox full of herbs will not keep you supplied with all you need for culinary use, but it's a fun feature and may extend the season of fresh herbs when those outdoors are no longer available. This windowbox contains (from left to right) basil, thyme, parsley, rosemary and variegated apple mint.*

BELOW RIGHT: *The vacant space on top of cupboards can be used for low-growing or trailing plants, but bear in mind that light levels are often low, trailers may interfere with opening doors and watering can be difficult.*

BELOW FAR RIGHT: *Codiaeums usually do well in a kitchen provided you avoid a position exposed to cold draughts.*

Bedrooms

IF YOUR ENTHUSIASM FOR PLANTS OUTGROWS THE SPACE AVAILABLE IN

TRADITIONAL DISPLAY AREAS SUCH AS THE LIVING-ROOM AND KITCHEN,

OVERCOME PREJUDICE AND MAKE YOUR BEDROOM MORE BEAUTIFUL, TOO.

Many people are deterred from placing plants in their bedroom on the grounds that they are 'unhealthy'. However, plants will not deprive you of oxygen, and the reluctance to use them in the bedroom is no more than prejudice. You will probably find it a more restful place with the added greenery of a few plants, and you can even wake up to the perfume of stephanotis or hyacinths.

Bedrooms are often kept cooler than living-rooms, and this is an advantage for many plants. Winter-flowering plants, in particular, often last much longer in a cool atmosphere.

Suitable plants

Plants in bedrooms are probably viewed less than those in other parts of the house. Although we spend many hours there, most of them will be spent asleep, which means the plants are sometimes neglected.

Bedrooms are an excellent place for a collection of cacti and succulents, and for large individual specimens of tolerant foliage plants such as aspidistras and scindapsus (epipremnums), which are unlikely to become stressed if forgotten for a day or two.

If you can discipline yourself to water and mist them regularly, however, even delicate ferns will often do well because the air is usually more humid than in a hot living-room.

Fragrant plants can be especially pleasing, and the strongest scents will be appreciated beyond the bedroom itself if you leave the door open.

Bedside tables and dressing tables

Plants can add the finishing touch to a dressing table or a bedside table, but these are usually areas where natural light levels are low. Table lamps can display the plant to advantage after dark, but these do little for plant growth (and if too near, may scorch the plant). Be prepared to move your plants around, giving them a week or two at most in these positions, then rotate them with other plants that have had a spell in better light.

A place for plants to rest
Although you will want your bedroom to look well-designed and furnished with pretty or attractive plants, you may want to use a spare bedroom as a resting place for all those plants that are so perfect for a short time but border on the unattractive for the rest of the year. 'Resting' orchids and ephiphyllums, and tender primulas that have finished flowering, for example, are among the candidates for a light position in a bedroom. You can move them into a prominent position when they come into bloom again.

OPPOSITE ABOVE: *Instead of using air fresheners, wake up to the fragrance of real flowers, provided by plants such as this* Stephanotis floribunda.

OPPOSITE BELOW: *Enjoy the delicate perfume of* Jasminum polyanthum *as you sit at your dressing table. Dressing-table plants should be used at their prime, then moved to a lighter and more appropriate position to recuperate.*

ABOVE RIGHT: *If you adore the heady scent of gardenias, try one on your bedside table. When flowering has finished, move it to a lighter position.*

RIGHT: *Many bromeliads bought in bloom are discarded after flowering, so they can be used on a table well away from the window. This one is* Vriesea splendens, *with a distinctive flower spike that can be 60cm (2ft) long. The yellow* Celosia plumosa *is an inexpensive annual which can be used as a short-term houseplant for a few weeks.*

Halls and landings

HALLS AND LANDINGS PRESENT BOTH PROBLEMS AND OPPORTUNITIES. THE LIGHT IS OFTEN POOR, SPACE SOMETIMES CRAMPED AND COLD BLASTS FROM THE OPEN FRONT DOOR IN WINTER ALL PROVIDE UNPROMISING CONDITIONS FOR PLANTS. BUT THERE ARE STILL SOME THAT WILL THRIVE AND EVEN LOOK GOOD ENOUGH TO MAKE YOU LINGER TO ADMIRE THEM. IF YOU ARE A HOUSEPLANT ENTHUSIAST YOU'LL WANT TO MAKE THE MOST OF ALL THE GROWING SPACE AVAILABLE.

In some centrally heated homes, halls and stairways are as warm as any other part of the house, in others they are often cold and lack sufficient natural light. Despite these drawbacks one survey showed that more than a third of people who grow houseplants have at least some of them in the hall, and probably many more would if they could find plants that would thrive there. The plants suggested here are tough enough to grow even where these imperfect conditions exist, but in any place where there is enough winter warmth, conditions can be improved by using plenty of artificial light to make a feature of your plants.

It is always better to have one or two well-displayed, tough evergreens that look really lush and healthy, than to struggle with lots of colourful exotics that end up looking sickly.

Large plants
One or two specimen plants used as focal points will impress visitors on their arrival. Depending on the layout of your hallway, place one at the end of the passage leading to the door, in the vestibule where the door opens, or on the landing or top of the stairs if there is space. Good plants for this purpose are large specimens of *Ficus benjamina* (a variegated variety is especially effective in this situation), *Monstera*

ABOVE: *Plants on stairs must always be used with caution, but where you have space, as with this turn in the stairs, a few plants will transform what would otherwise be a featureless part of the house.*

deliciosa, Dracaena deremensis, Schefflera actinophylla, Yucca elephantipes, or a tough palm such as *Howeia forsteriana* (syn. *Kentia forsteriana*). If the position is gloomy during the day, use fluorescent lights balanced for plant growth, or spotlights recommended for plants.

Make sure that your décor shows off specimen plants to their best advantage: a plain, light-coloured wall is particularly effective, and a mirror placed behind a plant will deflect the light, perhaps making the hall look larger, as well as reflecting the plant itself. A white or cream-coloured ceiling will also help to reflect light.

Climbers and trailers
Provided that using plants will never become a danger to anyone in this area, stairwells provide a great opportunity for luxuriant climbers and trailers to grow freely.

Troughs filled with trailers, placed on a balcony along the stairwell, will enable the plants to tumble over the edge to provide a living curtain. A climber in the hall or at the bottom of the stairs can sometimes be trained to grow along the banister.

Climbers that often thrive in hall conditions include *Rhoicissus rhomboidea* (syn. *Cissus rhombifolia)* and the small-leaved varieties of the ordinary ivy (varieties of *Hedera helix*).

You can let ivies trail too, but more interesting are *Philodendron scandens,* and *Epipremnum aureum* 'Neon', both of which will produce long trails of growth. *Plectranthus australis* and *P. coleoides* 'Marginatus' are also vigorous trailers that will soon produce a hanging curtain of foliage.

Table plants
One of the most popular positions for a hall plant is on a small table near the front door. If the door and the surrounding area are solid you might find cut flowers more successful here, but if they are mainly glass, conditions will be ideal for a plant that does not object to cold draughts. Be warned, however: the patterned glass sometimes used in this situation can act like a magnifying glass and scorch leaves directly in the sun's rays.

Dependable plants for a hall table with reasonable light are chlorophytums, and two tough ferns: *Cyrtomium falcatum* and *Asplenium nidus.*

ABOVE: *If you have a hall with an old-fashioned look or an ambience associated with antiques, choose a large plant for the entrance, such as a palm, large ficus, or even a tall bamboo, but make sure it will cope with blasts of cold air in the winter.*

RIGHT: *If you use white or pale walls to reflect the light, some plants will do quite well even away from a window. Here a fern makes a statement of elegance in an area that could otherwise look bare.*

FAR RIGHT: *Floor-standing plants for landings must be chosen with care. Although height is useful, it is important that the plant does not cause an obstruction. Try to position the plant in a corner. The white walls of this landing help to reflect light and show the plant off to advantage.*

Bathrooms

BATHROOMS ARE NOT THE PARADISE FOR PLANTS THAT SOME PEOPLE THINK.

ALTHOUGH THE HUMIDITY IS OFTEN HIGH, THERE ARE DRAWBACKS TOO, SO

CHOOSE YOUR PLANTS WITH CARE.

The average bathroom has conditions that prevail nowhere else in the home: short periods of high temperature and high humidity contrasting with much longer spells of quite cool conditions (especially if the central heating is not kept on permanently), and because the windows are often small, poor natural light. The plants may also have to contend with the use of aerosols and sprays containing a variety of chemicals for personal care, and often a liberal dusting of talcum powder too. These are not conditions in which the majority of houseplants will thrive.

Good positions

Try to keep foliage out of reach of splashes from the bath and washbasin. Pots perched on the edge or back of the bath are in a precarious position, and the chances are that the light will also be poor.

Make the most of the windowsill, especially for flowering plants. Further into the room, use tough foliage plants such as aspidistras and asparagus ferns, perhaps in front of a mirror, where they will receive reflected light and the mirror will make the plants look larger.

Tolerant trailers such as ivies and *Philodendron scandens* look good hanging from a high shelf, perhaps framing a mirror.

LEFT: *Plants may have to be concentrated near the window as bathrooms are not usually well illuminated with natural light, but by using plenty of plants on all available surfaces, the effect can be particularly pleasing.*

Use small flowering plants such as saintpaulias and kalanchoes on a make-up table or vanity unit, using attractive cache-pots that suit the setting. These will not make long-term bathroom plants, but they will look good for weeks before you have to move them on.

SUITABLE PLANTS

❧ The following plants generally do well:

❧ **Large plants**
Fatsia japonica, Monstera deliciosa and *Philodendron bipinnatifidum.*

❧ **Trailers**
Epipremnum aureum (syn. *Scindapsus aureus*), *Philodendron scandens* and small-leaved ivies.

❧ **Bushy plants**
Aglaonema species and varieties, *Aspidistra elatior* and *Chamaedorea elegans* (syn. *Neanthe bella*).

❧ **Short-term flowering plants**
Chrysanthemum, cyclamen and exacum.

ABOVE RIGHT: *Plants as diverse as the hardy ivy and tricky* Asplenium capillus-veneris *can thrive in a bathroom. The ivy is good for low light levels, and the fern will appreciate the frequent spells of high humidity.*

RIGHT: Philodendron scandens *is a good choice for a trailer, while a spathiphyllum always looks elegant with its glossy green leaves and white sail-like flowers. Flowering plants, such as the cyclamen, can be brought in as short-term plants.*

FAR RIGHT: *Use trailers with imagination. Bathrooms usually have small windows and tend to be relatively gloomy, but by rotating the plants between rooms periodically you can feature attractive plant displays in all areas of the home.*

A–Z
directory of
houseplants

BROWSE THROUGH THIS PARADE OF
HOUSEPLANTS TO CHOOSE THOSE THAT
APPEAL, THEN CHECK THEIR REQUIREMENTS
TO MAKE SURE YOU CAN PROVIDE SUITABLE
CONDITIONS.

THE FOLLOWING PAGES CONTAIN MOST
OF THE HOUSEPLANTS THAT YOU ARE LIKELY
TO FIND IN GARDEN CENTRES AND SHOPS,
AND EVEN MANY SPECIALIST NURSERIES.
IF YOU HAVE A PLANT THAT YOU CAN'T
IDENTIFY, THE CHANCES ARE YOU WILL
FIND IT HERE . . . THOUGH THE NATURE OF
THE HOUSEPLANT TRADE MEANS THAT FROM
TIME TO TIME YOU ARE LIKELY TO FIND A
PLANT THAT MAY NOT BE IN THE BOOKS.

Introduction

Most of the houseplants in the following pages can be found in garden centres and shops, and the many illustrations will allow you to use the book for identification as well as for practical advice. No book can be totally comprehensive, of course, and if you begin to collect particular groups of plants such as bromeliads, cacti or orchids, you will find many more varieties at specialist nurseries. In most cases, these varieties are likely to prefer similar conditions and care to those mentioned in this book.

Finding the right name

Sometimes botanists change the names of old favourites, and it is not unknown for other botanists to change them again – even back to the original name! Sometimes new names are taken up quickly, but often it is many years, even decades, before a new name becomes accepted by nurserymen and gardeners.

In this book the up-to-date names are mentioned to make the book as complete as possible, but the entry is likely to be found under the name by which the plant is commonly sold. Wherever applicable the names have been cross-referenced, so you should be able to find the plant whether you normally use the 'old' or 'new' name.

In common with many books, we have used the word 'variety' in its colloquial sense, rather than the more botanically correct 'cultivar', 'variety' or 'varietas', and 'forma', which make for difficult reading and are of no practical value to the gardener. The typographical presentation of the names is, however, correct.

If you know a plant only by its common name, look it up in the common name index. This will give you the Latin name under which you will find the entry.

Opposite: A selection of houseplants

Reading the entries

Genus This is equivalent to a surname, identifying the group of plants with common characteristics.

Species This is equivalent to a forename, identifying an individual plant within the genus. Sometimes there is only one species in a genus, but usually there are many – sometimes hundreds. Those listed are the species you are most likely to encounter when buying houseplants.

Temperature Except where a plant is frost-sensitive (when it is very important to prevent the plant freezing), the temperatures given are target minimums. But the majority of plants will not come to any harm if the temperature drops lower – they may not thrive or grow as well, but they are unlikely to die. Maximum temperatures are not given, as in most households it is not practical to reduce the summer air temperature significantly. When a high winter temperature caused by central heating may be detrimental – perhaps shortening the flowering period – a suggested maximum has been given.

Humidity The amount of moisture in the air can be crucial. Plants from tropical rain forests may demand very moist or humid air, yet desert plants will often tolerate air drier than you are likely to find in the home. Avoid those that require high humidity unless you can provide it . . . or are

Above: Columnea gloriosa

prepared to treat the plant simply as a short-term decoration for the home.

Position This can be crucial – if the light is bad many plants grow poorly and fail to thrive. Other plants will be scorched (develop brown burn marks on the leaves) or even die if placed in a hot and sunny spot.

Watering and feeding Never water by the calendar alone, and always use your own discretion when deciding whether a plant requires more water. This book indicates periods of high or low water needs. Feeding should never be neglected, but the advice here is based on periods of need rather than frequency of feeding. Frequency depends on the type of fertilizer being used – follow the instructions on the fertilizer label.

Care Useful hints and tips that will help you get the best from your plant.

Propagation Detailed propagation techniques are beyond the scope of this book, but the main methods used are given for guidance. If sowing seed, follow the information on the packet or in the catalogue. Cuttings are likely to require a heated propagator during cold months, but should root at air temperature during the summer. The best type of cutting may depend on the time of year it is taken, so consult a propagation book for the trickier subjects if in doubt.

Abutilon

These versatile evergreen shrubs are usually grown as foliage plants, but some are chosen primarily for their striking flowers. *A. megapotamicum* is grown as an outdoor wall shrub in mild areas.

Abutilon × hybridum
Most hybrid varieties, such as 'Canary Bird' or 'Yellow Belle', and 'Golden Fleece' or 'Moonchimer' (both yellow), are grown for their bell-like flowers. A few, such as 'Savitzii' (white and green blotched leaves) are attractive foliage plants. In a conservatory, plants may grow to 1.5m (5ft) or more, but smaller plants also flower well.

Abutilon megapotamicum
Small, pendent, red and yellow bell-like flowers for most of the summer. The plant will trail from a large hanging basket or can be trained against a conservatory wall. 'Variegatum' has yellow-splashed leaves.

Abutilon striatum
Although correctly known as *A. pictum,* you are more likely to find it sold under its traditional name. It is often grown in its variegated form 'Thompsonii', which has yellow-blotched leaves and pale orange flowers.

TOP: Abutilon *hybrid*

ABOVE: Abutilon striatum *'Thompsonii'*

LEFT: Abutilon megapotamicum *'Variegatum'*

HELPFUL HINTS
Temperature Aim for 12–15°C (53–59°F) from early autumn to late winter. Avoid high winter temperatures.
Humidity Mist occasionally.
Position Good light, but avoid exposing to direct sun.
Watering and feeding Water freely in summer, sparingly in winter. Feed regularly in summer.
Care Repot each spring, but use a pot only one size larger as the plant flowers best if the roots are constrained. If the plant has lost its beauty by spring, cut back long shoots at the same time to encourage new bushy growth. Tie in the shoots of *A. megapotamicum* in spring and summer if grown against a conservatory wall. Ventilate freely. The plant can stand in the garden for the summer.
Propagation Cuttings. Seed if you do not want a particular colour or variegation.

Acacia

Acacias are grown mainly for their feathery foliage and pretty yellow flowers. In their native habitat most make large trees, but many can be grown in a large pot and will make a bush about 1–1.5m (3–5ft) tall. They are more suitable for a conservatory than the home.

Acacia armata
Pale yellow, fragrant flowers, like small balls clustered along the stems, freely produced between mid winter and early spring. It makes a branching shrub to about 1.5m (5ft). More correctly known as *A. paradoxa* now, but usually found under its old name.

Acacia dealbata
Sulphur-yellow flowers, often sold by florists as mimosa, from mid winter to early spring. Attractive feathery foliage. This species is cold tolerant.

Above: Acacia dealbata

Helpful hints
Temperature Aim for a minimum 10°C (50°F). Avoid high winter temperatures.
Humidity Undemanding.
Position As much light as possible.
Watering and feeding Water sparingly in winter, freely at other times. Feed during the summer (generous feeding may stimulate too much growth).
Care To keep the plant compact, cut back shoots that have become too long when flowering is over. Repot every second year, after flowering. If you don't have a conservatory, stand the plant outside for the summer.
Propagation Seed; cuttings.

Acalypha

The acalyphas are a diverse group of plants, some grown for their bright coleus-like foliage, others for their spectacular drooping flowers.

Acalypha hispida
Red tassel-like flowers up to 50cm (20in) long. 'Alba' has whitish flowers. In a warm conservatory it can grow to a height of 1.8m (6ft) or more; in the home it is unlikely to grow to more than half this size.

Acalypha wilkesiana
Brightly coloured oval leaves about 15cm (6in) long. Most are attractively variegated in shades of red, and there are named varieties such as 'Godseffiana' (pale green), and 'Musaica' (patches of bronze, red and orange).

Helpful hints
Temperature Winter minimum 15°C (59°F).

Humidity High humidity is essential. Does best in a conservatory; if in a room, mist frequently (especially *A. hispida*).
Position Good light, but avoid exposing to direct sun.
Watering and feeding Keep the compost (potting soil) moist at all times, but avoid waterlogging. Feed from spring to autumn.
Care To keep compact, prune back by half in early spring or late summer. Repot in spring (topdress if the pot is already large). Deadhead *A. hispida* as the flowers die. Pinch out any flowers on *A. wilkesiana* before they open, and remove the tips of long shoots as necessary, to keep the plant compact and bushy.
Propagation Cuttings.

Above: Acalypha wilkesiana 'Ceylon'
Below: Acalypha hispida

ABOVE: Achimenes *hybrid*

Achimenes

True species are sometimes grown, but the plants you are most likely to find are hybrids. Specialist nurseries offer a large range of named varieties, and the rhizomes are often sold by bulb merchants and seedsmen.

Achimenes hybrids
The short-lived flowers, in shades of pink, purple, yellow, red, and white, are produced in abundance from early summer to autumn. The plants die down in winter but grow again the following spring.

HELPFUL HINTS

Temperature Undemanding as the plant dies down for the winter. Aim for a minimum 13°C (55°F) while growing.
Humidity Mist frequently when the flower buds are developing, then provide humidity without spraying by standing the pot on a tray of pebbles.
Position Good light, but avoid exposing to direct sun.
Watering and feeding Water with tepid, soft water during the growing season. Never allow the compost (potting soil) to dry out. Feed regularly.
Care Grow in a hanging pot if you want its weak stems to cascade, otherwise support them with thin canes. Stop watering when the plant begins to drop its leaves in autumn. Leave the rhizomes in the pot or remove and store in peat (moss peat) or sand in a frost-free place. Start into growth or replant in late winter or early spring.
Propagation Division of rhizomes; cuttings; seed (not named varieties).

Adiantum

These delicate-looking ferns include a few species that are frost-tolerant, but most are delicate plants that need warmth and high humidity and they can be difficult to keep for long in a living-room. The small ones do well in a bottle garden.

Adiantum capillus-veneris
Thin, feathery-looking fronds on dark stems. This fern is the toughest of those described. In some countries this is known commercially as *A. chilense*, though there is a distinct plant with this name.

Adiantum chilense *see A. capillus-veneris.*

Adiantum cuneatum *see A. raddianum.*

Adiantum hispidulum
A coarser-looking fern than most adiantums, although the new fronds are a delicate pinkish-bronze.

BELOW: Adiantum hispidulum

ABOVE: Adiantum raddianum 'Fragrantissimum', also known as 'Fragrans' (left), and 'Fritz Luthii' (right)
LEFT: Adiantum capillus-veneris

Care Most problems arise from dry or cool air. Never let the compost (potting soil) dry out, but do not leave the pot standing in water.
Propagation Division is the easiest method, but spores can be sown in spring.

Aechmea

The most widely grown species, *A. fasciata*, is one of the best-known of the bromeliads, with attractive foliage and a spectacular and long-lasting flower head.

Aechmea fasciata
Large green leaves banded silvery-grey, form an urn-like rosette. The spiky-looking flower head has pink bracts and small blue flowers that fade to lilac. The main flowering season is mid summer to early winter; individual heads can remain attractive for months, but the rosette dies afterwards. The plant is sometimes seen under its old name of *A. rhodocyanea*.

Aechmea rhodocyanea see *A. fasciata*.

Adiantum raddianum
One of the most popular species, with erect young fronds that later curve. If conditions suit, it will make a medium-sized pot plant. There are many varieties, with slight variations in leaf shape or colour and growth habit. 'Fragrantissimum' is slightly aromatic. 'Fritz-Luthii' has bright green fronds. Also known as *A. cuneatum*.

HELPFUL HINTS
Temperature A winter minimum of 18°C (64°F) is generally advisable for most species.
Humidity High humidity is essential for good results.
Position Shaded from direct sun and away from cold draughts.
Watering and feeding Water freely throughout the year. Apply a weak fertilizer from spring to early autumn.

HELPFUL HINTS
Temperature Winter minimum 5°C (59°F), unless you intend to discard the plant after flowering.
Humidity Undemanding.
Position Good light, but avoid exposing to direct sun.
Watering and feeding Keep roots moist at all times, top up water in funnel in summer, but empty it in winter unless the temperature is above 18°C (64°F). Feed with a weak fertilizer in summer.
Care Young plants raised at home will not flower for several years, but to stimulate flowering on a mature plant, enclose in a plastic bag with a couple of ripe apples for a few days. The gasses released may induce flowering. Mist only on hot days. After flowering, that part of the plant will die, but offsets will be produced that can be used for propagation.
Propagation Remove the young rosettes when about half the height of the parent. Pot up, retaining as much of the root system as possible.

BELOW: Aechmea fasciata

Aeschynanthus

Several species may be grown as houseplants, but the one described is among the most successful. Even this is better in a conservatory than a living-room. All have trailing stems with leathery leaves and clusters of red or orange flowers.

Aeschynanthus lobbianus

Dark green, fleshy leaves on trailing stems, with terminal clusters of bright flowers with brownish-purple calyces and red flowers lightly flushed with yellow. Flowering time is usually early summer.

Helpful hints

Temperature Warm in summer, cool in winter, but with a minimum of 13°C (55°F).
Humidity Mist frequently all year round, especially in hot weather.
Position Good light, but not direct sun.
Watering and feeding Water freely from spring to autumn, sparingly at other times. Use soft, tepid water if possible. Feed in summer.

Care After flowering, shorten the stems to prevent the plant becoming too straggly. Moving a plant in flower to a different position may sometimes cause the blooms to drop. It is a good idea to repot the plants every second or third year.
Propagation Cuttings.

Above: Aeschynanthus *hybrid 'Mona'*

Agave

Although often regarded as succulents, agaves are xerophytes (plants able to survive in areas with scanty water supplies). Some have magnificent flower spikes where they are able to grow outdoors, but they are regarded as foliage plants indoors. *A. americana* is often used in a tub as a patio plant, and in mild areas can sometimes be overwintered successfully outdoors.

Agave americana

Large grey-green or blue-grey, strap-like leaves, often 1–1.2m (3–4ft) long in favourable conditions, and with sharp spines. As a pot plant it is

Left: Agave americana
Opposite top: Agave victoriae-reginae

usually grown in one of its variegated forms such as 'Marginata', 'Mediopicta' or 'Variegata'.

Agave filifera
A rounded rosette of stiff, fleshy, pointed leaves that curve upwards, with thread-like growths.

Agave victoriae-reginae
Dull-green, white-edged triangular leaves, forming an almost spherical rosette. One of the best agaves as a houseplant.

HELPFUL HINTS
Temperature Winter minimum 10°C (50°F) is adequate for all species. Some will tolerate lower temperatures but keep frost-free.
Humidity Tolerates dry air.
Position Full sun.
Watering and feeding Water as required in summer, but keep almost dry in winter (water occasionally if the light is good). Feed occasionally during the summer.
Care Stand large plants such as *A. americana* outdoors for the summer (but beware of any spines if placing on a patio). Repot each spring.
Propagation Root the runners or separate the young plants that form around the bases of some species. Can be raised from seed, but growth tends to be slow.

Aglaonema

Clump-forming plants with spear-shaped leaves on short stems arising from the base. The plain green ones lack interest, but the variegated species and varieties make attractive and tolerant houseplants.

Aglaonema crispum
Green leaves with silvery-grey patches. 'Marie' has particularly good variegation.

Aglaonema commutatum
Green leaves crossed with silvery bands. Inconspicuous greenish-white flowers are sometimes followed by red berries.

Aglaonema hybrids
Some of the best aglaonemas to use as houseplants are hybrids. 'Silver Queen' has silver and green leaves, 'Silver King' has leaves almost entirely silvery-grey and spotted leaf stalks.

The nomenclature of aglaonemas has been confused, and you will sometimes find these listed as varieties of *A. treubii*.

HELPFUL HINTS
Temperature Aim for a winter minimum of 15°C (59°F), although plants will continue to grow at 10°C (50°F).
Humidity Needs high humidity. Mist regularly.
Position All-green aglaonemas tolerate low light levels, but variegated forms need only light shade. Avoid direct sun.
Watering and feeding Water freely spring to autumn, sparingly in winter. Feed from spring to autumn.
Care Best in shallow pots. The plants are slow-growing so repot only when necessary.
Propagation Cuttings. Division.

BELOW LEFT: Aglaonema crispum *'Marie'*

Aloe

Aloes are trouble-free succulents with a dramatic appearance, which makes them useful as specimen houseplants for a sunny windowsill.

Aloe arborescens
Erect growth with tentacle-like fleshy leaves, edged with sharp thorns. May produce spikes of attractive orange-red flowers. Will make a tall plant in time, but growth is relatively slow if restricted in a pot.

Aloe ferox
Thick, fleshy leaves with reddish-brown spines over the surface that give the plant a warty appearance. Mature plants produce branching red flower spikes. Grows to about 45cm (1¹/₂ft).

Aloe mitriformis
Fleshy blue-green leaves, conspicuously spined around the edge and on the back. Dull scarlet flowers in summer.

Aloe variegata
Forms a rosette of triangular, dark green, purple-tinged leaves with V-shaped white bands. Red flowers are sometimes produced. Makes a compact plant that grows to about 15–30cm (6–12in) tall.

HELPFUL HINTS
Temperature Cool but frost-free in winter. Aim for about 5°C (41°F).
Humidity Tolerates dry air.
Position Full sun. Can stand in the garden in summer.
Watering and feeding Water a couple of times a week in summer, sparingly in winter. Feed occasionally in summer.
Routine care Repot in spring every second or third year.
Propagation Offsets (sever carefully with as much root system as possible). Seed in spring.

LEFT: Aloe ferox
BELOW: Aloe variegata

Ananas

The ornamental pineapples grown as houseplants sometimes have small inedible fruits. These are an interesting bonus, but ananas are grown primarily as foliage plants indoors.

Ananas bracteatus striatus
Brightly striped, spiky leaves in green, cream and pink. Although this plant is often found under this name, you may also see it as the more correct *A. b. tricolor.*

Ananas comosus variegatus
This is a variegated form of the edible pineapple. The plain green species is an unattractive houseplant, but this variegated form with lengthwise cream banding is more compact and appealing.

HELPFUL HINTS
Temperature Aim for 15–18°C (59–64°F) in winter.

Anthurium

Some species, such as *A. crystallinum* and *A. magnificum,* are grown as foliage plants, but the ones you are most likely to find are sold as flowering plants. They are difficult to keep indoors, but their distinctive flowers make them popular where a dramatic effect is required.

Anthurium andreanum
The plants sold under this name are almost always hybrids. One may also find the name with its more correct spelling of *A. andaeanum.* Heart-shaped leaves are produced on long stalks. The flowers have a large, shiny, red, pink, or white spathe and generally a straight spadix. Flowering is between spring and later summer, and the blooms last for several weeks.

Anthurium scherzerianum
The plants sold under this name are almost always hybrids. The leaves are

Humidity Undemanding, but mist in very hot weather.

Position Good light. The variegation is often better in sun. If placing on a windowsill, beware of the spines, which tend to catch on net curtains.

Watering and feeding Water freely in summer, cautiously in winter, and allow the soil to dry out a little before watering. Feed from late spring to early autumn.

Care In summer, occasionally add a little water to the vase formed by the rosette of leaves. Mature plants can be encouraged to flower by placing them in a plastic bag together with a few ripe apples or bananas for a few days.

Propagation Commercially, plants are often raised from seed, but for just a few plants it is quicker to use the crown of leaves on top of the fruit.

RIGHT: Ananas bracteatus striatus

lance- rather than heart-shaped and the spadix is curled. Flowering time for these plants is the same as for the previous species.

HELPFUL HINTS

Temperature Winter minimum 16°C (60°F).

Humidity Needs high humidity. Mist frequently, but avoid spraying the flowers.

Position Good light, but avoid exposing to direct summer sun.

Watering and feeding Water freely in summer, sparingly in winter. If possible use soft water. Feed with a weak fertilizer during summer.

Care Repot every second year, in spring, using a fibrous compost (potting mixture), and avoid over-firming.

Propagation Division. Stem cuttings and seeds are possible methods, but much more difficult.

LEFT: Anthurium scherzerianum

Aphelandra

The only species widely grown is a useful dual-purpose plant with attractive foliage and flowers.

Aphelandra squarrosa
Large, glossy, dark green leaves striped white along the veins. Conspicuous flower spike with long-lasting yellow bracts surrounding shorter-lived yellow flowers. The bracts overlap, giving a tiled effect, and remain attractive for a month or more. Flowering is usually in the autumn, but plants may bloom from late spring onwards and are sometimes available in flower in winter. The true species is not usually grown, and you are most likely to find more compact varieties such as 'Dania' and 'Louisae'.

HELPFUL HINTS
Temperature Winter minimum 13°C (55°F).
Humidity Needs high humidity. Mist frequently.
Position Good light; not direct sun. Good light induces flowering.
Watering and feeding Water freely in summer, less often in winter, but never let the compost become dry. Use soft water if possible. Feed regularly from spring to autumn.
Care Deadhead when flowering has finished. To prevent the leaves falling keep warm and humid, and away from cold draughts.
Propagation Stem cuttings in a propagator, in spring. Stem sections with a single eye can also be used.

BELOW: Aphelandra squarrosa

Aporocactus

A small group of undemanding cacti, the species described here being the ones most usually found. Of these, *A. flagelliformis* is most common. Although these trailing plants can be grafted on a taller rootstock, they are usually grown on their own roots and cascade over the edge of the pot.

Aporocactus flagelliformis
Circular trailing stems, with sharp spines. The red or pink flowers, large in relation to the size of the plant, are produced in spring.

Aporocactus flagriformis
Stronger and thornier stems than the previous species (although this is not always regarded as a distinct species).

ABOVE: Aporocactus flagelliformis

Flowers are yellowish-red in bud and scarlet edged with violet when open.

HELPFUL HINTS

Temperature Winter minimum 5°C (41°F).

Humidity Tolerates dry air, but mist in very hot weather.

Position Full sun, but avoid intense afternoon sun. The plant can stand in the garden for the summer.

Watering and feeding Water freely in spring and summer, sparingly at other times.

Care Never move the plant once the buds have started to form, as this often causes them to drop. Keep in a cool, well-lit position in winter.

Propagation Cuttings; seed.

Araucaria

The species described is the only one normally grown as a pot plant, and is one of the few conifers used indoors. It makes a very large tree in the wild, but indoors grows into a majestic specimen plant of about 1.5m (5ft) after a few years. It needs space to grow symmetrically.

Araucaria excelsa see *A. heterophylla*.

Araucaria heterophylla
Tiers of stiff branches covered with prickly conifer needles about 1.5cm (⁵/₈in) long. It is still sometimes sold under its old name of *A. excelsa*.

HELPFUL HINTS

Temperature Aim for 5–10°C (41–50°F) in winter.

Humidity Needs high humidity. Does not do well in a dry, centrally-heated room without regular misting.

Position Good light; not direct sun. Stand plant in the garden in summer.

Watering and feeding Water freely from spring to autumn, sparingly in winter. Never let the soil dry out. Use soft water if possible. Feed with a weak fertilizer in summer.

Care Try to avoid a hot room in winter. Repot only every third or fourth year to prevent the plant becoming too large.

Propagation Tip cuttings in a propagator, but amateurs usually have a low success rate.

BELOW: Araucaria heterophylla

Asparagus

Although popularly called ferns, these useful houseplants belong to the lily family and are not true ferns at all. The feathery-looking foliage, reduced to needle-like scales in many species, gives some of them a ferny appearance and they are a useful choice for a position that demands a tougher plant than most ferns. The species below are the most common, but others are sometimes available.

Asparagus densiflorus
The 'leaves' (technically cladophylls and not true leaves) are a fresh green and larger than those of *A. setaceus*, creating a more striking plant. The thread-like stems arch and become more pendulous as the plant grows older. Small white or pink flowers are sometimes produced and may be followed by red berries. The variety usually grown is 'Sprengeri'. 'Meyeri', sometimes listed as a separate species and more correctly spelt 'Myersii', is more erect and compact in habit.

Asparagus meyeri *see A. densiflorus* 'Meyeri' (syn. 'Myersii').

Asparagus plumosus *see A. setaceus.*

ABOVE: Asparagus densiflorus 'Sprengeri' (*syn.* A. sprengeri)

Asparagus setaceus
Thread-like pale green 'leaves' (phyllodes) produce a feathery and ferny effect. Young plants are compact, but as they mature, long climbing shoots are produced. The plant is still widely known as *A. plumosus.*

Asparagus sprengeri *see A. densiflorus* 'Sprengeri'.

HELPFUL HINTS
Temperature Winter minimum 7°C (45°F). *A. setaceus* is best kept at a minimum 13°C (55°F).
Humidity Mist occasionally, especially in a centrally-heated room in winter. Mist *A. setaceus* in winter.
Position Good light or partial shade, but avoid exposing to direct sun.
Watering and feeding Water from spring to autumn, sparingly in winter. Feed from spring to early autumn.
Care Cut back by half a plant that has started to turn yellow or grown too large: it will often produce new shoots from lower down. Repot young plants every spring, older ones every second year.
Propagation Division; seed.

Aspidistra

Evergreen herbaceous plants with leaves that grow directly from soil level. The one species grown as a houseplant was once very popular because of its tough constitution and tolerance of poor growing conditions.

Aspidistra elatior
Large, dark green leaves about 45–60cm (1½–2ft) long, arising from the base. 'Variegata' has irregular creamy-white longitudinal stripes. Small purplish flowers sometimes appear at soil level in late winter or early spring, but usually go unnoticed.

HELPFUL HINTS
Temperature Keep cool but frost-free in winter, 7–10°C (45–50°F) is ideal.
Humidity Tolerates dry air.
Position Light or shade, but avoid exposing to direct sun.
Watering and feeding Water moderately from spring to autumn, sparingly in winter. Avoid waterlogging.
Care Wash or sponge the leaves occasionally to remove dust and improve light penetration. Repot only when really necessary – usually every four years or so.
Propagation Division.

BELOW: Aspidistra elatior

Asplenium

Of the many hundreds of species of this fern, including some that are hardy, only a few are regularly grown as houseplants. *Asplenium nidus* is especially popular because its thick, leathery leaves make it a much more tolerant houseplant than ferns with thinner and more delicate foliage.

Asplenium bulbiferum

Typical fern fronds, usually about 45–60cm (1½–2ft) tall. Small plantlets develop on the upper surfaces of mature leaves, which can be potted up to provide new plants.

Asplenium nidus

An epiphytic fern with glossy, undivided leaves that form a vase-like rosette. Mature plants may have brown spore cases on the undersides of the leaves.

HELPFUL HINTS

Temperature Winter minimum 13°C (55°F) for *A. bulbiferum*, 16°C (60°F) for *A. nidus*.
Humidity High humidity is essential.

ABOVE: Asplenium bulbiferum

Position Light or shade, but avoid exposing to direct sun.
Watering and feeding Water freely from spring to autumn, moderately in winter. Use soft water whenever possible.

Care Dust *A. nidus* leaves periodically. If brown or disfigured edges form on the leaves of *A. nidus*, these can often be successfully trimmed off with scissors – but avoid cutting into the green area.
Propagation Spores (difficult) or division. Pot up the plantlets of *A. bulbiferum*.

Aucuba

Frost-hardy shrubs widely planted in gardens, and often used as a houseplant for difficult situations where more tender plants would not thrive. You can plant them out in the garden if they grow too large, but acclimatize them first.

Aucuba japonica

Large, dark green, leathery leaves, blotched or spotted yellow in the varieties usually used as houseplants. There are many varieties, differing mainly in the amount of variegation. Popular ones, though often not identified on the label, are 'Crotonifolia' (boldly spotted and blotched gold), and 'Variegata' (speckled yellow). The inconspicuous flowers and red berries are seldom produced on indoor plants.

Although a large shrub of 1.5–1.8m (5-6ft) in the garden, it seldom grows to more than half this height when grown indoors in a pot.

HELPFUL HINTS

Temperature Undemanding and tolerates frost. Avoid high winter temperatures.
Humidity Tolerates dry air, but mist regularly in a warm room in winter.
Position Useful for shade but will grow in a light position. Avoid direct summer sun.
Watering and feeding Water freely spring to autumn, sparingly in winter.
Care Repot every second spring. Prune any over-long or sparse shoots at the same time.
Propagation Cuttings.

RIGHT: Aucuba japonica *variety*

Azalea

See Rhododendron.

Begonia – Foliage

Foliage begonias are attractive all year round. Although most foliage begonias will flower, the blooms are generally inconspicuous.

Begonia bowerae
Compact growth to about 15–23cm (6–9in), with small, bright green, brown-edged leaves, which are slightly serrated and hairy. Grows from a creeping rhizome. Single white flowers, tinged pink, in winter. Attractive hybrids include 'Tiger', heavily blotched bronze and green. Also spelled *B. boweri.*

Begonia listada
Lobed, dark green, softly hairy leaves with bright emerald green markings. A few white flowers in autumn and winter.

Begonia masoniana
Very distinctive, large, bright green, puckered leaves with a central brownish 'cross'. The flowers are insignificant.

Begonia rex
It is the hybrids of this important species that are now widely grown. There are named varieties, but the plants are usually sold as mixtures or unnamed. The asymmetrical leaves are about 23cm (9in) long and brightly variegated in shades of green, silver, brown, red, pink, and purple.

HELPFUL HINTS
Temperature Winter minimum 16°C (60°F).

Humidity Provide high humidity, but avoid spraying water directly onto the leaves.
Position Good light, but not direct sun.
Watering and feeding Water freely from spring to autumn, sparingly in winter.
Care Repot annually in spring.
Propagation Division; leaf cuttings.

Begonia – Flowering

Many begonias are grown for the beauty of their flowers – some for the prolific mass of small flowers over a long period (such as *B. semperflorens,* a very popular choice for a summer display in the garden); others, such as some of the tuberous hybrids, are grown for their less numerous, but larger, blooms.

Begonia × cheimantha *see B. lorraine hybrids.*

Begonia elatior hybrids
Single or double flowers in a wide colour range mainly in shades of red, pink, yellow, orange, and white. They are derived from crosses between *B. socotrana* and tuberous species from South America. The Rieger begonias belong to this group of hybrids, and these varieties are generally superior because they are less prone to mildew and bud-drop. The natural flowering period is winter, but commercial growers induce them to flower at all seasons. There are many named varieties.

This group of begonias is also known as *B. × hiemalis.*

Begonia × hiemalis *see B. elatior hybrids.*

Begonia lorraine hybrids
A cross between *B. socotrana* and *B. dregei,* and now botanically described as *B. × cheimantha,* this winter-flowering begonia has clusters of small pink or white flowers. 'Gloire de Lorraine', with its pink flowers, is one of the best-known varieties.

Begonia semperflorens
Low, mound-forming plant covered with small flowers all summer. Colours include shades of pink and red, as well as white, some with bronze foliage. Many varieties are offered by seed companies.

Begonia sutherlandii
Trailer with small lance-shaped leaves and a profusion of single orange flowers in loose clusters in summer.

Begonia × tuberhybrida
A group that includes large-flowered, double begonias used as both pot plants and for garden display. There are many varieties, including single and double Pendula trailers for hanging baskets, and Multifloras with masses of single, semi-double and double flowers. Colours include many shades of red, orange, pink, and yellow. All flower for many months during the summer.

HELPFUL HINTS
Temperature Aim for 13–21°C (55–70°F) for winter-flowering types. Tuberous types that die back need to be protected from frost, but only for the tubers.
Humidity High humidity is beneficial but not critical.
Position Good light, but out of direct summer sun. Provide the best possible light in winter.
Watering and feeding Water freely while the plants are in flower, cautiously at other times. Gradually withhold water from those that die

ABOVE: Begonia sutherlandii
OPPOSITE ABOVE: Begonia rex
OPPOSITE BELOW: *A group of foliage begonias. 'Cleopatra' (top left), 'Tiger' (top right),* B. listada *(centre),* B. masoniana *(bottom left), 'Red Planet' (bottom right)*

back and have a resting period once the foliage begins to yellow with age. Begonias are sensitive to over- and under-watering. Feed with a weak fertilizer while in bud and flowering.
Care Many types of begonia are prone to mildew. Spray at the first sign of the disease and keep in a well-ventilated position. Pick off any affected leaves. If growing large-flowered tuberous begonias as specimen pot plants, pick off the small female flowers behind the larger and showier male blooms. Deadhead regularly except small-flowered species, which make it impractical. Tuberous varieties can be saved and overwintered in a frost-free place, but other kinds are usually discarded after flowering.
Propagation *B. semperflorens* is raised from seed. Tuberous species can be raised from cuttings in spring or by dividing old tubers (some can also be raised from seed). Winter-flowering lorraine and elatior hybrids can be propagated by leaf or tip cuttings.

Beloperone

See Justicia.

Billbergia

Terrestrial bromeliads grown for their exotic-looking flowers. The plants described are easy houseplants, and *B. nutans* is especially tolerant. Flowering time depends on the growing conditions – spring is the normal season, but if subjected to cool temperatures they may not flower until late summer.

Billbergia nutans

Arching, pendulous clusters of yellow and green, blue-edged flowers hang from conspicuous pink bracts. Foliage grows in clusters of narrow, funnel-shaped rosettes.

Billbergia × windii

A hybrid between *B. nutans* and *B. decora*. Similar to the previous species but with larger flowers and particularly conspicuous pink bracts.

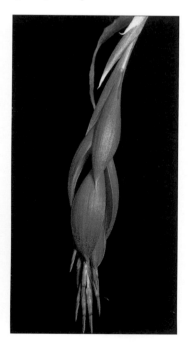

ABOVE: Billbergia nutans
BELOW LEFT: Billbergia × windii

HELPFUL HINTS

Temperature Winter minimum 13°C (55°F). Lower but frost-free temperatures are unlikely to kill the plant, but it may not grow or flower so well.
Humidity Tolerates dry air if necessary.
Position Good light, but not direct sun.
Watering and feeding Water freely from spring to autumn, sparingly in winter. In summer, pour some water into the leaf rosettes, but leave these dry at other times. Feed from spring to autumn.
Care Do not discard after flowering – often the case with flowering bromeliads grown as houseplants – as new offsets flower quickly. After a few years it will make a large clump that flowers reliably every year. Repot when the clump has filled the pot.
Propagation Offsets that form around the old rosette that has flowered. Separate from the parent when the new shoots are half as tall as the parent plant.

Blechnum

Distinctive ferns with a creeping rhizome or short stem or 'trunk' (on mature plants). The leaves are arranged in a funnel-shaped rosette.

Blechnum brasiliense

Rosette of reddish-brown young fronds, maturing to green. Makes a plant up to 1m (3ft) tall.

Blechnum gibbum

Rosette of large fronds that can be up to 1m (3ft) long on a mature plant. A distinct trunk develops with age.

HELPFUL HINTS

Temperature Aim for 13–18°C (55–64°F) in winter. High winter temperatures are detrimental.
Humidity Moderate humidity.
Position Light or partial shade. Avoid exposing to direct sun.
Watering and feeding Water freely in spring and summer, moderately at other times. Never let the roots dry out. Feed with a weak fertilizer in spring and summer.
Care Remove any dead or marked fronds to keep the plant looking attractive.
Propagation Division or spores.

RIGHT: Blechnum gibbum

Bougainvillea

Climbing shrubs grown for their colourful papery bracts rather than their true flowers, which are insignificant. Because of their size – 3m (10ft) or more in a border – they are better suited to a conservatory than indoors, although they can be grown successfully around hoops or supports in a small container for several years in a living-room. Besides the species and hybrids listed you will find many sold simply under varietal names, which may be varieties of the following species or be hybrids with others. They are all treated in the same way.

Bougainvillea × buttiana

A hybrid between *B. glabra* and *B. peruviana*. 'Mrs Butt' or 'Crimson Lake' are the best-known varieties, with scarlet, long-lasting, papery bracts in spring and summer. Other varieties sometimes offered include 'Miss Manila' (reddish-pink bracts), 'Mrs Helen McLean' (apricot to amber), and 'Scarlet O'Hara' (scarlet).

Bougainvillea glabra

Vigorous climber with thorny stems. Rose-red bracts in summer. There are varieties with purple to violet bracts, and 'Variegata' has variegated foliage. Varieties sometimes seen include 'Magnifica' (vivid purple), 'Rainbow' (coral red bracts becoming multicoloured as they fade), and 'Snow White' (white).

Bougainvillea spectabilis

A thorny, vigorous species, seldom grown as a houseplant. Reddish-purple bracts, but there are also varieties that are red, pink, white, and yellowish-orange.

Helpful hints

Temperature Winter minimum 13°C (55°F).

Humidity Mist regularly if in a heated room, and on hot summer days.

Position Good light. Tolerates direct sun if not too fierce, but avoid exposing to direct midday sun through glass.

Watering and feeding Water freely in summer, sparingly at other times. Avoid over-watering in spring when the new growth starts, as this may retard flowering. Feed regularly during the summer months.

Care Repot in spring if necessary. The plant rarely flowers for a second season if kept in living-room conditions, so move to a conservatory or greenhouse if possible when not in flower. Shorten the shoots in autumn to keep the plant compact, training new shoots to the support.

Propagation Cuttings.

LEFT: Bougainvillea *hybrid*
BELOW: Bougainvillea g.abra '*Alexandra*'

Browallia

A small group of mainly herbaceous plants, but the one most often grown is a semi-shrubby plant usually treated like an annual and discarded when it deteriorates.

Browallia speciosa

Pale or deep blue, or white or purple flowers on bushy plants about 30cm (1ft) tall. Its varieties, rather than the species itself, are usually grown. These vary in colour and compactness, and have larger flowers than the species. Can be had in flower for most of the year by staggering the sowings.

HELPFUL HINTS

Temperature Aim for 10–15°C (50–59°F). Plants flower for longer if the temperature is not too high.

Humidity Undemanding, but mist the leaves occasionally.

Position Good light. Tolerates some direct sun, but avoid direct sun through glass during the hottest part of the day.

Watering and feeding Water freely at all times. Feed regularly.

Care Grow one plant in a 10cm (4in) pot or three in a 15cm (6in) pot. Pinch out the growing tips periodically – especially when young – to encourage bushiness. Deadhead regularly. Discard the plant when flowering has finished.

Propagation Seed in late winter or early spring for summer and autumn flowering, and in summer for winter and spring flowering.

BELOW: Browallia speciosa

Brugmansia

Likely to be found under this name or its previous name datura. The species and hybrids likely to be grown as indoor or patio plants are large shrubs. Their large size – often 1.8m (6ft) or more even if pruned back each year – makes them more appropriate for a conservatory than a living-room. All parts of these plants are potentially poisonous, so they are not a good choice if there are small children in the home.

Brugmansia × candida

Large leaves, often 30cm (1ft) or more long, and huge, bell-shaped flowers up to 20cm (8in) deep. 'Plena' has double flowers. Very fragrant. Can be in bloom throughout the year if conditions are suitable, but summer is the main flowering period. Also sold as *Datura × candida.*

Brugmansia suaveolens

Similar to the above species, with even

larger white flowers. There is a double form. Very fragrant. Also sold as *Datura suaveolens.*

HELPFUL HINTS
Temperature Winter minimum 7°C (45°F).
Humidity Undemanding, but mist the leaves occasionally.
Position Good light, preferably with some direct sun.
Watering and feeding Water freely from spring to autumn, sparingly in winter. Feed regularly from spring to autumn.
Care Prune back hard at the end of the flowering season to keep the shrub compact. If possible, grow in a tub that can be moved out to the patio for the summer and brought back indoors for the cold months.
Propagation Cuttings.

RIGHT: Brugmansia suaveolens (*syn.* Datura suaveolens)

Bryophyllum

The two viviparous species described are grown as curiosities rather than plants of beauty. They become tall and leggy with age and their appeal lies in their ability to produce plantlets along the edges or at the tips of their leaves. These can be potted up to produce new plants. If you propagate these plants frequently and discard old specimens, they make interesting plants which are easy to grow. They also make ideal houseplants for children to grow. Like other bryophyllums, they are now more correctly called *Kalanchoe,* but you will still see them sold under their old name.

Bryophyllum daigremontianum
An erect, unbranching plant to about 75cm (2½ft), with succulent leaves blotched purple beneath and plantlets around the serrated leaf edges. Also known as *Kalanchoe daigremontiana.*

Bryophyllum tubiflorum
Erect growth with cylindrical, pale green leaves with darker markings. Plantlets are formed at the toothed ends. Also known as *Kalanchoe tubiflora;* now botanically named *K. dalagonensis.*

HELPFUL HINTS
Temperature Winter minimum 5°C (41°F).
Humidity Tolerates dry air.
Position Good light, but avoid exposing to direct summer sun.
Watering and feeding Water sparingly at all times, with enough moisture only to prevent the soil becoming completely dry in winter. Feed regularly in summer for a large plant: do no feed for a compact plant.
Care Remove plantlets that drop before they root.
Propagation Pot up the plantlets.

LEFT: Bryophyllum tubiflorum (*syn.* Kalanchoe tubiflora)

ABOVE: Bryophyllum daigremontianum (*syn.* Kalanchoe daigremontiana)

Calathea

Calatheas are exotic-looking rainforest plants, popular for their striking variegated foliage. They are demanding plants to grow in a living-room and are short-lived unless provided with sufficient warmth and humidity.

Calathea crocata
Dark green foliage with a reddish bloom, almost purple beneath the leaf. Long-lasting orange flowers.

Calathea insignis *see C. lancifolia.*

Calathea lancifolia
Lance-shaped leaves about 45cm (1½ft) long with alternating small and large darker green blotches along each side of the main vein. The reverse side is purple. This plant is also known as *C. insignis.*

Calathea lietzei
Slightly wavy oblong leaves about 15cm (6in) long, green with olive stripes above, reddish-purple beneath.

Calathea lubbersii
Large green leaves irregularly splashed with flashes of yellow along each side of the main vein.

Calathea makoyana
Long stalks bearing oval papery leaves, with feathery streaks of silver and dark green blotches running from the central vein. The reverse of the leaves is purple with similar markings. This plant is also known as *Maranta makoyana.*

Calathea medio-picta
Pointed oblong leaves about 15–20cm (6–8in) long, the upper surface dark

green with a whitish band along the central vein.

Calathea picturata

Oval, dark green leaves with white and yellowish-green streaks along the midrib and near the margins. 'Vandenheckei' has silvery streaks in the centre and on either side.

Calathea roseopicta

Large oval leaves about 20cm (8in) long, streaked pink and later fading to silvery-white. Red central vein and purplish reverse.

Calathea zebrina

Lance-shaped leaves 30–45cm (1–1½ft) long with dark green patches each side of the main vein. Grey-green or reddish-purple reverse.

Helpful hints

Temperature Winter minimum 16°C (60°F). Avoid sudden fluctuations in temperature.
Humidity Needs high humidity.
Position Partial shade or good light out of direct sun. Good light in winter, but avoid exposing to direct sun.
Watering and feeding Water freely,

Far left: Calathea crocata
Opposite above: Calathea lubbersii
Opposite below: Calathea zebrina
Above: Calathea picturata 'Vandenheckei' (left) and Calathea lancifolia (right)

using soft water if possible, from spring to autumn; sparingly in winter. Feed with a weak fertilizer in summer.
Care Repot annually in spring. Sponge the leaves occasionally.
Propagation Division.

Calceolaria

The only calceolarias widely grown as houseplants are hybrids, sometimes listed as *C. × herbeohybrida*. They are annuals that have to be discarded after flowering.

Calceolaria hybrids
Pouch-shaped flowers in shades of red, orange, yellow, pink, and white, usually attractively blotched or spotted. Height about 23–45cm (9–18in) according to variety. 'Grandiflora' varieties have flowers up to 6cm (2½in) across; 'Multiflora' varieties have flowers about 4cm (1½in) across. Seed companies offer many varieties.

HELPFUL HINTS
Temperature Aim for 10–15°C (50–59°F). Avoid high temperatures as much as possible.
Humidity Moderate humidity, but avoid wetting the blooms when the plant is in flower.
Position Good light, but avoid exposing to direct sun. Avoid draughts.
Watering and feeding Water freely. Never allow the plant to become dry.
Care Be alert for aphids, and spray promptly to control them if necessary. If possible, grow in a conservatory or greenhouse until just coming into flower. Discard the plant when flowering is over.
Propagation Seed in early summer. If you do not have a greenhouse or conservatory to raise plants, it is best to buy them ready-grown.

RIGHT: Calceolaria herbeo hybrida

Campanula

Most of this large group of plants are used in the herbaceous border or rock garden. *C. carpatica* is frost-hardy and best planted outdoors when flowering has finished. The other species listed here are trailing plants for the greenhouse or conservatory, but useful for short-term decoration indoors.

Campanula carpatica
Compact plant 15–23cm (6–9in) tall, covered with upward-facing, blue or white, cup-shaped flowers in summer. Often sold as a pot plant, but best planted in the garden after flowering.

Campanula fragilis
Trailing stems about 30cm (1ft) long, with blue flowers in early and mid summer.

Campanula isophylla
Trailing stems with soft blue, star-like flowers in mid and late summer. 'Mayi' has slightly larger flowers, 'Alba' is white.

HELPFUL HINTS
Temperature Winter minimum 7°C (45°F) for *C. fragilis* and *C. isophylla*. *C. carpatica* is hardy.
Humidity Undemanding, but mist the leaves occasionally.
Position Good light, but not direct summer sun.
Watering and feeding Water freely from spring to autumn, sparingly in winter.
Care Deadhead regularly. Plant *C. carpatica* in the garden when flowering is over. Cut the stems back to 5–7½cm (2–3in) at the end of the growing season to keep the plant compact and well clothed.
Propagation Seed; cuttings.

BELOW: Campanula isophylla

Capsicum

Only one species is used as a house-plant, an annual grown for its colour-ful fruits. Some varieties have round fruits, but most are cone-shaped.

Capsicum annuum

White, inconspicuous flowers in spring or summer, followed by green fruits that ripen to shades of yellow, orange, red, or purple; at their most attractive in early and mid winter.

HELPFUL HINTS

Temperature Winter minimum 13°C (55°F).
Humidity Mist the leaves regularly.
Position Good light with some direct sun.
Watering and feeding Water freely. Never allow the plant to become dry.

Care As the plant is uninteresting until the fruits ripen, keep in a green-house or conservatory if possible, and bring indoors as the fruits develop their colour. The fruits will be held for longer if kept in cool, humid conditions. Hot, dry air causes them to drop prematurely.
Propagation Seed.

BELOW: Capsicum annuum

ABOVE: Caryota mitis

Catharanthus

A small genus with a few species, only one of which is usually grown as a houseplant. Although perennial, this species is often grown as an annual.

Catharanthus roseus
Pink or white flowers about 2.5cm (1in) across with a dark eye, on compact plants that resemble the popular impatiens at a glance. Leaves have a prominent white vein. Catharanthus flower mainly between early summer and late autumn although they can be in bloom almost the year round. May also be sold as *Vinca rosea*.

HELPFUL HINTS
Temperature Minimum 10°C (50°F).
Humidity Moderate humidity.
Position Good light, but not direct sun during the hottest part of the day.
Watering and feeding Water freely at all times. Feed regularly.
Care The plant is easily raised from seed and is best discarded once it deteriorates. If you want to overwinter plants, cuttings taken in late summer will take up less space. Never let the roots become dry. Pinch out the growing tips of young plants to encourage a bushy shape.
Propagation Seed; cuttings.

BELOW: Catharanthus roseus

Caryota

Palms with distinctive fronds that look ragged and torn at the ends. Most caryotas make large plants given good conditions, but indoors they rarely grow to more than 1.2m (4ft).

Caryota mitis
Large fronds with individual leaflets about 15cm (6in) long and 10cm (4in) wide on a mature plant. The ends are ragged, giving a fishtail effect.

HELPFUL HINTS
Temperature Winter minimum 13°C (55°F).

Humidity Moderate humidity. Mist regularly in a centrally-heated room.
Position Good light, but avoid exposing to direct summer sun.
Watering and feeding Water freely from spring to autumn, sparingly in winter but always keep the roots slightly moist. Feed in summer.
Care Repot only when the roots have filled the pot and growth is beginning to suffer. Always ensure there is very good drainage when repotting. Sponge the leaves occasionally.
Propagation Suckers. Seed (can be difficult).

Celosia

Easy-to-grow, colourful flowering plants, often used for summer bedding outdoors but useful as a pot plant. Although strictly perennial they are almost always grown as annuals. Celosias are happier in a conservatory than in a living-room.

Celosia argentea *see C. cristata.*

Celosia cristata
Crested 'cockscomb' flowers, deeply crenated and ruffled, in shades of red, yellow, orange, and pink, in summer and early autumn. The Plumosa group has feathery flower plumes. Lance-shaped pale green leaves. The nomenclature has become confused, and you may find them listed as separate species (*C. cristata,* and *C. plumosa*) or as varieties of C. argentea.

Celosia plumosa *see C. cristata.*

HELPFUL HINTS
Temperature Aim for 10–15°C (50–59°F) if possible, although in summer the temperature will inevitably be

higher. Plants last better indoors than outside, and often have stronger colours if kept cool.
Humidity Moderate humidity.
Position Good light, but avoid exposing to direct summer sun through glass.
Watering and feeding Water moderately. The plant is vulnerable to both under- and over-watering. Feed regularly but cautiously: too much fertilizer with a high nitrogen content

ABOVE: Celosia cristata (*syn.* C. argentea). *These are the cockscomb type.*

may produce healthy leaves but poor flowers.
Care Discard after flowering. Best raised in a greenhouse to produce sturdy plants, but can usually be bought as young plants coming into flower.
Propagation Seed.

Cephalocereus

Ribbed, columnar cacti that rarely branch, grown mainly for the eye-catching profusion of long white hairs that they produce.

Cephalocereus chrysacanthus
Forms a large column with a green body and woolly top clothed with yellow hairs. Nine to fourteen ribs clothed with amber thorns. Red flowers are occasionally produced. Now more correctly called *Pilosocereus chrysacanthus.*

Cephalocereus senilis
Columnar growth that rarely branches, covered with long grey or white, slightly twisted hairs. Pink flowers, but these only produced on very large plants.

HELPFUL HINTS
Temperature Winter minimum 16°C (60°F).
Humidity Tolerates dry air but benefits from misting occasionally in summer.
Position Lightest possible position, benefits from direct sun.
Watering and feeding Water moderately in summer, keep almost dry in winter. Feed in spring and summer.
Care Repot only when necessary, and move into a pot only slightly larger. It may be necessary to support a tall plant with thin canes for a month or two after repotting.
Propagation Seed.

RIGHT: Cephalocereus senilis

ABOVE: Cereus peruvianus

Cereus

Columnar cacti, although in some varieties there is a disturbance of the growth point that gives them a congested and malformed appearance. In many species the flesh is covered with a whitish, green or bluish waxy layer that helps to minimize water loss through evaporation. Most are vigorous growers, and are sometimes used as rootstocks for other grafted cacti.

Cereus azureus
Upright habit with slender stems, the young ones covered with a bluish waxy bloom. The columnar stems have six or seven ribs. The large white flowers are brownish on the outside.

Cereus chalybaeus
Upright-growing columns that can be tall and 10cm (4in) across in suitable conditions, with a blue bloom. There are usually six ribs. The large flowers

are pink to red on the outside and white inside.

Cereus jamacaru
Fast-growing species with four to six ribs and stong yellowish-brown thorns. A blue waxy bloom is often noticeable. 'Monstrosus' has malformed growth that produces a mass of congested stems. Cup-shaped white flowers which open at night appear on mature plants.

Cereus peruvianus
Columnar growth with blue bloom and five to eight ribs. Clusters of sharp brown thorns, the central one up to 2cm (³⁄₄in) long. 'Monstrosus' develops a congested head of shoots that makes the plant look malformed. Old plants – often over 1m (3ft) tall – may produce flowers of 10–15cm (4–6in), red outside, white inside. The plant

sold as *C. peruvianus* is botanically considered to be *C. uruguayanus*.

Temperature Winter minimum 5°C (41°F).
Humidity Tolerates dry air.
Position Lightest possible position, benefits from direct sun.
Watering and feeding Water moderately in spring and summer, very sparingly in winter.
Care Repot only when necessary. Mist occasionally to help keep the plant looking clean and fresh. The plant can be stood in the garden in summer.
Propagation Seed; cuttings (for the branching species).

Ceropegia

Over 150 species are known but only a handful are cultivated. Some species have fleshy, erect-growing stems that may be leafless, but the best-known ones are succulent trailers.

Ceropegia radicans
Creeping succulent stems that root readily, with oval to oblong succulent leaves and long, tubular flowers striped green, white, and purple-red.

Ceropegia stapeliiformis
Upright, shrubby growth with succulent stems mottled grey-brown, and only rudimentary, scale-like. Funnel-shaped greenish-white flowers blotched purple-black.

Ceropegia woodii
Wiry purplish stems, up to 1m (3ft) long, with sparse small, heart-shaped, silver-mottled leaves. Inconspicuous 1–2cm (¹⁄₂–³⁄₄in) pinkish tubular flowers in summer. Small tubers sometimes form on the stems. Now considered to be *C. linearis woodii*.

HELPFUL HINTS
Temperature Winter minimum 10°C (50°F).
Humidity Tolerates dry air.

Position Good light. Tolerates both full sun and partial shade.
Watering and feeding Water sparingly at all times, especially in winter. Feed regularly with a weak fertilizer in summer.
Care Shorten spindly stems that have become bare in spring.
Propagation Seed; layering; cuttings from sections of stem containing a stem tuber.

Chamaecereus

A genus of just one species, an easy-to-grow cactus that flowers readily. It is now considered by botanists to be a species of *Echinopsis* and has been called *E. chamaecereus*.

Chamaecereus silvestrii

Clump-forming, with finger-like, densely spined stems that are often decumbent and tend to trail over the edge of the pot. Funnel-shaped bright red flowers in early summer. One of the most reliable cacti for flowering.

HELPFUL HINTS

Temperature Keep cool in winter. Aim for a minimum 3°C (37°F), although it will not be killed if a couple of degrees lower.
Humidity Tolerates dry air.
Position Good light, but not direct summer sun.
Watering and feeding Water freely from spring to autumn; keep practically dry in winter. Feed regularly with a weak fertilizer from mid spring to late summer.
Care Do not over-pamper in winter. If kept cold and dry the plant may shrivel but will probably bloom all the more prolifically afterwards.
Propagation Seed; cuttings.

BELOW: Chamaecereus silvestrii

Chamaedorea

A genus of more than 100 species, but only one is widely grown as a house-plant. *C. elegans* is widely popular because of its compact size and un-demanding nature.

Chamaedorea elegans
Bright green arching leaves growing from the base. On small plants these may be only 15–30cm (6–12in) long, but on a mature plant can be 60cm (2ft) or more. Flowers, like tiny yellow balls, may appear on quite young plants. Still sometimes listed under the name *Neanthe bella*.

RIGHT: Chamaedorea elegans

HELPFUL HINTS
Temperature Aim for 12–15°C (53–59°F) in winter.
Humidity Mist the leaves occasional-ly, even in winter if the room is centrally-heated.
Position Good light, but avoid ex-posing to direct sun.
Watering and feeding Water gener-ously from spring to autumn, but keep only just moist in winter. Feed regularly with a weak fertilizer in spring and summer.
Care Repot when its roots start to grow through the bottom of the pot. Avoid high winter temperatures as *C. elegans* benefits from a winter rest-ing period.
Propagation Seed; division.

Chamaerops

Palms with large fan-shaped leaves. Although older specimens may be sizeable if given ideal conditions, in a large pot or tub they rarely exceed 1m (3ft). Only one species is widely grown indoors as a houseplant.

Chamaerops humilis
Fan-shaped leaves on spiny stalks on top of a short trunk on an old speci-men, but in most plants of houseplant size the trunk is missing.

HELPFUL HINTS
Temperature Aim for 3–10°C (37–50°F) in winter. Avoid high winter temperatures. Will even tolerate a few degrees of frost if the roots are dry, although this is not recommended.
Humidity Benefits from high humid-ity. Mist the leaves regularly, espe-cially in a centrally-heated room.
Position Good light, but avoid ex-posing to direct summer sun.
Watering and feeding Water gener-ously from spring to autumn. Keep fairly moist in winter if the tempera-ture is high, almost dry if cold. Feed regularly in summer.
Care Can be stood outside for the summer, after careful acclimatization.

Sponge the leaves occasionally. Trim off any brown leaf tips, but do not cut into the green area. Repot young plants every two or three years.
Propagation Seed.

BELOW: Chamaerops humilis

Chlorophytum

A genus of about 200 or so species, but only a few are commonly grown as houseplants. *Chlorophytum comosum* is a native of South Africa, and it is the variegated forms that are almost exclusively used as pot plants.

Chlorophytum comosum

Linear leaves up to 2cm (¾in) wide and 30–60cm (1–2ft) long, arching to form a cascading habit. The flower stalk gradually curves as it lengthens, and as well as small star-shaped white flowers it usually bears small rosettes of leaves that form plantlets. 'Variegatum' and 'Vittatum' have white and green striped leaves.

LEFT: Chlorophytum com 'Vittatum'

HELPFUL HINTS
Temperature Winter minimum 7°C (45°F). Will withstand temperatures just above freezing, but for strong, healthy plants keep them above the recommended minimum.
Humidity Undemanding, but mist the leaves occasionally.
Position Good light, but avoid exposing to direct sun.
Watering and feeding Water generously from spring to autumn, sparingly in winter. Feed regularly from spring to autumn.
Care Repot young plants annually in spring, more mature ones only when the strong, fleshy roots show signs of cracking the pot or pushing the plant from its container.
Propagation Plantlets that form on the flowering stems. Large plants can be divided.

Chrysanthemum

The florist's year-round pot chrysanthemums need no introduction. By adjusting the day length and using dwarfing chemicals, commercial growers are able to produce compact plants in flower for every season. The correct botanical name for these plants is dendranthema, but you are unlikely to find them for sale under that name. The varieties used for year-round pot chrysanthemums are derived from many species, and although named varieties are used these are seldom specified at the point of sale. There may be several plants in a single pot to produce a better display.

Year-round pot chrysanthemums

Usually less than 30cm (1ft) high when grown as a houseplant. Single and double flowers in shades of red, pink, purple, yellow, and white. Grown normally, most of these make tall plants that flower in the autumn.

HELPFUL HINTS
Temperature Aim for 10–15°C (50–59°F). Plants tolerate a warm room but the display of flowers will be much shorter-lived.
Humidity Undemanding, but mist the leaves occasionally.
Position Undemanding. As you will probably discard the plant afterwards, place in any position.
Watering and feeding Keep moist at all times. Feeding is unnecessary.
Care Deadhead to keep the plant looking tidy. Discard after flowering unless you want to try them as garden plants in which case plant out in spring or summer. Some varieties will make good tall garden plants for autumn colour, others will die – so this is a gamble.
Propagation Cuttings, although it is not practical to raise your own indoor pot chrysanthemums year-round.

BELOW: *Chrysanthemum, year-round type*

Cineraria

See Senecio cruentus.

Cissus

A large genus of tropical plants with about 350 species, some succulents, others woody. Those used most often as houseplants are vigorous climbers grown for their foliage. Any flowers that appear in summer are usually green and inconspicuous.

Cissus antarctica
Climber with woody stems and shiny oval, dark green leaves up to 10cm (4in) long. Will grow rapidly to about 3m (10ft) and needs plenty of space.

Cissus discolor
Climber with red tendrils and stems, and heart-shaped, pointed leaves that combine violet-red with silvery-grey and olive-green variegation. Flushed purplish-red beneath.

Cissus rhombifolia
Vigorous climber with dark green leaves, the undersides covered in red-dish hairs. Leaves have three leaflets, the central one larger than the two behind. Still widely sold under the name *Rhoicissus rhomboidea*. 'Ellen Danica' is a widely grown variety with more deeply lobed leaflets.

Helpful hints
Temperature Aim for 7–13°C (45–55°F) in winter, with a minimum of 16°C (60°F) for *C. discolor.*
Humidity Undemanding, but mist occasionally, especially in summer.
Position Good light, but avoid exposing to direct summer sun. Provide light shade for *C. discolor.*
Watering and feeding Water generously from spring to autumn, more sparingly in winter.
Care Pinch out growing tips on young plants to stimulate new growth from low down. Keep new shoots tied to the support. Thin out overcrowded

stems in spring. Spray or sponge the leaves of *C. antarctica* periodically to keep them bright and dust-free. Other species also benefit from occasional leaf-cleaning.
Propagation Cuttings.

Top: Cissus rhombifolia
Above: Cissus antarctica

✕   Citrofortunella

A hybrid genus (*Citrus* ✕ *Fortunella*) of evergreen shrubs and trees grown mainly for their fruit. ✕ *C. microcarpa* (syn. *Citrus mitis*) is a popular pot plant producing miniature oranges on compact plants suitable for growing indoors where larger citrus fruits would be unsuitable.

✕   Citrofortunella   microcarpa

Glossy, dark green foliage. Small clusters of fragant white flowers, produced even on young plants, followed by miniature orange fruits about 4cm (1½in) across. These are rather bitter to taste. Summer is the usual flowering period, but both flowers and fruit may be produced almost all year round. It will reach about 1.2m (4ft) in time. May be seen under its older name of *Citrus mitis*.

✕   Citrofortunella mitis *see* ✕ *C. microcarpa*.

HELPFUL HINTS
Temperature Winter minimum 10°C (50°F).
Humidity Undemanding, but mist the leaves occasionally.
Position Good light, but avoid direct summer sun through glass.
Watering and feeding Water freely in summer, sparingly in winter. Feed regularly in summer. A fertilizer containing magnesium and iron may be necessary as the plants are prone to a deficiency of these elements.
Care Stand the plants outside for the summer, after careful acclimatization. Pollinate the flowers by dabbing with cotton wool or a small paintbrush.
Propagation Cuttings.

RIGHT: ✕ Citrofortunella microcarpa (*syn.* Citrus mitis)

Citrus mitis

See ✕ *Citrofortunella microcarpa*.

Clerodendrum

A large genus of about 400 mainly woody trees, shrubs and climbers, including a few that are hardy. Only *C. thomsoniae* is widely used as a houseplant, and even that is likely to prefer the conditions in a conservatory to the living-room.

Clerodendrum philippinum

Broad oval leaves up to 25cm (10in) long, and covered in hairs at the back. Fragrant white or pink flowers, at almost any time of the year.

Clerodendrum splendens

Wavy-edged, heart-shaped leaves up to 15cm (6in) long, dark green above, paler beneath. Pendulous red flower plumes between early winter and late spring.

Clerodendrum thomsoniae

Climbing stems that reach 2.4m (8ft) or more in a conservatory or green-house. Dark green, heart-shaped leaves. Distinctive red and white flowers in summer. The red corolla soon drops but the white calyx remains for many weeks.

HELPFUL HINTS
Temperature Aim for 13–15°C (55–59°F) in winter.
Humidity Mist the leaves regularly.
Position Good light, but not direct summer sun.
Watering and feeding Water freely spring to autumn, sparingly in winter. Feed regularly in spring and summer.
Care If required as a hanging or small bushy plant, cut back the stems by about half to two-thirds in late winter (by which time most of the foliage has probably dropped). Pinch out the growing tips of young plants if a bushy shape is required. Trail long stems around an upright support.
Propagation Cuttings; seed.

RIGHT: Clerodendrum thomsoniae

Colchicum

Corms with the ability to flower without soil, sometimes grown as a fun plant to flower on a windowsill in the late summer or early autumn. They are planted in the garden to grow normally once flowering indoors is over. The species described is the most common, but several other species can be treated in the same way.

Colchicum autumnale
Large crocus-shaped flowers in early autumn, usually in shades of pink. The colours are almost always paler when flowered dry indoors than when planted in the garden. The leaves do not appear until spring. Note that the corms and leaves are poisonous.

Helpful hints
Temperature Undemanding, as the plants are hardy and can be planted in the garden after flowering.
Humidity Undemanding. No special care needed.
Position A light windowsill, preferably out of strong direct sunlight.
Watering and feeding No watering or feeding necessary.
Care Place the dry corms in a saucer of sand or tray of dry pebbles to keep them upright. Set in a light position and leave the corms to flower – no water is needed. After flowering, plant in the garden in light shade, and cover with about 10cm (4in) of soil. Buy new corms each year rather than use the same ones again.
Propagation Seed; division of a large clump, but it is usually easier to buy new corms.

RIGHT: Colchicum autumnale

Coleus

A large genus of about 200 species, including perennials, annuals and evergreen sub-shrubs, many with bright and colourful foliage, but only one is widely grown. These are almost always listed as *C. blumei* hybrids, but botanists now list them as *Solenostemon* instead of coleus. However, you will almost always find them under their traditional name.

Coleus blumei hybrids
Perennial sub-shrub, but usually treated as an annual. Most have oval leaves that are gently serrated around the edge, but a few have deeply lobed foliage. Variegation varies enormously in colour and pattern, many incorporating shades of red, yellow, and green. There are named varieties, some of which have to be propagated from cuttings, but most seed mixtures produce a pleasing range of colours and patterns. Plants or cuttings are best overwintered in a greenhouse or conservatory if new stock is not to be raised from seed.

Helpful hints
Temperature Winter minimum 10°C (50°F).
Humidity Needs high humidity. Mist the leaves frequently.
Position Good light, but avoid exposing to direct summer sun during the hottest part of the day.
Watering and feeding Water freely from spring to autumn, keep the roots just moist in winter, and use soft water. Feed from spring to autumn.
Care Pinch out the growing tips of young plants to promote bushy growth. Pinch out several times more for really bushy plants. If an old plant has been overwintered, cut back hard and repot in spring to stimulate new growth from low down.

If you have raised your own plants from seed, you will probably have many, as they germinate easily. Once the plants are large enough to show their variegation clearly, retain the most appealing and discard the rest.
Propagation Seed in spring; stem cuttings in spring or summer.

RIGHT: Coleus *hybrids*

Columnea

A genus of creeping or trailing evergreen perennials or sub-shrubs, from the rain forests of Central America.

Columnea × banksii

Creeping or trailing stems with small, glossy leaves, green above and reddish beneath. Orange-red, two-lipped flowers, about 6cm (2½in) long, usually in winter and spring.

Columnea gloriosa

Long, limp, trailing stems with small leaves covered in red hairs. Scarlet flowers about 8cm (3in) long, with a yellow spot in the throat, usually in winter or spring.

Columnea hirta

Creeping or trailing stems that root readily. Red flowers about 10cm (4in) long in spring. The entire plant is covered with short, stiff hairs.

Columnea microphylla

Long, thin, trailing stems up to 1m (3ft) in length, with small almost circular leaves. Orange-red flowers in spring or summer.

HELPFUL HINTS

Temperature Winter minimum 13°C (55°F).
Humidity Needs high humidity. Mist the leaves regularly.
Position Good light, but avoid exposing to direct summer sun.
Watering and feeding Water freely from spring to autumn, sparingly in winter. Feed regularly in spring and summer months
Care Shorten the stems once flowering is over to keep the plant compact. Repot every second or third year.

Columneas do best planted in the humus-rich fibrous compost (potting soil) sold for bromeliads and orchids.
Propagation Cuttings.

TOP: Columnea microphylla
BOTTOM: Columnea gloriosa
MIDDLE: Columnea hirta

Cordyline

Evergreen shrubs and trees grown mainly for their foliage. Some of the species are sometimes sold as dracaenas, and there is often confusion between these two genera. If in doubt about whether a particular plant is a cordyline or a dracaena, check the roots. Cordylines have creeping roots that are knobbly and white when cut, while dracaenas have non-creeping roots that are smooth and yellow or orange if cut.

Cordyline australis
Sword-shaped green leaves that can be 1m (3ft) long. Some varieties are variegated, with red or yellow stripes along the green leaves. *C. a.* 'Purpurea' has reddish-purple leaves. Young plants grown indoors usually lack a distinctive trunk, which only develops on older plants. Young plants in the home are unlikely to flower.

Cordyline fruticosa
Old plants develop a clear stem or trunk, and grow large, but the young specimens usually sold as houseplants are leafy down to the base and remain compact for a long time. The species itself has plain green leaves, but there

ABOVE LEFT: Cordyline australis
ABOVE: Cordyline terminalis (*syn. C. fruticosa*) *'Kiwi'*

are many variegated varieties, heavily marked with red, pink, or cream, and sometimes a combination of these colours. Some have broad leaves, others narrower ones. Treat them all in the same way. This plant can be sold as *C. terminalis* or *Dracaena terminalis*.

Cordyline terminalis *see C. fruticosa.*

HELPFUL HINTS
Temperature Winter minimum 13°C (55°F) for tender species such as *C. fruticosa*, 3°C (37°F) for tough species such as *C. australis*.
Humidity *C. australis* is undemanding. Tropical species such as *C. fruticosa* require high humidity and should be misted regularly.
Position Good light, but avoid exposing to direct sun. *C. australis* will tolerate direct sun, but avoid summer sun through glass during the hottest part of the day.
Watering and feeding Water freely from spring to autumn, sparingly in winter. Feed tropical species regularly in spring and summer, *C. australis* less frequently.

Care Sponge leaves occasionally to remove dust and make them look brighter. Repot every second spring. *C. australis* and its varieties make attractive patio plants for the summer, but acclimatize them to outdoor conditions first. In mild areas where frosts are never severe they are sometimes successful when planted permanently in the garden, but they are best regarded as frost-tender, especially young plants.
Propagation Cuttings and stem sections with an eye, rooted in a propagator, are the best ways to increase the number of plants. An old specimen that has become leggy where leaves have fallen can be air layered.

Crassula

A large genus of about 300 succulents, ranging from dwarfs of less than 2.5cm (1in) to tall species over 5m (16ft). The species listed are just a selection of those sometimes grown as house and conservatory plants.

Crassula arborescens
Tree-shaped and will grow to about

BELOW: Crassula argentea

ABOVE: Crassula lycopodiodes
RIGHT: Crassula arborescens

1.8m (6ft) if conditions are suitable. Thick, greyish leaves edged with a red margin. White flowers, fading to pink, may appear in early and mid summer on a mature plant.

Crassula argentea *see C. portulacea.*

Crassula ovata *see C. portulacea.*

Crassula portulacea
Tree-shaped with a short 'trunk'. May grow to 1m (3ft) or more. Thick dark green succulent leaves about 2.5–5cm (1–2in) across, edged red. You may also find the plant under two other names: *C. argentea* and *C. ovata*.

Crassula lycopodioides
Distinctive fleshy stems forming an upright cluster, completely covered with minute fleshy, scale-like leaves arranged in four rows. Tiny greenish-yellow flowers in spring. The correct botanical name for this plant is now *C. mucosa.*

HELPFUL HINTS
Temperature Aim for 7–10°C (45–50°F) in winter. Avoid high temperatures in winter, otherwise the plants become lanky and leaves may fall.
Humidity Tolerates dry air.
Position Good light, in sun if possible. Species with very pale green leaves or a white bloom are best protected from strong direct sunlight through glass.

Watering and feeding Water sparingly at all times, and keep almost dry in winter. Feed with a weak fertilizer occasionally in summer.
Care Repot annually in spring while the plants are still young. Restrict watering for a while after repotting, otherwise the roots may rot.
Propagation Leaf and tip cuttings. Seed is an option but seldom used.

Crocus

Mainly spring-flowering corms, but some bloom in the autumn. It is the popular spring-flowering kinds that are almost exclusively used indoors.

Crocus chrysanthus
Typical crocus-shaped flowers, but smaller and earlier than the large-flowered varieties. The true species is seldom grown, but there are many varieties in a range of colours available for autumn planting. They bloom indoors in late winter. The grass-like leaves have a white central stripe.

Crocus, large-flowered
The typical large-flowered crocuses of spring, botanically derived from *C. vernus.* Grass-like leaves with a white

central stripe. There are many varieties to plant in autumn for late winter and early spring blooming.

HELPFUL HINTS
Temperature Keep cool. Leave in the garden until mid winter but protect from excessive freezing in cold climates, also rain that might waterlog the pots or containers. Maintain in cool conditions indoors until at least a third of the developing flower bud is visible.
Humidity Undemanding.
Position Good light once brought indoors. A sunny position will encourage the flowers to open fully.
Watering and feeding Water cautiously so that the corms do not start to rot.
Care After flowering, plant in the garden. Do not attempt to force the same corms for a second time – buy new ones each year.
Propagation Small offset corms; seed. Crocuses are seldom propagated by amateurs because it takes several years to produce plants of flowering size. It is more convenient to buy flowering-sized corms.

BELOW: Crocus, *large-flowered hybrid*

ABOVE: Crossandra infundibuliformis

Crossandra

A genus of tropical evergreen sub-shrubs with long-lasting, attractive flowers. Several species are grown as houseplants, but the one described here is the most commonly found.

Crossandra infundibuliformis
Bright heads of tubular soft orange flowers about 2.5cm (1in) across above glossy, dark green, oval to lance-shaped leaves. The plants flower while still young and may be in bloom from mid spring to autumn if conditions suit. Most plants reach about 30–60cm (1–2ft) indoors. Sometimes sold under its old name of *C. undulifolia*.

Crossandra undulifolia *see C. infundibuliformis.*

HELPFUL HINTS
Temperature Winter minimum 13°C (55°F).
Humidity High humidity is essential. Mist the leaves regularly.
Position Good light, but avoid exposing to direct summer sun.
Watering and feeding Water gener-ously in summer, less often in winter.
Care Deadhead regularly to prolong season of flowering. Repot in spring if necessary.
Propagation Stem cuttings; seed (used commercially but difficult in the home).

Cryptanthus

Genus of rosette-forming bromeliads, grown for their attractive foliage. The colouring often varies according to the light intensity.

Cryptanthus acaulis
Low-growing rosette of green, narrow, pointed leaves about 10–15cm (4–6in) long, the edges wavy and slightly serrated. Fragrant tubular white flowers sometimes appear from the centre of each rosette in summer.

Cryptanthus bromelioides
Large rosettes about 20cm (8in) or more tall, with strap-shaped and fine-ly toothed green leaves. White flowers are occasionally produced, usually in summer. More decorative is *C. b. tricolor*, which is suffused with carmine and striped white.

Cryptanthus zonatus
Flattish rosettes of wavy leaves about 20cm (8in) long, cross-banded dark sepia-green and silvery-white. A clus-

BELOW: Cryptanthus bromeliodes tricolor

ter of white flowers may be produced from the centre of rosettes in summer.

HELPFUL HINTS
Temperature Winter minimum 18°C (64°F).
Humidity Needs high humidity.
Position Good light, but not direct summer sun.
Watering and feeding Water freely in spring and summer, cautiously in autumn and sparingly in winter. Never allow the roots to dry out. Pour water into the rosettes in summer, but not in winter. Try to use tepid water. Feed regularly with a weak fertilizer in summer.
Care If the plant has to be repotted, choose a shallow container as cryptanthus have a shallow root system. Can also be grown as epiphytes in a basket or on a piece of bark. Old rosettes die once they have flowered, but young ones (offsets) will have formed around the centre of the old plants.
Propagation Offsets or plantlets which grow from the centre of the old plant in these species.

Ctenanthe

Evergreen perennials, mainly from Brazil, grown for their attractive foliage. The two species listed here are the ones most likely to be sold as houseplants.

Ctenanthe lubbersiana
Clump-forming with almost oblong leaves, about 20–25cm (8–10in) long, and on long stalks that end in an abrupt point. The leaves are irregularly splashed with pale yellow above, pale green below. Grows to about 60–75cm (2–2½ft) as a houseplant.

Ctenanthe oppenheimiana
Densely leaved, clump-forming plant with leaves usually more than 30cm (1ft) long, on tall stems that produce a plant about 1m (3ft) tall. The foliage is dark green above with irregular silvery-white bands each side of the

ABOVE: Ctenanthe lubbersiana
RIGHT: Ctenanthe oppenheimiana

midribs, and reddish-purple beneath. 'Tricolor' has large cream blotches over the green leaves.

HELPFUL HINTS
Temperature Winter minimum 16°C (60°F).
Humidity Needs high humidity.
Position Good light, but avoid exposing to direct sun.
Watering and feeding Water moderately at all times. Do not water if the surface is still damp, but never let the roots dry out. Use soft water if possible – for watering and misting. Feed in summer.
Care Sponge leaves occasionally to remove dust and to keep them looking bright. Cut out any leaves that have deteriorated.
Propagation Division.

Watering and feeding Water freely while the plants are growing actively. Gradually reduce the amount of water given once flowering has finished. During the resting period give just a little water occasionally to prevent the corm shrivelling. Feed regularly during the active growing and flowering periods.

Care Deadhead regularly, trying not to leave any stumps of flower stalk as these will be prone to rotting. Once the leaves have died, the corm goes into a dormant period, so keep the pot in a cool place (perhaps outside) and almost dry until mid summer. Then start watering again (repot if necessary, burying the tuber to half its depth), and bring indoors if the plant has been in the garden during the summer months.

Propagation Seed. Most varieties take 15–18 months to flower, but miniature cyclamen can be in flower in about 8 months.

Cymbidium

A genus of 45 or so species, including both epiphytes and semi-terrestrial orchids. There are a great many hybrids, and it is these that are normally grown in the home, where they are among the most reliable orchids to grow as houseplants.

Cymbidium hybrids
Upright spikes of large waxy-looking flowers, in colours such as green, yellow, pink, and white, usually attractively speckled or marked. Flowering time is usually between autumn and spring. Many named hybrids are grown by specialist orchid nurseries, but variety names may not be identified if you buy from a garden centre or superstore. However, all those widely sold as pot plants can be treated in the same way.

HELPFUL HINTS
Temperature Aim for 7–13°C (45–55°F) in winter.

Cyclamen

A small genus that includes hardy species with tiny flowers as well as the more popular florist's cyclamen. Those grown as pot plants are derived from *C. persicum*, which is native to the Middle East.

Cyclamen persicum
The species itself is not grown, but its hybrids and varieties are available in a range of pinks, reds, purples, salmon and white. The wide, reflexed petals are sometimes frilled or ruffled, and some of the varieties are fragrant. Leaf patterning is also variable, and often marbled or zoned white or silver. The main flowering time is autumn to

ABOVE: Cyclamen, *large-flowered hybrid*

early spring. Standard varieties grow to about 30cm (1ft), intermediate ones to about 23cm (9in), and miniatures to 15cm (6in) or less.

HELPFUL HINTS
Temperature Aim for 10–15°C (50–59°F) in winter. High temperatures will shorten the flowering period.
Humidity Moderate humidity. Plants benefit from misting when only foliage is present, but be careful not to spray the flowers. Humidity is best provided by standing the pot on pebbles over water.
Position Good light, but avoid exposing to direct sun.

Humidity Mist the leaves regularly. Humidity is best provided by standing the pot on pebbles over water.
Position Good light, but avoid exposing to direct sun.
Watering and feeding Water freely in spring and summer, sparingly in autumn and winter. Never let the roots dry out. Use soft, tepid water if possible. Feed during the flowering period.
Care Avoid a stuffy position and provide ventilation whenever it is warm enough. The plants – which are uninteresting out of flower – can be stood in a sheltered position outdoors for the summer. Repot only when the existing pot is full of roots, and use a special orchid mixture if possible.
Propagation Commercial growers use micropropagation but the easiest method for an amateur is division of an established clump, ideally after flowering.

BELOW: Cymbidium *hybrid*

Cyperus

A large genus with more than 600 species of rush-like plants, a few of which are grown as houseplants. They are a good choice for anyone who tends to overwater their plants, as they will actually thrive if the pot stands in a little water.

Cyperus albostriatus
Sedge with grass-like leaves, radiating out like the ribs of an opened umbrella, at the top of stems about 60cm (2ft) tall. This is the plant often grown as *C. diffusus*. 'Variegatus' has white-striped leaves.

Cyperus alternifolius
Grass-like leaves radiate from stiff stalks, resembling the ribs of an open umbrella. 'Variegatus' has white stripes along the length of its leaves. Height about 1m (3ft). Now more correctly called *C. involucratus,* but the name under which it is listed here is

ABOVE: Cyperus alternifolius

the one by which you are likely to purchase it.

Cyperus diffusus *see C. albostriatus.*

Cyperus involucratus *see C. alternifolius.*

HELPFUL HINTS
Temperature Winter minimum 7°C (45°F).
Humidity Mist the leaves regularly.
Position Good light, but not direct summer sun.
Watering and feeding Water freely at all times. Keep the roots moist. It will not matter if the pot stands in a little water. Feed from mid spring to early autumn.
Care Cut out any yellowing stems. Repot every spring.
Propagation Division.

Cypripedium

See Paphiopedilum.

Datura

See Brugmansia.

Davallia

A genus of evergreen or semi-evergreen, often epiphytic, ferns from tropical areas of Asia and Australia.

Davillia bullata
Divided fronds about 30cm (12in) long, sometimes with a puckered appearance.

Davallia fejeensis
A small to medium-sized fern with layers of delicate lacy fronds. Creeping rhizomes on the surface often grow over the edge of the pot.

HELPFUL HINTS
Temperature Winter minimum 7°C (45°F).
Humidity Mist the leaves regularly.
Position Partial shade or good light without direct sun.
Watering and feeding Water freely from spring to autumn, more sparingly in winter.
Care Remove dying or fading fronds.
Propagation Division; spores.

BELOW: Davallia bullata

Dendranthema

See Chrysanthemum.

Dieffenbachia

Bold foliage plants with poisonous or irritant sap that should be kept away from mouth, eyes and skin. The nomenclature of some dieffenbachias has become very confused, and you may find them sold under several synonyms. Many of the hybrids are listed simply under varietal name. As they can all be treated in the same way, this is not especially important horticulturally.

Dieffenbachia amoena
Large oblong leaves, often 60cm (2ft) long, on a thick stem. Dark green foliage with cream or white marbling along the side veins. 'Tropic Snow' is an example of a variety with heavier white variegation. You might find *D. amoena* listed as a variety of *D. seguine,* which is where some botanists now prefer to place it.

Dieffenbachia × bausei
Yellowish-green leaves about 30cm (1ft) long, marbled dark green with white patches.

Dieffenbachia bowmannii
Varieties of this species have dark and light flecks on the body of the leaves, overlaid with white or cream. The leaves can be up to 75cm (2½ft) long. There are varieties with bolder white variegation.

Dieffenbachia maculata
Large oval leaves up to 60cm (2ft) long and 20cm (8in) wide with ivory or cream blotches and markings – the variegation depending on the variety. 'Camilla' and 'Exotica' are popular varieties. For many years this species has been considered synonymous with *D. picta.*

Dieffenbachia picta *see D. maculata.*

TOP: Dieffenbachia maculata *'Camilla'*
ABOVE: Dieffenbachia maculata *'Exotica'*

Dieffenbachia seguine *see D. amoena.*

HELPFUL HINTS
Temperature Winter minimum 16°C (60°F).
Humidity Mist the leaves regularly.
Position Partial shade or good light without direct summer sun. Good light without direct sun in winter.
Watering and feeding Water freely from spring to autumn, sparingly in winter.
Care Wash leaves occasionally. Repot each spring. If the plant has become

bare at the base, try pruning back to leave a stump of about 15cm (6in) – it will often respond by producing new shoots.

Propagation Cane cuttings or stem cuttings. Air layering is a useful method for plants that have become bare at the base.

Dionaea

Insectivorous, rosette-forming perennials. The species described here is most widely sold as a fun plant. It does not make a good houseplant, however, and will probably die in a short time in a living-room.

Dionaea muscipula
Rosettes of modified hinged leaves fringed with large hairs along the edges. Insects landing on the plant can trigger the trap, which snaps closed. The two halves open again when the insect has been digested.

HELPFUL HINTS
Temperature Aim for 3–10°F (37–50°F) in winter. Keep plants frost-free, but avoid exposing to high temperatures.
Humidity High humidity is essen-

BELOW: Dionaea muscipula

tial. Mist regularly, and if possible provide additional humidity by other methods.
Position Good light, even direct sunlight, provided plants are screened from sun through glass during the hottest part of the day in summer. Best possible light in winter – supplementary artificial lighting can be beneficial, but should be of the type specially designed for use with plants.
Watering and feeding Keep constantly moist. Do not feed.
Care Repot if necessary, in spring but use an ericaceous compost (potting soil) (one for acid-loving plants) and mix with an equal volume of chopped sphagnum moss (the type used to line hanging baskets). Cover the surface with more moss.
Propagation Seed; division.

Dizygotheca

A genus of small evergreen trees and shrubs, the species below being the only one widely used as a houseplant.

Dizygotheca elegantissima
Graceful plant with dark green,

ABOVE: Dizygotheca elegantissima

almost black, leaves divided into seven to eleven finger-like serrated leaflets. On mature plants the leaflets tend to be broader, which alters their appearance slightly. In the home it will often make a plant 1–1.2m (3–4ft) tall. The plant used to be known as *Aralia elegantissima,* and some experts consider there is confusion among the plants in cultivation between this species and *Schefflera elegantissima.* However, you are most likely to find it sold as a dizygotheca.

HELPFUL HINTS
Temperature Winter minimum 13°C (55°F).
Humidity Mist the leaves regularly.
Position Good light; not direct summer sun at the hottest part of the day.
Watering and feeding Water moderately from spring to autumn, sparingly in winter.
Care Repot every second spring. If the plant becomes leggy, try cutting it down to about 10cm (4in) – it may be stimulated into producing new shoots from the base.
Propagation Seed or air layering in spring. Tip cuttings in summer.

Dracaena

The genus dracaena contains many species of palm-like plants from Africa and Asia, most of them creating the impression of an exotic plant while actually being quite tough. This has made them very popular indoor plants. The genus is sometimes confused with cordylines, but the dracaenas on the whole have less spectacularly coloured leaves and they rely on simple but very striking variegation and bold outline for their attraction. *D. godseffiana* is the odd one out, being distinctly shrubby and bearing oval rather than strap-shaped leaves.

Dracaena deremensis
Stalkless sword-shaped leaves growing directly from an upright stem. 'Janet Craig' is an all-green variety, but mostly the variegated varieties are grown. These include varieties with light or dark green leaves, and white, silver, yellow, or green stripes. Two well-known examples are 'Bausei' (white stripes on a dark green background), and 'Warneckii' (green and white central band and narrow white lines along the margins).

Dracaena fragrans
Similar to the previous species but the leaves are longer and broader and a distinct trunk forms even on young plants. The attractively variegated varieties are usually grown, such as 'Massangeana' (yellowish-green stripes along the centre of the leaf). The heavily scented flowers are unlikely to form on small plants in the home.

Dracaena godseffiana
Shrubby growth with pointed oval leaves on thin stems. The glossy green foliage is splashed and mottled with cream, but the colouring and extent of the variegation depends on the variety. Makes a bushy plant about 60cm (2ft) high, and flowers at an early age. These flowers are yellowish-green and fragrant, and may be followed by attractive red berries.

Dracaena marginata
Narrow trunk, often twisted; unbranched on young plants but in time may become branched and tall (perhaps to ceiling height). Narrow green leaves, edged purplish-red, 30–45cm (1–1½ft) or more long. More brightly coloured varieties include 'Colorama' (broad red band along each edge) and 'Tricolor' (green, cream, and red).

Dracaena sanderiana
Oval to lance-shaped leaves about 23cm (9in) long, edged with a broad creamy-white band.

Dracaena surculosa *see D. godseffiana.*

Dracaena terminalis *see Cordyline fruticosa.*

HELPFUL HINTS
Temperature Winter minimum 13°C (55°F); 10°C (50°F) for *D. godseffiana* and *D. sanderiana*.

Humidity Mist the leaves regularly. *D. godseffiana* tolerates dry air.
Position Good light, but avoid exposing to direct sun.
Watering and feeding Water freely from spring to autumn, sparingly in winter. Never let the roots dry out. Feed regularly in spring and summer.
Care Sponge the leaves occasionally to keep them clean and bright. Cease feeding by autumn to help give the plant a resting period of less active growth. Repot in spring if necessary.
Propagation Tip cuttings; air layering (for a leggy plant); cane cuttings.

BELOW: Dracaena deremensis *(right), and two of its varieties: 'Yellow Stripe' (centre) and 'White Stripe' (left)*
OPPOSITE ABOVE: Dracaena sanderiana
OPPOSITE MIDDLE: Dracaena fragrans *(right)* and D.f. *'Massageana' (left)*
OPPOSITE BELOW: Dracaena godseffiana
FAR RIGHT: Dracaena marginata *(right)* and D.m. *'Tricolor' (left)*

Echeveria

Rosette-forming succulents, grown mainly for their often attractive shape and colouring. Most species will flower, and although the flowers are not especially beautiful they are sufficiently appealing in most species to be a bonus. Of the more than 150 species and many hybrids, the ones listed below are just examples.

Echeveria elegans
Rosettes of fleshy bluish-white leaves up to 15cm (6in) across. Pink or red flowers, tipped yellow, from early spring to mid summer. Its correct botanical name is *E. secunda glanca*.

Echeveria glauca
Rosettes of waxy, spoon-shaped, blue-grey leaves. Yellow flowers tinged red in spring and early summer.

Helpful hints

Temperature Aim for 5–10°C (41–50°F) in winter.
Humidity Tolerates dry air.
Position Best possible light throughout the year. Will tolerate full sun.
Watering and feeding Water moderately from spring to autumn. Give enough water in winter to prevent the leaves shrivelling. Feed in spring and summer using a weak fertilizer.
Care Avoid getting water on the leaves if possible (it may damage the waxy layer and lead to rotting). Avoid high winter temperatures. If most of the lower leaves drop in winter, use the tips as cuttings and start again.
Propagation Tip cuttings; leaf cuttings; offsets (if the rosette produces them); seed.

LEFT: Echeveria elegans
BELOW LEFT: Echeveria glauca

Echinocactus

Slow-growing spherical to cylindrical cacti, usually with fierce but attractive spines. The plants rarely flower in cultivation.

Echinocactus grusonii
The best-known species, spherical when young, slightly more cylindrical

BELOW: Echinocactus grusonii

with age. Very old specimens in bota-nic gardens can be 1m (3ft) across, but in the home they usually remain small.

HELPFUL HINTS
Temperature Aim for 5–10°C (41–50°F) in winter.
Humidity Tolerates dry air.
Position Best possible light through-out the year. Tolerates full sun.
Watering and feeding Water mod-erately from spring to autumn, keep practically dry in winter. Feed with a weak fertilizer in spring and summer.
Care Repot only as necessary, and always use a special cactus mixture. Be careful because the roots are easily damaged.
Propagation Seed.

Echinocereus

Spherical to columnar cacti, freely branched with age. Different species vary considerably in appearance – some are practically bare, others are densely thorned or hairy.

Echinocereus pectinatus
Columnar growth with numerous ribs and small spines that are yellow at first but later become grey. Sometimes sparsely branched. Flowers freely in spring, with trumpet-shaped purple,

BELOW: Echinocereus salm-dyckianus

ABOVE: Echinocereus pectinatus

pink, or yellow blooms about 12cm (5in) across.

Echinocereus salm-dyckianus
Dark green stems, branching at the base, covered with yellowish thorns tipped red. Produces its orange flowers freely in spring. This is now consi-dered by botanists to be more correctly named *E. scheeri*.

HELPFUL HINTS
Temperature Aim for 10–13°C (50–55°F) in winter.
Humidity Tolerates dry air, but appreciates higher humidity than most cacti.
Position Best possible light through-out the year. Tolerates full sun.
Watering and feeding Water mod-erately from spring to autumn. Keep practically dry in winter. Feed reg-ularly in spring and summer with a weak fertilizer.
Care Repot only when necessary, us-ing a cactus mixture.
Propagation Cuttings if the species produces a sideshoot; seed.

Echinopsis

Spherical cacti, sometimes slightly columnar; generally freely branching.

Echinopsis eyriesii
Spherical at first, becoming more col-umnar with age. Numerous ribs with dark brown spines. Large, tubular, greenish-white scented flowers in spring or summer.

Echinopsis rhodotricha
Globular or columnar stems with 2.5cm (1in) long pale yellow spines tipped brown. Large white flowers in summer.

HELPFUL HINTS
Temperature Aim for 5–10°C (41–50°F) in winter.
Humidity Tolerates dry air.
Position Good light, but screen from very intense direct sunlight.
Watering and feeding Water mod-erately from spring to autumn. Keep practically dry in winter. Feed with a weak fertilizer in spring and summer.
Care Repot as necessary, using a cac-tus mixture. Avoid turning the plant when coming into flower (after flowering it does not matter). It is com-mon for the flowers to develop on the shady side.
Propagation Seed; cuttings.

BELOW: Echinopsis eyriesii

Epiphyllum

Genus of cacti with strap-shaped leaves, mainly from Central and South America and especially Mexico. The plants that are grown in the home, however, are almost always hybrids.

Epiphyllum hybrids

Erect, flattened, or triangular stems, sometimes winged or with a wavy edge, spreading outwards with age and often requiring support. Very large funnel-shaped flowers with a wide-flared mouth, in spring and early summer. Mainly in shades of red and pink, as well as white.

HELPFUL HINTS
Temperature Aim for 7–10°C (45–50°F) in winter. Avoid high winter temperatures.
Humidity Undemanding, but benefits from misting in spring and summer.
Position Good light, but avoid exposing to direct sun.
Watering and feeding Water freely from spring to autumn, sparingly in winter. Use soft water if possible. Feed regularly in spring and summer.
Care The plants are uninteresting out of flower so you may prefer to stand them in the garden for the summer. Avoid moving the plants once buds form, otherwise they may drop.
Propagation Cuttings.

ABOVE: Epipremnum aureum (*syn.* Scindapsus aureus)

Epipremnum

Woody climbers. The most popular species, described below, is often used in the home as a trailing plant.

Epipremnum aureum

Climber with aerial roots and heart-shaped glossy leaves, blotched or streaked with yellow. There are attractive variegated varieties such as 'Marble Queen' (white and green), and golden forms such as 'Neon'. This plant has been subject to several name-changes, and although you will find it in some shops and garden centres under the name given here, you will also find it sold as *Scindapsus aureus,* and it is sometimes listed as *Rhaphidophora aurea*.

HELPFUL HINTS
Temperature Winter minimum 13°C (55°F).
Humidity Undemanding, but benefits from occasional misting.
Position Good light, but avoid exposing to direct sun. Usually does well in poor light, but variegation is much improved in good light.
Watering and feeding Water freely from spring to autumn, sparingly in

BELOW: Epiphyllum *hybrids*

winter. Feed in spring and summer.
Care Repot in spring if necessary.
Long shoots can be shortened to keep
the plant compact.
Propagation Leaf bud or stem tip
cuttings; layering.

Erica

A very large genus of over 500 species,
many of them hardy plants used in the
garden, but only the two described
here are the ones most commonly used
as houseplants.

BELOW: Erica gracilis
BOTTOM: Erica hiemalis

Erica gracilis
Leafy spike of urn-shaped pink flowers
with white tips, in winter. The plant
grows to about 30cm (1ft). Needle-
like foliage.

Erica hyemalis
Small white, pink, or reddish bell-
shaped flowers on spikes with needle-
like leaves, in winter. Grows to about
30cm (1ft).

HELPFUL HINTS
Temperature Aim for 5–13°C (41–
55°F) during flowering period.
Humidity Mist the leaves regularly.
Position Good light. Will benefit
from winter sun.
Watering and feeding Water freely
at all times. Never allow the roots to
dry out. Use soft water if possible.
Care These are not practical plants to
keep in the home long-term, and are
usually bought in flower. Cool
temperatures will prolong flowering,
after which the plants are usually
discarded. They can sometimes be
kept successfully for another year by
trimming back the shoots after
flowering and keeping in a cool, light
position until early summer. Stand
the pot outdoors for the summer and
bring in again before the first frost.
Propagation Cuttings.

Euonymus

A genus that includes many hardy
trees and shrubs, and the species sometimes grown as a houseplant is a common hardy garden shrub. The variegated varieties make acceptable pot
plants for an unheated room or for a
cold porch, and these varieties can be
planted in the garden once they
become too large.

Euonymus japonicus
Oval leaves on upright stems, the
upper surface dark green and glossy,
the underside paler. The more attractive and less vigorous variegated
varieties are the ones usually grown

indoors, such as the small-leaved
'Microphyllus Albovariegatus' (white
variegation), and 'Microphyllus Aureovariegatus' (gold and green).

HELPFUL HINTS
Temperature Aim for 3–7°C (37–
45°F) in winter, although plants
should survive even if it drops below
freezing.
Humidity Undemanding, but mist
the leaves occasionally.
Position Good light, with or without
direct sun.
Watering and feeding Water freely
from spring to autumn, sparingly in
winter. Feed regularly in spring and
summer.
Care It is a good idea to stand the
plants in the garden for the summer
months, to keep the growth sturdy
and the variegation strong.
Propagation Cuttings.

BELOW: Euonymus japonicus
'Mediopictus'

Euphorbia

There are about 2,000 species of euphorbia ranging from annuals to shrubs, hardy border plants to tender houseplants including the poinsettia (*E. pulcherrima*). Others, such as *E. milii,* are succulents.

Euphorbia milii
Succulent shrub with woody and very thorny stems, bearing inconspicuous true flowers surrounded by bold, bright red bracts. Flowering time is spring to mid summer. The plant can grow to about 1m (3ft), but it will remain compact for many years. The sap is poisonous. May also be found under its old name of *E. splendens.*

Euphorbia obesa
Unusual-looking spherical succulent, dark green often chequered with light green, with eight flat ribs dividing the body in sections from top to bottom. A crown of cup-shaped, greenish-yellow flowers in summer.

Euphorbia pulcherrima
Erect shrubby plant grown for its colourful red, pink, or white bracts in winter (the true flowers are insignificant). Most plants bought in flower are a compact 30–60cm (1–2ft) but dwarfing chemicals will have been used. If you keep the plant for another season it will be taller.

Euphorbia splendens *see E. milii.*

Euphorbia trigona
Candelabrum-shaped succulent with triangular or winged stems. Pale green stem markings. Small oval leaves that are deciduous.

Helpful hints
Temperature Winter minimum 13°C (55°F) for most species, although the succulent kinds will usually tolerate temperatures of 10°C (50°F) quite happily.
Humidity High humidity for *E. pulcherrima* – mist the leaves regularly.

Above: Euphorbia milii
Above left: Euphorbia trigona
Left: Euphorbia obesa

Succulent species tolerate dry air, but mist *E. milii* occasionally in spring and summer.
Position Best possible light for all species in winter, but avoid direct summer sun for *E. pulcherrima.* Succulent species tolerate direct sun.
Watering and feeding Water succulent species freely from spring to autumn, sparingly in winter. Water *E. pulcherrima* freely when in flower and in summer, moderately at other times but never let the roots dry out. Feed succulent species with a weak fertilizer in summer; feed *E. pulcherrima* in summer and until it is in full flower.
Care Succulent varieties need little extra care apart from repotting when it becomes necessary. *E . pulcherrima* needs careful cultivation if it is to flower another year. Cut back the stems to leave 10cm (4in) stumps when flowering is over, and keep the roots only just moist, to induce a resting period. Repot in late spring and start watering more freely, feeding regularly as new growth is stimulated. Thin excess stems to leave about four or five on each plant. To induce flowering in early winter again, control the amount of light received from early or mid autumn. Eliminate light (using a black plastic sack, for instance) for 14 hours each day. Put the cover on in the evening and remove the next morning. Continue this treatment for eight weeks, then grow the plant on normally.
Propagation Cuttings of *E. pulcherrima* and *E. milii.* Seed is the best method for the other succulent species mentioned.

Eustoma

A genus of annuals and perennials with poppy-like flowers. The species listed is often grown as a cut flower but can also be found as a pot plant.

Eustoma grandiflorum

Open, poppy-like flowers in shades of blue, pink, and white, in summer. There are also double varieties. Small lance-shaped green leaves, about 5cm (2in) long. Compact varieties that grow to about 30–45cm (1–1½ft) are best for pots. Other names are *Lisianthus russellianus* and *E . russellianum*.

BELOW: Eustoma grandiflorum (*syn.* Lisianthus russellianus)

HELPFUL HINTS
Temperature Winter minimum 7°C (45°C).
Humidity Mist occasionally.
Position Good light, but avoid direct summer sun.
Watering and feeding Water with care at all times, making sure the compost (potting soil) never becomes dry or waterlogged. Feed regularly once the nutrients in the initial potting soil become depleted.
Care Although technically perennials, these plants are treated as annuals and discarded when flowering has finished.
Propagation Seed. Plants can be divided in autumn, but it is more satisfactory to raise fresh ones from seed.

ABOVE: Exacum affine

Exacum

A genus of about 40 species, including annuals, biennials and perennials. Only one species, however, is now widely grown, mainly because it is so easy to raise from seed and because it flowers well in a pot.

Exacum affine

Masses of small, pale purple (sometimes white), slightly fragrant flowers with yellow centres. The main flowering period is from mid summer to late autumn. Small, fresh green leaves 2–4cm (¾–1½in) long.

HELPFUL HINTS
Temperature Aim for 10–21°C (50–70°F).
Humidity Mist the leaves regularly.
Position Good light, but avoid exposing to direct summer sun.
Watering and feeding Water freely at all times. Feed regularly once the nutrients in the initial potting soil become depleted.
Care Deadhead regularly. Discard after flowering (although they can sometimes be kept growing into the second year, it is best to start with new plants).
Propagation Seed.

× Fatshedera

A bigeneric hybrid from a cross between *Fatsia japonica* and *Hedera helix* 'Hibernica'.

× Fatshedera lizei

Shiny, five-fingered, hand-shaped leaves. The shoots grow upwards initially, then tend to become decumbent. Rounded heads of creamy-white flowers are sometimes produced in autumn on mature plants. Will grow to 1.8m (6ft) or more if conditions are suitable, and is hardy enough to grow outside where frosts are not severe. The variegated varieties, such as 'Variegata', are slower-growing and more attractive as houseplants.

HELPFUL HINTS
Temperature Winter minimum 3°C (37°F). Keep below 21°C (70°F) if possible.
Humidity Undemanding in a cool position, mist the leaves occasionally in a warm room.
Position Good light, but avoid exposing to direct summer sun. Best possible light in winter.
Watering and feeding Water freely from spring to autumn, sparingly in winter. Feed in spring and summer.
Care Repot each spring. Provide a support if you want to grow it like an ivy, but pinch out the growing tips each spring if you prefer a more bushy plant.
Propagation Cuttings.

RIGHT: × Fatshedera lizei '*Pia*'
BELOW: × Fatshedera lizei '*Anne Mieke*'

Fatsia

A genus with only one species, a useful evergreen for the garden where winters are not harsh and a good houseplant for a cool and shady position.

Fatsia japonica

Deeply lobed, glossy dark green leaves, 20–40cm (8–16in) across. Variegated varieties make less vigorous and more attractive houseplants.

HELPFUL HINTS
Temperature Winter minimum 3°C (37°F), although it is not critical if the plants are exposed to a little frost. Variegated varieties are more cold-sensitive and are best in a winter minimum of about 13°C (55°F). Keep below 21°C (70°F) if possible.
Humidity Moderate humidity.
Position Good light, but not direct summer sun. Tolerates shade well.
Watering and feeding Water freely from spring to autumn, sparingly in winter. Feed in spring and summer.
Care Sponge the leaves once a month.
Propagation Cuttings; air layering; seed (for the green form).

ABOVE: Fatsia japonica

Faucaria

South African succulents with semi-cylindrical or angled fleshy leaves, and golden-yellow, daisy-like flowers in autumn.

Faucaria tigrina
Fleshy green leaves about 5cm (2in) long, speckled white and with deeply-toothed edges that create a jaw-like appearance.

HELPFUL HINTS
Temperature Winter minimum 5°C (41°F). Avoid high winter temperatures, if possible.
Humidity Tolerates dry air.
Position Brightest possible position, benefits from direct sun.
Watering and feeding Water freely in summer, sparingly in autumn and spring, and keep practically dry in winter. Feed regularly with a weak fertilizer in summer.
Care Rest the plant once the leaves begin to shrivel in autumn, and keep the compost (potting soil) and air dry

BELOW: Faucaria tigrina

to reduce the risk of rotting. Repot the plant every third year, using a cactus mixture.
Propagation Cuttings; seed.

Ferocactus

Slow-growing spherical cacti that become columnar with age. Curved, colourful spines. Specialist nurseries will offer several species, but the one described here is among those most commonly grown as houseplants.

Ferocactus latispinus
Blue-green body, spherical on small plants, with about 20 prominent ribs that bear large hooked spines. The red flowers rarely appear on specimens kept as houseplants.

HELPFUL HINTS
Temperature Winter minimum 5°C (41°F).
Humidity Tolerates dry air.
Position Brightest possible position, benefits from direct sun.
Watering and feeding Water moderately from spring to autumn. Keep practically dry in winter. Use soft water if possible.
Care Repot in spring, using a cactus mixture.
Propagation Seed; offsets.

BELOW: Ferocactus latispinus

Ficus

A huge genus with more than 800 species, most of them originating in Asia and Africa, and including the edible fig. Those used as houseplants are grown for foliage effect, and for many years *F. elastica* was one of the most popular of all houseplants. The larger species still make some of the finest focal-point plants for a room, while the trailers make useful plants for hanging pots and bottle gardens.

Ficus benghalensis
Resembles the more popular *F. elastica* but the 20cm (8in) leathery leaves are hairy. They make immense trees in the wild, and in the home will reach ceiling height after a few years if conditions are suitable.

Ficus benjamina
A tall tree with a broad crown and trailing branches in the wild, but as a pot plant the pendulous shoots give the whole plant the appearance of a small weeping tree and will seldom grow to more than 2.4m (8ft) indoors. In the species the 10cm (4in) long, pointed leaves are green, but the variegated varieties are more popular. 'Starlight' is a variety with particularly bold white markings.

Ficus deltoidea
Dark green, leathery leaves about 6–8cm (2½–3in) long, tapering towards the base and blunt at the tip. Makes a branching shrub to about 75cm (2½ft) in cultivation. May also be found under the name *F. diversifolia*.

Ficus diversifolia *see F. deltoidea.*

Ficus elastica
Large oval leaves about 30cm (1ft) long, glossy and dark green. The young leaves are sheathed in red stipules, which drop as the leaf opens. The species itself is seldom grown, and the green varieties usually sold are 'Decora' and 'Robusta', which have broader leaves, often more densely spaced. Variegated varieties include 'Doescheri' and 'Tricolor'. 'Black Prince' has very dark foliage.

Ficus lyrata
Large, waxy leaves shaped like an upside-down violin, about 50cm (20in) long. A tall plant, usually reluctant to branch, that will reach ceiling height after a few years.

Ficus pumila
Trailing plant with thin wiry stems and heart-shaped leaves about 2.5cm (1in) long. The foliage on mature plants has thicker and longer leaves, but it is almost always seen as a houseplant with its juvenile foliage. Will also climb by means of clinging roots. 'Minima' has smaller leaves and

Ficus radicans
Trailing, wiry stems with pointed leaves about 7.5–10cm (3–4in) long. The limp stems will trail or climb by rooting at the leaf joints. 'Variegata' has narrower leaves marked with white. More correctly known as *F. sagittata.*

Ficus religiosa
A large tree in the wild, with prop roots growing from the branches. Dull green 10–15cm (4–6in) leaves with long, slender, almost thread-like tips.

Ficus repens *see F. pumila.*

Ficus sagittata *see F. radicans.*

HELPFUL HINTS
Temperature Winter minimum 13°C (55°F).
Humidity Mist the leaves occasionally. *F. lyrata*, *F. pumila* and *F. radicans* benefit from regular misting.
Position Good light for tree and shrub types, but avoid direct summer sun through glass during the hottest part of the day. Partial shade for creeping and climbing types.
Watering and feeding Water all varieties freely from spring to autumn, but sparingly in winter. Use tepid water if possible, especially in winter. Feed in spring and summer.
Care Repot young plants every second year. Occasionally sponge the leaves of species with large, glossy foliage.
Propagation Cuttings; air layering of woody species.

LEFT: Ficus lyrata
OPPOSITE ABOVE: *Three varieties of* Ficus elastica: *'Belgica' (left), 'Robusta' (centre), 'Black Prince' (right)*
OPPOSITE BELOW: *Three varieties of* Ficus benjamina: *'Exotica' (left), 'Starlight' (centre), 'Reginald' (right)*
FAR RIGHT ABOVE: Ficus benghalensis
FAR RIGHT BELOW: Ficus deltoidea

ABOVE: Fittonia verschaffeltii

Fittonia

Non-woody, creeping ground cover plants that originate from the tropical rain forests of Peru. Although small yellowish flowers may appear in spring they are inconspicuous and the plants are grown for foliage effect.

Fittonia argyroneura *see F. verschaffeltii.*

Fittonia verschaffeltii
This species has olive green leaves about 5cm (2in) long, with deep pink veins. *F. v. argyroneura* (often sold simply as *F. argyroneura*) has pale green leaves with white veins. *F. v. argyroneura nana* (frequently sold as *F. argyroneura nana*) also has white veins on light green leaves, but these are only about 2.5cm (1in) long. Large-leaved forms grow to about 10cm (4in), the small-leaved variety only half this height.

HELPFUL HINTS
Temperature Winter minimum 16°C (60°F).
Humidity Needs high humidity.
Position Partial shade. Avoid direct sunlight.
Watering and feeding Water freely from spring to autumn, sparingly in winter. Use tepid water if possible. Feed from spring to autumn with a weak fertilizer.
Care Pinch back long, straggly shoots to keep the plant compact. Repot each

spring. Difficult to keep unless the humidity is high, but plants do well in a bottle garden.
Propagation Division; cuttings; or just pot up plants where the creeping stems have rooted.

Fuchsia

A genus of evergreen and deciduous trees and shrubs, grown mainly for their attractive pendent flowers.

Fuchsia hybrids
The hybrid fuchsias need little description as their usually bell-shaped flowers with flared 'skirts' are so well known as garden and greenhouse plants. There are single, semi-double and double varieties in a wide range of colours, but mainly pinks, reds, purples and white. The ones likely to be grown as pot plants will be hybrids, most of which will make a compact plant about 45–60cm (1½-2ft) tall. Old specimens are best discarded unless trained as a standard, when they should be repotted each spring.

HELPFUL HINTS
Temperature Aim for 10–16°C (50–60°F) in winter. Avoid high winter temperatures.
Humidity Mist the leaves occasionally when the plant has foliage.
Position Good light, but not direct summer sun.
Watering and feeding Water freely from spring to autumn while the plant is growing vigorously, sparingly early and late in the season. Water very sparingly in winter if the plants are dormant – just enough to prevent the soil drying out completely. Continue to water cuttings in leaf sufficiently to sustain growth. Feed from late spring to late summer.
Care It is natural for the leaves to fall in autumn. If possible, keep the plants in a cool, light position for the winter. New growth will appear in spring. Shorten the old shoots just before, or as, new growth starts, to keep the plant compact and bushy. The pruning can be severe as the flowers form on new growth, which is freely produced.
Propagation Cuttings.

RIGHT: Fuchsia *hybrid*

Gardenia

Evergreen shrubs and small trees. The shrub described here is widely grown for its fragrant flowers.

G. augusta *see G. jasminoides.*

Gardenia jasminoides

Fragrant semi-double to double white flowers about 5cm (2in) across, usually borne in summer although there are varieties that flower in winter. Glossy green leaves up to 10cm (4in) long. Will make a shrub of about 1.5m (5ft) in a conservatory, but as a houseplant grows no taller than 45cm (1½ft).

HELPFUL HINTS
Temperature Winter minimum 16°C (60°F).
Humidity Mist the leaves regularly.
Position Good light, but not direct summer sun during the hottest part of the day.
Watering and feeding Water freely from spring to autumn, sparingly in winter, but never let the roots become dry. Use soft water if possible. Feed

ABOVE: Gardenia jasminoides

from spring to autumn.
Care Avoid widely fluctuating temperatures when the buds are forming, as this may cause them to drop. Deadhead regularly – the blooms turn yellowish with age. After flowering the plant can be placed in a sheltered spot outside for the summer. Repot every second or third year, using an ericaceous (lime-free) compost (potting soil).
Propagation Cuttings.

Gerbera

Herbaceous perennials with daisy-like flowers. There are about 45 species but only one is grown as a pot plant.

Gerbera jamesonii

Single or double, daisy-type flowers about 5cm (2in) across, in bright colours such as red, orange, pink, yellow, and white, with a yellow centre. Main flowering time is early summer to late autumn, but they are sometimes sold

in flower in winter. Lobed hairy leaves about 15cm (6in) long arise from the base. Some grow to about 60cm (2ft) tall, but compact varieties about 25–30cm (10–12in) tall are more suitable as houseplants.

HELPFUL HINTS
Temperature Aim for 10–21°C (50–70°F) during flowering.
Humidity Mist the leaves regularly.
Position Good light, with direct sun for at least part of the day.
Watering and feeding Water freely while the plant is growing actively, more cautiously when it is resting, but never allow the roots to dry out. Feed regularly while the plant is in active growth.
Care It is difficult to keep the plant for another year when flowering has finished, unless you have a conservatory. As old plants tend to flower poorly, they are usually discarded.
Propagation Seed is the usual method, but division is an easy technique if you have an old plant.

BELOW: Gerbera jamesonii *hybrid*

Gloxinia

See Sinningia speciosa.

Guzmania

Epiphytic bromeliads, mainly from the tropical rain forests of South America. They are usually grown for their showy flower heads. The species described here is one of the most popular, but others are also sold as pot plants.

Guzmania lingulata
Rosette of foliage with strap-shaped leaves about 15–20cm (6–8in) long. The flower stalk, up to about 30cm (1ft) long, is topped by bright red or orange bracts with small yellowish-white flowers in the centre, and usual-ly blooms in summer, although commercial growers can produce plants in flower throughout the year. *G. l. minor* is a smaller plant, often only about 15cm (6in) tall.

HELPFUL HINTS
Temperature Winter minimum 16°C (60°F).
Humidity Mist occasionally in winter, regularly in summer.
Position Light shade in summer, good light in winter.
Watering and feeding Water freely from spring to autumn, sparingly in winter. Feed with a weak fertilizer in spring and summer.
Care In summer pour water into the 'vase' formed by the rosette of leaves.
Propagation Offsets; seed.

BELOW: Guzmania lingulata

Gymnocalycium

A genus of cacti with about 50 species. Many of them will produce their funnel-shaped flowers at an early age, but the ones most often sold are grafted forms that lack enough chlorophyll to thrive on their own roots. The grafted forms are grown for their curious appearance rather than their flowers, which tend to be less freely produced.

Gymnocalycium mihanovichii
Normally has a grey-green ribbed body with small curved thorns, and yellowish-green flowers. *G. m. friedrichii* has pink flowers. The 'curiosity' varieties have yellow, orange, red, or almost black bodies, and these are sold grafted onto a green stem from a different cactus.

ABOVE: Gymnocalycium mihanovichii

HELPFUL HINTS
Temperature Aim for a winter temperature of 5–10°C (41–50°F).
Humidity Tolerates dry air.
Position Good light, full sun in winter, but avoid direct summer sun during the hottest part of the day for coloured grafted varieties.
Watering and feeding Water moderately in summer, very sparingly at other times (just enough to prevent the body shrivelling). Feed with a weak fertilizer in summer.
Care Use a special cactus mixture if repotting.
Propagation Offsets from those species that produce them freely; coloured varieties that lack chlorophyll are best grafted.

Gynura

A genus of about 25 herbaceous or shrubby plants, from tropical areas of Asia, but only the species with attractive purple hairs are usually grown as houseplants.

Gynura aurantiaca
Dark green leaves about 15cm (6in) long, covered with purple hairs that create a velvety appearance. Upright growth to about 45-90cm (1½–3ft). Orange flowers with an unpleasant smell in winter.

Gynura procumbens *see G. sarmentosa.*

Gynura sarmentosa
Similar to previous species but smaller leaves about 7.5cm (3in) long on trailing or climbing stems. Will reach 60cm (2ft) or more with a support. May also be listed as *G. procumbens*. The plant grown as *G. sarmentosa* in cultivation is likely to be the variety *G.* 'Purple Passion'.

HELPFUL HINTS
Temperature Winter minimum 10°C (50°F).
Humidity Mist occasionally.
Position Good light, but not direct summer sun.
Watering and feeding Water freely from spring to autumn, more sparingly in winter.
Care Pinch out the growing tips periodically if you want to keep the

ABOVE: Gynura sarmentosa
BELOW: Gynura *'Purple Passion'*

plant compact and bushy. Pinch out any flowers as soon as the buds appear, as they smell unpleasant.
Propagation Cuttings.

Haworthia

A genus of clump-forming succulents with a basal rosette of warty leaves.

Haworthia fasciata
Rosette of thick, slightly incurving, finely-pointed leaves with pearly warts on the lower surface. These appear to form crosswise white bands.

Haworthia margaritifera
Similar to the previous species, but with broader rosettes, about 13cm (5in) across; the warts are arranged more randomly and do not appear to form bands.

Helpful hints

Temperature Aim for 10-13°C (50–55°F) in winter.

Humidity Tolerates dry air.

Position Brightest possible position, benefits from full sun.

Watering and feeding Water moderately from spring to autumn, very sparingly in winter. Feed with a weak fertilizer or a cactus food while plant is growing actively.

Care Repot in spring, but only when the rosette has grown too large for the pot.

Propagation Offsets; seed.

BELOW: Haworthia margaritifera

Hedera

A small genus of self-clinging climbers, but with many varieties. Plants will climb or trail, depending on how you grow them.

Hedera algeriensis *see H. canariensis.*

Hedera canariensis
Large, slightly lobed leaves, with white margins in 'Variegata', often sold under its other name of 'Gloire de Marengo'. Botanists now consider the correct name for this plant to be *H. algeriensis* 'Gloire de Marengo', but you are unlikely to find it sold under this name.

Hedera helix
This plant – the common ivy – needs no description. The leaves are much smaller than those of the previous species, and varieties are available with foliage of many different shapes and markings.

Helpful hints

Temperature Cool but frost-free is ideal, although plants are frost-hardy if suitably acclimatized. Avoid warm rooms in winter – plants are more likely to thrive in an unheated room.

Humidity Mist the leaves occasionally, regularly in summer if possible.

Position Good light or some shade.

extend the season considerably. Individual blooms are short-lived but there is a constant succession of them. Will make a shrub of 1.5m (5ft) or more given suitable conditions, but more often seen as a compact plant less than half this height indoors.

HELPFUL HINTS
Temperature Winter minimum 13°C (55°F).
Humidity Mist occasionally.
Position Good light, but not direct summer sun through glass during the hottest part of the day.
Watering and feeding Water freely from spring to autumn, sparingly in winter, but never allow the roots to dry out. Feed regularly in summer.
Care Deadhead regularly. Shorten long shoots after flowering, or in late winter. Do not turn or move the plant once buds have formed as this may cause the buds to drop. Repot each spring. The plant can be placed in a sheltered spot outdoors for the summer months.
Propagation Cuttings; seed.

BELOW: Hibiscus rosa-sinensis

OPPOSITE ABOVE: Hedera helix *'Goldchild'*
ABOVE: Hedera canariensis *'Variegata'*

Will tolerate poor light for short periods. Benefits from good light in winter, but avoid direct summer sun.
Watering and feeding Water freely in warm weather, moderately in cool temperatures. Never allow the roots to dry out. Feed regularly from spring to autumn.
Care Repot each spring unless the plant is already in a large pot. Pinch out the growing tips periodically if you want a bushy plant.
Propagation Cuttings.

Helxine

See Soleirolia.

Heptapleurum

See Schefflera.

Hibiscus

A genus that contains evergreen and deciduous trees and shrubs, herbaceous perennials, and annuals. Just one species is widely grown as a houseplant, a shrubby plant widely grown in gardens in subtropical regions.

Hibiscus rosa-sinensis
Large, double or single showy flowers about 10–13cm (4–5in) across, with stamens on a prominent central column. Colours include red, pink, orange, yellow, and white. 'Cooperi' has variegated foliage and red flowers. The main flowering time is summer, but commercial growers are able to

Hippeastrum

A genus of about 70 bulbous species from tropical and subtropical parts of America, but the plants with huge trumpet-shaped flowers grown as pot plants are hybrids. Although these are popularly known as amaryllis, this is really the botanical name of a different plant that is sometimes grown in the garden.

Hippeastrum hybrids
Clusters of three to six huge, trumpet-shaped flowers on strong stems about 60cm (2ft) tall. Colours include shades of red, pink, and white, some bicoloured. There are a few semi-double varieties. The large, strap-shaped leaves usually emerge once the flowers have started to open. It can be forced into flower in winter without the need for a period in the dark.

HELPFUL HINTS
Temperature Needs warmth to start into growth (*see* Care), but the flowers will last for longer in a cool room.
Humidity Undemanding.
Position Good light.
Watering and feeding Water moderately when the bulbs are growing, keep almost dry when resting. Feed regularly once the leaves start to grow, and cease when the resting period is due (see Care).
Care Bulbs prepared for early flowering should be planted when available, and they will bloom in winter. Unprepared bulbs planted at the same time will flower later. Bulbs planted in late winter or early spring will flower in mid or late spring. A soil temperature of 21°C (70°F) is required to start dormant bulbs into growth. If the roots look very dry, soak the bulbs for a few hours before potting up, burying only about half the bulb.

As soon as the flower stalk is 15–20cm (6–8in) tall, keep in a very light position. Cut off the flower stalk when blooming is over. The plant will then look unattractive and is best

ABOVE: Hippeastrum *hybrid*

placed in a conservatory or greenhouse, or outdoors for the summer once there is no risk of frost. Reduce watering in early autumn and allow the leaves to die back. Start into growth again by resuming watering a month or two later.
Propagation Offsets (which may bloom after three years); seed (unpredictable results and flowering even slower).

Howea

Evergreen palms, also occasionally seen under their old name of kentia.

Howea belmoreana
Thin green stems and arching pinnate foliage, the edges covered in woolly hairs. Will eventually grow to ceiling height indoors if conditions suit. May also be listed as *Kentia belmoreana*.

Howea forsteriana
Similar to previous species, but with broader leaflets and less arching fronds. May also be listed as *Kentia forsteriana*.

HELPFUL HINTS
Temperature Winter minimum for

RIGHT: Howea belmoreana (*syn.* Kentia belmoreana)
ABOVE RIGHT: Howea forsteriana (*syn.* Kentia forsteriana)

H. belmoreana 16°C (60°F), for *H. forsteriana* 10°C (50°F).

Humidity Mist the leaves regularly.

Position Good light, but not direct summer sun through glass during the hottest part of the day. Tolerates some shade. Good light in winter.

Watering and feeding Water moderately in summer, sparingly in winter. Keep the soil just moist. Feed in summer.

Care Sponge the leaves occasionally. The plant benefits from being stood outside in a light summer shower. Avoid using leaf shines, as some can damage the fronds.

Propagation Seed (difficult).

Hoya

Evergreen climbers, trailers, or lax shrubs, but only three out of over 200 species are grown as houseplants. The two listed are the ones most commonly grown.

Hoya bella

Fleshy leaves about 2.5cm (1in) long. Pendulous clusters of fragrant white, waxy-looking, star-shaped flowers with purplish-red centres. Flowering time is usually between late spring and early autumn. The correct botanical name for this plant is *Hoya lanceolata bella,* although you are unlikely to find it under this name.

Hoya carnosa

Similar to the previous species but with slightly larger, pale pink flowers, which are also fragrant. Leaves about 7.5 cm (3 in) long. There is a variegated variety.

HELPFUL HINTS

Temperature Aim for 10–13°C (50–55°F) in winter for *H. carnosa*, and a winter minimum of 18°C (64°F) for *H. bella.*

Humidity Mist the leaves regularly, but not when plant is in bloom.

Position Good light. Some direct sun is beneficial, but avoid summer sun

ABOVE: Hoya bella

through glass during the hottest part of the day.

Watering and feeding Water freely from spring to autumn, sparingly in winter. Feed sparingly when the plant is in flower as over-feeding can inhibit flowering.

Care Provide suitable support if the plant is to be grown as a climber. A trellis or moss pole is suitable, but *H. bella* can also be grown in a hanging basket. Do not move the plant once flower buds form. Do not repot until absolutely necessary as root disturbance is resented.

Propagation Semi-ripe tip cuttings or eye cuttings *H. bella* is sometimes grafted onto *H. carnosa.*

Hyacinthus

A small genus of bulbous plants, from Asia Minor and around the Mediterranean. Only one is widely grown, but its varieties are among the most popular indoor bulbs for winter colour and fragrance

Hyacinthus orientalis

The dense spikes of the hyacinth need no description. There are many varieties in shades of red, pink, mauve, blue, yellow, and white. Multiflora varieties produce several small spikes from each bulb instead of one large one. Flowering time ranges from early winter to mid spring, depending on variety, planting time, and

whether the bulb has been specially prepared for early flowering. Consult a bulb catalogue for specific varieties, planting and flowering times.

HELPFUL HINTS

Temperature Hardy. Keep as cool as possible unless advancing flowering, and then only force once the bud has emerged. Once in bloom, the cooler the room, the longer the flowers will last.

Humidity Undemanding.

Position Good light once flower buds start to show colour. Once in full flower, can be positioned anywhere as a short-term houseplant.

Watering and feeding Ensure the roots do not dry out at any time. Feeding is not necessary unless you want to save the bulbs to plant in the garden.

Care Hyacinths should be regarded as short-term houseplants. If you want to plant the bulbs in the garden after flowering, continue to water and feed regularly until the leaves begin to die down. At this stage, place in a garden frame to acclimatize to outside conditions and then plant in the garden. Do not use again indoors.

Propagation Offset bulbs can be grown on, but this is not practical for propagating houseplants. Buy fresh bulbs each year.

BELOW: Hyacinthus orientalis *variety*

Hydrangea

A genus of over 20 deciduous shrubs and deciduous and evergreen climbers, but only the species below is used as a pot plant.

Hydrangea macrophylla

Shrub with broad oval, coarsely toothed deciduous leaves about 15cm (6in) long, and ball-shaped flower heads in shades of blue, pink, and white. Mophead varieties have rounded heads of flowers that all look the same; Lacecap varieties have an outer ring of open flowers. Although they make shrubs of at least 1.5cm (5ft) in the garden, these plants are only used indoors while small. Hydrangeas are usually sold as flowering pot plants in flower in spring, but specially-treated plants may be available in bloom at other times of year.

HELPFUL HINTS

Temperature Frost-hardy, but indoors these plants are best in a winter minimum of 7°C (45°F). Move them to a warm, bright position in mid winter, when you can increase watering. If possible, avoid a very warm room.
Humidity Mist occasionally.
Position Good light or light shade. Some direct sun is beneficial in winter but avoid hot summer sun.
Watering and feeding Water freely from spring to autumn, sparingly in early winter. Use soft water if possible. Feed regularly while plants are growing actively.
Care Flower colour can be affected by the acidity of the compost (potting soil). Use an ericaceous (acidic, humusy, lime-free) mixture if you want blue flowers. You can also buy proprietary blueing compounds but plants must be treated before they flower. Never allow the roots to dry out during the growing season. Cut back the stems to half their height after flowering. The plants are not particularly attractive when flowering has finished, so stand in the garden for the summer.
Propagation Semi-ripe cuttings.

BELOW: Hydrangea macrophylla

ABOVE: Hymenocallis × festalis

Hymenocallis

A genus of about 40 bulbous plants, only a few of which are sometimes grown as pot plants. You can buy the bulbs from specialist bulb suppliers.

Hymenocallis × festalis

Large white central cup surrounded by backward-curving petals, in late spring or summer. Fragrant. Strap-shaped leaves die down in autumn. A hybrid between *H. narcissiflora* and *H. longipetala*.

Hymenocallis narcissiflora

Clusters of three to six pendulous white flowers with a white funnel-shaped fringed cup surrounded by backward-curving slender petals. Fragrant. Leaves die down in autumn.

HELPFUL HINTS

Temperature Winter minimum 15°C (59°F), although the plant may be dormant for most of that time.
Humidity Undemanding.
Position Good light, but avoid direct summer sun through glass during the hottest part of the day.
Watering and feeding Water freely during the growing season. Keep the

species that die back practically dry in winter and water those that retain their foliage cautiously. Feed regularly when active growth starts.
Care More likely to be available as dry bulbs than growing plants. Start the bulbs into growth in late winter or early spring.
Propagation Offsets.

Hypocyrta

A small genus of about nine species, which has since been divided by botanists into other varieties. Only one of these is widely grown.

Hypocyrta glabra
Shiny dark green, leathery leaves, about 3cm (1¼in) long on compact plants 15–23cm (6–9in) tall. Small orange, waxy-looking flowers appear along the stems in summer. Now considered by botanists to be more correctly *Nematanthus,* although you are much more likely to find it sold under the name used here.

BELOW: Hypocyrta glabra

HELPFUL HINTS
Temperature Winter minimum 10°C (50°F).
Humidity Mist the leaves regularly.
Position Good light, but do not expose to direct summer sun during the hottest part of the day. Best possible light in winter.
Watering and feeding Water moderately from spring to autumn, sparingly in winter.
Care Cut back after flowering, shortening the shoots by about a third. Avoid high winter temperatures as the plant benefits from a rest at this time.
Propagation Cuttings; division; seed.

Hypoestes

A genus of mainly evergreen perennials and sub-shrubs, only two of which are grown as houseplants. The one described here is the species most commonly seen.

Hypoestes phyllostachya
Pointed, oval leaves about 6cm (2½in)

ABOVE: Hypoestes phyllostachya (*syn.* H. sanguinolenta)

long, covered with red or pink spots and blotches. The intensity of variegation depends on variety and growing conditions: some appear mainly pink, red or white, with areas of green, others are mainly green with more distinct spots of pink or white. Colouring is usually more vivid with some direct sunlight. Can be kept to 30–60cm (1–2ft) by regular pruning. Also sold as *H. sanguinolenta,* although strictly this is a different plant.

Hypoestes sanguinolenta *see H. phyllostachya.*

HELPFUL HINTS
Temperature Winter minimum 13°C (55°F).
Humidity Mist the leaves regularly.
Position Good light, but avoid direct summer sun through glass during the hottest part of the day.
Watering and feeding Water freely from spring to autumn, sparingly in winter. Feed regularly in summer. Over-feeding may encourage tall, spindly growth.
Care Pinch out the growing tips and cut back straggly shoots from time to time to keep the plant compact. If it becomes tall and straggly, cut it back – shoots will regrow from near the base. Pinch out flowers as they will spoil the plant's compact shape.
Propagation Cuttings; seed.

Impatiens

A large genus of about 850 species, but those used as houseplants are mainly derived from the single species *I. walleriana*. These plants have been subject to intensive breeding; apart from compact and floriferous varieties (used for summer bedding as well as pot plants), foliage plants such as the New Guinea hybrids have extended the range of impatiens that are suitable for the home.

Impatiens hybrids

Masses of spurred, flat flowers, 2.5–5cm (1–2in) across, at any time of the year if the temperature can be maintained above 16°C (60°F). Blooms are mostly in shades of red, orange, pink, and white, of which many are multi-coloured and some double. Small pale green leaves on brittle stems. The New Guinea hybrids have large, more lance-shaped, bronze or variegated leaves and generally make taller plants, of 30–60cm (1–2ft). The blooms on New Guinea hybrids are usually fewer but larger.

Helpful hints

Temperature Winter minimum 13°C (55°F); 16°C (60°F) if you want to keep plants flowering.
Humidity Mist the leaves occasionally, but try to keep water away from the flowers.
Position Good light, but not direct summer sun during the hottest part of the day. Will tolerate shade, but the plants will be taller and lankier and the blooms less prolific.
Watering and feeding Water freely from spring to autumn, sparingly in winter.
Care If an old plant has become tall and lanky, cut it back to within a few inches of the base – it will usually regrow. Repot old plants in spring if necessary. As impatiens are so easy to grow from cuttings and seed, however, it is generally preferable to raise new plants regularly and to discard old ones.

Top: Impatiens *hybrid*
Above: Impatiens, *a New Guinea hybrid*

Propagation Seed; cuttings. Most New Guinea hybrids can only be raised from cuttings, although a few varieties can be grown from seed.

Iresine

A genus of evergreen perennials grown for their colourful foliage, widely used as formal bedding in countries where frosts do not occur.

Iresine herbstii

Spatula-shaped leaves about 7.5cm (3in) long, dark reddish-brown with carmine veins. 'Aureoreticulata' has green leaves with yellow veins, on red stems. Grows to about 60cm (2ft), but is kept smaller by pruning.

Iresine lindenii

Narrow, glossy deep red leaves with prominent veins. Uncommon.

Helpful hints

Temperature Winter minimum 13°C (55°F).
Humidity Mist the leaves regularly.
Position Good light, but not direct summer sun through glass during the hottest part of the day.

Watering and feeding Water freely from spring to autumn, sparingly in winter. Feed from spring to autumn.

Care Pinch out the growing tips occasionally to encourage compact and bushy growth. Will tolerate regular clipping if necessary. Can be stood outdoors for the summer. Overwintered plants often look unhappy by spring, but cuttings root easily and it may be more practical to start again with new plants.

Propagation Cuttings.

BELOW: Iresine lindenii

Iris

A large group of plants that includes hardy border plants with rhizomes and some that form bulbs. Those sometimes used as short-term houseplants are hardy dwarf bulbous species useful for providing spring colour indoors.

Iris danfordiae

Fragrant yellow flowers on stems about 10cm (4in) tall appear before the leaves. The grass-like foliage grows to twice this height, but plants are normally placed outside before the foliage becomes obtrusive.

Iris reticulata hybrids

Slightly fragrant blue or purple flowers (depending on variety) with yellow markings. About 15cm (6in) tall in flower, although the grass-like foliage later grows taller.

HELPFUL HINTS

Temperature Frost-hardy. Keep cool to prolong flower life.

Humidity Undemanding.

Position Good light once the buds begin to open.

RIGHT: Iris reticulata 'Harmony'
BELOW: Iris danfordiae

Watering and feeding Keep the potting mixture moist but not wet.

Care Plant the bulbs in early or mid autumn, in pots or bowls, and place outside or in a garden frame. Once the shoots are through bring the bulbs indoors and keep in a light place. Discard or plant out in the garden once flowering is over. Do not reuse the bulbs indoors.

Propagation Offsets, but for growing in pots or bowls it is best to buy fresh bulbs each year.

Jasminum

A genus of about 200 species, mainly deciduous and evergreen woody climbers. Being vigorous climbers, they are more suitable for a conservatory than a living-room, especially if you want to keep them as long-term plants.

Jasminum officinale
Deciduous climber with divided leaves and loose sprays of fragrant white flowers about 2.5cm (1in) across in summer. 'Grandiflorum' (which may also be seen as *J. o. affine*), with larger flowers tinged pink on the outside, is a form commonly sold. Can be grown outdoors where winters are mild.

Jasminum polyanthum
Similar to the previous species, but usually pink in bud, with plumes of

ABOVE: Jasminum polyanthum

fragrant white flowers in winter.

HELPFUL HINTS
Temperature Winter minimum 7°C (45°F).
Humidity Mist the leaves regularly.
Position Good light with some direct sun.
Watering and feeding Water freely from spring to autumn, but in winter keep compost (potting soil) only moist enough to prevent it from completely drying out. Feed regularly during periods of active growth.
Care Grow in a large pot with a suitable support. Prune back to contain size if necessary – jasminums will soon reach 3m (10ft) or more if left to grow unchecked. Avoid high winter temperatures. Can be stood outside in summer.
Propagation Cuttings.

Justicia

Genus of evergreen perennials, shrubs and sub-shrubs, from tropical and sub-tropical regions, but only the species described here is widely grown as a pot plant. You are just as likely to find it sold under its other name of *Beloperone guttata*.

Justicia brandegeana
Small white flowers surrounded by reddish-brown bracts that overlap like roof tiles. These bracts are the main reason for growing the plant, as they

Kalanchoe

A genus of about 125 perennial succulents or shrubs with fleshy leaves, which includes a number of popular and undemanding houseplants.

Kalanchoe blossfeldiana hybrids
Small, leathery, serrated oval leaves, which often turn reddish in strong sunlight. Clusters of long-lasting, short-stalked small flowers in shades of red, orange, yellow, and lilac. Although naturally spring-flowering plants, commercial growers are able to produce flowering specimens throughout the year.

Only hybrids are grown, and most of these make compact plants 15–30cm (6–12in) tall. There are also miniatures.

Although there are many named varieties, they are usually sold simply by colour.

Kalanchoe daigremontiana *see Bryophyllum daigremontianum.*

Kalanchoe manginii
Lance- or spatula-shaped leaves about 2.5cm (1in) long, on upright stems that gradually arch over. Larger, pendent, bell-like orange-red flowers in arching sprays.

Kalanchoe tubiflora *see Bryophyllum tubiflorum.*

remain attractive for a long period. The plants can be bought in flower every month of the year. Old plants can reach 90cm (3ft) or more, but in the home they tend to be discarded before they reach this size and are usually only half this height.

HELPFUL HINTS

Temperature Aim for 10–16°C (50–60°F) in winter.
Humidity Mist occasionally.
Position Good light, including some

LEFT: Justicia brandegeana

direct sun, but not direct summer sun through glass during the hottest part of the day.
Watering and feeding Water freely from spring to autumn, sparingly in winter. Feed regularly from spring to autumn.
Care Repot each spring. At the same time, prune the shoots back by one-third to half to keep the plant a compact shape.
Propagation Cuttings.

ABOVE: Kalanchoe blossfeldiana *hybrid*
RIGHT: Kalanchoe manginii

HELPFUL HINTS

Temperature Winter minimum 10°C (50°F).
Humidity Tolerates dry air.
Position Good light, including some direct sun, but avoid direct summer sun through glass during the hottest part of the day.
Watering and feeding Water freely from spring to autumn, sparingly in

winter. Feed regularly from spring to autumn.
Care Repot after flowering if saving an old plant, and shorten the shoots to keep growth compact. As they are easy to raise and cheap to buy, however, most people treat them as annuals and discard them when flowering is over. If raising your own plants they will only develop flower buds when

day length is less than 12 hours. It is possible to adjust flowering time by artificially controlling daylight hours.
Propagation Cuttings; seed.

Kentia

See Howea.

Lilium

A genus of bulbous plants widely grown in gardens. Most species, especially those chosen as pot plants, are hybrids. They have become more popular as commercially grown houseplants with the introduction of compact varieties and new techniques with growth regulators to keep the plants dwarf. Apart from the hybrids, species such as *L. auratum*, *L. longiflorum*, *L. regale*, and *L. speciosum* are sometimes grown in pots.

Lilium hybrids
Most hybrids have trumpet-shaped or backward-curving petals, in shades of red, orange, yellow, and white, usually spotted, mottled, or flushed with another colour. There are hundreds of varieties, with new ones introduced annually. Consult a good bulb catalogue for the most appropriate varieties to grow in pots, and choose the most compact ones for the home. You may find it difficult to keep home-grown plants as compact as those produced by nurseries: special facilities and chemicals are used to produce small plants in full bloom.

HELPFUL HINTS
Temperature Aim for 3–10°C (37–50°F). Avoid high temperatures.
Humidity Mist occasionally.
Position Good light, but avoid exposing to direct summer sun.
Watering and feeding Keep the compost (potting soil) moist during the period of active growth, and feed regularly.
Care Bulbs are usually planted in autumn or mid to late winter, according to when they are available. Pot up large ones singly, smaller ones three to a pot. There should be at least 5cm (2in) of compost (potting soil) beneath the bulb and about 10cm (4in) above, but lilies vary in the way they form roots, so be guided by any instructions that come with the bulb or

LEFT: Lilium *hybrid*

in the catalogue. Keep the planted bulbs in a cool place, such as a garden frame, cellar or basement, with the soil just moist. Ensure there is good light once shoots appear, and keep at the recommended temperature once buds can be seen. When the buds show colour the pots can be moved to a warmer room, but avoid high temperatures that will shorten the life of the blooms. Plant in the garden after flowering.

Propagation Offsets or scales, but this is a slow job requiring an area where they can be grown on. Buy new bulbs each time for use indoors.

Lisianthus russellianus

See Eustoma grandiflora.

Lithops

Prostrate succulents with pairs of fused swollen leaves, which eventually grow into small clumps. They are interesting plants that mimic stones or pebbles, but are slow-growing. Many species are available but the one described below is typical of those you are likely to find.

BELOW: Lithops bella

Lithops bella
Pairs of pale brownish-yellow, fused leaves with slightly depressed darker patches. White daisy-like flowers in late summer or early autumn. About 2.5cm (1in) high.

HELPFUL HINTS
Temperature Winter minimum 7°C (45°F).
Humidity Tolerates dry air.
Position Good light with plenty of sun. Tolerates full summer sun.
Watering and feeding Water carefully at all times, only moderately in summer and not at all in winter. Start watering again when the old leaves split to reveal the new ones beneath. Feeding is seldom necessary, but if the plants have been in the same pot for many years, feed occasionally with a cactus fertilizer.
Care Repot only when the pot has become filled with leaves. Lithops look attractive if grown in a landscaped container with the surface decorated with gravel or pebbles to blend in with the plants.
Propagation Seed.

Lobivia

A genus of spherical to columnar cacti, forming clumps with age. Lobivias flower at an early age.

Lobivia densispina
Densely thorned, short-cylindrical body, sometimes branched. Wide, funnel-shaped, flowers. More correctly named *Echinopsis kuehnrichii*.

Lobivia famatimensis
Cylindrical body with about 20 ribs and yellowish thorns. The flowers appear in early summer, but are short-lived. More correctly named *Rebutia famatimensis*.

Lobivia hertrichiana
Spherical body with 11 notched ribs covered with yellow thorns. Red, short-lived flowers in early summer.

TOP: Lobivia densispina
ABOVE: Lobivia hertrichiana

HELPFUL HINTS
Temperature Aim for 5–7°C (41–45°F) in winter. Avoid high winter temperatures, but keep frost-free.
Humidity Tolerates dry air.
Position Best possible light, including some direct sun.
Watering and feeding Water moderately in summer, sparingly from autumn to spring. Keep practically dry in winter. Use soft water if possible. Feed with a weak fertilizer in summer.
Care Pay special attention to winter temperatures to encourage the plant to flower well. Repot young plants each spring.
Propagation Offsets (unrooted ones can be used as cuttings); seed.

Lytocaryum

See Cocos.

Mammillaria

A genus of about 150 hemispherical, spherical, or columnar cacti, most of which are compact in growth and free-flowering. Cacti specialists offer a wide range of species, and those described here are only a selection of those available.

Mammillaria bocasana
Spherical or cylindrical, maturing to form a clump, covered with hooked thorns and white hairs. Reddish flowers that are white inside.

Mammillaria elongata
Clump-forming with columnar stems, densely covered with yellow to brown spines. Cream flowers in summer.

Mammillaria wildii
Clump-forming, branching columnar stems with white thorns and long hairs. Rings of small white flowers appear in spring.

Mammillaria zeilmanniana
Clusters of short, cylindrical stems, with dense covering of hooked spines.

Bell-shaped flowers, deep purple to pink, sometimes white in spring.

HELPFUL HINTS
Temperature Winter minimum 7°C (45°F).
Humidity Tolerates dry air.
Position Best possible light, with some sun.
Watering and feeding Water moderately from spring to autumn, but keep almost dry in winter.
Care Repot young plants annually in spring; older ones will not require such frequent repotting.
Propagation Cuttings; seed.

ABOVE: Mammillaria zeilmanniana
BELOW: Mammillaria bocasana *(left)*
and M. wildii *(right)*

TOP: Maranta leuconeura erythroneura
(*syn.* 'Erythrophylla' *and* M. tricolor)
ABOVE: Maranta leuconeura
kerchoveana

Maranta

A small genus of tropical plants from regions of Central and South America, grown for their attractive foliage.

Maranta bicolor
Round to oval leaves up to 15cm (6in) long, with five to eight brown blotches on either side of the main vein and purple undersides. Small white flowers are sometimes produced.

Maranta leuconeura
A tuberous plant with slightly smaller leaves than the previous species. Varieties of this species most commonly grown include *M. l. erythroneura* (syn. 'Erythrophylla', sometimes sold

as *M. tricolor)*, which has prominent red veins and yellow markings near main vein, and *M. l. kerchoveana,* with brown blotches turning green with age.

HELPFUL HINTS
Temperature Winter minimum 10°C (50°F).
Humidity Needs high humidity. Mist the leaves regularly.
Position Good light, but avoid exposing to direct summer sun. Best possible light in winter.
Watering and feeding Water freely from spring to autumn, sparingly in winter. Use soft water if possible. Feed regularly in summer.
Care Repot every second spring.
Propagation Division.

Microcoelum

See Cocos.

Mimosa

A large genus of shrubs, trees, climbers and annuals, including plants with very varied characteristics and requirements, but the one most likely to be grown as a houseplant is the species described here.

Mimosa pudica
Feathery-looking leaves with leaflets, which are highly responsive to being touched. First the leaflets fold, then the whole leaf droops (at night they fold naturally). After about a half to one hour the leaves resume their original position. Small flowers like pink balls are produced in summer. Although a short-lived shrub, it is usually treated as an annual, when it seldom exceeds 60cm (2ft).

HELPFUL HINTS
Temperature Winter minimum 16°C (60°F).
Humidity Mist the leaves regularly.
Position Good light with some direct sun, but avoid direct summer sun during the hottest part of the day.
Watering and feeding Water freely from spring to autumn, sparingly in summer. Use soft water if possible. Feed regularly in summer.
Care Repot in spring, but as plants are easily raised from seed, they are best treated as annuals.
Propagation Seed; cuttings.

BELOW: Mimosa pudica

ABOVE: Monstera deliciosa

Monstera

Woody climbers, most growing as epiphytes, from tropical regions of America.

Monstera deliciosa
Climber with thick stems and aerial roots by which it clings. The large leaves, up to 60cm (2ft) across, are entire and heart-shaped initially, but become incised and perforated with age. There is also a variegated variety. White lily-like flowers sometimes appear, but usually only on plants grown in a greenhouse or conservatory. Will easily grow to ceiling height. May be found under its old name of *Philodendron pertusum.*

HELPFUL HINTS
Temperature Winter minimum 10°C (50°F).
Humidity Mist the leaves regularly.
Position Good light or shade, out of direct sunlight.
Watering and feeding Water freely from spring to autumn, sparingly in winter.
Routine care Provide a suitable climbing support, such as a moss-covered pole. Lightly sponge the leaves occasionally.
Propagation Cuttings; air layering.

Nematanthus

See Hypocyrta.

Narcissus

A genus of well-known bulbous plants that includes the popular daffodil. Suitable varieties can be grown in pots for early flowering indoors.

Narcissus hybrids
There are hundreds of varieties, ranging from traditional trumpet daffodils to miniatures, mainly in the usual shades of yellow or white. Consult a bulb catalogue for varieties suitable for forcing in pots. 'Paperwhite' (white with yellow eye, fragrant) and 'Soleil d'Or' (yellow, with deep yellow centre) are sold primarily for indoor use.

HELPFUL HINTS
Temperature Aim for 15–21°C (59–70°F) for the varieties mentioned above. Garden varieties being used in the home should be kept cool until the flower buds have emerged from the bulb (*see* Care), then brought into warmth.
Humidity Undemanding.
Position The varieties mentioned above should be kept in good light all the time. Normal varieties should be in good light when the buds have emerged, but may be placed anywhere once in flower as they are short-term houseplants.
Watering and feeding Water moderately while the bulbs are growing. If keeping the bulbs to grow in the garden, continue watering until planted out. Feeding is unnecessary.
Care The two varieties mentioned specifically can be grown in pots, but are sometimes grown in bowls of water, supported by pebbles or marbles (keep base of bulb above the water). These are kept indoors, and will flower very early. Garden varieties forced in pots should be potted up then kept in a cool, dark place until rooted – aim for 7–10°C (45–50°F) at this

ABOVE: Narcissus '*Cheerfulness*'

stage. Bring indoors or into the warmth only when the flower buds have clearly emerged from the bulbs.
Propagation Offsets and scales (bulb-cuttings), but this is impractical in the home. Buy fresh bulbs each year.

Neanthe

See Chamaedorea.

Neoregelia

Rosette-forming epiphytic bromeliads, mainly from Brazil.

Neoregelia carolinae
Leaves about 40cm (16in) long and 5cm (2in) wide form a broad rosette, normally green but those that surround the top of the 'vase' created by the rosette are flushed red when the plant is in flower (usually in summer). *N. c. tricolor* has slightly narrower leaves streaked yellow along their length. The purple-blue flowers nestle in the water-filled 'vase'.

HELPFUL HINTS
Temperature Winter minimum 13°C (55°F).
Humidity Mist the leaves regularly.
Position Good light, but avoid exposing to direct sun.

BELOW: Neoregelia carolinae

Watering and feeding Water the compost (potting mixture) moderately at all times, but keep the 'vase' topped up with water. Use soft water if possible. Use a weak fertilizer (add it to the soil or 'vase') in summer.
Care The plant will die after flowering, so once in bloom it does not matter much where you place it. But if you want to propagate new plants from the offsets produced from around the parent, continue to feed and grow in good light. These are not easy plants to keep long-term in the home. It is best to grow them to flowering stage in a greenhouse or conservatory, bringing them indoors only when they begin to show colour.
Propagation Offsets.

Nephrolepis

Genus of about 30 terrestrial and epiphytic, evergreen or semi-evergreen ferns, distributed over tropical regions in all parts of the world. The species below is the only one widely grown as a pot plant.

Nephrolepis exaltata
Pinnate leaves about 45–60cm (1½-2ft) long, forming a dense clump. There are variations on the basic plant, including 'Bostoniensis', with more gracefully drooping leaves than the true species, 'Teddy Junior', with

LEFT: Nephrolepis exaltata *'Bostoniensis'*

crimped and undulating leaflets, and 'Whitmanii', with deeply incised, lacy-looking leaflets.

HELPFUL HINTS
Temperature Winter minimum 18°C (64°F).
Humidity Mist the leaves regularly.
Position Good light, but not direct sun.
Watering and feeding Water freely in summer, cautiously in winter, but with care at all times. The plant is vulnerable to over- and under-watering, so try to keep the roots moist without being wet. Use soft water if possible.
Care Repot in spring if the plant becomes too large for its pot, but do not be surprised if the plant deteriorates before this stage is reached – it is difficult to keep in good condition in the home. Provide a position away from draughts.
Propagation Plantlets, which develop at intervals along the rhizomes. Spores can be used only for the species, and not the varieties.

Nerium

A genus of evergreen shrubs grown for their flowers. The species described here is widely grown as a pot plant, and is a very popular outdoor shrub in southern Europe and America.

ABOVE: Nerium oleander

Nerium oleander
Leathery, willow-like leaves 15–20cm (6–8in) long, arranged around the stem in groups of three. Clusters of white, red, pink, or lilac flowers. There are many varieties, including those with double blooms. Will make a large shrub of 1.8m (6ft) or more in suitable conditions, and, when fully grown, is more suitable for a conservatory than the home.

HELPFUL HINTS
Temperature Winter minimum 7°C (45°F).
Humidity Undemanding.
Position Good light, with some direct sun.
Watering and feeding Water freely spring to autumn, cautiously in winter; do not allow roots to become dry. Feed regularly in spring and summer.
Care The plant can be stood outdoors, perhaps on the patio, for the summer. Acclimatize it gradually, and bring in before the nights become cold. In autumn, shorten stems that have flowered by about half to keep the plant compact and encourage bushiness.
Propagation Cuttings.

Nertera

A small genus of creeping perennials grown for their bead-like berries. Only one species is cultivated.

Nertera depressa *see N. granadensis.*

Nertera granadensis
Mound-forming plant with creeping stems and small rounded leaves about 6mm (¼in) long. Tiny greenish-white flowers in spring followed by bright orange berries in autumn. You may find it sold under its other name of *N. depressa.*

HELPFUL HINTS
Temperature Winter minimum 7°C (45°F).
Humidity Mist the leaves from time to time.
Position Good light, with some direct sun.
Watering and feeding Water freely from spring to autumn, sparingly in winter. Never allow the roots to dry out completely.
Care The plant is unattractive until the berries appear, but you can stand it outdoors from early summer until the berries form. The plants are usually bought when in fruit and discarded afterwards, but they can be overwintered with care.
Propagation Division; seed.

BELOW: Nertera granadensis

Nidularium

Rosette-forming epiphytic bromeliads, similar to neoregelias.

Nidularium billbergioides citrinum
A rosette of arching strap-shaped leaves, to about 45–60cm (1½–2ft). The true flowers are white and inconspicuous, but the head of yellow bracts is bright and long-lasting.

Nidularium fulgens
Spreading rosettes of broad, strap-shaped, spiny-toothed leaves. Tubular white and purple flowers nestle in the 'vase' formed by the rosette of foliage, mainly in summer. When the plant is flowering the bright red bracts surrounding the 'vase' are the plant's main feature.

Nidularium innocentii
Similar to the previous species, but the undersides of the leaves are purple and the flowers white. The bracts also colour well at flowering.

LEFT BELOW: Nidularium innocentii striatum
LEFT ABOVE: Nidularium fulgens
ABOVE: Nidularium billbergiodes citrinum

HELPFUL HINTS
Temperature Winter minimum 10°C (50°F).
Humidity Mist occasionally.
Position Good light, but not direct sun.
Watering and feeding Water freely from spring to autumn, sparingly in winter. Keep the 'vase' topped up with water from spring to autumn. Feed with a weak fertilizer in summer.
Care The parent plant will die after flowering, and young plants propagated from offsets take a few years to make attractive specimens. If you do not have a greenhouse or conservatory where you can grow them on, it may be best to buy plants in flower and discard them afterwards.
Propagation Offsets.

Notocactus

A small genus of mainly spherical cacti, often ribbed and densely spiny, that flower young and prolifically.

Notocactus apricus
A small species forming a flattened and much-ribbed sphere. Very spiny. Yellow flowers about 7.5cm (3in) across in summer. Now also known as *Parodia concinna*.

Notocactus ottonis
A ribbed spherical body with stiff spines. Golden yellow flowers about 7.5cm (3in) across in summer. Now also known as *Parodia ottonis*.

HELPFUL HINTS
Temperature Winter minimum 10°C (50°F).
Humidity Tolerates dry air.
Position Good light but only limited direct sun. Provide shade from bright direct sun in spring; in summer a mixture of sun and some shade.

TOP: Notocactus apricus
ABOVE: Notocactus ottonis

Watering and feeding Water freely from spring to autumn, more sparingly in winter.
Care Generally trouble-free, but do not keep too warm in winter.
Propagation Seed; cuttings in species that produce offsets.

Odontoglossum

Epiphytic orchids from the mountain forests of tropical America. The species below is often particularly successful in a living-room, others can be more demanding in the home.

Odontoglossum grande

Large brown, yellow, and white flowers, up to 15cm (6in) across, produced in autumn. There are a number of varieties of this species. Now considered to be more correctly named *Rossioglossum grande*.

HELPFUL HINTS

Temperature Winter minimum 13°C (55°F).

Humidity Mist occasionally.
Position Good light, but not direct summer sun. Best possible light in winter.
Watering and feeding Water freely from spring to autumn, and very sparingly in winter (just enough to prevent the pseudobulbs from shrivelling). Use soft water if possible. Feed with a weak fertilizer from spring to autumn.
Care Use a special orchid compost (potting soil) when repotting. This becomes necessary when growth begins to wilt and die back.
Propagation Division.

BELOW: Odontoglossum grande
RIGHT BELOW: Opuntia microdasys

Opuntia

A large genus of more than 200 cacti, ranging from low ground-cover to tree-sized plants. Many of these are popular with collectors.

Opuntia cylindrica

Cylindrical stems which become branching with age. Older plants – usually those over 1.8m (6ft) tall – produce saucer-shaped, reddish-pink flowers in spring or early summer.

Opuntia microdasys

Flat, pale green pads, usually growing to about 30cm (1ft) as a houseplant, with tufts of tiny hooked barbs known as glochids. There are several varieties, and in *O. m. albinospina* the glochids are white. Flowers are usually yellow, about 5cm (2in) across, but only produced on larger plants than are usually found in the home.

Opuntia phaeacantha

Oval to round pads up to 15cm (6in) long, with brownish-yellow glochids. Yellow flowers. Cold tolerant.

Opuntia vestita

Cylindrical joints, the sections easily

ABOVE: Opuntia vestita *(left)*, O. cylindrica *(centre)*, O. phaeacantha *(right)*

broken off, with conspicuous wool and long hairs. Small, deep red flowers.

HELPFUL HINTS

Temperature Winter minimum 7°C (45°F).
Humidity Tolerates dry air.
Position Good light. Benefits from direct sun.
Watering and feeding Water moderately from spring to autumn, very sparingly in winter. Feed with a weak fertilizer, or one formulated for cacti, in summer.
Care Repot in spring if necessary – those with flat pads usually do well in an ordinary loam-based compost (potting soil), others prefer a cactus mixture. Avoid warm temperatures in winter. Some species can be grown outdoors if frosts are not severe.
Propagation Cuttings (detach pads from species that have them); seed.

Oxalis

A large genus of tuberous-, rhizomatous-, and fibrous-rooted perennials, most combining attractive foliage with pretty flowers. Some species are troublesome as garden weeds.

Oxalis deppei

A clover-like plant with four green leaflets blotched pinkish-brown at the base. Red or purplish-violet small, funnel-shaped flowers in late spring or summer. Frost-hardy. Is now considered by botanists to be more correctly named *O. tetraphylla,* but is still widely sold under the name given here.

Oxalis tetraphylla *see O. deppei.*

HELPFUL HINTS

Temperature Winter minimum 7°C (45°F). Some species are hardy, but indoors they are best kept at the minimum suggested.
Humidity Undemanding.
Position Good light or partial shade, out of direct summer sun.
Watering and feeding Water freely while in active growth. Feed regularly during the growing season.
Care Avoid high temperatures – otherwise the plant will be short-lived. Plants are sometimes sold for winter decoration indoors, but hardy species are best planted in the garden when flowering has finished.
Propagation Offsets.

BELOW: Oxalis deppei

Pachystachys

A genus of evergreen perennials and shrubs, with only one species being grown as a houseplant.

Pachystachys lutea
Cone-shaped yellow flower heads, about 10cm (4in) long, over a period from late spring to autumn. The true flowers are white and protrude from the longer-lasting yellow bracts. Pointed oval leaves.

HELPFUL HINTS
Temperature Winter minimum 13°C (55°F).
Humidity Mist the leaves regularly in summer.
Position Good light, but not direct summer sun during the hottest part of the day.
Watering and feeding Water freely from spring to autumn, sparingly in winter. Feed regularly in summer.
Care Cut off the flower heads when flowering is over, and shorten long shoots in spring to keep the plant compact. Repot annually in spring.
Propagation Cuttings.

BELOW: Pachystachys lutea

Paphiopedilum

A genus of about 60 orchids, but it is the hybrids that are usually grown.

Paphiopedilum hybrids
Striking flowers, about 5–10cm (2–4in) across, with a lower lip that forms a pouch, and wing-like petals. Colours vary according to variety but are usually in shades of brown, orange, amber, green, and purple, often heavily streaked or spotted. Most bloom in winter or spring. You may sometimes find paphiopedilums sold under their old name of cypripedium.

HELPFUL HINTS
Temperature Winter minimum 13°C (55°F).
Humidity Mist occasionally.
Position Good light, but avoid exposing to direct sun.
Watering and feeding Water freely from spring to autumn, sparingly in winter. Use soft water if possible. Feed with a weak fertilizer while growing actively.
Care Remove any old and yellowing leaves periodically and keep a watch for slugs, which may spoil the foliage.
Propagation Division.

RIGHT: Paphiopedilum *'Green Gable'*

Parodia

Rounded cacti, some becoming cylindrical with age, with ribs and usually thorns. You may find that some plants have been grafted.

Parodia aureispina
A spherical body up to about 10cm (4in) across, with many conspicuous white and yellow thorns. Yellow flowers about 2.5cm (1in) across in spring.

Parodia chrysacanthion
A spherical body up to about 10cm (4in) across, sometimes flattened with age, with bristle-like spines. Yellow flowers in spring.

Temperature Aim for 7–12°C (45–53°F) in winter.

Humidity Tolerates dry air.

Position Best possible light. Benefits from full sun.

Watering and feeding Water moderately from spring to autumn, keep practically dry in winter. Use soft water if possible. Feed in summer with a weak fertilizer or cactus food.

Care Plants are slow-growing, but if they need repotting use a special cactus mixture if possible.

Propagation Seed.

FAR RIGHT: Parodia chrysacanthion
RIGHT: Parodia aureispina

Pelargonium – Flowering

There are about 250 species of pelargonium, mainly from South Africa. However, those widely grown as flowering pot plants and for summer displays in our gardens, are hybrids that are the result of many years of intensive breeding.

Pelargonium grandiflorum (P. domesticum) hybrids

The result of crossing *P. grandiflorum, P. cordatum,* and other species. They are more popularly known as Regal or Martha Washington pelargoniums. The flowering season (early spring to mid summer) is shorter than in the zonal pelargoniums, but the blooms are larger, frillier, often more showy, and commonly bicoloured. The scalloped leaves with a serrated edge are about 7.5cm (3in) across and lack a distinctive zone. They make plants 30–60cm (1–2ft) tall in pots.

Pelargonium peltatum hybrids

Straggly, cascading stems, with shield-shaped, five-lobed leaves. Single or double, star-shaped flowers,

ABOVE LEFT: *A zonal pelargonium*
BELOW: *Regal pelargonium*

usually in shades of pink or red, sometimes white. Usually grown in a hanging basket or on a pedestal.

Pelargonium zonale hybrids

The traditional geraniums so widely grown as summer bedding. Rounded, slightly lobed leaves about 7.5–10cm (3–4in) across (smaller in miniatures), often attractively zoned and sometimes golden or variegated. Rounded heads of single or double flowers in shades of pink, orange, red, purple, and white. There are hundreds of varieties with variations in flower shape and size as well as colour and leaf patterning. Miniatures, growing only 15–23cm (6–9in) tall, are particularly useful for a windowsill.

HELPFUL HINTS

Temperature Winter minimum 7°C (45°F). Zonal pelargoniums will tolerate a few degrees lower, but are best maintained at the temperature recommended.
Humidity Tolerates dry air.
Position Good light with some sun.

Tolerates full sun.
Watering and feeding Water moderately from spring to autumn; pelargoniums will tolerate dry soil more happily than most houseplants and are not demanding in this respect. Regal or Martha Washington pelargoniums need more water in summer than the other types. Feed regularly from spring to autumn.
Care Plants grown for the garden are often overwintered in a greenhouse, and kept in a semi-dormant state. Those grown as pot plants indoors can be kept in leaf and looking attractive if given sufficient – warmth at least 13°C (55°F) – and good light. Repot in spring if necessary. Deadhead regularly. Shorten long shoots in spring (autumn for Regal or Martha Washington types). Pinch out the growing tip of young plants to encourage bushy growth.
Propagation Cuttings; seed (some varieties).

ABOVE: Pelargonium peltatum *hybrid*
OPPOSITE: *Scented-leaved pelargoniums. Left to right:* P. odoratissumum, P. graveolens, P. crispum *'Variegatum'*

Pelargonium – Foliage

Some of the zonal pelargoniums have attractive foliage as well as flowers, and are generally better looking than those grown specifically for their scented leaves. Pelargoniums with scented leaves sometimes have small flowers but these tend to be unexciting, and the foliage itself is often uninspiring although some varieties are variegated. They are grown for the strong aromas released when you brush against the leaves (and sometimes even when you don't).

Descriptions used to classify the scents sometimes appear to contradict one another, at other times to be fanciful, but this is largely because scent can be perceived differently from one person to another, and some of the plants give off a blend or mixture of smells. The best way to choose scented species and varieties is simply to follow your nose.

A selection of different species is listed here, but you will find many more scented species and hybrids at specialist nurseries.

Pelargonium capitatum
Deeply lobed leaves, smelling of roses. Mauve flowers. Will grow to about 90cm (3ft) if conditions suit.

Pelargonium crispum
Small, slightly lobed, green and cream leaves, with a lemon fragrance. Pink flowers. Grows to about 60cm (2ft).

Pelargonium graveolens
Deeply divided, lobed leaves, smelling of roses. Pink to rose-red flowers. Grows to about 90cm (3ft).

Pelargonium odoratissimum
Apple-scented foliage. White flowers. Grows to about 30cm (1ft).

Pelargonium tomentosum
Large, rounded, slightly lobed leaves, smelling of peppermint. Small white flowers. Grows to about 60cm (2ft).

Pellaea

Deciduous, semi-evergreen or evergreen ferns, generally found in dry areas of South America, South Africa and New Zealand. Being adapted to dry conditions, most species are better able to cope with conditions found in the home than most other types of fern.

Pellaea rotundifolia
Small, round, leathery leaflets on long arching fronds that grow from a creeping rootstock. The leaflets become more oval in shape with age. Low, spreading growth.

Pellaea viridis
More like a traditional fern than the previous species, with larger and more divided feathery fronds.

HELPFUL HINTS
Temperature Aim for 13–16°C (55–60°F) in winter.
Humidity Mist the leaves occasionally. Although better adapted to dry conditions than most ferns, growth will usually be improved if reasonable humidity is provided.
Position Good light, but avoid exposing to direct sun.
Watering and feeding Water moderately at all times. Never allow the roots to dry out entirely, but avoid very wet compost (potting soil). Feed with a weak fertilizer in summer.
Care If repotting use a shallow container or a hanging basket. In the wild they often grow in rock crevices.
Propagation Division; spores.

RIGHT: Pellaea rotundifolia
BELOW: Pellaea viridis

Pellionia

A small genus of evergreen creeping perennials, a few of which may be used in large terrariums or bottle gardens, or as trailers for a hanging pot.

Pellionia daveauana
Creeping plant with oval leaves, olive green around the edge with a pale

central area. You may also find it more correctly called *P. repens.*

Pellionia pulchra

Creeping plant with almost oblong leaves about 4–8cm (1½–3in) long and 2.5cm (1in) wide. These have a mottled appearance with dark green veins over an olive-green background, and the reverse is brownish-purple.

Pellionia repens *see P. daveauana.*

HELPFUL HINTS

Temperature Winter minimum 13°C (55°F).
Humidity Mist the leaves regularly. Needs very high humidity.
Position Semi-shade or good light but no direct sun.
Watering and feeding Water freely from spring to autumn, sparingly in winter. Never allow the roots to become dry. Feed regularly in summer.
Care Misting alone is unlikely to provide sufficient humidity, so use other methods too, such as standing the pot over a dish of water, supporting the pot on marbles or pebbles to avoid direct contact.
Propagation Cuttings; division.

ABOVE: Pellionia daveauana

ABOVE: Pentas lanceolata

Pentas

A genus of about 30 mainly evergreen perennials and shrubs, generally found in areas such as the Middle East and tropical Africa.

Pentas carnea *see P. lanceolata.*

Pentas lanceolata

Small, star-shaped flowers in heads about 7.5–10cm (3–4in) across. Pink or red are the usual colours, but some varieties have white or mauve flowers. May be seen in flower in any month of the year, but winter is the most usual time. Hairy oval leaves about 5–7.5cm (2–3in) long. Also sold under its other name of *P. carnea.*

HELPFUL HINTS

Temperature Winter minimum 10°C (50°F).
Humidity Mist occasionally.
Position Good light with some sun, but not direct summer sun during the hottest part of the day.
Watering and feeding Water freely from spring to autumn, sparingly in winter. Never allow the roots to become dry. Feed regularly in summer.
Care Pinch out the growing tips of young plants to make them bushy. If you want the plant for winter flowering, pinch out early buds that form in autumn. Repot annually in spring.
Propagation Cuttings; seed.

Peperomia

Peperomias form a large genus of about 1,000 species, mainly from tropical and subtropical America. Some are epiphytes that grow on trees, others terrestrial plants from tropical rain forests. Some are annuals, but most are evergreen perennials. Some of the most popular ones used as houseplants are listed below, but you may sometimes find others that are equally pleasing in the home. Most of those that you are likely to find are undemanding to grow, and their variation in leaf shape, colouring and size makes them interesting to collect. Small poker-like, creamy-white flower spikes are sometimes produced, but on most species these are of marginal interest and they are grown mainly as foliage plants.

Peperomia argyreia
Shield-shaped leaves with dark green

and silver blades and red stalks. Forms a neat, bushy clump. May also be found under its synonym *P. sandersii.*

Peperomia caperata
Heart-shaped leaves about 2.5cm (1in) long, deeply corrugated and grooved between the veins. Bushy, clump-forming growth. Varieties have variations in leaf shapes and colouring.

Peperomia clusiifolia
Leathery leaves about 7.5cm (3in) long, edged purple-red. *P. c.* 'Variegata' has cream and red margins. Upright growth to about 20cm (8in).

Peperomia fraseri
Circular to heart-shaped leaves, usually arranged in whorls on upright stems. The flower spikes are white and fragrant.

Peperomia glabella
Trailing stems with broadly oval,

glossy, bright green leaves.

Peperomia griseoargentea
Heart-shaped to almost circular leaves on long pinkish stalks. Deep corrugations between the veins create a quilted look. The under surface is pale green. You are also likely to find this plant sold under its other name of *P. hederaefolia* (or *P. hederifolia*).

Peperomia hederaefolia (also P. hederifolia) *see P. griseoargentea.*

Peperomia magnoliaefolia (also P. magnoliifolia) *see P. obtusifolia.*

Peperomia nummulariifolia *see P. rotundifolia.*

Peperomia obtusifolia
Thick, fleshy leaves about 5–10cm (2–4in) long, on short stalks. The plain green form is not often grown as there are several variegated varieties

with yellow or cream markings. Up-right but sprawling growth to about 25cm (10in). The nomenclature of these plants is confused – you will sometimes find them sold as *P. magnoliaefolia* (or *P. magnoliifolia*), and while some experts consider them synonymous others list them as distinct species, whatever the label.

OPPOSITE: *Peperomias: P. hybrid 'Columbiana' (far left), P. hybrid 'Rauvema' (second from left), and three varieties of* P. caperata
BELOW: *Peperomias: P. pereskiifolia (top left), P. obtusifolia 'USA' (top right), P. clusiifolia 'Jeli' (bottom left), P. clusiifolia variety (bottom right)*

Peperomia pereskiifolia
Whorls of dull green leaves tinged dull red. Spread to 30cm (12in).

Peperomia rotundifolia
A trailing species with round, bright green leaves, about 1cm (½in) across. Also known as *P. nummulariifolia*.

Peperomia verticillata
Distinctive upright growth to about 30cm (1ft) with the 2.5cm (1in) leaves in whorls of four to six along the stems. Foliage covered with fine hairs.

HELPFUL HINTS
Temperature Winter minimum 10°C (50°F).

Humidity Mist the leaves occasionally in warm weather, not in winter.
Position Semi-shade or good light, but not direct summer sun.
Watering and feeding Water moderately throughout the year, cautiously in winter. Use soft water if possible. Feed from spring to autumn.
Care Most peperomias have only a small root system and annual repotting is unnecessary. When necessary, move to a slightly larger pot in spring. A peat-based (peat moss) compost (potting mixture) is preferable to one based on loam.
Propagation Cuttings; leaf cuttings from species with rosettes of fleshy leaves.

Philodendron

A genus of about 350 evergreen shrubs and woody climbers from the rain forests of Central and South America. Although most of the species listed here are climbers and will reach ceiling height, many are fairly slow-growing and will put on less than 30cm (1ft) in a year, so they will give years of pleasure before they outgrow their space. Some of the non-climbing species can make large, spreading plants, and may be too large for a small home.

Philodendron angustisectum
Vigorous climber with large heart-shaped leaves, about 45–60cm (1½–2ft) long, incised almost to the main rib. Will readily grow to ceiling height. May also be found under its other name of *P. elegans.*

Philodendron bipennifolium *see P. panduriforme.*

Philodendron bipinnatifidum
Non-climbing species with a straight stem densely clothed with leathery, heart-shaped, deeply lobed leaves about 45–60cm (1½-2ft) long. Will make a large plant that can be 1.8m (6ft) or more across and about 1.2m (4ft) tall.

Philodendron domesticum
Climber with glossy, bright green leaves about 30–45cm (1–1½ft) long, arrow-shaped on young plants but with more prominent basal lobes when it matures. Will readily reach ceiling height. Also listed under its alternative name of *P. hastatum.*

Philodendron elegans *see P. angustisectum.*

Philodendron erubescens
Climber with young leaves surrounded by attractive rose-red sheaths that drop as the foliage expands. Arrow-shaped to heart-shaped, dark green leaves with a purple sheen and red edge. There are also named selections

with either greener or redder foliage than in the normal plants. Will easily reach ceiling height.

Philodendron hastatum *see P. domesticum.*

Philodendron hybrids
There are hybrids and selections usually sold just by their varietal name, such as 'Blue Mink', 'Burgundy', and 'Pink Prince'. These are generally climbers with large, attractive leaves, and can be treated in the same way as the other climbing species listed here.

Philodendron melanochrysum
Climber with heart-shaped leaves about 60cm (2ft) long, with a coppery surface and white veins. Fairly slow-growing but will easily reach ceiling height. The heart-shaped leaves become increasingly elongated as the plant matures.

Philodendron panduriforme
Climber with leaves about 23–30cm (9–12in) long, deeply lobed, with a distinct 'waist' on mature foliage. May also be named *P. bipennifolium.*

Philodendron pertusum *see Monstera deliciosa.*

Philodendron scandens
Climber or trailer with 7.5–13cm (3–5in) heart-shaped, glossy green leaves. Fairly rapid growth and will reach ceiling height if given a support, but is most often seen as a trailer.

Philodendron selloum
A non-climbing species, with leaves 60–90cm (2–3ft) long, deeply incised and with ruffled edges. Grows to about 1.5m (5ft).

HELPFUL HINTS
Temperature Winter minimum 13°C (55°F), but many, such as *P. melanochrysum,* prefer warmer temperatures and for these 18°C (64°F) or higher is preferable.
Humidity Mist the leaves regularly.
Position Good light, but not direct summer sun. *P. scandens* tolerates low light levels well.
Watering and feeding Water freely from spring to autumn, moderately in winter. Use soft water if possible. Feed from spring to autumn, but avoid high-nitrogen feeds if you want to limit the plant's growth.
Care Provide a suitable support for climbing species – moss poles are a popular method. Aerial roots that form low down on the plant can be trained to grow into the pot.
Propagation Cuttings; air layering.

ABOVE: Philodendron scandens
RIGHT TOP: Philodendron *hybrid 'Red Emerald'*
RIGHT MIDDLE: Philodendron *hybrid 'Blue Mink'*
RIGHT BOTTOM: Philodendron domesticum
FAR RIGHT: Philodendron *hybrid 'Purple Prince'*

Phlebodium aureum

See Polypodium aureum.

Phoenix

A genus of about 17 palms. Most become large trees where they grow outdoors, but some can make attractive pot plants while young.

Phoenix canariensis
Feathery fronds, stiff and erect at first, arching later, with narrow leaflets.

Phoenix dactylifera
The edible date. Similar to previous species, but not normally grown as a houseplant.

Phoenix roebelenii
Gracefully arching fronds, on a compact plant that seldom grows larger than 1.2m (4ft).

HELPFUL HINTS
Temperature Winter minimum 7°C (45°F); 16°C (60°F) for *P. roebelenii.*

BELOW: Phoenix canariensis

Humidity Tolerates dry air.
Position Good light. Benefits from direct sun.
Watering and feeding Water moderately from spring to autumn, sparingly in winter. Feed regularly from spring to autumn.
Care Repot only when the plant becomes pot-bound as the plant resents unnecessary root disturbance. Roots often penetrate through the bottom of the pot, and for this reason these plants are often planted in deeper containers than normal. Trim off any dead or yellowing leaves that are spoiling the plant's appearance.
Propagation Seed; division for *P. roebelenii.*

Pilea

A genus of about 600 bushy or trailing annuals and evergreen perennials from tropical regions, a small number of which are grown as foliage houseplants.

Pilea cadierei
Elliptical to oval leaves about 7.5–10cm (3–4in) long, with silver markings that look as though they have been painted on the green background.

Pilea hybrids
Some pileas are likely to be found with just their varietal name. The botanical status of these is sometimes confused or debatable, and more than one species may have been involved in their breeding. These vary in colouring and variegation, but the general cultural advice given below applies to them.

Pilea involucrata
Oval, slightly fleshy leaves, about 5–7.5cm (2–3in) long and deeply quilted. The species has dark green foliage with a coppery sheen and pale green margins, but varieties include 'Moon Valley' (bronze above, reddish-green below), and 'Norfolk' (bronze in good light, almost green in poor light,

with several lengthwise white bands). You may find the latter listed as a variety of *P. spruceana.* They make bushy plants about 15–23cm (6–9in) tall.

Pilea microphylla
Small, pale green leaves only 2–6mm (1/8–1/4in) long, on much-branched stems, forming a mass of fern-like foliage. Forms a dense, compact plant about 15cm (6in) tall. May also be found under its old name *P. muscosa.*

Pilea muscosa *see P. microphylla.*

Pilea nummulariifolia
Creeping reddish stems with round leaves about 1cm (1/2in) across, with a quilted surface, purplish on the underside. Grows to about 5cm (2in) tall.

ABOVE: Pilea microphylla
LEFT: Pilea spruceana '*Bronze*' *(left) and*
Pilea repens *(right)*
LEFT BELOW: Pilea cadierei

Pilea spruceana

Oval, wrinkled leaves 5–7.5cm (2–3in) long. Most likely to be seen in one of its varieties, such as 'Bronze'. 'Norfolk' is often listed as a variety of this species, but other authorities consider it a variety of *P. involucrata*.

HELPFUL HINTS
Temperature Winter minimum 10°C (50°F).
Humidity Mist the leaves regularly.
Position Good light or partial shade, out of direct summer sun.
Watering and feeding Water freely while in active growth. Feed regularly from spring to autumn.
Care Pinch out the growing tips of young plants, and repeat the process a month or two later, to encourage bushy growth. Repot in spring.
Propagation Cuttings.

Pinguicula

A genus of more than 50 species of insectivorous plants that work on the fly-paper principle.

Pinguicula grandiflora

Broad, flat ground-hugging, spatula-shaped leaves about 7.5–10cm (3–4in) long, slightly curled at the edges.

BELOW: Pinguicula moranensis

Long-spurred pink flowers on slender stems about 10cm (4in) long, carried well above the foliage.

Pinguicula moranensis

Rounded to oval leaves about 15cm (6in) long. Crimson, magenta or pink flowers with white throat.

HELPFUL HINTS
Temperature Winter minimum 7°C (45°F).
Humidity Needs moderate humidity. Occasional misting is useful, but standing the plant in a water-filled saucer will also help.
Position Good light, but avoid exposing to direct sun.
Watering and feeding Water freely at all times. These plants are used to damp or bog conditions and will react badly if the roots become dry. This is one of the few plants that benefits if the saucer in which the pot stands is kept topped up with water so that the soil in the pot is always moist.
Care Do not worry if some of the older leaves start to die, as these are recycled by the plant and new leaves are formed. Provided the young leaves look healthy, the whole plant is in good health.
Propagation Division; leaf cuttings (lay cuttings on chopped sphagnum moss); seed.

Platycerium

A small genus of epiphytic ferns whose natural habitat is high up in trees in tropical rain forests. Usually grown in cultivation in a hanging basket or wired to a piece of cork bark.

Platycerium alcicorne *see P. bifurcatum.*

Platycerium bifurcatum
The roots are hidden behind shield-shaped, sterile fronds that appear to clasp the plant's support. The broad, fertile fronds, which stand forwards, are divided and look like a stag's antlers. The plant may also be found under the name *P. alcicorne*.

HELPFUL HINTS
Temperature Winter minimum 10°C (50°F), although a few degrees lower should not harm plants.
Humidity Mist the leaves occasionally, more often in hot weather, but it is not as vulnerable as most ferns in dry air.
Position Good light, but avoid exposing to direct sun.
Watering and feeding Water freely from spring to autumn, sparingly in winter. Use soft water if possible. Feed with a weak fertilizer while growing actively. If you are growing

ABOVE: Platycerium bifurcatum

the fern on a piece of cork bark in the home, the easiest way to water it is to plunge the bark and fern in a bucket of water, and then allow it to drain before rehanging.
Care Although it can be grown in a pot, this fern looks much better displayed in a more natural way. In a greenhouse or conservatory, hanging baskets are satisfactory, but in the home a piece of cork bark is a better choice. Drill holes and insert wires for hanging the cork bark and to hold the plant securely in place. Pack plenty of sphagnum moss around the root-ball and wire in position on the piece of bark.
Propagation Offsets; spores.

Plectranthus

A genus of trailing or bushy evergreen perennials. Most of those grown as houseplants have variegated foliage.

Plectranthus coleoides
Low-growing creeper with green, scalloped leaves about 5cm (2in) long. It is the variegated varieties that are normally grown. The leaves of 'Marginatus' have white margins. Now more correctly named *P. forsteri*.

P. forsteri *see P. coleoides.*

Plectranthus fruticosus
Light green, oval to heart-shaped leaves, with a scalloped edge, up to 15cm (6in) long, on stems that grow to about 90cm (3ft). Spikes of lilac-blue flowers may grow in winter.

Plectranthus oertendahlii
A creeping plant with oval to round leaves about 2.5cm (1in) across, green with white veins above, purple-red on the reverse.

HELPFUL HINTS
Temperature Winter minimum 10°C (50°F).
Humidity Mist occasionally.
Position Good light or semi-shade, but not direct sunlight.
Watering and feeding Water freely from spring to autumn, sparingly in winter. Feed from spring to autumn.
Care Pinch stems back to keep trailing varieties compact and bushy.
Propagation Cuttings.

BELOW: Plectranthus coleoides *'Marginatus'*

ABOVE: Polypodium aureum

Polypodium

A large and diverse group of deciduous, semi-evergreen and evergreen ferns. The species described here is the one you are most likely to find grown as a houseplant.

Polypodium aureum
Blue-green, deeply-cut leaves sometimes 60cm (2ft) or more long. The creeping rhizomes are densely covered with orange-brown 'fur'. Although normally beneath the soil, these are sometimes visible. You may also find this plant sold or listed under its other name of *Phlebodium aureum*.

HELPFUL HINTS
Temperature Winter minimum 16°C (60°F).
Humidity Mist the leaves occasionally. Polypodium are more tolerant of dry air than most ferns.
Position Good light, but avoid exposing to direct sun.
Watering and feeding Water moderately from spring to autumn, sparingly in winter. Use soft water if possible. Feed regularly from spring to autumn.
Care Repot annually in spring.
Propagation Division of the rhizome; spores.

Polyscias

A genus of more than 70 evergreen trees and shrubs, a few of which are grown as houseplants. Unfortunately they can be difficult to grow successfully in the home.

Polyscias balfouriana
Leaves usually have three leaflets, which are dark green and speckled grey or paler green. Each leaflet, on a 15cm (6in) stalk, is about 7.5cm (3in) across and almost circular. 'Pennockii' has white veins, 'Marginata' has a white edge. Shrubby growth habit. Now considered to be more accurately named *P. scutellaria* 'Balfourii'.

Polyscias fruticosa
Compound leaves usually with three leaflets, each about 15cm (6in) long and spiny-toothed, creating a feathery appearance. Makes a large bushy, upright plant in time.

HELPFUL HINTS
Temperature Aim for 13–16°C (55–60°F) in winter.
Humidity Mist the leaves regularly, and provide as much additional humidity as possible.
Position Good light, but avoid exposing to direct sun.
Watering and feeding Water freely from spring to autumn, moderately in winter. Use soft water if possible. Feed regularly in summer.
Care Use an ericaceous (lime-free) compost (potting soil) when you have to repot the plant.
Propagation Cuttings.

BELOW: Polyscias balfouriana

Polystichum

A large group of evergreen, semi-evergreen and deciduous ferns, distributed over most parts of the world. Many species are used as hardy garden plants, and the two listed below cannot withstand severe frosts.

Polystichum falcatum
Tough, glossy fronds 30–60cm (1–2ft) long with large leathery leaflets. 'Rochfordianum' has more numerous holly-shaped leaflets. Although classed as a polystichum by some, you are likely to find it sold as *Cyrtomium falcatum,* which is considered by other botanists to be its correct name.

Polystichum tsus-simense
Broadly lance-shaped, semi-evergreen fronds with delicate-looking, spiny-edged leaflets. Grows to a height of about 30cm (1ft).

HELPFUL HINTS
Temperature Winter minimum 5°C (41°F), although short periods below this are unlikely to be detrimental.
Humidity Mist the leaves regularly, although these plants are not as demanding as many other ferns.

Position Semi-shade or good light, but not direct sun.
Watering and feeding Water freely from spring to autumn, sparingly in winter. Feed regularly in summer.
Care Remove faded or damaged

ABOVE: Polystichum falcatum (*syn.* Cyrtomium falcatum) *'Rochfordianum'*

fronds to keep the plants looking at their most attractive.
Propagation Division; spores.

Primula

A large genus with about 400 species of annuals, biennials and perennials, many of them hardy garden plants. Those listed below are popular commercial pot plants which you are most likely to come across.

Primula acaulis *see P. vulgaris.*

Primula malacoides
Dainty flowers about 1cm (¼in) across, arranged in two to six tiers along the flower stalk, in shades of pink, purple, lilac, red, and white, with a yellow eye. Flowers are carried on stems about 30–45cm (1–1½ft) tall, above toothed oval leaves. Winter flowering.

Primula obconica
Large, rounded heads of 2.5–4cm (1– 1½in) flowers mainly in shades of pink and blue, on stems about 23–30cm (9–12in) tall, appearing in winter and spring. The pale green hairy leaves may cause an allergic reaction in some people.

Primula vulgaris hybrids
The true species is the common primrose, with yellow flowers nestling in the rosette of leaves. These are unsuitable as houseplants. The modern hybrids, however, have large, colourful blooms in many shades, mainly yellows, reds, pinks, and blues, most with a bold contrasting eye, on stems

RIGHT: Primula obconica

carried higher above the leaves than in the species. These are widely sold as pot plants, and although they are not suitable for long-term use indoors they make a pretty short-term display in winter and spring.

HELPFUL HINTS
Temperature Winter minimum 13°C (55°F). To prolong the display, avoid high temperatures while plants are in flower.
Humidity Mist the leaves occasionally, especially if the air is dry.
Position Good light with some sun, but no direct summer sun during the hottest part of the day.
Watering and feeding Water freely from spring to autumn, but sparingly in winter. Feed quite regularly during the flowering season using a weak fertilizer.
Care The *P. vulgaris* hybrids should be bought in flower or raised in a greenhouse and taken indoors once the buds begin to open. After flowering they are best discarded or planted in the garden. The other primulas listed here are also often treated as short-term plants raised afresh each year and discarded after flowering. You can, however, successfully keep *P. obconica* from year to year. Keep it cool and out of strong sunlight, and water sparingly during the summer when it has its resting period. Resume normal watering in autumn.
Propagation Seed.

Pteris

A genus of about 280 deciduous, semi-evergreen and evergreen ferns from tropical and subtropical regions around the world.

Pteris cretica
Deeply divided green fronds with slender, slightly serrated leaflets on arching stems, growing to about 30cm (1ft). There are many varieties and these are more often grown than the species. Examples are 'Albolineata'

(pale stripe down the centre of each leaflet), and 'Alexandrae' (variegated but with the ends of the leaflets cut and fringed).

Pteris ensiformis
Similar to the previous species, but with darker leaves. There are variegated varieties, such as 'Evergemiensis' (broad white lengthwise bands on the leaflets) and 'Victoriae' (similar to the previous variety but with less pronounced markings).

HELPFUL HINTS
Temperature Winter minimum 13°C (55°F) for plain green forms, 16°C (60°F) for variegated varieties.
Humidity Mist the leaves regularly.
Position Good light, but not direct sun. Plain green forms will tolerate poorer light than the variegated varieties.
Watering and feeding Water freely from spring to autumn, sparingly in winter. Use soft water if possible. Feed regularly with a weak fertilizer from spring to autumn.
Care Be especially careful never to allow the roots to become dry.
Propagation Division; spores.

ABOVE: Pteris ensiformis *'Evergemiensis'*
BELOW: Pteris cretica *'Albolineata'*

Radermachera

A small genus of vigorous evergeeen trees and shrubs native to South-east Asia. The species below is the only one you are likely to find.

Radermachera sinica

Doubly pinnate foliage with individual leaflets about 2.5cm (1in) long, distinctly pointed at the ends. Makes a bushy plant about 60cm (2ft) tall in most home conditions. May sometimes be listed or sold as *Stereospermum suaveolens*.

HELPFUL HINTS
Temperature Winter minimum 13°C (55°F).
Humidity Undemanding.
Position Good light, but not direct summer sun during the hottest part of the day.
Watering and feeding Water freely from spring to autumn, moderately in winter.
Care Pinch out the growing tip of a young plant to encourage more compact, bushy growth.
Propagation Cuttings.

RIGHT: Radermachera sinica

Rebutia

Cacti originating from northern Argentina and parts of Bolivia, where they grow at high altitudes. There are about 40 species.

Rebutia minuscula

Spherical body, usually about 5cm (2in) across and somewhat flattened. Short white spines. Red to orange-red flowers about 2.5cm (1in) long, in spring and early summer.

Rebutia pygmaea

Oval to finger-shaped ribbed body,

RIGHT: Rebutia senilis *(left)* and Rebutia miniscula *(right)*
FAR RIGHT: Rebutia pygmaea

with tiny spines. It is often only about 2.5cm (1in) tall, but old specimens will reach 10cm (4in). Purple, pink, or red flowers, about 2.5cm (1in) long, in late spring and early summer.

Rebutia senilis
A flattened sphere, densely covered with white thorns. Bright-red, trumpet-shaped flowers, over 2.5cm (1in) long, in spring and summer. There are varieties with yellow, lilac, and orange flowers. Grows to about 7.5cm (3in).

HELPFUL HINTS
Temperature Winter minimum 5°C (41°F).
Humidity Tolerates dry air, but appreciates a humid atmosphere in spring and summer.
Position Good light. Benefits from direct sun.
Watering and feeding Water moderately from spring to autumn, keep practically dry in winter. Feed in summer with a weak fertilizer or a special cactus food.
Care Repot in spring when it becomes necessary, using a cactus mixture.
Propagation Cuttings (from offshoots); seed.

Rhaphidophora aurea

See Epipremnum aureum.

Rhipsalidopsis

A small genus of epiphytic cacti from the tropical forests of southern Brazil.

Rhipsalidopsis gaertneri
Flattened, segmented stems bearing clusters of bell-shaped scarlet flowers with multiple petals in mid and late spring. May sometimes be listed as *Schlumbergera gaertneri*, and now considered by botanists to be more correctly named *Hatiora gaertneri*.

ABOVE: Rhipsalidopsis gaertneri (*syn.* Schlumbergera gaertneri)

HELPFUL HINTS
Temperature Winter minimum 10°C (50°F).
Humidity Mist leaves occasionally.
Position Good light, but not direct summer sun.
Watering and feeding Water freely while in active growth. In winter give sufficient water only to prevent the stems from shrivelling. Feed with a weak fertilizer in spring and summer.
Care A cool resting period is essential for good flowering – so avoid keeping the plant in a hot room in winter. Do not move the plant once the buds have formed. Stand in a shady spot outdoors for the summer months.
Propagation Cuttings; seed.

Rhododendron

A very large genus of evergreen and deciduous shrubs, ranging from small alpine species to large plants of tree-like stature. Many of them are hardy and popular garden plants, especially the hybrids. Only a couple of species have been developed as houseplants, however, and these are popularly known as azaleas.

Rhododendron × obtusum
Semi-evergreen, with glossy leaves 2.5–4cm (1–1½in) long. Single or double, funnel-shaped flowers in clusters of two to five blooms, in late winter and spring. Varieties are available in a range of colours. They usually grow 30–45cm (1–1½ft) tall when kept as a pot plant.

Rhododendron simsii
Evergreen leathery leaves, about 4–5cm (1½-2in) long. Profusion of 4–5cm (1½-2in) single or double flowers in a range of colours, mainly pinks and reds, as well as white, in winter and spring. They grow to about 30–45cm (1–1½ft) tall as a pot plant.

HELPFUL HINTS
Temperature Aim for 10–16°C (50–60°F) in winter.
Humidity Mist the leaves regularly.
Position Good light, but avoid exposing to direct sun.
Watering and feeding Water freely at all times, using soft water if possible. Feed regularly in summer.
Care Pay special attention to watering – plants are often sold in a very peaty (peat moss) mixture that is difficult to moisten once it dries out. Always use an ericaceous (lime-free) compost (potting soil) for repotting, which is best done about a month after flowering has finished. Place the plants in a shady and sheltered spot in the garden once all danger of frost is past. *R. × obtusum* varieties can be planted permanently in the garden in sheltered areas where the winters are not very severe. *R. simsii* varieties must be brought indoors again in early autumn. If you stand the plants in the garden, plunge the pots into the ground to conserve moisture – don't forget to keep them watered and fed.
Propagation Cuttings.

BELOW: Rhododendron × obtusum
BOTTOM: Rhododendron simsii

Rosa

Roses are universally popular plants, and although there are only about 200 different species, there are thousands of hybrids and varieties. However, even dwarf and miniature varieties make only short-term houseplants.

Rosa, miniature hybrids
A scaled-down rose 15–30cm (6–12in) tall, with single, semi-double, or double flowers about 1–4cm (½–1½in) across. They are available as bushes or trained as miniature standards. Most are derived from *R. chinensis* 'Minima', but the breeding of those available today is complex and they will usually be sold simply with a variety name, or perhaps just labelled 'miniature rose'. Some are true miniatures, growing less than 15cm (6in) high, but the treatment is the same however they are labelled when you buy them.

Helpful hints
Temperature Frost-hardy. Aim for 10–21°C (50–70°F) when the plants are growing actively.
Humidity Undemanding, but it is beneficial to mist occasionally.
Position Best possible light. Will tolerate full sun.
Watering and feeding Water freely from spring to autumn, while they are in leaf. Feed regularly in summer.
Care The plants are best kept outdoors for as long as possible. After flowering stand them on the balcony or patio and keep watered, or plunge the pot in the garden soil. Pots kept on a balcony or patio for the winter may need some protection to prevent the root-ball from freezing solid. Re-pot in autumn if necessary. Prune in spring as you would an ordinary rose – although with very small plants it may be sufficient simply to remove dead or crossing shoots. Bring indoors again in late spring, or as soon as flowering starts.
Propagation Cuttings.

RIGHT: *Rose, miniature hybrids*

Saintpaulia

A small genus of rosette-forming perennials, just one species of which is well known. The large colour range and variation in flower form are the result of introducing genes from other species such as *S. confusa*, although they are usually all listed as varieties of *S. ionantha*. The original species is not grown as a houseplant.

Most of the saintpaulias sold in shops and garden centres will lack a specific name, but if you go to a specialist supplier you will have a choice of hundreds of varieties, all accurately named.

The huge range of varieties available, in many colours and variations in flower form and growth habit, make saintpaulias an ideal plant for collectors. They can be induced to flower throughout the year if you can provide suitable light intensities.

Sizes

Large varieties grow to 40cm (16in) or more across. Standard saintpaulias are the ones most often bought and generally grow between 20–40cm (8–16in) across. Miniatures are only 7.5–15cm (3–6in) across. There are also varieties intermediate in size, and microminiatures less than 7.5cm (3in) across when mature. Trailers have more widely spaced foliage than normal varieties, with drooping stems that tend to arch over the pot.

Flower shapes

Single flowers are the most common type. Semi-double flowers have more than five petals, but the centre is still clearly visible. Double flowers have at least ten petals, and the yellow centre is not visible. Frilled flowers have petals with a wavy edge. Star flowers have five equally sized and spaced petals, instead of the more usual two small and three large petals.

Leaf shapes

These are just a few of the leaf shapes identified by specialists. Boy leaves are plain green, and do not have a spot at the leaf base. Girl leaves are the same shape as boy leaves, but have a small white spot or blotch at the base. Lance leaves are longer and more pointed at the end. Spoon leaves have a rolled-up edge. Variegated leaves are mottled or speckled with white or cream.

HELPFUL HINTS

Temperature Winter minimum 16°C (60°F).

Humidity Saintpaulias appreciate high humidity, but regular misting is not appropriate as water may lodge on the hairy leaves and cause rotting. Provide the humidity in other ways, such as standing the pot over a saucer of water on pebbles or marbles so that the compost (potting soil) is not in direct contact with the water.

Position Good light, but not direct summer sun during the hottest part of the day. Strong light without direct sun is ideal. Saintpaulias grow very well under suitable artificial light (at least 5,000 lux).

Watering and feeding Water freely from spring to autumn, moderately in winter, but never allow the roots to remain wet – try to let the soil surface dry out a little before watering again. Use soft water if possible. Try to

ABOVE, OPPOSITE TOP LEFT AND ABOVE LEFT: *Saintpaulia hybrids*
OPPOSITE BELOW: *Saintpaulias, showing the diversity of flower shapes and colouring, including a double. A miniature is shown bottom right.*
OPPOSITE ABOVE RIGHT: *Saintpaulias: 'Maggie May' (left), 'Fancy Pants' (centre), 'Colorado' (right)*

water without wetting the leaves – use the immersion method or direct the spout of the watering-can below the rosette of leaves. Feed during active growth. However, if the plant produces lots of leaves and few flowers despite adequate light, you may be overfeeding – switch to a low-nitrogen fertilizer.

Care Most windowsill plants flower in spring and summer, when the light is good, but by supplementing the light they will continue blooming for most of the year. If you have the ability to maintain high light levels, however, it is best to rest the plant for about a month: lower the temperature close to the minimum, reduce watering and shorten the day length. After a month, place in good light to start into active growth again. Remove any old leaves that are marring the plant.

Propagation Leaf cuttings; seed.

Sansevieria

A small genus of evergreen rhizomatous perennials with stiff, fleshy leaves. These are desert plants that can tolerate poor conditions.

Sansevieria trifasciata

Tough, sword-like leaves, slightly crescent-shaped in cross-section, that can be 1.5m (5ft) long in good conditions, but usually only grow to half this height in the home. Dull green leaves with paler cross-banding that creates a mottled appearance. A more popular form is the variety 'Laurentii' which has yellow leaf margins. 'Hahnii' is a low-growing variety with a short, funnel-shaped rosette of leaves; 'Golden Hahnii' is similar but with broad yellow stripes along the edge of each leaf. Spikes of white flowers are sometimes produced.

BELOW: Sansevieria trifasciata *'Laurentii'*

HELPFUL HINTS

Temperature Winter minimum 10°C (50°F).
Humidity Tolerates dry air.
Position Best in bright, indirect light, but will tolerate direct sun and also a degree of shade.
Watering and feeding Water moderately from spring to autumn, very sparingly in winter. Always allow the soil to dry out slightly before watering. Feed regularly in summer.
Care Repotting is seldom required, as plants respond well to cramped conditions. However, always repot if the roots show signs of splitting the pot.
Propagation Division; leaf cuttings (but yellow-edged varieties will revert to the green form).

Sarracenia

Carnivorous plants with just eight species in the genus. Demanding as a houseplant, but grown as a curiosity.

Sarracenia flava

Leaves like long trumpets, hooded at the top, grow to about 30–60cm (1–2ft) long indoors. Insects are lured into the trap, attracted by nectar in special glands, and by the yellow colouring developed by the leaf traps. They are digested by enzymes and bacteria. Unusual yellow or cream flowers are sometimes produced in spring.

Sarracenia purpurea

Rosette-forming plants with erect to semi-prostrate growth to about 30cm (12in). Inflated green traps with red or purple veins and markings. Purple flowers in spring.

HELPFUL HINTS

Temperature Winter minimum 5°C (41°F).
Humidity Mist the leaves regularly, and try to maintain a humid atmosphere around the plant.
Position Good light with or without direct sun, but not direct summer sun

ABOVE: Sarracenia purpurea

during the hottest part of the day.
Watering and feeding Water freely from spring to autumn (when the plant likes to be kept constantly wet), sparingly in winter. Feeding is not normally necessary.
Care The plant is likely to do better in a greenhouse or conservatory than in a centrally-heated living-room.
Propagation Seed.

Saxifraga

A large genus with hundreds of species, mostly alpines, but only one is commonly grown as a houseplant.

Saxifraga sarmentosa *see S. stolonifera.*

Saxifraga stolonifera

Rounded leaves about 4–5cm (1½-2in) across, broadly toothed, olive green with white veins above, reddish beneath. 'Tricolor' has green and red or pink leaves with silver or white markings, reddish beneath. Height is up to about 23cm (9in), but plantlets will cascade if grown in a hanging pot. May also be found under its older name of *S. sarmentosa.*

ABOVE: Saxifraga stolonifera

HELPFUL HINTS
Temperature Winter minimum 7°C (45°F).
Humidity Mist occasionally.
Position Good light, but avoid exposing to direct sun.
Watering and feeding Water freely from spring to autumn, sparingly in winter. Feed regularly in summer.
Care The species listed above is frost-hardy and will grow in the garden where winters are mild. 'Tricolor' is more delicate, however, and is best kept indoors. Trim off long runners if they look untidy.
Propagation Plantlets (peg down into pots).

Schefflera

A large genus of evergreen shrubs and trees, a few of which are grown as focal-point houseplants.

Schefflera actinophylla
Although a large tree where it grows outdoors, in the home it makes a bushy plant up to ceiling height. Large, spreading leaves with 5–16 leaflets (the older the plant, the more it is likely to have), each of them about 10–20cm (4–8in) long.

Schefflera arboricola
Erect, well-branched growth with 7–16 oval leaflets which radiate from the top of the leaf stalk like an umbrella. There are several widely available varieties with variegated foliage. You may also find this plant sold or listed as *Heptapleurum arboricola*.

BELOW: Schefflera arboricola *'Aurea'*

HELPFUL HINTS
Temperature Winter minimum 13°C (55°F).
Humidity Mist the leaves regularly.
Position Good light, but avoid exposing to direct sun.

Watering and feeding Water freely from spring to autumn, sparingly in winter. Feed regularly in summer.
Care Can be trained as an upright, unbranching plant if you stake the plant and do not remove the growing tip, or can be made to bush out by removing the growing tip. Repot annually in spring.
Propagation Cuttings.

Schizanthus

A small group of annuals from Chile. Most of the plants grown in pots are hybrids, evolved through many years of breeding by seed companies.

Schizanthus hybrids
Feathery, light green leaves, divided and fern-like in appearance. Exotic-looking, open-mouthed flowers, often described as orchid-like. Flowers multicoloured and very freely produced. Height depends on variety – dwarf varieties are most appropriate for the home, and you should be able to restrict them to little more than 30cm (1ft). Some greenhouse varieties grow to 1.2m (4ft).

Helpful hints
Temperature Aim for 10–18°C (50–64°F).
Humidity Mist occasionally.

Below: Schizanthus *hybrid*

Position Best possible light. Will tolerate some direct sun.
Watering and feeding Water freely at all times. Remember to feed regularly.
Care If raising your own plant, pinch out the growing tips while the seedlings are still young in order to produce bushy growth. Repeat again later if the plants seem to be lanky. Move younger plants into larger pots to avoid checking their growth. Avoid very high temperatures. Discard plants when flowering has finished.
Propagation Seed.

Schlumbergera

See Rhipsalidopsis and Zygocactus.

Scindapsus aureus

See Epipremnum.

Sedum

A large genus of over 300 species, from temperate zones throughout the world. Many of them are fleshy or succulent, including the majority of those used as pot plants.

Sedum bellum
A small plant to about 7.5–15cm (3–6in), with leaves folded like buds that eventually spread apart and become spatula shaped. Small star-like white flowers in spring.

Sedum morganianum
Cascading growth with closely-packed grey-green, succulent cylindrical leaves that overlap like tiles, creating a tail-like appearance. Pink flowers may appear in summer.

ABOVE: Sedum sieboldii
'Mediovariegatum'
LEFT ABOVE: Sedum pachyphyllum
LEFT BELOW: Sedum × rubrotinctum

Sedum pachyphyllum

Erect with pale blue-green cylindrical leaves about 2.5cm (1in) long, slightly upturned and flushed red at the tips. Yellow flowers may appear in spring.

Sedum × rubrotinctum

Similar to the previous species, but more of the leaf tends to be flushed red, especially in strong sunlight.

Sedum sieboldii

Thin, flattish leaves, in groups of three, blue-green with a white edge. In the variety 'Mediovariegatum' the leaves have a central creamy-white blotch. Pink flowers may appear in late summer or autumn. Botanists have now moved this to another genus and called it *Hylotelephium sieboldii*, but it is still sold as a sedum.

HELPFUL HINTS

Temperature Winter minimum 5°C (41°F).
Humidity Tolerates dry air.
Position Best possible light.

Watering and feeding Water sparingly from spring to autumn, and keep practically dry in winter (water only to prevent the leaves from shrivelling up). Feeding is not normally necessary.
Care Repot in spring, using a potting soil that drains freely. A cactus mixture suits well.
Propagation Leaf cuttings (for varieties with large, fleshy leaves such as *S. pachyphyllum* and *S. morganianum*); stem cuttings.

Selaginella

A genus of about 700 species of moss-like perennials, most of them coming from tropical rain forests.

Selaginella kraussiana

Creeping stems with filigreed green foliage, yellowish-green in 'Aurea'. Individual stems may be 30cm (1ft) long, and they root readily as they spread over the surface.

Selaginella lepidophylla

Looks like a ball of rolled-up, dead foliage in its dry state (the form in which it is often sold as a curiosity plant). Within hours of being given water it opens to a rosette shape, and the green colouring gradually returns.

Selaginella martensii

Upright-growing stems to about 30cm (1ft), which later become decumbent and produce aerial roots. Frond-like sprays of feathery green foliage. There are variegated varieties, such as 'Watsoniana', which has silvery-white tips.

HELPFUL HINTS

Temperature Winter minimum 13°C (55°F).
Humidity Mist the leaves regularly. Additional humidity from other sources must be provided.
Position Partial shade – avoid direct sun all year round. Plants do well in bottle gardens and terrariums, where the atmosphere is humid and protected.
Watering and feeding Keep moist at all times, but reduce watering in winter to suit the lower temperatures. Feed occasionally in summer using a foliar feed.
Care Provide as much humidity as possible and avoid cold draughts and very hot, sunny windows. Do not be surprised if plants are short-lived in living-room conditions.
Propagation Division (pot up rooted pieces).

BELOW: Selaginella lepidophylla
BELOW LEFT: Selaginella martensii

Senecio

A very large group of plants, with over 1,000 species, distributed throughout the world. It includes plants as diverse as annuals and perennials, succulents and non-succulent perennials, evergreen shrubs, sub-shrubs and climbers. Relatively few are used as houseplants.

Senecio cruentus hybrids
Dense head of colourful daisy-like flowers in winter and spring. Colours include shades of red, pink, purple, white, and blue. Large, irregularly lobed, hairy leaves, which can almost be hidden when a compact plant is in full flower. Height ranges from about 23–75cm (9–30in), and flower size from 2.5–7.5cm (1–3in) depending on the variety. Choose compact varieties for the home. You will usually find this plant called cineraria. Although botanists have now reclassified it as *Pericallis cruenta*, it is not sold under this name.

Senecio macroglossus
Trailer or climber with small succulent, roughly triangular leaves resembling common ivy *(Hedera helix)*. 'Variegatus' has white margins.

Senecio mikanioides
Trailer or climber similar to the previous species, but the leaves have five

ABOVE: Senecio rowleyanus
BELOW: Senecio macroglossus 'Variegatus'

to seven sharply pointed lobes. Now reclassified as *Delairea odorata*.

Senecio rowleyanus
Trailer with pendent, thread-like stems clustered with pea-like leaves that resemble beads.

HELPFUL HINTS
Temperature Winter minimum 7°C (45°F). Try to keep *S. cruentus* varieties below 13°C (55°F).
Humidity Succulent types are tolerant of dry air, but mist *S. cruentus, S. macroglossus*, and *S. mikanioides* occasionally.
Position Best possible light, but not direct sun for *S. cruentus. S. rowleyanus* should receive some direct sun. The other species listed here need good light but not direct summer sun, and

will tolerate semi-shade, but in winter provide as much light as possible.
Watering and feeding Water the non-succulent types freely from spring to autumn, sparingly in winter. Water *S. rowleyanus* sparingly at all times, and keep practically dry in winter. Feed all types when they are growing actively.
Care *S. cruentus* will die after flowering, so discard once blooming is over.
Propagation Although you can raise senecios from seed in the greenhouse, they are difficult to grow on from seed in the home. Most people buy them in flower if they cannot keep them in a greenhouse until flowering starts.

Sinningia

A small genus of tuberous perennials and deciduous sub-shrubs. Those commonly grown are widely known and sold as gloxinias, and have been bred from *S. speciosa*.

Sinningia speciosa
Large, oval to oblong leaves arising directly from the tuber, about 20–25cm (8–10in) long and hairy. The underside is sometimes reddish. Large, showy, bell-shaped flowers about 5cm (2in) long, in pink, red, blue, purple, or white, some with contrasting rim, others attractively speckled.

HELPFUL HINTS
Temperature Minimum 16°C (60°F) during growing season.
Humidity Mist around plants regularly, but avoid wetting the leaves or blooms. Provide as much humidity as possible by other methods.
Position Good light, but avoid exposing to direct sun.
Watering and feeding Water freely once the tubers have rooted well. Decrease watering at the end of the growing season (*see* Care). Feed regularly in summer.
Care When flowering has finished, gradually reduce the amount of water given and stop feeding. Remove the

ABOVE: Sinningia speciosa

sometimes mottled. Height in flower is usually about 30–38cm (12–15in).

HELPFUL HINTS
Temperature Winter minimum 13°C (55°F).
Humidity Mist regularly, but try not to over-wet the leaves. Use soft water if possible.
Position Good light, but avoid exposing to direct sun.
Watering and feeding Water freely from spring to autumn, while plants are growing. Keep almost dry in winter if the top growth has died down. Feed regularly in summer.
Care After flowering, gradually reduce the amount of water given and stop feeding. Leave the rhizome in its old pot for most of the winter, but repot and start into active growth again in late winter.
Propagation Division of rhizomes; leaf cuttings.

leaves when they have turned yellow. If you have space, store the tubers in the pot in a frost-free, place ideally at about 10°C (50°F).

Repot afresh in the spring, making sure you plant them the right way up and at about the same depth as before.
Propagation Leaf cuttings; seed.

Smithiantha

Only a few species are known, and these come from humid mountain forests in Mexico and Guatemala. These have been used to provide some attractive hybrids, however, that are especially worth growing if you have a conservatory. They are not easy to grow in a living-room.

Smithiantha hybrids
Loose heads of pendent, tubular flowers about 5cm (2in) long, with a slightly flared mouth, in autumn. Hairy, round to heart-shaped leaves, usually about 10cm (4in) long and

RIGHT: Smithiantha × hybrida

Solanum

A genus of about 1,400 species, from all parts of the world, and including annuals, perennials, shrubs, sub-shrubs and climbers. The only ones used in the home are the two species described below. These are grown for their decorative fruits, which are poisonous.

Solanum capsicastrum
A sub-shrub usually grown as an annual, generally reaching 30–60cm (1–2ft) as a pot plant, but this depends on variety. Lance-shaped leaves about 5cm (2in) long, and small white star-shaped flowers in summer. These are followed by egg-shaped or round green fruits that turn orange-red or scarlet by winter.

Solanum pseudocapsicum
Very similar to the previous species, but the stems are smoother and the fruits usually larger.

Helpful hints
Temperature Aim for 10–16°C (50–60°F) in winter.
Humidity Mist the leaves regularly.
Position Best possible light. Tolerates some direct sun.
Watering and feeding Water freely

BELOW: Solanum capsicastrum

throughout the growing period. Feed regularly in summer.
Care Most people buy the plants already in fruit, but they are easy to raise from seed. As they are uninteresting until the fruits colour, and conditions indoors are not really suitable, it is best to raise them in a greenhouse to take indoors later. If you want to try to keep an old plant, cut the stems back to half their length after flowering and water sparingly until spring, when you can repot the plant. Stand the plant in a garden frame or outside in the garden for the summer, but spray the flowers with water to try to assist pollination. Bring indoors in autumn, before the evenings turn cold.
Propagation Seed; cuttings.

Soleirolia

There is only one species in this genus, a native of Corsica. It is frost-hardy, but easily damaged or killed by hard winter frosts so is only suitable for growing outdoors in mild areas.

Soleirolia soleirolii
Creeping, ground-hugging plant with very small round leaves that give a mossy appearance from a distance. The species itself is green, but there are silver and gold varieties that masquerade under several names. The silver form 'Variegata' is also sold as 'Argentea' and 'Silver Queen'. The golden form 'Aurea' is also sold as 'Golden Queen'. They all grow to form compact mounds not more than 5cm (2in) tall. You are also likely to find the plant under its older name of *Helxine soleirolii*.

Helpful hints
Temperature Frost-hardy, but aim for 7°C (45°F) when growing it as a pot plant.
Humidity Mist the leaves regularly.
Position Good light, but avoid exposing to direct sun.
Watering and feeding Water freely

Top and above: Soleirolia soleirolii

at all times. Feeding is normally unnecessary.
Care Repot in spring. A low, wide container is better than a normal pot, as the growth quickly spreads and hangs over the edge.
Propagation Division.

Solenostemon

See Coleus.

Sparmannia

A small group of evergreen trees and shrubs. The only species normally grown as a pot plant is the one pictured and described on this page, *Sparmannia africana.*

Sparmannia africana

Large, pale green downy leaves up to 25cm (10in) across. Long-stalked clusters of white flowers with yellow and purplish-red stamens in spring. Makes a large plant that will reach ceiling height.

HELPFUL HINTS
Temperature Winter minimum 7°C (45°F).
Humidity Mist occasionally.
Position Good light, but not direct summer sun during the hottest part of the day.
Watering and feeding Water freely from spring to autumn, sparingly in winter. Feed regularly in spring and summer.
Care Cut back the stems when flowering is over – this helps to keep the plants compact and may encourage a later flush of flowers. When you repot, you can cut it back severely to a height of about 30cm (1ft) if necessary. Young plants may need repotting several times in a year. The plant can be stood outdoors for the summer, but choose a sheltered position out of direct sun, and bring indoors again before the evenings turn cold. Pinch out the growing tip of a young plant if you want to encourage a bushy shape.
Propagation Cuttings.

Right: Sparmannia africana

ABOVE: Spathiphyllum wallisii

Spathiphyllum

Rhizomatous evergreen perennials, grown for their arum lily-like flowers. Other species and hybrids are available, but the one below is compact and one of the most popular.

Spathiphyllum wallisii
Tuft-forming clusters of thin, lance-shaped leaves arising from soil level. Arum lily-type flowers with a sail-like white spathe and fragrant florets on a white spadix, in spring and sometimes autumn. Height 30–45cm (1–1½ft).

HELPFUL HINTS
Temperature Winter minimum 16°C (60°F).
Humidity Mist the leaves regularly. Provide additional humidity by other means too.
Position Best possible light in winter, semi-shade in summer, out of direct summer sun.
Watering and feeding Water freely

from spring to autumn, sparingly in winter. Feed regularly in summer.
Care Pay special attention to providing high humidity, and avoid cold draughts. Repot annually, in spring.
Propagation Division.

Stapelia

A genus of about 100 clump-forming succulents, most of them from South and South West Africa.

Stapelia variegata
Angular, fleshy green stems arising from the base of the plant and forming a small clump, usually about 10–15cm (4–6in) long. Star-shaped flowers about 5–7.5cm (2–3in) across, variable in colour but usually blotched or mottled yellow, purple, and brown, appearing in summer or autumn. Now reclassified as *Orbea variegata*, but likely to be sold as a stapelia.

HELPFUL HINTS
Temperature Winter minimum 10°C (50°F).
Humidity Tolerates dry air.
Position Best possible light.
Watering and feeding Water freely from spring to autumn, sparingly in winter. Feeding not necessary if plant is repotted periodically.
Care Repot in spring, annually if growth is good.
Propagation Cuttings; seed.

BELOW: Stapelia variegata

ABOVE: Stephanotis floribunda

Stephanotis

A small genus of climbers. The species described below is the one most commonly grown. This is a popular plant for bridal bouquets in some countries.

Stephanotis floribunda
Glossy, oval leaves 7.5–10cm (3–4in) long. Clusters of very fragrant star-shaped tubular white flowers in spring and summer. Will reach 3m (10ft) in good conditions. Often trained around wire hoops as a small plant, but is a vigorous climber requiring a proper support in a conservatory.

HELPFUL HINTS
Temperature Aim for 13–16°C (55–60°F) in winter. Avoid high winter temperatures.
Humidity Mist occasionally.
Position Best possible light, but not direct summer sun during the hottest part of the day.

Watering and feeding Water freely from spring to autumn, sparingly in winter. Feed regularly in summer, only in moderation if the plant is already large and seems too vigorous.
Care Train plant to a support. Shorten over-long shoots in spring, and cut out overcrowded stems at the same time. Repot every second spring.
Propagation Cuttings.

Stereospermum suaveolens

See Radermachera sinica.

Strelitzia

A small genus of large and exotic-looking plants from South Africa. Only the species described here is grown as a houseplant.

Strelitzia reginae
Clump-forming with large paddle-shaped leaves about 90cm (3ft) tall, including the stalk. Spectacular and long-lasting orange and blue flowers sitting in a boat-like bract. Spring is the main flowering period, but they may bloom at other times.

Helpful hints
Temperature Aim for a winter temperature of 13–16°C (55–60°F).
Humidity Mist occasionally.
Position Best possible light, but not direct summer sun during the hottest part of the day.
Watering and feeding Water freely from spring to autumn, sparingly in winter. Feed regularly from spring to autumn.
Care Repot as infrequently as possible as the roots are easily damaged. Be patient if you buy a small plant or raise your own from seed, as they can take four or five years to flower.
Propagation Division; seed.

Below: Strelitzia reginae

Streptocarpus

A genus of woodland plants from South Africa and Madagascar, but the ones grown in the home are almost always hybrids.

Streptocarpus hybrids
Long, stemless, strap-shaped leaves, 20–30cm (8–12in) long, growing more or less horizontally and often arching over the edge of the pot. Trumpet-shaped flowers about 5cm (2in) across in shades of pink, red, and blue, on stems about 23cm (9in) tall. Late spring to late summer is the normal flowering time. The leaf sap sometimes causes an irritating rash.

Streptocarpus saxorum
Woody-based perennial with whorls of small, oval, hairy leaves. Lilac flowers, like a smaller version of the hybrids, in summer and autumn.

HELPFUL HINTS
Temperature Winter minimum 13°C (55°F).
Humidity Mist the leaves occasional-ly, lightly so as not to soak them.
Position Good light, but not direct summer sun.
Watering and feeding Water freely from spring to autumn, sparingly in winter. Feed regularly in summer.
Care Benefits from a dormant winter season, with the compost (potting soil) only slightly moist and the temperature close to the minimum suggested. Repot in mid spring.
Propagation Leaf cuttings; seed.

Stromanthe

A small genus, from the maranta fami-ly, native to tropical regions of South America. They are easily confused with some species of ctenanthe and calathea.

Stromanthe amabilis
Pale green oval leaves, attractively cross-banded either side of the midrib with grey streaks. The reverse of the leaf is grey-green. This has now been reclassified as *Ctenanthe amabilis*.

Stromanthe sanguinea
Stiff, erect growth, with glossy, lance-shaped leaves about 38cm (15in) long, olive green above with a pale central vein. The reverse is purplish-red. Many-stemmed flower heads may be produced in spring. The true flowers are small and white, but the conspi-cuous bracts are vivid scarlet.

HELPFUL HINTS
Temperature Winter minimum 18°C (64°F).
Humidity Mist the leaves regularly,

Above: Stromanthe amabilis
Opposite above: Streptocarpus saxorum
Opposite below: Streptocarpus *hybrid*

and supplement with other methods of raising the humidity level.

Position Good light, but not direct summer sun during the hottest part of the day.

Watering and feeding Water freely from spring to autumn, sparingly in winter. Use soft water if possible. Feed regularly in summer.

Care These are difficult plants to care for indoors. If you have a heated greenhouse or conservatory, keep them there for most of the year, only bringing them into the home for short periods. When repotting, use a soil mixture that drains freely.

Propagation Division.

Syagrus weddeliana

See Cocos weddeliana.

Syngonium

A genus of about 30 species, from tropical rain forests in Central and South America. These woody climbers have leaves that change shape according to the plant's stage of growth, and adult leaf forms are often much more lobed than the juvenile forms usually seen on small pot plants.

Syngonium podophyllum

Foot-shaped compound leaves, arrow-shaped on young plants. There are several variegated varieties, the main differences being in the position and extent of the cream or white markings. Some leaves are almost entirely white or yellow. Grows to about 1.8m (6ft) with a suitable support.

Below: Syngonium *hybrid 'White Butterfly'*

HELPFUL HINTS

Temperature Winter minimum 16°C (60°F).

Humidity Mist the leaves regularly.

Position Good light, but not direct sun. Tolerant of low light levels.

Watering and feeding Water freely from spring to autumn, sparingly in winter. Feed regularly in spring and summer.

Care If you prefer the juvenile foliage, cut off the climbing stems that develop – the plant will remain bushy rather than climb, and the leaves will be more arrow-shaped. Repot every second spring.

Propagation Cuttings; air layering.

Tillandsia

About 400 species of mainly epiphytic plants. Many of those that derive nutrients from air alone are now popular as novelty plants, and are often used as decorations even by non-gardeners. These are usually displayed for sale glued or wired to accessories such as shells, mirrors or pieces of wood. A few of the species planted in pots are grown for their interesting or unusual flowers.

Air plant tillandsias

These interesting plants have special scaly leaves, capable of trapping moisture from the air, and they can even absorb nutrients from dust and any nutrient-rich moisture that may be about. *T. usneoides* grows best in a humid greenhouse, but the other species listed here are compact and tough enough to grow in the home.

The scales that give the air plants their unique quality reflect light in such a way that the plants all tend to look grey in colour. For that reason they are sometimes referred to as the grey tillandsias. The species listed here provide a cross-section of some of the most popular, but specialist suppliers will offer many more.

Tillandsia argentea
Rosettes of very narrow, thread-like leaves, with a bulb-like base. Loose sprays of small red flowers may appear in summer.

Tillandsia caput-medusae
Thick, twisted, reflexed leaves, broadening at the base to form a bulb-like structure. Quite showy red flowers in blue bracts in summer.

Tillandsia ionantha
Compact rosettes of silvery arching leaves. The inner leaves turn red when the small spikes of violet-blue flowers emerge in summer.

Tillandsia juncea
Tufts of rush-like foliage reflexing outwards, forming a thick, bushy rosette.

Tillandsia magnusiana
Thread-like leaves covered in grey scales, bulbous at base.

Tillandsia oaxacana
Dense rosette of rolled grey-green foliage. Flowers not a feature.

Tillandsia usneoides
Cylindrical leaves about 5cm (2in) long on slender drooping stems. Forms a long cascading chain of grey leaves suspended from the plant's support. There are inconspicuous yellowish-green flowers in summer, which tend to be lost among the foliage.

Opposite far left: Tillandsia
usneoides
Opposite above: Tillandsia
magnusiana
Oppostie middle: *Tillandsias. From left
to right:* T. oaxacana, T. caput-medusae,
T. juncea, *and* T. ionantha
Opposite below: Tillandsia argentea

Flowering pot tillandsias

Tillandsias grown for their flowers are very different in appearance to air plant species. Although their root systems are not extensive, they are grown in pots like a conventional houseplant.

Tillandsia cyanea
Rosette of narrow, grass-like leaves, reddish-brown at the base and striped brown along the length. Blade-like flower spike in summer, from which purple-blue, pansy-shaped flowers appear along the edge of the spike from the pink or red bracts. The plant grows to about 25cm (10in).

Tillandsia lindenii
Similar to the previous species, but the blue flowers have a white eye.

Helpful hints
Temperature Winter minimum 13°C (55°F) for air plant tillandsias, 18°F (64°F) for the flowering species.
Humidity Mist regularly. This is especially important for the air plants, as these depend on atmospheric moisture. If possible, provide additional humidity by other methods as well
Position Good light, but not direct sun in summer. The air plants can tolerate quite low light levels.
Watering and feeding Air plants receive their moisture by regular – preferably daily – misting. Water the

Above: Tillandsia cyanea

other species freely from spring to autumn, sparingly in winter. Use soft water if possible. Air plants are fed via the leaves using a mister, but use a very weak solution of the fertilizer, and only apply when the plants are growing actively. Feed pot-grown species in the same way, or by adding the fertilizer to the soil.
Care Air plants are often wired into position on a bromeliad 'tree' or suitable support. If you want to fix them to a mirror or ornament, use adhesives sold for the purpose by many garden centres. Other species can be potted in spring. Although the flowered part will die, other shoots will appear.
Propagation Offsets.

Tolmiea

The single species below is the only one in the genus, a native of the west coast of North America. It is hardy enough to be grown in the garden.

Tolmiea menziesii
Bright green foliage arranged in a rosette and forming a mound of heart-shaped lobed leaves about 5cm (2in) across. The leaf stalks are long and when the plant is grown in a hanging pot this sometimes gives the plant a cascading appearance. Young plantlets form at the base of the leaf blade. 'Taff's Gold' is a variegated variety that you may also find under the names 'Goldsplash', 'Maculata', and 'Variegata'. It is sometimes semi-evergreen.

HELPFUL HINTS
Temperature Hardy, but usually requires a winter minimum of 5°C (41°F) when grown as a houseplant. Avoid high winter temperatures.
Humidity Mist occasionally.
Position Good light or semi-shade, but not direct sun.

ABOVE: Tolmiea menziesii

Watering and feeding Water freely from spring to autumn, sparingly in winter. Feed regularly in summer.
Care If the plant becomes too large and its stems are congested, try cutting it back in spring to allow new leaves to grow from the base. Repot annually in spring. The plant can be stood outside for the summer, but choose a position out of direct sun.
Propagation Division, or pot up plantlets.

Tradescantia

A genus of about 70 species, including hardy border plants as well as tender trailers. It now includes *Zebrina pendula,* another popular trailing houseplant.

Tradescantia albiflora *see T. fluminensis.*

Tradescantia blossfeldiana
Narrowly oval, slightly fleshy leaves 5–10cm (2–4in) long in two distinct

rows on hairy, trailing stems. In the species the leaves are glossy green above and sometimes tinged purple beneath. It is the variegated varieties that are usually grown, however, and 'Variegata' has longitudinal cream stripes. The flowers are pink with a white base. This species is now more correctly *T. cerinthoides.*

Tradescantia cerinthoides *see T. blossfeldiana.*

Tradescantia fluminensis
Trailing, rooting, hairless stems, with short-stalked green leaves about 5–7.5cm (2–3in) long, sometimes tinged purple beneath. It is the variegated varieties that are grown, however, and these include 'Albovittata' (creamy-white lengthwise stripes), 'Quicksilver' (clear white markings), and 'Tricolor' (white and pale purple stripes). The white flowers are unspectacular. This species was once considered distinct from *T. albiflora* (colourless sap in *albiflora,* violet in *fluminensis*), but they are now classed by botanists as one species. You may find them under either name.

Tradescantia zebrina

Pointed oval leaves about 5cm (2in) long on creeping or trailing stems. The upper surface is pale green with a silvery sheen and lengthwise purple stripe, and the underside is purple. Small white or rose-red flowers. This plant is still widely known and sold as *Zebrina pendula*. The variety 'Purpusii' is a little larger and more robust, with purple-tinged, bluish-green leaves and pink flowers. This is likely to be found also as *Zebrina purpusii* or *Tradescantia purpusii*.

HELPFUL HINTS
Temperature Keep temperature in

LEFT: Tradescantia blossfeldiana *'Variegata'*
BELOW: Tradescantia fluminensis *'Albovittata'*
BOTTOM: Tradescantia zebrina

winter to a minimum of 7°C (45°F).
Humidity Mist occasionally.
Position Good light, including some direct sun. Variegation will be inferior in poor light.
Watering and feeding Water freely from spring to autumn, sparingly in winter. Feed regularly from spring to autumn.
Care The plants soon look untidy with tangled growth, and if conditions are not good the leaves may turn brown or shrivel. Trim them back by pinching out unattractive shoots – this will encourage bushy new growth from near the base.
Propagation Cuttings.

Tulipa

Although there are only about 100 species of tulip, breeding has produced a huge range of hybrids and varieties that are planted in their millions every year. None of them can be considered true houseplants, but some are forced for early flowering in winter and may be used as a short-term houseplant.

Tulipa hybrids

The tulip needs no description, but there are many kinds. Consult a good bulb catalogue for those varieties suitable for growing in pots for early flowering – these will usually be compact types such as early singles and early doubles, and specialists will also offer bulbs that have been specially treated or 'prepared' so that they come into flower early. Florists and garden centres also offer pots of tulips that are just coming into flower, and these are a useful option.

HELPFUL HINTS
Temperature Hardy, and once in flower the cooler the room, the longer the flowers should last. See below for advice on earlier treatment.
Humidity Undemanding.
Position If brought indoors just as the flowers open, they can be placed anywhere you choose.

ABOVE: *Tulip, early double*

Watering and feeding Water moderately while in the home.
Care In early or mid autumn, plant the bulbs with their necks just below the compost (deep planting is impractical in a pot). Place in a sheltered position outdoors, and cover with fine gravel, pulverized bark, or some other suitable mulch, to a depth of at least 5cm (2in). Keep the soil in the pots just moist but be careful not to overwater. When the shoots are about 4–5cm (1½–2in) tall, or as soon as you can detect signs of a bud, bring into the light. Keep the pots in a light place at about 15°C (59°F) – ideally in a greenhouse or conservatory – until the buds show colour. Then bring them into the home. Discard or plant in the garden once flowering is over.
Propagation Bulb offsets, but this is not a practical option in the home. Buy fresh bulbs each year.

Veltheilmia

There are only a handful of species in this genus of bulbous plants, which originate from South Africa.

Veltheilmia capensis
Strap-shaped, wavy-edged leaves approximately 30cm (1ft) in length. The flower spike, consisting of about 60 small, bell-like, pink or red blooms, arises from the centre of the plant in winter.

HELPFUL HINTS
Temperature Winter minimum 10°C (50°F), but at higher than 13°C (55°F) the flowers tend to drop.
Humidity Undemanding.
Position Good light, including sun in winter.
Watering and feeding Water cautiously until growth appears, moderately throughout the growing period, then gradually reduce the amount of water given in late spring or early summer. The leaves will then die down as the bulb enters its dormant period.

Once growth is well established, feed regularly until flowering is over.
Care Plant the bulbs in autumn, and keep at about 21°C (70°F) until growth starts. After the bulbs have flowered and entered their resting period, keep the pots practically dry

ABOVE: Veltheilmia capensis

until early autumn. During the dormant stage you can stand the pots in a sheltered position outdoors.
Propagation Bulb offsets; seed (slow).

Vriesea

Bromeliads with about 250 species in the genus, occurring naturally in Central and South America.

Vriesea hieroglyphica
A species grown for foliage effect. Large rosette of wide, strap-shaped leaves with very dark green, sometimes almost black, markings. Seldom flowers in cultivation.

Vriesea hybrids
Hybrids are sometimes available ('Elan' is illustrated). Others include 'Perfecta' (a cross between *V. carinata* and *V.* 'Poelmannii') and 'Poelmannii' (a cross between *V. gloriosa* and *V. vangertii).

OPPOSITE ABOVE: Vriesea splendens
LEFT: Vriesea *hybrid 'Elan'*

Vriesea splendens
Rosette of arching, strap-shaped leaves, 30–45cm (1–1½ft) long on a mature plant, with brown cross-bands. The bright red flower head, 60cm (2ft) long, rises above the rosette of leaves. The true flowers are yellow but the plant is grown for the colourful red bracts, which appear mainly in summer and autumn.

HELPFUL HINTS
Temperature Winter minimum 15°C (59°F).
Humidity Mist the leaves regularly.
Position Light shade or good light out of direct sun.
Watering and feeding Water freely from spring to autumn, sparingly in winter. Keep the 'vase' formed by the leaves topped up with water from mid spring to mid autumn. Use soft water if possible. Feed with a weak fertilizer in summer.
Care The species grown for their colourful flower spikes are often discarded after flowering, but offsets will form around the old plant and these can be grown on to flower in due course. They are difficult to grow successfully in the home throughout their lives, however. If repotting, use an ericaceous (lime-free) mixture. You can also grow them attached to a bromeliad 'tree' made from an old branch, if you have space.
Propagation Offsets.

Washingtonia

A very small genus of just two species of tall palms. Both are occasionally used as a houseplants, but the species described below is the one you are most likely to find.

Washingtonia filifera
Fan-shaped, long-stalked, grey-green leaves with fibrous threads at the ends. Will make a large specimen if conditions suit, but is often short-lived in the home.

BELOW: Washingtonia filifera

HELPFUL HINTS
Temperature Winter minimum 10°C (50°F).
Humidity Undemanding.
Position Best possible light, with some direct sun, but avoid sunlight through glass during the hottest part of the day in summer.
Watering and feeding Water freely from spring to autumn, sparingly in winter. Feed regularly in summer.
Care The plant will appreciate being stood outside, perhaps on the patio, for the warmest months. In winter, the plant is better in a cool conservatory than in a living-room.
Propagation Seed (difficult).

Yucca

A genus of about 40 species of evergreen trees and shrubs, some of which are hardy. The two species listed below are the ones most commonly seen as houseplants.

Yucca aloifolia
The leaves, up to 50cm (20in) long, grow in a dense rosette, and have very sharp points. A pronounced trunk gives it a tree-like shape.

Yucca elephantipes
Similar to the previous species, but the leaf tips are not sharp. This is the species commonly sold, and in Europe large quantities of the sawn stems are imported from countries such as Honduras. These 'trunks' are then started into growth like giant cuttings, to produce attractive plants with a thick trunk. Commercial growers sometimes refer to this species as *Y. elegantissima* but you are unlikely to see this name used.

HELPFUL HINTS
Temperature Winter minimum 7°C (45°F).
Humidity Tolerates dry air.
Position Good light with some sun.
Watering and feeding Water freely from spring to autumn, sparingly in winter. Feed regularly in summer.
Care Repot small plants if necessary, large ones can remain in the same container for many years, but in this case it is worth removing and replacing the top 2in (5cm) of the compost (potting mixture). The plant will be happy standing on the patio for the summer, but keep in shade for the first few weeks to acclimatize.
Propagation Sideshoots can be used as cuttings. The large-trunked plants seen in shops are raised from imported stems.

BELOW: Yucca elephantipes

Zebrina

See Tradescantia.

Zephyranthes

A genus of bulbous plants from Central and South America. Growing plants are not often sold, but you can obtain the bulbs easily from specialist bulb companies.

Zephyranthes Candida
Fine, grass-like leaves, and crocus-like white flowers, sometimes with a hint of purple, in autumn. Grows to about 15cm (6in).

BELOW: Zephyranthes grandiflora

ABOVE: Zephyranthes candida

Zephyranthes grandiflora
Similar to the previous species but with larger, rosy-pink flowers with a yellow throat on 30cm (1ft) stems, in early summer.

HELPFUL HINTS
Temperature Winter minimum 5°C (41°F).
Humidity Undemanding.
Position Best possible light, with some direct sun.
Watering and feeding Water freely when the bulbs are growing actively, sparingly when they are resting. Never let the soil become completely dry even during the resting period.
Care If necessary, repot when the bulbs are dormant, but do not repot unnecessarily. The display is usually better when the pot is densely planted with bulbs.
Propagation Division; seed.

Zygocactus

Forest cacti with flattened stems. The plants widely grown for the home are hybrids of *Z. truncatus,* but you may also find them allocated to the genus schlumbergera. Some may be hybrids between more than one genus.

Zygocactus truncatus hybrids
Flattered, winged segments forming arching branches. Exotic-looking flowers with two tiers of reflexed petals and forward-thrusting stems and stigma. The flowers, up to 7.5cm (3in) long, are borne on the tips of the shoots. Bright violet flowers are most common, but they vary from orange to lilac, as well as white. Late autumn and winter are the main flowering times. Also labelled under what some consider to be their more correct name of *Schlumbergera truncata.*

HELPFUL HINTS
Temperature Winter minimum 13°C (55°F).
Humidity Mist the leaves regularly.
Position Good light, but not direct summer sun.
Watering and feeding Water freely from late autumn, sparingly from late winter onwards. Increase the amount of water given again when buds start to form in the autumn. Use soft water if possible. Feed with a weak fertilizer during the period of active growth.
Care Stand the plant outdoors in a shady spot for the summer, but bring in before the evenings turn too cold. Avoid turning or moving the plant once the buds are well developed as they may drop. Repot young plants each spring, mature ones only every second or third year.
Propagation Cuttings.

BELOW: Zygocactus truncatus (*syn.* Schlumbergera truncata)

Glossary

Aerial root A root that grows from the stem above ground level. Plants such as philodendrons use them to assist climbing, as well as to absorb moisture and nutrients.

Air layering Method of propagating a plant by encouraging a stem to root while still on the plant. After careful wounding the stem is protected with sphagnum moss or other moisture-holding material and covered with plastic or foil until roots form.

Alkaline compost A growing medium containing lime, and having a high pH.

Annual A plant that lives for only one year.

Areole A small depression or raised, cushion-like area on a cactus that bears spines or wool.

Aroid A member of the *Araceae* family, which includes anthuriums, philodendrons and monsteras among the houseplants.

Bloom When used to describe the appearance of a leaf or fruit, a whitish or bluish powdery or waxy coating, which is easily removed by rubbing or handling.

Bract A modified leaf, often brightly coloured and petal-like, associated with flowers that themselves lack size or colour. Some bracts are small and scale-like, however, and serve mainly to protect buds.

Bromeliad A member of the *Bromeliaceae* family. Most are ephiphytic, and the leaves usually form a rosette.

Bulb Although the term is often used to include corms and tubers, strictly speaking, a bulb is a structure consisting of modified leaves that protects the next season's embryo shoots and flowers.

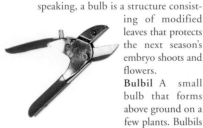

Bulbil A small bulb that forms above ground on a few plants. Bulbils can be removed and potted up to grow into normal bulbs.

Callus A growth of corky tissue that forms over a wound, sealing and healing it.

Cane cuttings Method of propagation using a piece of stem cut into small lengths placed horizontally in the rooting medium.

Capillary mat An absorbent mat that holds a lot of water. Plants placed on it can draw up moisture by capillary action.

Chlorophyll The green pigment in plants which enables them to manufacture food from sunlight (photosynthesize).

Chlorosis An unhealthy yellowing of the foliage, usually caused by a deficiency of iron or other trace elements. Often appears in lime-hating plants which have been grown in an alkaline medium.

Cladode *See Cladophyll*

Cladophyll Also called a cladode. A modified stem that simulates a leaf in appearance and function. They can be found in the garden plant *Ruscus aculeatus*. One of the best-known houseplants with cladophylls is *Asparagus densiflorus*.

Compost (potting soil) The medium in which pot plants are grown.

Corm A swollen stem base that usually remains underground and stores food during the dormant season. If cut across, no distinct layers of leaves can be seen, unlike a bulb.

Corolla A term applied to the petals of a flower, or the inner ring of them, the petals being either separate or fused.

Crocks Pieces of broken clay pot (also known as shards), placed over the drainage hole of a clay pot to prevent the compost (potting soil) from being washed through the hole.

Crown The point at which stem and roots meet.

Dormant period The time when growth slows down and the plant needs less warmth and water. Some plants have no discernible dormant period, but with others – such as cyclamen – it is pronounced.

Epiphyte A plant that grows above ground level, usually in trees. Epiphytes are not parasites and only use their host for physical support.

Epiphytic A plant that grows on other plants without being parasitic.

Ericaceous When used specifically the term applies to members of the *Ericaceae* family, but is sometimes applied broadly to include similar plants. If applied to potting soils (potting composts) it means one specially formulated with a low pH to suit acid-loving plants.

Eye A term with several meanings. If used with reference to a flower it indicates that the centre of the bloom is a different colour. In propagation it refers to a stem cutting with a single lateral bud. If applied to a tuber, it is used to describe a dormant (undeveloped) bud on its surface.

Eye cuttings Method of propagation using a short section of ripened stem with a growth bud, the cutting being placed horizontally in the rooting medium.

Foliar feed A quick-acting liquid fertilizer that can be absorbed through the leaves as well as the roots.

Genus A group of species with enough common characteristics to group them together like a 'family'.

Glochid A tiny barbed spine or bristle, usually occurring in tufts on the areoles of some cacti. These penetrate the skin easily and can often set up irritation, making some cacti hazardous to handle. A good way to remove them from the skin is to lay a surgical plaster or tape over the area then peel it off.

Hardy Frost-tolerant.

Hormone, rooting hormone An organic compound that stimulates a cutting into forming roots.

Humidifier A device for raising the humidity in a room. Sometimes a tray of evaporating water is used, but more

sophisticated humidifiers are electrically powered.

Hydroponics A method of growing plants in nutrient solutions, without compost (potting soil).

Loam-based compost (potting soil) A soil mix in which the main ingredient is sterilized loam, to which peat (peat moss), sand and fertilizer are added.

Lux The scientific unit by which light levels are measured.

Mulch A protective covering for soil. In this book it refers to a loose covering of chipped bark, peat (peat moss), or similar material used to cover bulbs planted in pots, giving them a period of darkness in preparation for early flowering.

Offset A small plant that is produced alongside its parent.

Peat-based compost (peat-moss-based potting soil) A soil mix in which peat is the main ingredient. Sometimes sand and other substances are added, and the mixture always includes fertilizers and something to neutralize the acidity of the peat. Peat substitutes, such as coir, are increasingly used to avoid depletion of natural peat reserves.

Perennial A plant that lives for more than two years.

Perlite An inert growing medium, sometimes used as a compost (potting soil) additive or for rooting cuttings.

Petiole A leaf stalk.

pH A scale expressing the degree of acidity or alkalinity of a substance. It runs from 0 to 14, 7 being technically neutral, though most plants prefer a pH of about 6.5. Above 7 is alkaline, below 7 is acid.

Photosynthesis The mechanism by which plants convert sunlight into energy.

Phyllode A leaf stalk that takes on the function and appearance of a leaf. They are commonly found in acacias.

Pinnate A compound leaf with the leaflets arranged in parallel rows.

Pot-bound A term used to describe a plant whose growth is being inhibited by roots that have filled the pot.

Prop roots Special roots that arise above ground level and help to give the mature plant stability.

Pseudobulb A thickened, bulb-like stem found on some orchids, used by the plant for water storage. They vary considerably in shape and size and can be long and narrow or short and rounded. They are always produced above the ground.

Relative humidity The amount of water contained in the air at a particular temperature. It is calculated against the maximum amount of water that could be held in the air at that temperature.

Resting period *see* **Dormant period**

Rhizome A special, modified stem, sometimes thick and fleshy but not always, that lies close to the surface of the soil (except in epiphytes) and produces both roots and aerial parts such as leaves and flowers. You can tell that a rhizome is not a root by the presence of nodes (joints) and often scale-like leaves or buds.

Root-ball A mass of roots and compost (potting soil) together.

Spadix A special type of fleshy flower spike, found in aroids and palms, in which small flowers are more or less embedded. In aroids it is surrounded by a spathe, and in this case forms a single erect organ. In palms it is often branched.

Spathe The term usually refers to the conspicuous bract that protects a spadix (see above). In aroids (members of the *Araceae* family, such as philodendrons and monsteras) it is leafy, more or less fleshy, and often brightly coloured. The term is sometimes used for palms (in which it could be fleshy or woody) and other plants – for example, the membranous sheath that surrounds a daffodil bud is technically

a spathe. In this book it is always used in the sense described for aroids.

Sphagnum moss A moss belonging to the genus *Sphagnum*, found in boggy places and capable of holding a large amount of water.

Spores Minute reproductive structure found on non-flowering plants such as ferns and mosses. Can be sown like seeds but need special treatment.

Stem cutting Method of propagation using a length of stem. There are many kinds, including soft, unripened wood, hardwood, and semiripe cuttings, the length varying according to the type of plant.

Stipule A leafy or bract-like appendage at the base of a leaf stalk. It is usually small and inconspicuous.

Sucker A shoot growing from a plant's roots or underground stem, producing leaves of its own. Suckers can be a problem on grafted plants in the garden, but for pot plants they usually provide a useful method of propagation. The term also applies to a group of insects, but is not used in that sense in this book.

Terrestrial Growing in soil – a land plant.

Tip cutting Method of propagation using only the soft tips of actively growing plants.

Tuber A swollen underground stem or root used by plants to store food during the dormant period.

Vermiculite An inert growing medium, sometimes used as a compost (potting soil) additive or for rooting cuttings.

Viviparous Producing live young. When applied to plants it refers to buds or bulbs that become plantlets while still attached to the parent plant. It also refers to seeds that germinate while on the parent plant.

Whorl Three or more organs, such as leaves, arranged in a circle around the same axis.

Index of common plant names

Pineapple, ivory – *Ananas comosus*
   'Variegatus'
Plantain lily – Hosta
Plume flower – *Celosia plumosa*
Poinsettia – *Euphorbia pulcherrima*
Polka dot plant – *Hypoestes sanguinolenta*
   (syn. *H. phyllostachya*)
Poor man's orchid – Schizanthus
Powder puff cactus – *Mammillaria bocasana*
Prairie gentian – *Eustoma grandiflorum*
Prayer plant – Maranta
Prickly pear – Opuntia

Primrose – *Primula vulgaris*
Pygmy date palm – *Phoenix roebelenii*
Queen's tears – *Billbergia nutans*
Rabbit's ears – *Opuntia microdasys*
Rainbow star – *Cryptanthus bromelioides*
Rat tail plant – *Crassula lycopodioides*
Rattlesnake plant – *Calathea lancifolia*
Regal pelargonium – *Pelargonium* x
   domesticum
Resurrection plant – *Selaginella lepidophylla*
Ribbon fern – Pteris
Ribbon plant – *Dracaena sanderiana*
Rosary vine – *Ceropegia woodii*
Rose of China – *Hibiscus rosa-sinensis*
Rose pincushion – *Mammillaria zeilmanniana*
Rubber plant – *Ficus elastica*
Scarlet star – *Guzmania lingulata*
   (and hybrids)
Sensitive plant – *Mimosa pudica*
Sentry palm – *Howeia belmoreana*
   (syn. *Kentia belmoreana*)
Shrimp plant – *Beloperone guttata*
Silk bark oak – *Grevillea robusta*
Silver jade plant – *Crassula arborescens*
Silver net leaf – *Fittonia verchaffeltii*
   argyroncura

Slipper flower – *Calceolaria* hybrids
Slipper orchid – Cypripedium
   (syn. Paphiopedilum)
Snakeskin plant – Fittonia
Spade leaf – *Philodendron domesticum*
Spanish bayonet – *Yucca aloifolia*
Spanish moss – *Tillandsia usneoides*
Spathe flower – Spathiphyllum
Spider lily – *Hymenocallis* x *festalis*
Spider plant – *Chlorophytum comosum*
Spineless yucca – *Yucca elephantipes*
Spiraea, perennial – Astilbe
Spotted laurel – *Aucuba japonica*
Spreading clubmoss – *Selaginella kraussiana*
Stag's horn fern – *Platycerium bifurcatum*
Star of Bethlehem – *Campanula*
   isophylla
Starfish flower – *Stapelia variegata*
Stonecrop – *Sedum*
Stove fern – *Pteris cretica*
Strawberry geranium – *Saxifraga stolonifera*
   (syn. *S. sarmentosa*)
String of hearts – *Ceropegia woodii*
Sundew – *Drosera capensis*
Sunset cactus – *Lobivia famatimensis*
Swedish ivy – *Plectanthus oertendahlii*
Sweetheart plant – *Philodendron scandens*
Swiss cheese plant – *Monstera deliciosa*
Sword fern – *Nephrolepis exaltata*
Table fern – *Pteris cretica*

Temple bells – Smithiantha
Ti tree – *Cordyline fruticosa*
Tiger jaws – *Faucaria tigrina*
Tiger orchid – *Odontoglossum grande*
Torch thistle – Cereus
Transvaal daisy – *Gerbera jamesonii*
Tree ivy – X *Fatshedera lizei*
Tree philodendron – *Philodendron*
   bipinnatifidum
Tsus-simense holly fern – *Polystichum*
   tsus-simense
Tulip – Tulipa
Umbrella plant – Cyperus
Umbrella plant – *Schefflera actinophylla*
Urn plant – *Aechmea fasciata*
Velvet plant – Gynura
Venus fly trap – *Dionaea muscipula*
Voodoo lily – *Sauromatum venosum*
   (syn. *S. guttatum*)
Wandering Jew – Tradescantia Zebrina
Washington palm – Washingtonia
Watermelon plant – *Peperomia argyreia*
Wax begonia – *Begonia semperflorens*
Wax flower – Hoya, *Stephanotis floribunda*
Wax privet – *Peperomia glabella*
Wax vine – *Senecio macroglossus*
Weeping fig – *Ficus benjamina*
Whorled peperomia – *Peperomia*
   verticillata
Winter cherry – *Solanum capsicastrum*,
   S. pseudocapsicum
Zebra plant – *Aphelandra squarrosa*,
   Calathea zebrina
Zonal pelargonium – *Pelargonium zonale*

Plant guide

* All plants marked with an asterisk need protection from frost.

TREES AND SHRUBS FOR CONTAINERS
Acer palmatum
Apple (dwarf)
Bay
Berberis thunbergii 'Atropurpurea Nana',
   B. darwinii
Box
Camellia
Ceratostigma plumbagoides
Chamaecyparis pisifera
Choisya ternata
x *Citrofortunella microcarpa**
Convolvulus cneorum
Cordyline*
Cotoneaster conspicuus
Datura*
Euonymous fortunei
Fuchsia
Hebe
Holly
Hydrangea
Lantana*
Lavender
Potentilla
Rhododendron
Rosemary
Rose
Skimmia

CLIMBERS FOR CONTAINERS
Bougainvillea*
Clematis alpina, C. macropetala
*Cobaea scandens**
Gynura*
Ivy
Jasmine
Stephanotis*

Thunbergia alata
Trachelospermum jasminoides

HARDY PLANTS FOR PERMANENT PLANTING IN CONTAINERS
Anemone blanda
Aquilegia alpina
Arabis ferdinandi-coburgii 'Variegata'
Asplenium crispum
Athyrium nipponicum
Berberis thunbergii 'Atropurpurea Nana',
   B. darwinii
Bergenia
Box
Ceratostigma plumbagoides
Chamaecyparis pisifera 'Filifera Aurea', 'Sungold'
Choisya ternata
Convolvulus cneorum
Cotoneaster conspicuus
Crocus
Day lily
Dianthus
Dryopteris filix-mas
Euonymous fortunei 'Emerald and Gold'
Euphorbia
Foxglove
Hebe
Helianthemum
Heuchera 'Palace Purple', 'Bressingham Bronze'
Holly
Hosta
Hydrangea
Inula
Iris reticulata
Ivy
Lamium
Lavender
Lily-of-the-valley
Narcissus
Nepeta mussinii
Ophiopogon planiscapus 'Nigrescens'
Pachysandra terminalis
Polygonum affine

Polystichum acrostichoides
Potentilla
Primula auricula
Rosemary
Salix alpina
Sedum ewersii
Sedum 'Ruby Glow'
Sempervivum
Skimmia japonica 'Rubella'
Thyme
Trachelospermum jasminoides
Veronica peduncularis
Vinca minor

TRAILING PLANTS FOR HANGING BASKETS
Ageratum*
*Begonia semperflorens**
*Bidens ferulifolia**
Brachycome iberidifolia
*Campanula isophylla**
*Chaenorhinum glareosum**
*Convolvulus sabatius**
Erigeron mucronatus
Felicia*
Fuchsia (lax varieties)*
Gazania*
Glechoma hederacea
*Helichrysum petiolare**
Lampranthus*
Lantana*
Lobelia*
*Lotus berthelotti**
Lysimachia nummularia
Nasturtium
Osteospermum*
Pelargonium*
Petunia*
Sedum ewersii
*Senecio maritima**
Sweet peas
Verbena*
Vinca minor

SPRING-FLOWERING PLANTS FOR CONTAINERS
Anagallis
Anemone blanda
Aquilegia
Arabis ferdinandi-coburgii 'Variegata'
Bluebells
Crocus
Day lily
Euphorbia
Forget-me-not
Iris reticulata
Lily-of-the-valley
Narcissus
Polyanthus
Primroses
Primula auricula
Snowdrops
Tulips
Vinca minor
Viola
Wallflower

AUTUMN AND WINTER COLOUR
Arabis ferdinandi-coburgii 'Variegata'
Berberis thunbergii 'Atropurpurea Nana',
    B. darwinii
Bergenia
Ceratostigma plumbagoides
Chamaecyparis pisifera 'Sungold'
Convolvulus cneorum
Euonymous fortunei
Euphorbia
Ferns
Heuchera 'Palace Purple', 'Bressingham Bronze'
Hakonechloa macra 'Alboaurea'
Hebe
Holly
Iris unguicularis
Ivy
Pachysandra terminalis
Polygonum affine
Salvia greggii
Sedum 'Ruby Glow'
Vinca minor

PLANTS FOR SHADE
Anemone blanda
Begonia semperflorens
Bergenia
Box
Campanula isophylla
Chamaecyparis pisifera
Digitalis
Euonymous
Euphorbia
Ferns
Glechoma hederacea
Heuchera
Holly
Hosta
Hydrangea
Impatiens*
Ivy
Lily-of-the-valley
Narcissus
Ophiopogon planiscapus
Pachysandra terminalis
Primrose
Primula auricula
Skimmia
Sorrel
Thunbergia alata
Trachelospermum jasminoides
Vinca minor
Viola

PLANTS FOR HOT CONDITIONS
Aloe*
Alyssum
Argyranthemum*
Arundinaria pygmaea
Crassula ovata
Diascia*
Erigeron mucronatus
Gazania*
Hakonechloa macra 'Aureola'
Helianthemum
Inula
Lavender
Lotus berthelotti
Mesembryanthemum
Osteospermum*

PLANTS WITH DECORATIVE FOLIAGE
Berberis thunbergii
Bergenia
Chamaecyparis pisifera
Choisya ternata

Convolvulus cneorum
Euonymous fortunei
Euphorbia
Fuchsia magellanica
Glechoma hederacea
Hebe
Hedera helix 'Hibernica'
Helichrysum petiolare
Heuchera
Holly
Hosta 'Blue Moon'
Lotus berthelotti
Lysimachia nummularia
Nasturtium 'Alaska'
Pachysandra terminalis
Pelargonium, ivy-leaved
Salvia officinalis
Senecio maritima
Thymus 'Silver Queen', 'Archer's
    Gold'
Vinca minor

FRAGRANT PLANTS
Alyssum
Bidens atrosanguinea
Cheiranthus
Choisya ternata
x *Citrofortunella microcarpa*
Dianthus
Heliotrope
Jasmine
Lavender
Lilies
Lily-of-the-valley
Nicotiana
Pelargonium, scented-leaved varieties*
Rosemary
Sweet pea
Thyme
Trachelospermum jasminoides
Viola odorata

Index

Page references in italic indicate illustrations and/or their captions. Page references in bold indicate entry in A–Z plant directory.

C

L. regale, 24, 39
Lily-of-the-valley, 30, *30*, 110
Liners for hanging baskets, 29
Liquid fertilizers, 295
Lisianthus russellianus see Eustoma grandiflora
Lithops, 445
   L. bella, 445
Living-rooms, 362–3
Loam-based composts (potting mixes), 18, 296
Lobelia, 24, 275
   colour schemes, 36, *54*, 63
   in other plantings, 123, 169, 179, 205, 222, 226
Lobivia, 268, 445
   L. densispina, 445
   L. famatimensis, 445
   L. hertrichiana, 445
Lotus berthelotii, 78
Lysimachia
   L. congestiflora, 89
   L. nummularia 'Aurea', 86, 182, 220
Lytocaryum see Cocos

M

Mahonia x *media* 'Charity', 32
Mail order plants, 17
Mammillaria, 268, 446
   M. bocasana, 446
   M. elongata, *289*, 446
   M. wildu, 446
   M. zeilmanniana, 229, 446
Maranta, 265, 288, 307, 317, 446–7
   M. bicolor, 446
   M. leuconeura, 446
Marjoram, 175, 364
Matteuccia struthiopteris, 181
Mealy bugs, 22, *22, 328*, 329
Mesembryanthemum, 186, 218
Microcoelum *see* Cocos

Mildews, 23, 331, *331*
Miltonia, 246, 278
Mimosa, 447
   M. pudica, 280, 447
Mimulus, 86, 182
Mint, 153, 155, 170
Misting of plants, 287, *287*
Monstera, 307, 447
   M. deliciosa, *261*, 322, *355*, 368, 371, 447
Moss baskets, *358*, 359
Mulches, 21

N

Narcissus, *42*, 103, 106, *361*, 448
   N. 'Paperwhite', *272*, 277
   N. 'Tête-à-Tête', 112
Nasturtium *see* Tropaeolum
Neanthe *see* Chamaedorea
Nematanthus *see* Hypocyrta
Nemesia, 114
   N. 'Confetti', 96, 200
   N. 'Orange Prince', 127
Neoregelia, 264, 270, 448–9
   N. carolinae, 270, 448
Nepeta mussinii, 194
Nephrolepis, 307, 339, *342, 345*, 449
   N. exaltata, 266, *267*, 449
Nerium, 32, 288, 449
   N. oleander, *272*, 348, 360, 449
Nertera, 288, 450
   N. granadensis, 450
Nicotiana, 119, 123
Nidularium, 450–1
   N. billbergioides citrinum, 450
   N. fulgens, 450
   N. innocentii, 450
Notocactus, 268, 451
   N. apricus, 451
   N. ottonis, 451
Nymphaea tetragona, 195

O

Odontoglossum, 452
   O. grande, 452
Offsets, 320–1
Ophiopogon planiscapus 'Nigrescens', 90, 197, 200
Optunia, 229, 452–3
   O. cylindrica, 452
   O. microdasys, 452
   O. phaeacantha, 452
   O. vestita, 452–3

Oranges, *277, 349*
Orchids, 246, 278, 279, 288, 367
   propagation, 324, *324*
   see also individual genus
   e.g. Cymbidium
Origanum, 154, 175
Ornamental cabbage, *34, 43, 358*
Osteospermum, 24, 197
   O. 'Buttermilk', 82, 185
   O. 'Pink Whirls', 76
   O. 'Whirligig', 62
Over-feeding, 295
Overwatering, *293*, 322, 332, 335
Overwintering, 26, 32, *32*
Oxalis, 153, 453
   O. deppei, 453

P

Pachysandra terminalis, 144
Pachystachys, 454
   P. lutea, 454
Palms, 234, 262–3, 291, 345, 348, *349*, 355
   see also individual genus e.g. Caryota
Papaver, *34*
   P. alpinum, 191
Paphiopedilum, 278, 454
Parodia, 268, 454–5
   P. aureispina, 454
   P. chrysacanthion, 454
Parsley, 87, 120, 153, 155, 159, 162, 164, 167, 235
Peat-based composts, 18, 296
Pebble trays, 346–347
Pedestals, 342–3, *342*
Pelargonium, 24, *24*, 456–7
   colour schemes, 56, 58, 64, 67, 68, 70, 72, 73, 80, 86
   indoors, *272*, 277, 288, 360, *361*
   other plantings, 206, 221, 222
   propagation, *312*
   scented plantings, 171, 174, 236

Acknowledgements

The Container Garden

All projects were created by Stephanie Donaldson and photographed by Marie O'Hara unless stated below.

Contributors Clare Bradley: pp 217, 221, 222, 223, 224, 225, 226, 228, 229, 232, 233. Blaise Cooke: pp 16, 17, 38, 44l, 47br, 60, 74, 75, 201, 204, 210, 211, 227, 248, 249. Tessa Evelegh: pp 24, 30t, 33, 34t, 37, 39, 40, 42, 43, 47t. Peter McHoy: pp 36, 41, 44r, 229, 231, 232, 233, 240, 241, 242, 243, 244, 245. Lesley Harle: p 48. Karin Hossack: pp 49, 50. Liz Wagstaff: p 51, 52.

Photographers John Freeman: pp 16, 17, 18, 21r, 24m, 24b, 25b, 26r, 27mr, 30m, 32, 38, 46tl, 47br, 60, 74, 75, 103, 104, 105, 107, 108, 109, 110, 111, 122, 130, 134, 135, 138, 139, 142, 143, 144, 145, 146, 147, 149, 150, 155, 160, 161, 163, 169, 176, 177, 195, 196, 197, 201, 204, 206, 207, 208, 209, 21, 211, 212, 213, 217, 221, 222, 223, 224, 225, 226, 227, 228, 229, 234, 235, 237, 238, 239, 245, 246, 247, 248, 249, 250, 251. Don Last: p 23r, 231, 232, 233, 240, 241, 242, 243, 244, 245. Debbie Patterson: pp 24m, 24b, 25b, 26l, 30t, 32, 34t, 36t, 36m, 37, 39, 42, 43, 47, 48, 49, 50, 51, 52, 61. Peter McHoy: pp 22, 23l, 31, 36, 41, 44r.

Success with Houseplants

All photography by John Freeman, with additional photographs, as follows.

Peter McHoy: pp 268b, 271t, 272t, 274b, 275tl br, 276b, 277tl tc tr b, 278t, 279b, 280t b, 281t c bl br, 287t, 294, 295cr br, 306, 307, 311b, 312, 318br, 319, 321cl cr bl br, 328tr bc, 329tl tc bl, 330b, 331tr, 332bl br, 333tl tr bl, 347bl, 348, 349tr, 351tl bl br, 352, 360b, 361b, 376c b, 377cr, 389, 390bl, 393t, 397, 402b, 408t, 423bl cl, 432, 433b, 436tc, 441tr br, 453b, 455t, 456b, 472t b, 478bl, 485, 495t b. The Garden Picture Library/ Erika Craddock: p 374. The Garden Picture Library/John Sira: pp 450, 494. The Garden Picture Library/Mayer Lescanff: p 482. A–Z Botanical: p 452. Photos Horticultural: pp 129tl, 438t, 463bl, 481b.

t=top, b=bottom, m=middle, l=left, r=right